EXPANDED 2ND EDITION

Inspiring ACTIVE LEARNING

A COMPLETE HANDBOOK FOR TODAY'S TEACHERS

MERRILL HARMIN *with* MELANIE TOTH

Association for Supervision and Curriculum Development
Alexandria, Virginia USA

Association for Supervision and Curriculum Development
1703 N. Beauregard St. · Alexandria, VA 22311-1714 USA
Phone: 800-933-2723 or 703-578-9600 · Fax: 703-575-5400
Web site: www.ascd.org · E-mail: member@ascd.org
Author guidelines: www.ascd.org/write

Gene R. Carter, *Executive Director;* Nancy Modrak, *Director of Publishing;* Julie Houtz, *Director of Book Editing & Production;* Genny Ostertag, *Project Manager;* Georgia Park, *Senior Graphic Designer;* Cynthia Stock, *Typesetter;* Dina Murray Seamon, *Production Specialist/Team Lead*

PAPERBACK ISBN-13: 978-1-4166-0155-5   ASCD product #103113   s7/06
PAPERBACK ISBN-10: 1-4166-0155-4
Also available as an e-book through ebrary, netLibrary, and many online booksellers (see *Books in Print* for the ISBNs).

Quantity discounts for the paperback edition only: 10–49 copies, 10%; 50+ copies, 15%; for 1,000 or more copies, call 800-933-2723, ext. 5634, or 703-575-5634. For desk copies, e-mail member@ascd.org.

Library of Congress Cataloging-in-Publication Data

Harmin, Merrill.
    Inspiring active learning : a complete handbook for today's teachers /
Merrill Harmin with Melanie Toth. — Expanded 2nd ed.
        p.   cm.
    Includes bibliographical references and index.
    ISBN-13: 978-1-4166-0155-5 (pbk. : alk. paper)
    ISBN-10: 1-4166-0155-4 (pbk. : alk. paper)   1. Teaching—Handbooks,
manuals, etc.   2. Motivation in education—Handbooks, manuals, etc.   3.
Active learning—Handbooks, manuals, etc.   I. Toth, Melanie.   II. Title.

    LB1025.3.H37 2006
    371.102—dc22

                                                        2006009539

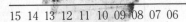

15 14 13 12 11 10 09 08 07 06   1 2 3 4 5 6 7 8 9 10 11 12

EXPANDED 2ND EDITION

INSPIRING ACTIVE LEARNING

A COMPLETE HANDBOOK FOR TODAY'S TEACHERS

List of Strategies

Strategies recommended for first attention are indicated by ◆〉.

A Personal Note on Using This Book

This book brings good news to teachers. No longer need teaching be so stressful. No longer need we struggle with our unmotivated students and passive learners. No longer must we abandon so many of our ideals. We now know how we can run our classrooms so students will *want* to cooperate, will *want* to do good work, will in fact want to do the very best they can for us.

Some background: I started off as a math teacher and, I thought, I was a pretty good one. No one complained too much and my students produced good test scores. But then I visited my colleague Peter's classroom. At the time, Peter was teaching a group of students I had taught the year before, a group I was particularly fond of. And as I watched those students in Peter's classroom, I noticed they were much more actively involved in learning than they ever were in my class. Many more hands waved to answer teacher questions. Eyes were brighter with attention. No one was fussing in his or her seat or looking aimlessly out the window. How come Peter got more from those students than I ever did?

I took that question with me when I became a teacher educator, wondering especially how some teachers motivated even the most reluctant and resistant of students to do good work. The answer to the question seemed to involve more than the methods those teachers used; other teachers could use the same methods without producing nearly the same results. And it seemed to involve more than the personalities of the teachers; teachers with many different personalities, from warm to cool, organized to disorganized, demonstrated that gift to motivate learning. And it was clearly more than a matter of educational knowledge; some of the brightest teachers lacked the gift and some of the most poorly prepared had it. What was it?

Being in the business of training teachers, my interest soon shifted from seeking an abstract answer to that question to seeking ways all teachers could develop more of that inspirational ability. Since it was obviously *possible* to run classrooms that motivated even the most unmotivated of our students—some teachers clearly had the knack—what could the rest of us do to move more closely to that outcome?

For many years, my colleagues and I played with various ideas, finally crafting an approach that led to the first edition of this book. A decade later, now with much more experience available to us, we offer this revised and expanded edition—and offer it with more assurance than ever. Yes, almost any teacher, K–12, can run a highly inspiring classroom. The profession now knows in practical detail how we can conduct a classroom that naturally, steadily draws even the most unmotivated of today's students toward active, cooperative, self-responsible learning.

But this is not to be taken on faith. You can easily test the idea for yourself. This book will show you how to do just that. More specifically, the book offers

• *Clarity about what makes a classroom inspiring to students.* What is at the heart of an inspiring classroom? If it's not our personality or teaching methods, what is it? That is the first question to address, and it's the focus of Chapter 1.

• *A simple, four-step process for making your classroom more inspiring.* That is the focus of Chapter 2. It presents a straightforward process for you to give this material a brief test for yourself. Then if you like what's showing up, you can use that process to gradually move ahead and create your own style of a highly inspiring classroom.

• *Practical strategies for running an inspiring classroom.* All the chapters after the first two contain examples of teacher-tested strategies that have been shown to be effective in the running of an inspiring classroom. They illustrate how we can handle almost all our daily tasks in a way that keeps eliciting the most positive response from students. Scan the Table of Contents and you'll see the complete list of teacher tasks for which strategies are provided.

Note that six of the most far-reaching of our teaching tasks are grouped in Part II, Strategies for Handling Six Fundamental Teaching Tasks. Because teaching is so much easier when those fundamental tasks are well handled, it's valuable to consider those chapters before the others. After that, you can jump around among the other strategy chapters according to your personal interests.

However, you need not look at every strategy in every chapter. The introductory paragraphs in each chapter specify a few strategies to look at first. Each of those is marked with an arrow like this: ·····▸)

The best preparation for being a happy or useful man or woman is to live fully as a child.
—*Plowden Report*

You can then dip into the other strategies if you need more examples. You may discover that once you become familiar with the inspiring approach to running a classroom, it will be easy to invent your own strategies.

As you will see, many of the strategies in the book will be familiar to you. That's because the intent here was not to present *new* strategies but *effective* strategies, and many standard and familiar practices can be used to run a highly inspiring classroom or can be tweaked to do so. In general, my intent was to take the best wisdom from research and theory and the best practices from experienced teachers and craft these ideas into a handbook that shows us how we might handle all our teaching tasks in a way that keeps eliciting the best students have in them.

Some of our teaching tasks can be handled with one-step strategies. Such tasks include motivating a class to start thinking and getting a student to stop disrupting. Other tasks are more complex and require multistep strategies. Examples: Conducting whole-class lessons, preparing students for a high-stakes test. You will note that several of the one-step strategies are also included in multipart strategies, so don't be surprised when you run into some strategies more than once in these pages. Indeed, you can safely assume that strategies used more than once were found by our field teachers to be especially flexible and valuable.

You can quickly find a definition of all the strategies in the book by looking into the glossary that begins on p. 439.

My good friend Melanie Toth gets most of the credit for the book's organization and for preparing much of what went into this expanded second edition. It was a task well beyond my ability. I hope you appreciate the job she did as much as I do. Yet when it comes to credit, most of it goes to the many teachers who shared their best ideas with us and tested our field editions. The book would certainly not exist without all of them.

They have given us an encyclopedic array of strategies for handling our many teaching tasks. It's an array that I think you will find particularly useful whenever you need something extra or face an unusually challenging group.

Like the first edition, this second edition is dedicated to a most remarkable educational innovator, Grace H. Pilon, the creator of Workshop Way. She was the first person who demonstrated to me that almost *any* teacher could teach a large classroom of unwilling students in a way that never discouraged anyone and, instead, inspired everyone, including those of us who do the teaching. We bless you, Grace.

—Merrill Harmin, White Plains, New York

Two Keys for Running an Inspiring Classroom

This part of the book provides an overview of an approach that increases active learning. It also offers you an efficient way to test the approach yourself.

The language we use as we handle our teaching tasks makes a difference. What wording will inspire students to be most actively, constructively engaged? Consider the impact these three messages have on students:

Least inspiring: "The rules and consequences in this class are as follows. If you cannot obey these rules, you will be punished accordingly."

In between: "I want you all to respect one another here, and I know you can do that. What are some guidelines that can help us?"

Most inspiring: "I expect us to respect one another in this classroom, and I'm going to begin by pledging to respect each of you. If you ever feel I've slipped, please speak to me confidentially so I can learn to do better."

Clarity About What Makes a Classroom Inspiring to Students

1

In a fantasy world, all students would march in on the first day of school, quietly seat themselves, and promptly look up, bright eyed, ready and willing to get to work. But this is the real world. In this world, students show up with a variety of motivations, such as

1. *The fully active learners.* Some students will be ready and willing to dive into schoolwork. When we assign four problems for homework, such students will not only do all four but do them with style. They might even recopy their work before handing it in, so it's very neat, or attach a cover sheet to make it look professional. Students in this category may not be the brightest in the classroom, and they may not get the highest exam scores. But they are our go-getters, self-motivated, ready to do the best work they possibly can. These students are a joy to teach.

2. *The responsible students.* Other students will enter the classroom ready to do whatever we ask, but not much more than that. When we assign these students four problems for homework, they will do all four carefully, but rarely will we get the sense they did their very best. These are dutiful, respectful students, more motivated to please us than to put themselves fully into their work. These students are easy enough to teach.

3. *The halfhearted workers.* Our class is also likely to contain students who are, at best, halfhearted workers. Give them four problems and they complete only two. Or, if they do all four, their work will be sloppy, full of careless errors. These students are often slow to start work and quick to give up, and they can be quite frustrating to teach.

4. *The work avoiders.* Finally, we might have students who will do little or no work. Indeed, some will do their best to avoid work altogether. Give these students

four problems for homework and they are likely to groan and then lose the assignment. They are the students most likely to become discipline problems, the ones most likely to drive us batty.

This is the array of motivations that we are likely to find when our students first arrive. Unfortunately, it is also the array of motivations we are likely to see in the last days of the school year. Despite all the books that have been written about motivation and all the teacher meetings devoted to the issue, most of us still have a hard time turning work avoiders and halfhearted workers into responsible students and fully active learners.

But this is not so for all teachers.

Learning from Great Teachers

Some teachers, those we might call our great teachers, have a knack for moving students up those motivation levels. If we visited their classrooms, we would see, week by week, fewer and fewer students working at levels three and four, more and more at levels one and two. Somehow these teachers are able to inspire students to work harder than they were initially inclined to work. As a result, the students tend to climb what we call the Active Learning Ladder (Figure 1).

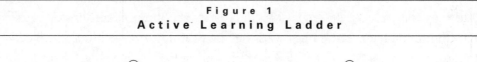

Figure 1
Active Learning Ladder

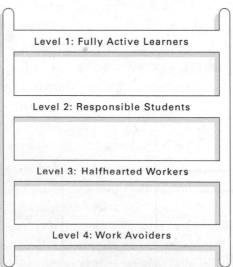

Level 1: Fully Active Learners

Level 2: Responsible Students

Level 3: Halfhearted Workers

Level 4: Work Avoiders

You probably remember having such teachers yourself. Most schools have at least a few. They are the ones who elicit such comments from students as

- I liked coming to class. I hated being absent.
- She turned us on to history and made it come alive.
- I never worked so hard in my life.
- I didn't expect to like that class, but I really did.

We might reasonably conclude, therefore, that it is possible to inspire students to become more fully active learners. Clearly, some teachers manage to do it. Might we do it, too? If so, how?

Interestingly, those great teachers don't achieve their results in any standard way. Look at a group of great teachers and you will notice that some do a lot of lecturing, others very little. Some are strict and demanding, others lenient and accepting. Some appear to be warm, others to be distant. Apparently, there is no one way to motivate students to do the best work they are capable of doing. This is good news for those who would like to inspire active learning. It suggests that we need not change our teaching personality or follow any standard model. Rather, we can create our own brand of great teaching, motivating higher levels of active learning in our own way. That is assuming, of course, we have a clear, realistic sense of how to go about doing so.

One of the *unrealistic* suggestions bantered about would have us start with students' interests and base all instruction on topics students are already motivated to learn more about: space travel, baseball, popular music. Another suggestion would have us build units around real-life issues that naturally motivate students: making friends, staying healthy, encouraging world peace, or the like. A third suggestion recommends that we convince students of the importance of grammar, history, or whatever else we want to teach them, so that the students will want to learn it.

These suggestions can help some of the time with some topics and some students, but rarely are they sufficient to move a classroom of students steadily up the Active Learning Ladder. Students need to be touched more deeply if they are to be inspired to do the best work they are capable of doing.

An Inspiring Approach

After years of experimentation, we have crafted a practical approach that does stir the deep positive abilities of students. Our approach resembles those that recommend a focus on the natural needs of students (deCharms, 1976; Havighurst, 1952; Maslow, 1999; Raths, 1972; Thelen, 1960; White, 1959).

The most powerful factors in the world are clear ideas in the minds of energetic men of good will.

—*J. Arthur Thomson*

Yet our approach is distinct in several ways. First, our focus is squarely on the *highest* needs of students, such as the need for students to become fully functioning or to be the best persons they can be. It does not ignore other needs, including what Maslow (1999) calls students' *deficiency needs,* such as the need for food and safety. But we place those needs in the background. We want to concentrate on the heart of the matter, on bringing out the very best students have in them, which often includes positive qualities the students themselves do not yet know they possess. In this regard, we agree with Erich Fromm when he says that the heart of education is "helping the child realize his potentialities." By aiming high we also take advantage of Goethe's wisdom: "Treat people as if they were what they ought to be, and you help them to become what they are capable of being."

A second key difference in our approach is that our target is not to bring out students' best potentials in a general way. We are teachers. We have jobs to do. Our approach is grounded in classroom realities. Our target, then, is very practical: to see students apply their best potentials to *daily schoolwork.*

A final difference is that our target is made more concrete and manageable by focusing on five student potentials that teachers have the power to influence and that directly contribute to school success. These five student abilities are dignity, energy, self-management, community, and awareness. We refer to them collectively as DESCA.

Five Key Student Abilities

All students have an inherent ability to live with *dignity,* to engage tasks with *energy,* to be appropriately *self-managing,* to work in *community* with at least some others, and to be *aware* of what is going on around them. Collectively, these DESCA abilities point to the heart of students' best, most productive selves.

D Is for Dignity

Students have an innate ability to live and work with dignity, as do we all. Moreover, deep down, students *want* to live and work with dignity. They do not want to feel belittled, demeaned, diminished, unimportant, unworthy. Yet traditional school practices can fail to take advantage of this ability to work with dignity. Some practices, in fact, frustrate students' impulses to do so. Our task, if we want to inspire students to be fully active learners, is to run our classrooms in a way that is comfortable to us, nourishing, never depressing, students' ability to work with dignity. We might, for example, take care to

Habit is habit, and not to be flung out of the window by any man, but coaxed downstairs a step at a time.
—*Mark Twain*

• Avoid embarrassing students, as by temporarily backing off when some feel blocked or are otherwise unable to learn what we are asking them to learn.

• Use only those discipline procedures that communicate care and high respect for students.

• Find practical ways to give students credit whenever they do the best they can, even when that falls far short of mastery.

• Announce high expectations without raising unproductive anxieties in low-ability students.

Practically speaking, can we do those things? Is it, for instance, realistic to expect us to avoid embarrassments and to discipline in ways that always communicate care? Yes, it is, as the strategies presented later in this book should make abundantly clear.

E Is for Energy

Students also have a natural ability to engage life energetically. They, in fact, *want* to engage life energetically. They suffer when they must sit still or stand around for too long with nothing much to do. We do well to nurture that ability to live energetically. It's after all what we, too, want. We certainly do not want students handling schoolwork apathetically or slumping in class listlessly. Nor do we want them running wildly out of control. Rather, we want students to engage schoolwork with a comfortable, steady flow of energy. To build on and draw out students' ability to do that, we might, for example

• Use very small groups, preferably pairs, to reduce chances that some students will be left uninvolved in group work.

• Adopt instructional procedures that allow students to occasionally move about so they can vent any built-up restlessness.

• Use whole-class choral work for information we want students to memorize.

S Is for Self-Management

All humans also have the ability to self-manage, and we would do well to develop this in our students. We do not want students asking us every little question that comes to mind. Rather, we want them to think for themselves, managing themselves as intelligently as they can. This is what they, too, want. They do not want to be bossed. Nor do they want to fly about out of control. To nurture students' self-managing ability, we might

- Include choices in each homework assignment; for example, give options on how many questions to answer or on how to handle a topic.
- Allow students to select their own work partners, chairs in the room, or focus for a small-group discussion.
- Ask each student to make a personal plan to tutor a younger student.

C Is for Community

Students, as do we all, have an ability to get along and relate comfortably with at least some others. And they want to do so. They do not want to be rejected or isolated. Rather, they want to be in community with at least some others. If, then, we want to elicit students' more cooperative and generous abilities, we might

- Structure lessons so students can often help one another.
- Encourage talkative students to create enough space for all students to be able to speak out.
- Set up support groups in which students learn to support one another over an extended time period.

A Is for Awareness

Finally, all students are aware beings. They have the ability to be alert, wakeful, observant, attentive. And they have an innate *longing* to be aware. They are not meant to be bored. Indeed, it is their very nature to *avoid* boredom. And we, of course, want students to stay alert and aware. That recommends we do not repress but rather develop this awareness ability. To do so, we might

- Find a way to help slower learners without boring faster learners.
- Change whatever we are doing whenever we notice student attention sliding, as by changing topics or procedures.
- Avoid having quick thinkers answering all our questions, as by having all students jot an answer on scrap paper or share answers in pairs before we discuss correct answers.
- Include activities students are highly interested in completing, as by asking students to construct a toothpick model of an idea, teach a concept to a younger student, or solve a real problem showing up in school.

Measuring Active Learning

Teachers have a great deal of control over the degree to which students will express those DESCA potentials and apply them to daily schoolwork. And we can measure how successfully we do that.

Several instruments can provide such measurements. One, the DESCA Scale for Rating a Class (Figure 2 on p. 10), is useful when we want to assess our own classes. We might also give the scale to observers so they can rate our students' current ability to engage in active and constructive learning.

Teachers who want to know the perceptions of their students often prefer to use something closer to the second form, the DESCA Questionnaire (Figure 3 on p. 11).

Also useful is a simple Active Learning Scale (Figure 4 on p. 12). Some options for using this scale:

• Each student completes the form every day, anonymously. Slips are put in an envelope. The teacher (or a mature student, volunteer parent, or office staff member) sorts slips and makes a chart to show progress over time. The teacher aims to gradually eliminate 1's and 2's and increase 3's and 4's.

• The above procedure is done on three random days each month. The three-day scores are averaged to give one monthly score. Scores are then charted for September, October, and so on, with the aim, as before, to show progress toward eliminating 1's and 2's and increasing 3's and 4's.

• To simplify scoring, ratings 1 and 2 could be collapsed and charted as "low involvement." Similarly, ratings 3 and 4 could be collapsed and charted as "high involvement." The aim, then, is to eliminate low-involvement scores.

Moving Education Forward

The strategies you will find in this book illustrate practical ways we can increase the scores on such measures. They show in some detail how each one of us, in our own ways, can run a classroom that keeps eliciting those DESCA abilities. Our field tests, by now involving hundreds of teachers in all kinds of schools and at all grade levels, show that when we do that, good things tend to happen. Students tend to climb up that Active Learning Ladder, so we see fewer and fewer working halfheartedly or not at all. As a result, students' time on task increases. Test scores rise. Discipline problems fade. Attendance improves. And, not insignificantly, we enjoy teaching far more.

Indeed, the benefits seem to stretch far beyond current classrooms. Consider the life-changing influence of a former 1st grade teacher, identified in the research only as "Miss A" (Pedersen, Faucher, & Eaton, 1978). The school in which Miss A taught was in the middle of a run-down neighborhood near the bus station in downtown Montreal. It was a neighborhood dotted with many taverns, few grocery stores. Some years ago researchers wondered if that school made much of a difference in the lives of its students, almost all of whom were living in poverty.

A teacher affects eternity; he can never tell where his influence stops.

—Henry Adams

Figure 2
DESCA Scale for Rating a Class

Dignity

| 1 | 2 | 3 | 4 | 5 |

Students have low self-worth: Students slouch or mope, as if feeling unimportant, weak, or hopeless. Or they act as if they will be worthless without success or others' approval. They show little evidence of self-confidence, self-respect, self-esteem.

Students work with full dignity: Talented or not, students sit and walk tall, self-assured. Students are confident they can succeed and can handle it when they don't. Students seem secure in their self-worth.

Energy

| 1 | 2 | 3 | 4 | 5 |

Students are lifeless or anxious: Tempo of class is too slow, with much inactivity, waiting, apathy, time wasting. Or the mood is too frantic, stressful, exhausting, anxious.

Student energy flows comfortably: Students keep busy, engaged, active. The mood is comfortably alive, with no evidence of clock watching. Time seems to fly.

Self-Management

| 1 | 2 | 3 | 4 | 5 |

Students only follow orders: Students show no evidence of self-responsibility, initiative, self-direction, personal choice. Students work passively, without personal commitment.

Students are self-managing: Students make appropriate choices, guide and discipline themselves, work purposefully and persistently. Students aren't bossed.

Community

| 1 | 2 | 3 | 4 | 5 |

Students are totally self-centered: Students act only for personal advantage, unconcerned with others' welfare. They show no evidence of sharing, teamwork, belonging, or kindness among peers or toward the teacher.

A togetherness mood prevails: Students display much sharing, cooperation, kindness, interdependence. There is no antagonism, teasing, rejection. Students often act to support one another and the teacher.

Awareness

| 1 | 2 | 3 | 4 | 5 |

Students are bored or occupied by mindless busywork: Class is dull. Students seem unaware, unresponsive, or narrow-minded, shallow. There is little or no thinking, searching, concentrating; much inattentiveness. Student talk is impulsive or thoughtless.

Students are aware and alert: Students show much evidence of concentration, observing, listening, thinking, noticing, evaluating, creating. Students appear to be mindful, aware of what is going on. They have a high level of attentiveness. Student talk is thoughtful.

Figure 3
DESCA Questionnaire

Dear Student:

How was class for you today? Please check one item in each category.

Dignity
____ I had strong, good feelings about myself.
____ I felt fairly positive and secure.
____ I am unsure how I felt.
____ I didn't feel very good about myself.
____ I thought I was inadequate, hopeless, bad, or stupid.

Energy
____ I was comfortably active and energetic all the time.
____ I was comfortably active and energetic most of the time.
____ I am unsure how I felt.
____ I did not put much energy into my work.
____ I felt inactive and low, or anxious and stressed.

Self-Management
____ I made many choices, managed myself, always felt self-responsible.
____ I was rather self-managing, somewhat self-responsible.
____ I am unsure how I felt.
____ I drifted along, not using much of my own willpower.
____ I was controlled or bossed, not at all self-responsible.

Community
____ I felt that I was a part of the group and wanted to help others.
____ I had generally positive feelings about others.
____ I am unsure how I felt.
____ I did not feel fully accepted by others and didn't much want to help them.
____ I felt only selfishness and rejection from others.

Awareness
____ I was aware and alert all the time.
____ I was aware and alert most of the time.
____ I am unsure how I felt.
____ I often was unresponsive or bored.
____ I paid little attention. I was very unresponsive or bored.

> When a person praises punishment, 9 times out of 10 this means he is prepared to administer it rather than submit to it.
>
> —*Anonymous*

To answer their question, the researchers looked up adults who had attended the school 25 years earlier. What they learned was not encouraging. Even after 25 years of adulthood and a general increase in society's economic welfare over that period, only 29 percent of the former students that the researchers located lived in reasonably decent housing or had more than menial jobs. Thirty-eight percent

---

Figure 4
Active Learning Scale

How were you in class today?
(Circle one number.)

1	2	3	4
Very inactive or bored	Sometimes active and alert	Usually active and alert	Very active and alert

---

of those former students were still suffering at the lowest levels of survival, typically homeless and unemployed.

Yet that did not include all the students. It did not include the students who had been in classrooms taught by Miss A. The researchers noticed something curious about Miss A's former students. Whereas only 29 percent of the students of the other teachers lived in decent housing and held more than menial jobs, a full 64 percent of the students who had Miss A were that well off. Furthermore, although 38 percent of the students from other classrooms were found to be living at the lowest economic levels, *none* of the students who had Miss A was living at that level. (See Figure 5.)

Clearly, one 1st grade teacher had a dramatic, long-term influence on students. She was doing much more than teaching reading, writing, and arithmetic. Perhaps she was doing what Marva Collins (1992) terms Hot Teaching. "When we make lessons come alive," Collins observes, " with what I call Hot Teaching, every child becomes a winner." (For more research on the long-term impact of excellent teachers, see Schweinhart, Montie, Xiang, Barnett, Belfield, and Nores, 2005.)

We believe that every teacher can now aim to make every child such a winner. The teaching profession has amassed enough practical wisdom to make that a real possibility. As a result, it is no longer necessary to struggle so fruitlessly with unmotivated and undisciplined students. It is no longer necessary to push and pull so doggedly, trying to force reluctant and resistant learners to change. The profession now knows how such students can be *inspired* to become more actively, responsibly involved. That is, the profession knows how teachers can do all they must do each day—from taking attendance to assigning homework, from collaring the troublemakers to smiling at the achievers—in a way that steadily draws out the best that students have in them.

This inspiring approach may be the most efficient way to move education ahead. Indeed, it may be the only way. It is difficult to see how schooling can

Schoolteachers are not fully appreciated by parents until it rains all day Saturday.

—E. C. McKenzie

Figure 5
Long-Term Impact of One Great Teacher
on Students in Poverty

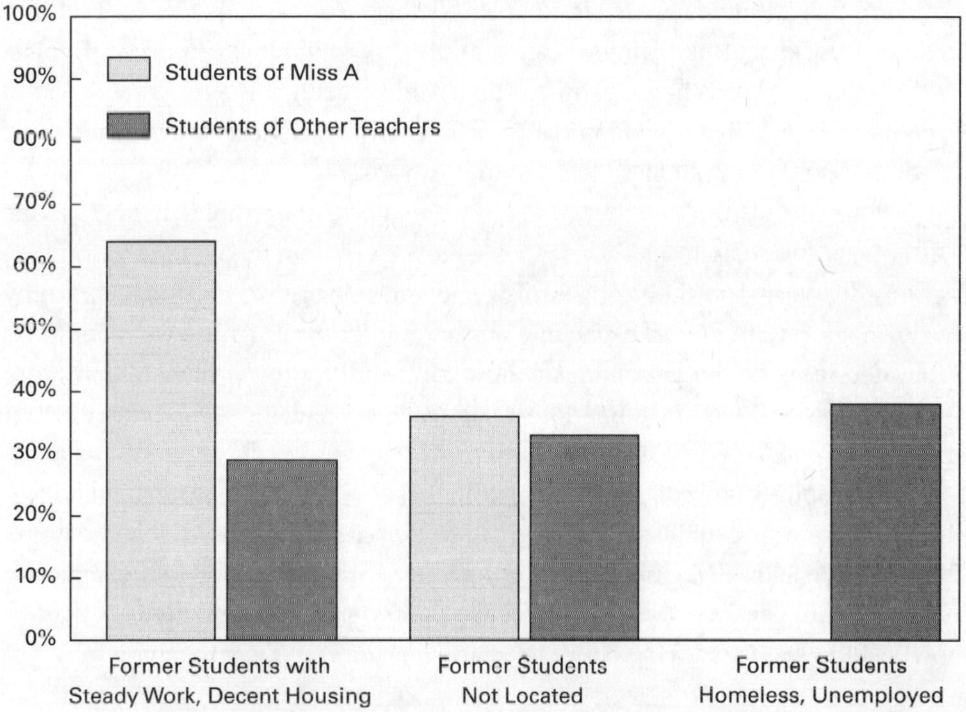

become much more effective if more of the constructive, positive abilities of students are *not* drawn into schoolwork.

Compare this approach to motivation with one based mainly on extrinsic rewards and punishments. How might a reward-punishment school treat students who have not been putting much effort into their schoolwork? It would likely threaten them in some way, perhaps threaten to send those who do not shape up to summer school or, ultimately, to make them repeat the grade. How effective are those threats? Do they spark the kind of constructive, self-responsible learning teachers really want to see in their classrooms? Not in our experience. Threats are more likely to add to classroom negativity, resentment, and depression, among both students and teachers.

Not that the inspiring approach excludes rewards and punishments. Rewards, smiles, and token prizes, we find, can well be inspiring to students. And a suitable punishment can be the best way to inspire someone to pay attention and consider a change in attitude. But to have a positive effect, the punishment must rest in a context of genuine care. Students must be certain—at some level of awareness—that punishment is not retaliation or the result of frustration or anger. They must understand that punishment is, instead, the result of the teacher's sincere concern that students learn more actively and self-responsibly, and of the teacher's belief that punishment can spark a new willingness to do so. Punishment in that context is healing, not hurting. And, as such, it is a tool that fits comfortably into our inspiring approach, as will be clear from the examples of effective discipline strategies included in this book.

So the issue is not whether to use rewards and punishments as motivators. The issue is about *our* motivations. Are we motivated more by our care for our students' education and their long-term well-being? Or are we motivated more by our own short-term needs, especially our need to control? And if we *want* to be motivated more by our genuine care, how can we move toward that target? More pointedly, given the many demands we face, *can* we realistically move toward it? Indeed, we can.

This inspiring approach to motivation is something to test for yourself. A three-week trial is usually enough for you to begin enjoying at least some benefits. Psychologists tell us that 21 days is the length of time needed to create a new habit. The next chapter details an effective procedure for conducting such a test and, just maybe, for moving closer to your own brand of great teaching.

DESCA as an Integrating Theme

Before turning to the next chapter, consider the possibility that DESCA might serve us as an integrating theme. So many new ideas come our way—constructivism, computer learning, brain research, accountability testing, cooperative learning. It's easy to see those as a series of disconnected developments, even fads that come and go, each replacing the one before. They are not so easily seen as developments that might complement one another and contribute to one whole thrust for our professional development.

Yet teaching is one of the helping professions. Regardless of our grade level or subject specialty, our job, in essence, is to help students. Like physicians, we certainly want to do no harm. Putting it more specifically, common to our mission is the goal of helping students learn in a way that develops what's positive and constructive in them—such as their abilities to live and work with personal *dignity*, steady *energy*, intelligent *self-management*, feelings of *community*, and open *awareness*. We certainly don't want to suppress those DESCA abilities or, worse, tempt students to conclude they cannot ever be developed.

Might it be useful, then, for us to take each improvement idea that comes along and ask, How might it help us teach whatever it is we teach in a way that serves students' DESCA growth? Might that question aid us in making innovations more cumulatively helpful? By giving each idea a role in our ongoing task of doing the best we can, might it not help us avoid forgetting the older ideas and, instead, keep all ideas alive and functional for us?

A Four-Step Process to Make a Classroom More Inspiring

A foreign dignitary visited President Clinton in the White House. Because the dignitary hardly spoke English, he was carefully coached beforehand. "When you meet the President," his coach explained, "simply shake hands and say, 'How are you, Mr. President?' After he replies, you say, 'Me, too.'"

Unfortunately, when the time came, the dignitary asked, "Who are you, Mr. President?" Gracefully, Clinton smiled and answered lightly, "I'm Hillary's husband." The dignitary then also smiled, gave a slight bow, and said, "Me, too."

The moral: It's easy to make mistakes when trying something new. And because we don't like to make mistakes, especially when we risk being criticized, we often don't explore new ways. We would rather stick with the familiar.

That reality became strikingly clear to us early in our workshops with teachers. We would demonstrate new motivation strategies, and the teachers would role-play those strategies. They would experience the power of the strategies and understand their value. The teachers said they planned to use some of the strategies, those they thought would work well in their classrooms. But guess what? Many did not do so. Apparently, breaking free of established routines was harder for those teachers than even they realized.

That, of course, is the classic problem in professional development. Despite all the graduate courses we take, despite the many inservice programs we attend, despite the best exhortations of education leaders, many of us end up taking the path of least resistance and repeating this year what we did last year. Thus can we become stagnant in our teaching, unable to take advantage of the best ideas available.

In working with teachers, we wanted to make it easier for them to move beyond their existing habits. And we wanted teachers to feel strong, not anxious, when they explored promising innovations. We wanted them to step out in the spirit of confident, open-minded explorers. But how can we help teachers do that? After much experimentation, we finally crafted a process that works very well. We recommend you consider using it during your test of the active-learning approach. The process will make it easier for you to put the ideas of this book into practice. It will also help you develop the skills of a confident, self-guided professional.

What Helps Us Be Self-Guided Professionals?

Self-guided professionals are those who ask questions, try new ideas, and keep improving their own effectiveness. They need not rely on others to initiate improvement. They are lifelong learners. More specifically, we find they are particularly skillful at

- *Targeting.* Self-guided professionals maintain clear standards for themselves, are in touch with their ideals, know the direction they want to go, and notice fairly quickly when they drift or are thrown off track.
- *Adjusting.* Self-guided professionals are able to adjust their teaching when they choose to do so and are not reluctant to explore something new if they sense it might help them better serve their ideals.
- *Balancing.* Self-guided professionals maintain a fair measure of personal balance and, when they become stressed or depressed or are otherwise thrown off balance, they are able to regain their balance.
- *Supporting.* Self-guided professionals are willing to share ideas and talk with colleagues about professional questions, including their personal confusions and weaknesses, and they feel supported by that collaborative process.

Consider giving yourself two assignments to help you practice and sharpen those four skills while you explore the strategies in this book. We think you will find each assignment straightforward and perhaps even intriguing. Together, the assignments illustrate a potent four-part process that will greatly facilitate your professional development.

Assignment 1: A Personal Adjustment List

The first assignment is designed to make the inspiring approach to motivation, discussed in Chapter 1, vivid and real for you. This assignment will also guide you in making a list of specific teaching adjustments you might want to try.

A man without a goal is like a ship without a rudder.

—*Thomas Carlyle*

As you'll see, Chapters 3 through 8 deal with basic teaching tasks. The first few strategies in each chapter, marked with an arrow, are strategies that teachers have found particularly effective in motivating more students to be active learners. Read at least those strategies from Chapters 3 through 8 and, as you do so, start a list called Possible Adjustments.

As you read a strategy, if a teaching idea pops up that you might want to try someday—or that you at least want to think more about—add it to your list. If you recall teaching practices you once thought of trying but never got around to, add those as well. Your goal is to build a list of new and old ideas that might help you to better handle your teaching tasks.

Learn from the mistakes of others. You won't live long enough to make them all yourself.

—*Anonymous*

By the way, some teachers find it useful to keep such a list throughout their careers. From time to time they add new ideas to the list and eliminate those tried. And, in that way, they keep their professional outlook fresh and exciting.

However, for the purposes of this assignment, it's usually best not to actually try any of the adjustment ideas quite yet. At this point we recommend you merely aim to clarify and expand your image of what a highly inspiring classroom might look like for you. Assignment 2 will guide you in trying some of those ideas in a way that maximizes chances you will have delightfully successful experiences.

If you can find a buddy or two to engage in this assignment with you, please do so. It's often fun to share discoveries with others and to hear of their discoveries. Besides, you may have questions as you read about the strategies in Chapters 3 through 8, and it's good to have someone to talk them over with. Make your lists alone, but then occasionally sit together and share thoughts and questions.

Take as much time as you need for Assignment 1. It will prepare you well for Assignment 2.

Assignment 2: Stepping Forward Smartly

Sometimes one action does not solve a problem. With a severe infection, for example, we may need to take medicine, drink lots of water, and get lots of bed rest. Similarly, we've learned that several things—four, to be exact—are required if most teachers are to smoothly and successfully advance in professional effectiveness. Accordingly, Assignment 2, which deals with trying some of the ideas on your Possible Adjustments List, has four parts to it. One for each of the four key skills of the effective lifelong professional learner: *targeting, adjusting, balancing,* and *supporting,* or TABS for short. The challenge, then, is to find a way to do all four parts of this assignment simultaneously.

TABS
The four skills of self-guiding
professionals

Targeting steadily on a single, encompassing goal, such as seeing all students learning with high DESCA.

Adjusting as you find opportunities to more easily or quickly move toward that target.

Balancing yourself when stressed, angry, guilty, or otherwise thrown off balance.

Supporting your efforts by enlisting at least one buddy with whom to share your thoughts and concerns.

Introduction

If you are like most others, the reading you did for Assignment 1 suggested several strategies you might want to experiment with. That is the typical reaction of those who look over Chapters 3 through 8. But for any given teacher, even the best strategy can be highly effective or a complete flop. What makes the difference? In large part, the intention or motivation of the teacher using the strategy. In the same way that someone greeting us cheerfully on the phone can either relax us or put us on guard, depending on whether that greeting comes from an old friend or a new salesman, the purpose behind the action makes all the difference in the world.

Consider three common teacher intentions, based on three common teacher targets (Figure 6 on p. 20). For some teachers, the ideal is a problem-free day at school. Such teachers may have many pressures in their lives unrelated to teaching and may feel a need to conserve their energy to handle those pressures. Or they may have large numbers of students who cause problems, so they may feel a need to get their classrooms under control before they can do more. Or they may simply be bored with teaching and want to get through each day with as little fuss as possible. In any case, these are the teachers who aim to run classrooms

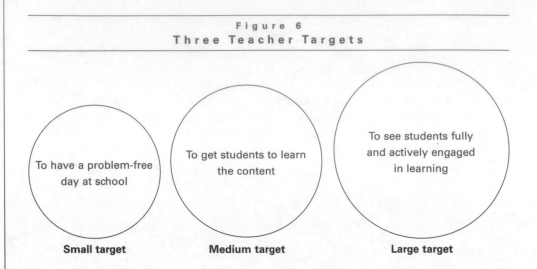

Figure 6
Three Teacher Targets

To have a problem-free day at school

To get students to learn the content

To see students fully and actively engaged in learning

Small target   **Medium target**   **Large target**

in a way that minimizes their daily difficulties. We might call this a relatively *small* target for a teacher. Unfortunately, although understandably, when we visit schools we see many teachers who, especially after they get tenure, settle for this target.

For other teachers, the target each day is to get students to learn specific content. This is a popular target, often recommended as the prime one for all teachers, and it's certainly a worthy one. We would expect the students of teachers who center on this target to learn more than the students of teachers who merely want problem-free days. We might call this a *medium* target.

For yet other teachers, the ideal is seeing students fully, actively engaged in learning, doing the very best they can each day. We might call that a *large* target, for when teachers succeed in reaching it, they automatically serve the small and medium targets mentioned above. That is, students who are fully active learners automatically produce fewer problems for teachers; they are, after all, generally busy learning. Furthermore, students who are fully, actively engaged in learning are likely to master the content of their courses as well as they possibly can.

When we hold that large target as our priority, then, we automatically take care of many of our other concerns. In that sense it's an encompassing, efficient target, which thereby simplifies teaching for us. And, as you can demonstrate for yourself, it is a target that inspires students to respond positively to our efforts.

Here, for example, is a teacher who holds that large target. She is addressing the first class of the year.

I want to see you all doing your very best work each day. That is my main concern. I want you to invest all your energy and creativity in our daily lessons. I want you to give our lessons the best you have in you. Do that and you'll be sure to learn as much as you possibly can.

That may be easy for you if you like the material we're covering. It may be a challenge if the material is difficult for you or not interesting to you. I remember having to memorize spelling words when I was in school; that was very hard for me. Some things might be like that for you. If so, you'll really have to be persistent and creative to find ways of attacking those lessons with your full energy and care. But it will be good practice, for often, in real life, we must do things that are hard for us or that we really don't like doing. Can anyone think of a time when you faced something that was hard for you or that you didn't like doing, yet you still gave it your all and did the very best you could? That is something I want you to learn how to do in this class.

Few of us want to go through our days pretending we are something we are not. Nor do we want to suppress parts of our natural abilities. We want to engage life as our full, comfortable selves. Consequently, when, as teachers, we target on helping students apply their full, comfortable selves to schoolwork, we harmonize what we want for ourselves with what we want for our students. And it is pleasing to live in such harmony. It's a way to define integrity.

In any case, it is the large target that we recommend you make your priority as you test the strategies in this book.

Part 1: On Targeting

First, choose some way of keeping in mind that one of your prime aims is to hit that large target. For example, we might target on seeing more students fully engaged in learning each day or, to be more precise, on seeing more students engaging their daily lessons at high levels of dignity, energy, self-management, community, and awareness (DESCA). What might help you keep that target in mind as you go through a busy teaching day? Different teachers use different methods. For example, you might

• Review the DESCA Scale for Rating a Class (Figure 2 on p. 10) each morning or evening, imagining what a high DESCA classroom would look like. Hold that picture inside your mind for a moment or two. Then, during the day, occasionally scan the class for evidence of high and low DESCA involvement.

• Pick one or two of the DESCA abilities—dignity, energy, self-management, community, awareness—and pay particular attention to improving those areas. Perhaps give approximate class ratings each day for each ability you picked.

• Call to mind a few students who are on the low rungs of the Active Learning Ladder (Figure 1 on p. 4). During the day, stay aware of those students and aim for your teaching actions to be especially valuable to them.

If [the teacher] is indeed wise he does not bid you enter the house of his wisdom, but rather leads you to the threshold of your own mind.

—Kahlil Gibran

• Post a copy of the Active Learning Ladder and announce to your class that you want everyone to join you in a challenge: to produce more class moments when all students are at the top half of that ladder. Make that a class project. Ask for student suggestions and assistance. Check in with students from time to time, perhaps asking, "How's it going?" Or asking, "How can we do better?"

• Make the experiment more concrete by actually charting active learning each day. You might measure active learning by using the DESCA Scale for Rating a Class, perhaps having three students make a classroom estimate at the same time each day. Or by using the DESCA Questionnaire (Figure 3 on p. 11). Or by using the Active Learning Scale (Figure 4 on p. 12). Or by using the Active Learning Ladder, perhaps by having students judge their own spots on the ladder each day and having a pair of students chart and post that information.

The principle here: If we are to harness the full power of the strategies in this book, and if we are to make progress without lots of backtracking and wandering, we must be very clear about our priorities and hold them steadily in mind. We must hold high the priority of inspiring more students to become fully, actively engaged. Because there are so many demands on us as teachers, it's not always easy to keep that large target in mind. It may help to remember that when we do so, we automatically serve many other goals we also care about—such as minimizing our discipline problems and maximizing student test scores.

Part 2: On Adjusting

If you want to give this inspiring approach a three-week test, during the next 15 teaching days try several adjustments to your standard way of teaching. Strive to get some new things to work for you. Proceed at your own pace, no matter how slowly, but do risk moving beyond your old habits. You might

• Plan to use one or more items from your Possible Adjustments List each day. Also, if you are so moved, make adjustments that occur to you spontaneously while teaching. Be as creative as you can.

• Identify a problem in your classroom, search for a strategy that might help you handle that problem, and then give the strategy a try.

• Try again if something does not work one day but still holds promise, perhaps by trying it somewhat differently. Don't give up too easily.

• Try adjustments other than the ones suggested in this book. Perhaps recall some of your own old ideas, which you might have put aside because they seemed inappropriate at the time. You might also find possibilities worth trying from the innovations currently popular—brain research, computer use, multiple intelligences, or whatever new research comes along. And, of course, other teachers might have ideas for you once you get into this project, especially if you cooperatively share your experiences with them.

The intent of this assignment is not for you to make a change in your teaching every day. But it is to try some new adjustments and, more significant, to break any habit or assumption that has been limiting your readiness to change, such as "I already have too much to do" or "I'm about as good a teacher as I can ever be." You want to deliberately seek to make changes for 15 teaching days because it often takes that long to repattern unproductive thinking. After 15 days, you should quite naturally remain on the lookout for improvement possibilities, ready and able to take advantage of the opportunities that show up, ready even to *create* new opportunities to be the kind of teacher that, deep down, you always longed to be.

Of course, as you engage this second assignment, keep in mind the target discussed in the first assignment: to see more students actively engaged, that is, learning with high DESCA. (If you have yet to begin teaching, we recommend you arrange some kind of role-play or practice teaching situation for yourself; it's difficult to advance something as complex as teaching competence without practice.)

Part 3: On Balancing

Take a few moments each day before school, during school, or after school to check the state of your personal balance. If you are feeling stressed, guilty, depressed, overburdened, frazzled, confused, or have in any other way been thrown off balance, find ways to regain your balance. You might

- Take six deep breaths, close your eyes, and imagine a positive scene.
- Go for a walk. Enjoy nature. Enjoy music. Get outside of your thoughts for a while.
- Talk out your feelings, write them out, or just let them go and turn your attention to something more peaceful.
- Exercise.
- Meditate.
- Give yourself extra free time.
- Give yourself more respect. Acknowledge your efforts and recognize a job well done.
- Say no to some temptations or requests, recognizing you can't do it all. Step off the fast pace of today's society.

• Write several times, "I am now regaining my fully peaceful self" or "No need for me to pretend so much. I intend to be true to myself." Or write any other affirmation that you find leads you to better balance.

• Remind yourself of the truth embedded in the Serenity Prayer: "Grant me the serenity to accept the things I cannot change, the courage to change the things I can, and the wisdom to know the difference."

When you are not your fully peaceful self, you will not be the best you can be for others or yourself. It's true: You must sometimes take care of yourself before you can effectively take care of others. The key here is not to struggle along in a state of imbalance as you try to improve your teaching.

In a way, your target for yourself should be similar to your target for your students: to bring out the best that is in you. Not incidentally, one way to bring out the best in yourself is to commit to *more* than yourself, as when you dedicate yourself to bringing out the best in your students. You then not only do good work; you give expression to your best self.

> Take the first steps in faith. You don't have to see the whole staircase. Just take the first step.
> —*Martin Luther King Jr.*

Part 4: On Supporting

This part of the assignment is simple: Talk over your experiences and questions each day with at least one supportive buddy. You might

• Ask one or two colleagues to have lunch with you daily and to give you 10 minutes to reflect on your day. You might report one thing you liked about the day and one thing you want to do differently. Or you might talk about your successes and failures, joys and frustrations, victories and fears. If your colleague is also engaging in these assignments, so much the better. You could then offer reciprocal support.

• Ask a friend or relative to be your listening ear for 10 minutes after school.

• Invite two to four teachers to form a small support team and meet at least once a week for a more extended sharing of ideas and progress. It's especially useful to share lesson plans, asking your team how your lessons can be made even more inspiring than they now are. Even more valuable is asking a colleague to observe your teaching and to suggest alternative ways you might proceed. Few of us have as many good ideas as have all of us. And few of us see ourselves as objectively or clearly as others see us.

• E-mail colleagues or friends regularly to communicate your thoughts.

The key here is not to go it alone. The reality is that it's much more difficult to change habits of thinking or acting when we attempt to proceed alone. It is almost always easier and more pleasant when we have a supportive person or two with whom we can share our daily experiences and questions.

A Checklist for Assignment 2

During this assignment, many teachers find it useful to create a checklist for themselves. To do this, you might draw a grid with five columns like the one shown in Figure 7. The first column is for dates of the 15 teaching days you plan to engage this assignment. Across the top, insert the four skills to practice each day: targeting, adjusting, balancing, and supporting, or TABS. Then aim to check each box each day as you take the steps that will lead you where you want to go. Perhaps give a box two check marks if you did exceptionally well with one of the TABS skills on that day.

Figure 7
Checklist for Becoming a Self-Guided Professional

Enter the date and place a check mark in the appropriate skills column as you practice each task.

Date	Skills of Self-Guided Professionals			
	Targeting	Adjusting	Balancing	Supporting

You have brains in your head. You have feet in your shoes. You can steer yourself any direction you choose. You're on your own, and you know what you know. And you are the one who'll decide where you'll go.

—Dr. Seuss

Future Assignments

Your three-week trial should give you the clear sense that your students' constructive, positive abilities can, in fact, be drawn into daily schoolwork. Perhaps students at the top of the Active Learning Ladder, those who were fully active learners, will show hints of new aliveness. Or those who were responsible students will show new initiative and dedication. Perhaps the halfhearted workers will show hints of new diligence, or the work avoiders will begin to show evidence of new cooperativeness and willingness.

Your next assignment, then, might be to continue to adjust your teaching so your classroom inspires active learning even more fully. You might want to make a new schedule for yourself and read ahead in this book in some systematic way, perhaps using other resources or coordinating your work with colleagues who also want to move further ahead. Or, if you were working alone up to now, you might want to share your experiences with others and invite them to join you.

You may also want to continue to make that four-step growth process part of your professional life. Your training may not have prepared you very well to escape the grasp of unproductive habits or to overcome the tendency to go along with other teachers, no matter how unprofessional those teachers might act. Accordingly, you may want to continue practicing some or all of the TABS skills included in the two assignments: *targeting* on a clear, large ideal; *adjusting* whenever a new idea shows promise of helping you reach your ideal; *balancing* in a way that allows you to be your most resourceful, fully peaceful self; and *supporting* your efforts by actively sharing, not trying to go it alone. That process should help you move toward more effective teaching and, as we think you will discover, toward more deeply satisfying teaching as well.

If you continue on this path, we believe you will be mastering the heart of the art of teaching—the ability to elicit the best students have in them. We each, of course, must approach that target from where we now are. And we must move toward it at our own speed. When we do so, we gradually develop our own brand of great teaching.

PART II

Strategies for Handling
Six Fundamental
Teaching Tasks

Certain teaching tasks are fundamental. When we can't handle them well, all our teaching days are likely to suffer. This part of the book focuses on six such tasks: preparing effective lessons, motivating student participation, motivating student cooperation, structuring class time efficiently, taking advantage of small groups, and preventing discipline problems. This part of the book, then, helps us build a solid foundation for the entire school year.

In terms of inspiring active learning, note that the language we use each day makes a difference. What language activates the best motives students carry within them? Consider these three comments and imagine the impact each might have on students:

> *Least inspiring:* "We'll cover a lot of material in this class, and if you expect a decent grade you must do decent work. The grading system will be as follows . . ."

> *In between:* "We'll cover a lot of material in this class. Here, for example, are the main questions we will answer . . ."

> *Most inspiring:* "We'll cover a lot of material in this class, and you will all learn a lot. It's important to me that you *enjoy* doing that learning. I want us to work together and find ways of making this class so satisfying you will *want* to come here every day. Let's get started."

Creating Lessons That Inspire Active Learning

3

One of the everyday tasks of teachers is planning lessons that inspire all students to stay actively, productively involved. Or, to be more specific, we might say the goal is to craft lessons that inspire students to work with high *dignity*, steady *energy*, intelligent *self-management*, feelings of *community*, and alert *awareness*. But considering the great variety of students in the classroom, how is that possible? The five strategies in this chapter can help us answer that question. Based on our field tests, we recommend giving first attention to the first four strategies, each of which is marked with an arrow.

Note that some of the strategies include references to other strategies that are explained fully in later chapters. All strategies are numbered by chapter—for example, Strategy 16-3 refers to the third strategy in Chapter 16.

Strategy 3-1: Action Flow Lessons

Purpose: To keep a variety of students actively and constructively engaged in learning.

Description: Planning lessons around active-learning strategies that flow together smoothly, coherently, interestingly.

Imagine a classroom in which students sit through long lectures or endless, repetitive discussions or in which students struggle through worksheet after worksheet. Boredom will likely be a common experience. The remedy turns out to be quite simple: adding more variety to our lessons. To accomplish this, consider what we call Action Flow Lessons.

As the name suggests, Action Flow Lessons are high on energy and movement. The aim is to get enough action going so students naturally remain involved, so neither threats nor rewards are necessary to keep students on task. A typical Action Flow Lesson moves quickly and contains much variety. One lesson includes some of this and some of that. If *this* does not capture the attention of a student, perhaps *that* will.

The following are some examples of such lessons. Imagine how students might experience each one and you'll get the feel for this kind of lesson.

Action Flow Lesson 1: Think-Share-Learn

1. Question, All Write (Strategy 16-3)

Whole class, 1–2 minutes. Pose a thought-provoking question to the class, such as "What makes a good paragraph?" or "What do we all know about planets and stars?" or "How can we tell the difference between a courageous act and a foolish act?" or "What are some ways we can dream up to make mental addition easier?" or "How might we improve the lunchroom?" Then ask each student to respond to the question by making notes. Ask with confidence, expecting all students to follow your direction. Do not be concerned if some do nothing at first; rely on the flow of the action to eventually capture all students' attention.

2. Productive Discussion (Strategy 16-2)

Whole class, time as appropriate. When three or four students have finished writing, announce, "Just one more minute, please," or say something like, "Just finish the thought you are now writing." Do not wait until most students finish. Rather, keep the pace upbeat; remain confident that students will soon realize they are not expected to write every idea they have. Then say something like, "I'd like to have a few share their ideas. Who's willing to go first?"

Do not let the discussion go too long. When you sense involvement may soon slump, move on, knowing it's better to have a discussion too short than to have some students tuning out.

3. Sharing Pairs (Strategy 7-1)

Small groups, 5–6 minutes. After the discussion, ask students to pair up with someone nearby and share their thoughts or notes. Tell them they have just a few minutes for this sharing. Say "Go!" as if starting a race, to zip up the class energy level.

Students pick their own partners. Help only those who can't manage. (If students have great difficulty pairing up, make a mental note to have them practice that procedure another time, so they master it and so you can use the procedure efficiently in the future.)

> Don't be afraid to give up the good to go for the great.
> —*Kenny Rogers*

When you see that two or three pairs have finished talking, announce, "Just one more minute, please," or say something like, "Just finish the thought you are now on." Then firmly call the class together. Do not worry if some students have not even started talking on the topic; trust that when students realize you do not give excess time for small-group talk, they will move into their discussions more quickly.

4. Productive Discussion/Attentive Lecture (Strategies 16-2 and 13-1)

Whole class, time as appropriate. Without waiting for all pairs to be ready (you want activity to catch students up, and waiting is not an activity), ask, "Who will share something you or your partner talked about?" This question usually leads to a Productive Discussion.

Then say something like, "Here are some thoughts I have about this." Continue your lecture only as long as the class remains attentive. Move on to the next step as soon as you sense some students are beginning to tune out; the plan is to maintain active learning, and students who are tuned out are not learning actively.

After the lecture segment, move on to either Step 5a or 5b.

5a. Question, All Write (Strategy 16-3)

Whole class, 1–2 minutes. Pose a new issue for students to respond to, perhaps a question designed to advance student thinking.

5b. Productive Discussion (Strategy 16-2)

Whole class, time as appropriate. Pose a discussion opener such as this: "Is anyone willing to share reactions or questions about what I said or to share any other ideas you have?"

6. Outcome Sentences (Strategy 21-1)

Whole class, 1–2 minutes. Conclude by saying something like, "Please think back over what we have done so far. See if you can write two or three things you got from the lesson. Perhaps write some endings to phrases like *I learned* . . . , or *I was surprised* . . . , or *I'm beginning to wonder* . . . , or *I rediscovered* . . . , or *I feel* . . . , or *I promise* . . . , or anything like that." Write these sentence stems on the board as you say them or point to a chart you prepared that contains those sentence stems. Then say, "See what you can get for yourself from this lesson. Go!"

7. Whip Around, Pass Option (Strategy 16-4)

Whole class, 2–3 minutes. When a few students seem ready, say, "One more minute, please." This will alert students that the lesson will soon move on. Then

> If we succeed in giving the love of learning, the learning itself is sure to follow.
>
> —*John Lubbock*

say something like, "Let's start with Bob here in the first seat and whip around at least part of the class. When it's your turn, either say, 'I pass' or read one Outcome Sentence you wrote. Bob, will you please begin?"

If time permits, you can conclude with the following optional step.

8. Sharing Pairs (Strategy 7-1)

Small groups, time as appropriate. Ask students to sit with their partners again and to take turns sharing what they wrote and, if they like, discussing the issues they found particularly interesting.

Summary

The Think-Share-Learn sequence illustrates one kind of high-involvement lesson. We would, of course, need to adjust the steps for various grade levels and subject specialties. The general format is simple: Questions are raised to stimulate student interest *before* we give information. This contrasts with lessons that start with a presentation, which in effect give students answers before they even wonder about the questions.

Action Flow Lesson 2: Guided Practice and Review

1. Choral Work (Strategy 11-2)

Whole class, 3–5 minutes. Display the top card of a set of cards, each one containing a math fact, a chemical symbol, a spelling word, a phrase illustrating proper language usage, or any other material students are to internalize. Have students chant out the content of each card as you display it. Turn the cards briskly and encourage high energy with an occasional request for "a little more power, please."

2. Guided Discovery (Strategy 14-4)

Whole class, 3–15 minutes. Pose a problem to be solved from yesterday's lesson, with each student working alone. As soon as students begin to write their solutions, quietly write the correct solution on the board. As students finish, they check their own work by looking at what you have written. If you sense students need more practice, pose another similar problem and, again, while students work it out at their desks, write your solution on the board. Continue until some students seem ready for new work.

Perhaps after a brief discussion, pose a problem that leads the students into new material. Have them try to solve it while you quietly write the correct solution on the board. The process continues in this way, with the focus on students discovering

> Boredom is the bitter fruit of too much routine or none at all.
>
> —*Brendan Francis*

solutions and practicing solving problems. Avoid extended discussion to keep the pace from lagging. Don't expect that all students will master the new material during this lesson, but do monitor the state of mastery as the lesson proceeds, so you know how fast to introduce new material and when to stop. Continue moving the process forward until you sense confusion rising or it's time to move on.

If you notice confusion among the students, go on to Step 3a or 3b. Time permitting, use both steps.

3a. Think Aloud (Strategy 14-3)

Whole class, time as appropriate. Work through a problem aloud, to model the thinking you use to solve it. An example in math: "Because I don't know what to put here, I think I'll try an estimate. I see I need something larger than 6 because . . ." An example in science: "How should I approach this? How would it work if I . . . Oops, that doesn't work. Let me try . . ."

3b. Learning Pairs (Strategy 7-2)

Small groups, time as appropriate. Ask students to pick a partner and to help each other with a set of problems, or, if both understand, to create new challenges for each other. Circulate among students, helping where needed.

4. Review Test (Strategy 11-1)

Whole class, 4–8 minutes. To review and reinforce prior material, ask students to solve five problems that deal with old material. Present the first problem. While students solve the problem by themselves, write out the correct solution on the board so students can silently correct their own work. Proceed in this way through the set of five review problems. No instruction or grading is involved. Instead, focus on review, self-correction, and personal challenge. Keep the pace sufficiently brisk to inspire high student involvement.

5. Voting Questions (Strategy 9-3)

Whole class, 1 minute. Ask students such questions as "How many of you did some good risk taking during today's lesson? How many of you strengthened old understandings? How many of you like the way you handled the work today?" The idea is to give students a moment to assess their own learning processes and to share their assessments. Do not give grades or rewards for excellence. Do not communicate dismay at those who are not yet doing excellent work. If appropriate, do say something like, "Remember that no one need have mastered this material quite yet. We'll review it many more times."

Action Flow Lesson 3:
Cushioning–Underexplain–Learning Pairs

1. Cushioning Questions (Strategy 4-2)

Whole class, 1–2 minutes. Begin the lesson by saying something like this: "Today we will talk about something new. You do not need to understand this completely right now. We will review and help one another later on, so relax and let's just see what happens today. Why do you think it would be OK with me if you made a mistake while learning this?" Discuss very briefly.

2. Underexplain and Learning Pairs (Strategy 14-2)

Whole class, 5–15 minutes. Present a concept or principle. An example: "There are many ways to get a balance beam like this to balance. You can move this center point or the position of the weights, as I am doing here. You can invent your own system, but one general rule that works is . . ." Continue your explanation, but keep it brief, so perhaps only half of the class is likely to understand. Then say something like, "Now get together in pairs. Help each other figure out how to do this. When you both get it, do some practice problems. If both of you remain stuck, ask another pair for help."

3. Attentive Lecture/Productive Discussion (Strategies 13-1 and 16-2)

Whole class, time as appropriate. Ask students how they did, what they figured out, and what questions they still have. Follow up with discussion or explanation as appropriate, but only as long as student involvement remains high.

4. Ask a Friend (Strategy 5-3)

Individual work, time as appropriate. Ask students to work on their individual worksheets and to practice good thinking. Conclude with this simple direction: "If you get stuck, ask any friend for help."

Action Flow Lesson 4: Lecture-Share-Learn

1. Attentive Lecture (Strategy 13-1)

Whole class, 15 minutes. Begin a lecture. An example from a history class: "The Enlightenment, which took place more or less in the 18th century, was also called the Age of Reason. What happened was . . ." Continue until you reach a natural break in the material, but for no more than five minutes. Then say, "Take a moment to write the key ideas you have heard so far, or any questions you may have."

When three or four students have finished writing, say, "One more minute, please."

Resume your lecture, continuing to the next natural break point, but not so long that students cannot hold the new material comfortably in mind. Then ask students to again jot down notes about what they heard or questions they have.

The process continues: You lecture briefly. Then pause while students make notes. And you repeat that sequence until you have completed your presentation or you notice students becoming less attentive, whichever comes first.

2. Summarizing/Sharing Pairs (Strategies 19-6 and 7-1)

Small groups, 5 minutes. Ask students to pair up and share with their partner a summary of what they heard, or what they consider the important points, or any questions they may have.

3. Lecture Summary

Whole class, 2–5 minutes. Summarize what you would most like students to understand—what you consider to be the main points of your lecture.

4. Productive Discussion (Strategy 16-2)

Whole class, time as appropriate. Ask students if anyone would be willing to share ideas, reactions, or questions.

5. Outcome Sentences (Strategy 21-1)

Individual work, 2–3 minutes. Say something like this: "Reviewing the lesson, make note of some key things you were able to get from it. You can use the starter phrases *I learned . . .* , *I rediscovered . . .* , or any phrases on the Outcome Sentence chart I posted."

6. Whip Around, Pass Option (Strategy 16-4)

Whole class, time remaining. Say something like, "Starting at this wall, let's whip around as much of the class as we have time for. When it comes your turn, read one of your Outcome Sentences or, if you prefer, say, 'I pass.'"

The Power of Action Flow Lessons

Those Action Flow Lessons were meant to illustrate how a lesson can flow with high levels of activity. The sequences are not entirely new. For example, the first sequence, Think-Share-Learn, is similar to the "Think, Pair, Share" series developed

> One looks back with appreciation to the brilliant teachers, but with gratitude to those who touched our human feelings. The curriculum is so much necessary raw material, but warmth is the vital element for the growing plant and for the soul of the child.
>
> —*Carl Jung*

by Frank Lyman at the University of Maryland (McTighe & Lyman, 1988), and the second sequence, Guided Practice and Review, is similar to Barak Rosenshine's (1976, 1979) "guided practice" in his seven-step direct instruction model.

Stevenson and Stigler (1992), exploring why Chinese and Japanese students do so well on math and science exams, found that their teachers similarly use a great variety of strategies in each lesson. In particular, they often intersperse explanations and problem solving with work that involves concrete materials and manipulatives. A typical lesson, for example, starts with the teacher posing a provocative problem and asking students to suggest alternative solutions. The teacher then asks students to discuss the value of each solution, its pros and cons. When it is practical to do so, students are asked to test the solution they prefer, to see if it works as anticipated. In the process, especially as students hear other students' contributions, they learn from one another. As a result, write Stevenson and Stigler, "Asian teachers are able to accommodate individual differences in learning abilities even though instruction is not tailored to each student" (p. 197).

That is the power of the Action Flow Lesson. Each lesson contains enough interesting activities to inspire a whole class of differing students to get involved and stay involved. Time on task is then high—and so is learning. Not insignificantly, students also tend to be deeply satisfied, happy to attend such classes.

▲ **TEACHER COMMENT**

I guess I followed what other teachers did and fell into what I now recognize were stale classroom procedures. I never thought to include so many activities in one lesson. After playing with your book for a few weeks, I can now see it's not so hard. My aim is to plan lessons now that have much more variety and, I hope, much more vitality.

—*High School History Teacher*

 ## Strategy 3-2: Teaching in Layers, Not Lumps

Purpose: To maintain high standards without frustrating students who cannot learn something right now.

Description: Planning not for mastery at any one time, but rather planning to return to topics as often as necessary until mastery is reached.

A quick pace during lessons need not result in inadequate learning. You can avoid lack of mastery by returning to a topic frequently enough so students eventually learn it fully and deeply. You can overlap content and spiral ahead to mastery. You can teach in layers, not lumps.

For example, as illustrated in Action Flow Lesson 2, students could handle material by taking part in Choral Work, by engaging in Guided Discovery, by hearing the teacher Think Aloud, and by completing a Review Test. Teaching in layers helps students learn content in much the same way that people learn their native language—dealing with it again and again, allowing mastery to develop gradually.

Adopting this strategy means planning lessons that keep touching on prior material until students reach sufficient mastery. Do not belabor a point and risk turning off some students. And when it comes to learning skills, avoid excessive massed practice in favor of more frequent distributed practice (Anderson, 1983; LaBerge & Samuels, 1974).

Strategy 3-3: Quick Pace

Purpose: To prevent students from tuning out because the pace is too slow.
Description: Noticing when students are losing interest and promptly making a change.

Life seems to be speeding up nowadays, and many students have internalized that fast pace. Few have patience for the slow and deliberate. As a result, teachers report more learning occurs when lessons proceed fairly quickly.

Many teachers make a classic error in this regard. In their teaching, they explain something, realize they could say it another way, and then go ahead and offer the new explanation. Then they ask, "Any questions?" which prompts some students who understood the first explanation to get restless, wondering if the teacher is about to explain it a third time. Sometimes other students say, yes, they do have questions. Then the teacher is stuck. Does the teacher refuse the students' request for assistance? Usually not. Most often the teacher explains a third time, which bores students who already understood—and students who were not interested in learning in the first place.

To reduce boredom and increase active learning, we suggest you avoid asking, "Any questions?" Instead, perhaps ask, "How many still have questions and would like us to come back to this another time?" Or you might say, "Pair up with someone nearby and talk over your understandings, helping those who still have questions." In general, it works best to return to topics many times—that is, to teach in layers, not lumps—so students do not need to master a topic in one teaching session.

It is also helpful to use strategies that provide alternative ways of helping students slow to understand. This book includes a number of such strategies, including Ask a Friend (Strategy 5-3), Sharing Pairs (Strategy 7-1), Learning Pairs (Strategy 7-2), Support Groups (Strategy 7-8), Review Test (Strategy 11-1), I Say Review (Strategy 11-3), and Class Tutors (Strategy 17-12).

Education is a social process; education is growth; education is not a preparation for life but is life itself.

—*John Dewey*

The quick pace preferred by many students often means presenting daily lessons in a number of small steps that involve a change in either topic or procedure. It is advisable to make that change as soon as you sense a slackening of student attention or dips in the classroom's energy level. It is almost always better to make such a change sooner, not later. Once students become disengaged, it takes extra effort to involve them again.

We also recommend using the power of expectations. Expect students who dally to speed up to your pace. Do not slow down to theirs. Move ahead at a pace that energizes student awareness and keeps as many as possible actively involved. Run your classes in ways that allow you to return to topics again and again, so students expect they will understand later what they do not understand now.

Is it ever a good idea to slow down? Yes, indeed. For those of us whose minds tend to move too fast or who talk too fast, slowing down may be a wise adjustment. This is the adjustment to make, too, when topics require more mulling over than usual. When we ask students to invent a way to solve a problem, for example, we must give them plenty of time to consider and create. If the problem begins to frustrate some students and they begin to give up, we might ask students to pair up and exchange ideas with a partner; pairing up usually keeps students on task longer. It's wise to slow down, too, when students become frazzled; students occasionally need to be calmed.

The key is to adjust the pacing so it is responsive to student realities. Figure 8 summarizes this concept. But note: More teachers are likely to belabor a point rather than to rush through it. They also are more likely to re-explain something than to let it go and return to it another day. So for most teachers, most of the time, boredom is what to watch for. When you see it, speed up or make another change that maintains high involvement.

Strategy 3-4: Efficient Classroom Structures

Purpose: To develop efficient routines for student learning.
Description: Settling on a few classroom routines that maximize learning and ease teaching.

Figure 8
Three Levels of Pacing

Boredom setting in. Students tuning out. **PACING TOO SLOW** *Speed up* or change to more involving activity.	**GOOD PACING**	Frustration rising. Students giving up. **PACING TOO FAST** *Slow down* or change to more manageable activity.

Some lesson plans work so well that they can be profitably turned into regular classroom routines. Once students learn these routines, the classroom develops a structure that is familiar to students, and that often eases our teaching chores and maximizes student learning. As examples, below are three structures for a day's learning experiences that teachers have found particularly efficient.

Structure 1: Highlighting Independent Work Time

The first structure is especially noteworthy because it provides time for students to learn independently both before and after the new lesson of the day. This structure uses eight elements. A discussion of each element follows the classroom example.

A Classroom Example

1. *Immediate work assignment.* Students know that as soon as they enter the classroom they are to begin work on the posted Do Now task (Strategy 6-1). Today's Do Now includes a quote. Students are to write a reaction to it in their personal journals. While students are doing this, the teacher can take attendance and attend to other housekeeping chores.

2. *Independent homework review.* After finishing their Do Now task, students know they are then to form pairs. With their partner they compare answers to yesterday's homework, using a strategy called Homework Sharing Pairs (Strategy 10-1). If pairs have questions they cannot answer, they ask another pair for assistance. Students know that if they did not complete the previous night's homework, they should skip Homework Sharing Pairs and move immediately to the next step.

When emotionally upset, people cannot remember, attend, learn, or make decisions clearly. As one management consultant put it, "stress makes people stupid."

—*Daniel Goleman*

3. *Independent tasks.* As students finish their homework review, they work with individually created sets of Study Cards (Strategy 6-3), which they use to review and memorize facts. They work individually until the teacher calls the class together. *In this sample class, students spend about 10 minutes on these first three elements.*

4. *Attention gathering.* The teacher uses a nonverbal Hand-Raising Signal (Strategy 9-1) to call the class together. When the class is fully attentive, the teacher asks for two volunteers to read what they wrote in response to the day's quote, using Set of Speakers (Strategy 16-5). *About 2 minutes.*

5. *Quick review.* The teacher asks five quick questions that review prior material. For each question, students write a response on scrap paper and then compare what they wrote with the correct response, which the teacher put on the board while the students were writing (Review Test, Strategy 11-1). *About 5 minutes.*

6. *Daily lesson.* The teacher then introduces the new material of the day, which today involves a lecture-discussion. At the end of the lesson, the teacher asks students to write what they learned in the form of Outcome Sentences (Strategy 21-1). *About 15 minutes.*

7. *Independent tasks.* When students finish writing, they return to independent tasks. Most continue working with their Study Cards, although some choose another task from a posted list of options (which includes work at learning centers and independent reading). *About 5 minutes.*

8. *Wrap-up.* The teacher announces the day's homework assignment and then has a few students report one of their Outcome Sentences, using Whip Around, Pass Option (Strategy 16-4). *About 3 minutes.*

Discussion

A few comments on each of the above elements:

• *Immediate work assignment* is a way to get students productively engaged as soon as they enter the room. Assignments are generally brief and easily managed. The Do Now strategy in this example is elaborated in Chapter 6.

• *Independent homework review* is a time for students to check homework and help one another with it. We might, for example, instruct students to use this time to compare answers with a partner (Strategy 10-1, Homework Sharing Pairs) or, if we have posted an answer key for the homework, ask them to check their work against the key (Strategy 10-2, Homework Self-Correcting). Chapter 10 contains several strategy options for this element. While students are handling homework, we may, of course, circulate through the room to get a general sense of class understanding and to assist as appropriate. Afterward we might initiate a homework discussion, perhaps by asking some Voting Questions to Assess Understanding (Strategy 16-6): "How many had trouble with last night's assignment? How many are confused about a particular question?" This helps determine whether a further discussion of the assignment is wise or necessary.

- *Independent tasks* ensure that students always have something to do when, for example, they finish an assignment before others, or we want to work with a small group or with individuals, or we have administrative chores to attend to. Note that Structure 1 includes two time slots for independent tasks, which is valuable because independent tasks tend to encourage students to take responsibility for their own learning. More options for employing independent tasks are discussed in Chapter 6.

- *Attention gathering* is used at the beginning of class and as necessary afterward. Chapter 9 contains options for doing this.

- *Quick review* is time to briefly review and refresh prior learning, something that facilitates Teaching in Layers, Not Lumps (Strategy 3-2). A Review Test (Strategy 11-1), as in the example above, accomplishes this without generating the kind of anxiety that a quiz might. Chapter 11 discusses options for quick reviews.

- *Daily lesson* is the time to introduce new material and help students begin to digest it. Parts IV and V of this book contain numerous strategies for handling this task.

- *Wrap-up* is a time to bring the group to a satisfying, collective closure. It also helps students clear their minds and get ready for the time ahead. For this we might, for example, ask students to reflect on the day's experiences (perhaps by writing Outcome Sentences, Strategy 21-1) or to share thoughts or questions (perhaps using a Concluding Whip Around, Strategy 21-4). This is also a convenient time for giving homework assignments. More wrap-up possibilities can be found in Part VI.

This structure can fit into a 50-minute class period. It can also easily be modified to accommodate a 90-minute period or, by extending the time students spend on independent tasks, to a half-day session. Such an extension would give the teacher more time to meet with individuals or small groups. In an elementary classroom, for instance, teachers could use the time to meet with different reading groups.

In general, the variety of student experiences provided by the structure we call Highlighting Independent Work Time tends to reduce teaching pressures and bring out the best in students. In terms of DESCA, it helps students feel *dignified,* for they are given many responsibilities to handle on their own. It helps them stay *energized,* for they are steadily called upon to be active. It helps them to be *self-managing,* for the several tasks they face often call on them to make their own decisions. It helps them feel part of a *community,* especially when they help one another learn. And it helps them to stay *aware,* for they must handle many small tasks in one time period.

Structure 2: Highlighting the Spin-off Procedure

Structure 2 is built around the spin-off procedure. In this classroom example, the teacher "spins off" quick learners into another activity when further direct instruction would no longer serve those students.

A Classroom Example

1. *Attention getting.* The teacher asks a series of Voting Questions (Strategy 9-3) that students respond to by raising their hands. For example, the teacher asks, "How many of you had a good day so far? How many are wearing something new? How many play baseball?" Questions may or may not be related—the main objective is to get the attention of all students. *About 2 minutes.*

2. *Daily lesson/independent tasks.* The teacher then introduces the day's lesson, which today is on multiplying fractions. "Please watch and listen as I solve this problem. There is no need for you to write anything just yet." The teacher thinks aloud as she works a problem on the board. When she's finished, she says, "Now try working the next two with me." She continues as before, thinking aloud as she works.

"Now try the next two problems on your own." The teacher circulates around the room to observe students working, and when a few have finished, she continues. "Let's see how we did with those last two." As before, she thinks aloud as she works the problems on the board, but this time she works more quickly.

The teacher then introduces the independent tasks component and spins some students into that. "All those who feel they understand, take a practice sheet from the back of the room," she says. "Please stay in the back or move to one side of the room and begin working on that sheet. If you have trouble, ask a friend for help. If you're still stuck after that, simply move back into my group." The teacher tells the students that when they finish, they should check with someone else who is finished to see if they agree on the right answers. "Then, alone or with a partner, begin working on the posted textbook challenge problems or go back to working on your Independent Learning Assignment." (See Strategy 6-4.)

The teacher gathers the remaining students for more careful instruction on the daily lesson. Anytime she senses some students are ready to move on, she spins them off to work on independent tasks, just as she did with the first group. Some students never get to independent tasks. *A total of about 35 minutes.*

3. *Attention gathering.* The teacher announces, "One more minute, please," and then uses a silent Hand-Raising Signal (Strategy 9-1) to quiet and reconvene the group. *About 1 minute.*

4. *Wrap up.* The teacher gives the day's homework assignment and concludes by asking some Voting Questions to Assess Understanding (Strategy 16-6): "How many of you would like more practice with this material? How many of you feel ready to move on to something new? Who still has a question?" She answers some student questions but leaves others for another day. *About 4 minutes.*

Discussion

In that example, the teacher kept all the slower learners with her for further instruction. Alternatively, we could keep only *some* of the slower learners with us and pair up others—those who might learn better from a peer—with one of the faster learners for one-on-one tutoring. Such a peer-tutoring procedure works best if, early in the year, we have introduced a "How to Tutor" project for students (for suggestions, see Strategy 17-12, Class Tutors, and Strategy 17-13, Tutor Training). Then, when the time is right, students who understand well can be asked to help those who do not. This also frees us to concentrate on the students who best learn directly from the teacher.

By the way, some teachers, building on the idea of a "three-ring circus," say something like this: "Class, let's now use our 'three-ring structure.' I'd like to work with the following students . . . As for the rest of you, if you think you could benefit from more practice, work at . . . If not, move to one of the learning centers, working there alone or in pairs, whichever you think is best for you."

In our own workshops, we often use such a three-ring structure. We might, as an example, ask participants to divide themselves into three groups: Group 1 to learn some new inspiring strategies. Group 2 to role-play using inspiring strategies previously discussed, to get a better feel of them. And Group 3 to brainstorm inspiring solutions to problems currently faced. Similarly, any teacher might have one group of students learning a new topic. Another group of students working at drill materials to master a former topic. And a third group working on a creative task, perhaps drawing something that illustrates a concept from a former topic. See Clear-to-Muddy Groups, Strategy 17-1, for another useful way to divide a class into three groups.

You can rest assured that if you devote your time and attention to the highest advantage of others, the Universe will support you, always and only in the nick of time.

—*R. Buckminster Fuller*

Structure 3: Highlighting Discovery Learning

As the name implies, this structure is built around discovery-type lessons. A discussion of the seven elements follows the example.

A Classroom Example

1. *Attention gathering.* As students enter the classroom, the teacher asks, "Anything new or good in your lives?" and calls on a few volunteers to respond, acknowledging each reply with "Thank you" or "I can appreciate that" (Strategy 9-4, New or Goods). When all students are present, the teacher shifts to the Lesson Agreement approach (Strategy 9-5), briefly stating his plan for the day: "First I'd like to quickly go over your homework. Then I have a problem for you to think about. Is this OK as a plan for today?" *About 3 minutes.*

2. *Homework review.* The teacher asks students to check their own work, then says, "If you answered correctly, give yourself a check. If you answered incorrectly, simply write the correct answer next to your response. The answer to number one is . . ." (See Strategy 10-2, Homework Self-Correcting.)

To gauge class understanding, the teacher then asks a few Voting Questions to Assess Understanding (Strategy 16-6): "How many had 10 correct responses? How many had less than 10 correct, but more than 5?" and so on. If students seem to be struggling, the teacher makes a mental note to use Reteach Review (Strategy 11-7) in the near future. *A total of about 5 minutes.*

3. *Problem posing.* The teacher draws a diagram of an isosceles triangle on the board and asks, "How can we find the area of this triangle?" That problem becomes the focus of the day's lesson. *About 1 minute.*

4. *Independent puzzling.* The teacher continues: "Please take a minute or two to think about this problem on your own and make some notes or calculations. Perhaps write about something you already know that might help you. Or jot down any questions you have. Just a few minutes for this. Go!" (This is Strategy 16-3, Question, All Write.) As soon as three or four students have stopped writing, the teacher says, "One more minute, please" to signal that time is almost up. *About 2 minutes.*

5. *Group puzzling.* The teacher says, "Please form pairs and share what you wrote. After you do that, brainstorm other possibilities for finding the area of that triangle. If you are stuck, ask another pair for help. Go!" The teacher circulates around the room observing students' work, providing encouragement and guidance when appropriate. *About 7 minutes.*

6. *Whole-class discussion/instruction.* The teacher asks for a few volunteers to share possible solutions. Through discussion and Guided Discovery (Strategy 14-4), the teacher leads students to discover why each offered solution would or wouldn't work and, finally, which are the best solutions. He then leads the whole class in solving two practice problems, using Think Aloud (Strategy 14-3) as he works at the board. *About 20 minutes.*

7. *Wrap-up.* The teacher gives the homework assignment for the day: "Use an effective formula to find the area of the triangles on page 176." He then uses a Like/Might Review (Strategy 21-2), asking students to write what they liked about how they handled today's problem and what they might do differently next time. *About 2 minutes.*

Discussion

* *Problem posing* introduces a new problem to the class. In the example, the students discover the problem's solution before the end of the lesson. However, with a more complicated problem, several lessons may be based upon the same problem. Challenge Opener (Strategy 12-4) contains additional suggestions for problem posing.

* *Independent puzzling* gives students time to begin playing with the problem. Question, All Write (Strategy 16-3) is useful here because the students' written responses become the basis for the group sharing of ideas.

* *Group puzzling* provides an opportunity for students to share ideas, get feedback, brainstorm additional possible solutions, and discuss questions or confusions. Rotating Pairs (Strategy 7-3) is often useful here, for it guarantees students will have several chances to discuss and brainstorm possibilities. Although this classroom example used pairs—the group size that usually works best for keeping students actively engaged—groups of three or four might be preferable when problems are so complex that they require more than two brains.

* *Whole-class discussion/instruction* gives us a chance to address questions and provide guidance as we lead students to discover the problem's solution. If the problem is complex, we might spend several days discussing and considering possibilities before moving ahead to instruction and practice. In such cases, students might continue puzzling about the problem for homework.

Each teacher must design his or her own class structures, of course, and the combination of elements is endless. Nonetheless, it is wise to choose such structures

Be sincere; be brief; be seated.

—*Franklin D. Roosevelt*

thoughtfully, for they can make instruction a lot easier for teachers and make learning a lot richer for students.

Strategy 3-5: Personal Inspiring Power

Purpose: To maximize our personal power to inspire.
Description: Learning to bring out our own best selves in the classroom.

Describing the composer and music director Leonard Bernstein, someone once said, "He was the gentle teacher, the logical, compassionate, caring, and articulate teacher, who inspired you so that you wanted to please him more than life itself." Bernstein had inspiring power.

Try recalling some teachers, coaches, or leaders you wanted to please, people for whom you wanted to do the best you could. Chances are they also had inspiring power.

You, too, have that power. And if you are like most other teachers with whom we've worked, you can unwrap more of it and use it to great advantage. Doing so will allow you to make the most of the strategies in this book, for it is your inspiring power that will give the strategies the hearty, robust flavor that will inspire students to do the best work they can (Goleman, 1995; Ostrander & Schroeder, 1994). How do you release more of that power? You take care of yourself so you can better take care of others.

Our goal, of course, is to bring out the best in our students. Or, stated more specifically, we want to see our students engaging daily lessons with dignity, energy, self-management, community, and awareness (DESCA). Similarly, we want to bring out the best in ourselves. Why? When we can radiate our best selves in the classroom each day, we naturally elicit the best response from students. It's the way to nurture and free our own style of charisma.

This inspiring power is especially intertwined with our ability to be caring. To sense the power of a caring person, recall two or three adults who, when you were younger, truly cared for you. They may not ever have said they cared, but you could tell they did. It might have been a parent or other relative who paid close attention to your needs. Or it might have been a teacher or a neighbor who demonstrated care by, perhaps, remembering your name, asking about things that mattered to you, taking time to listen to you. Perhaps jot down the names or initials of such caring persons.

Then think of two or three adults who you sensed really *did not* care for you very much. They might have *acted* as if they cared, but you knew they didn't. If they listened to you, for example, or gave you a gift or a compliment, you knew it was just to be polite or to get something *they* wanted, perhaps approval from others, perhaps the self-satisfaction of doing what "good" people do. Then compare the influence on you of those persons who cared and those who didn't. Which ones brought out the best in you?

It's obvious. We respond best to those who truly care for us. And it's to the caring teacher that students give their best efforts. And note: It is not enough for a teacher to care that students learn their lessons. Our care must be broad enough to include an honest concern for students as individuals, even if they never learn their lessons (Csikszentmihalyi, 1990; Gardner, 1993).

It's useful to remember that being caring does not necessarily mean smiling a lot and giving a lot of compliments. We can be strict and stern and yet be highly caring. The question is not how we appear on the outside but what our motivations are from the inside (Walberg & Greenberg, 1997). Is our prime concern our own welfare, or is it the welfare of the students we teach? Do we want high test scores for our own welfare, well-behaved students for our own comfort? Or is our primary concern to elicit the best our students carry within them, which may well maximize test scores and good behavior but, even if it doesn't, expresses what is good and caring inside us? In short, are we motivated by the best that is inside us?

Consider testing this proposition by bringing more of your best self into the classroom and staying alert for emerging benefits. Here are some ways you might do that.

- *Take time to tune into students as individuals.* Perhaps occasionally stroll about and ask individual students what they like about the class. Or ask about their hobbies or interests. Or initiate class discussions about what is interesting about their personal lives—something readily done with two strategies found in Chapter 9, Voting Questions (Strategy 9-3) and New or Goods (Strategy 9-4). It is easier to be caring and therefore inspiring to people you know well than to people you know only superficially.

- *See potential stars.* See your students' best potential, not the surface behavior they currently demonstrate. Perhaps imagine that all students have stars painted on their foreheads, signifying their future stardom. Or visualize them with the word *dignity* floating above their heads, signifying that each is a fully dignified human being, worthy of your most respectful treatment. Or imagine that each student is a slightly different version of someone you truly love. Perhaps start by seeing one student that way. See what that does for you.

A problem is a chance to do your best.

—*Duke Ellington*

- *Affirm your intention to reveal your inspiring power.* Perhaps write a daily affirmation for yourself, such as "I will be caring and respectful of my students today" or "I intend today to awaken the best in each student" or "I will inspire more students to learn actively today." Maintain a positive perspective and watch to see if students rise to meet your expectation. Treat it as an experiment. See if the results please you.

- *Extend your trust of students.* Caring is, of course, different from smothering. When we care about the welfare of another, we do not want to suffocate that person. We do not want to be overly controlling. We want to give the person enough room to live his or her own life, just as we wanted that from the adults who cared for us. Consider if you are sufficiently trusting of students. Perhaps experiment occasionally and relax some classroom controls. You might, for instance, decrease how often you check homework, give tests, and evaluate student work and increase how often you use strategies that get students to check and evaluate their own work. Trust that all students, at heart, want to be self-responsible. See if the response of your students confirms Ralph Waldo Emerson's statement: "Trust men, and they will be true to you; treat them greatly, and they will show themselves great."

- *Extend your trust in life.* Is it possible that you are too certain you know what is best for all others? Might it be better if you were less arrogant, more humble, less anxious, less worried, less pessimistic, more trusting of life's processes? If so, consider focusing more on the sunny side for a while, trusting that, somehow, things will work out the best for all concerned without your interference, trusting that nature has its ways, ways that we may well not understand. See what happens.

- *Maintain high expectations.* High expectations are signs that you strongly care. When you give up on students or accept halfhearted work, you tell students you do not care about their welfare all that much. Try being like a coach who might address a class this way: "I very much want you succeed in this class, and in the future, too. I want you prepared to be a winner. Each day I want us all to do the very best we can. You each have more talent and ability than you likely even know you have. Let's work together to make this a great learning experience for us all. I know we can do it. Let's get to it!" But note: High expectations require high acceptance. We must be fully accepting of those not yet ready or able to reach our high expectations. We can aim for the mountaintop. But unless we accept our need to go step by step, resting when necessary, stopping if necessary, we will soon be filled with more resentment and anxiety than inspiration.

- *Extend your inclusiveness.* It's important to include in your caring not only the cooperative students but also those who are resistant, even those who are

Don't take life too seriously; you'll never get out of it alive.

—Elbert Hubbard

aggressively antagonistic. "It's tough working in this school," reports one woman teaching in a chaotic urban school, "but I can't bear to walk away from these kids." That is a teacher who cares. And unless more teachers in such schools find a way to keep their inherent sense of caring alive, it's unlikely that the worst schools will improve very much, for students will reveal and develop their best abilities only for teachers who genuinely care. (For specific strategies for handling chronically disruptive students in an inspiring way, see Chapter 34.)

• *Monitor your stress level.* A friend wrote that she had lost patience with her own children. "I got snappy, and it wasn't the girls' fault. It was just that I was too bummed out." She then adjusted, she wrote, and cut back on outside obligations. "The girls and I are now much closer. It was just too hard to spend quality time with them when I was suffering all those pressures." Her experience can be a good reminder to us. Teaching is easier when our own stress level is under control. Our natural care for others can disappear when we're swamped by our own problems. You do well, then, to monitor your level of stress, and if it gets high, to adjust. It's one of the best ways to do good for both your students and yourself. (For specific strategies, see Chapter 29.)

• *Use instructional strategies that make it easy for students to stay actively engaged.* When, for example, you plan lessons that flow with a lot of action; teach in layers, not lumps; maintain a quick pace; and structure learning experiences efficiently—using the first four strategies in this chapter—students react positively. This approach, in turn, makes teaching easier—which relaxes you; which in turn brings out more of your best qualities, including more of your ability to be truly caring; which in turn elicits even *more* of a positive response from students. Check it out for yourself. See if when you strive to bring out the best in students, you notice that you are automatically bringing out the best in yourself.

Our experiences are consistent. We find again and again that the more often we can stand tall before our students as teachers who honestly care, the more we release our powers to inspire students to do the best they can possibly do. So what is good for students is good for us, and what is good for us is good for students. Not a bad deal.

▲ TEACHER COMMENT

I'm not a social person, and my classes were always businesslike. But I risked experimenting with my 3rd period class. On all Mondays this quarter I asked if anyone had anything good happen over the weekend. We then took a few minutes to hear some reports, mostly of parties and ball games. I also sometimes talked about my personal life, which I rarely did before. I found that I liked what was happening. The class atmosphere became warmer. Students smiled more. And although I was using some time for nonacademic talk, I covered as much material as I ever did. I'll now do this with other classes, too.

—*Bob Hendricks, High School Science Teacher*

Establishing a Climate That Inspires Full Participation

The strategies in Chapter 3 automatically invite high levels of student participation. But to ensure such participation, all students, especially those who tend to be timid or lack self-confidence, must feel safe enough to risk full engagement. How can we create such a secure climate? The 10 strategies in this chapter can help with this important task.

Our field tests show that the first two strategies, each marked with an arrow, are particularly effective. We recommend them for your first consideration.

Strategy 4-1: Truth Signs

Purpose: To make it easier for students to become intelligent, relaxed, self-responsible learners.

Description: Posting and discussing signs that remind students of core truths about learning.

If we want to learn something—for example, French or biology—we want a class in which we can relax and participate with an assurance that we will not feel embarrassed or apprehensive. Summarizing the relevant research, Wang, Haertel, and Walberg (1992) and Brophy (1983) emphasize the importance of reducing learning anxiety, especially fear of failure, and building learner confidence. Few things do that better than Truth Signs.

Truth Signs are not the usual signs posted in classrooms. They do not tell students what to do ("Think before you act" or "Respect the rights of others"). They do not moralize. Nor do they threaten ("One infraction = 10 minutes off free time"). Instead, these signs remind students of important truths about living and learning. The following example depicts one teacher introducing five particularly valuable Truth Signs to a class. Notice especially the care the teacher takes to make the meaning of each sign clear to students.

A Sample Lesson

The teacher points to a sign posted on the wall and reads it aloud:

> Everyone needs time
> to think and learn.

"Now let's read this together," the teacher says. A scattering of students read the sign along with her. "Let's say it again, with power," she says. The class repeats the words with more intensity.

"Yes, it is true," the teacher continues. "When we hear something or try something, we don't usually learn it right away. It takes a little time for us to make sense of it, to get it inside us. Even if I say something simple, like 'My mother was born in England,' it might take a second for you to make sense of what those words mean."

The teacher tells the students that she posted the sign in the classroom so everyone will remember what it says. "It's an important truth. It can help us keep our learning climate healthy. You can use it as a reminder to give yourself enough time when you want to learn something. You don't want to rush. Why?" The class discusses this. The teacher concludes the discussion by saying, "We don't want to rush because, as the sign says, 'Everyone needs time to think and learn.'" She asks the students to read the words aloud again.

The teacher then asks the students to look at another sign:

> We each learn in our own ways,
> by our own time clocks.

She asks the students to read the words aloud, then again "with more power." She explains, "This sign, too, is true. We each learn in our own ways, no one quite like

The more mistakes I make, the smarter I get.

—*Jennifer, age 13*

the other. Some learn best from words, some from pictures, some from experimenting, some from talking with other people. We each have our own favorite ways."

The teacher continues by explaining how people also learn according to their own "time clocks," some fast, some slow—and only when the time is right. As an example, she recounts her own experience with spelling, explaining that she didn't learn to spell well until she was much older than her classmates. Eventually, "when the time was right," she became a fairly good speller. She asks the students to share similar experiences they may have had, in which they tried to learn something or were expected to learn something, but they didn't succeed until the time was right. She reiterates the importance of remembering the sign's message and asks the students to read it aloud again, "with energy."

The teacher tells the students that the sign will remain posted in the classroom along with the first one, to remind them that people learn in different ways and at different times. She reassures them by saying, "Please don't get down on yourself if you don't learn the way other people learn or if you don't learn *when* other people learn. That would be foolish, for we each learn in our own ways, by our own time clocks, right?"

Then the teacher introduces another sign:

> It's OK to make mistakes.
> That's the way we learn.

Again she asks the students to read the sign aloud, then to repeat it. She helps them to understand the truth of the message by presenting a familiar example: "Even the first time we walk, we stumble around, fall down, get up, try again. The first time we try anything new we are likely to make a mistake until we get it." She tells them that it makes no sense for people to get down on themselves when they make a mistake. "We can eventually get so afraid of making mistakes that we are afraid even to try. And that is silly. Making mistakes is just what happens when we start learning." She asks the students to read the sign aloud again, and then a second time, "Like you mean it!"

Then the teacher invites the students to consider a fourth sign:

> It's intelligent to ask for help.
> No one needs to do it all alone.

She points out that she doesn't have to be able to manufacture cars and grow food and construct roads and paint pictures and design shirts. She simply needs to know how to do what she does. "No one has to know it all," she says. She tells the students that if she needs something done that she can't do herself, she asks for help from someone who can do it—because that is the intelligent thing to do. "Then I get what I need and, often, the other person gets the pleasure of helping. Don't you sometimes feel good when you can be helpful to someone?" She tells the students that such helping is what characterizes a community of people. "One person delivers the mail. Another mows the lawn. One cooks. Another builds. Old folks sit outside and smile at us. Young people play outside and act silly. It takes all of us to make a community. No one has to do it all alone. We can help one another."

She repeats the point that asking for help is the "intelligent" choice, and says that trying to do everything alone is "not at all intelligent." She urges the students to ask for help if they don't know what to do or they need an explanation for something. "Everything works better that way," she says. "We can become one happy team, one community that way." She asks the students to join her in saying the sign's message aloud, and then one more time, "with a lot of power!"

The teacher asks the students to look at one last sign:

> It is OK to fail, but it is not OK to give up.
> —*Kate, age 8*

> We can do more and learn more
> when we're willing to take a risk.

To explain the concept, the teacher provides an example. "Let's say you want to do something—try something new, or talk to someone, or speak up in class. What you want to do might seem like a good thing, but it can also feel risky. This often happens. We want to do something, but our feelings tell us to hold it, that it's risky." The teacher points out that sometimes the risk really is too great—someone might get hurt, for example—and then it would be smart to stop. But sometimes the risk is not that dangerous. It just *feels* risky. In such situations, she suggests, "we can call on our courage and move right through the anxiety. Speak out, or join a new group, or jump into the swimming pool—or do whatever else we want to do.

"The key is a *willingness* to risk," continues the teacher. "Notice that the sign talks about being *willing* to take a risk. If we are willing to sometimes take a risk, then we can stop and think if the act we now face is too dangerous or just *feels* dangerous and is really not all that dangerous. If we are *not* willing to act, we will not even stop to think about it. The risk will fill us with an anxiety that will turn off our thinking ability, and we will automatically turn away and do nothing. Our life space then becomes smaller. We get stuck in inaction. As the sign says, we can do more and learn more when we are *willing* to risk." She invites students to give some examples of times they faced a risk and did or did not think about whether the risk was worth taking.

The teacher reiterates the truth of the sign's message, and then points out a way to make risk taking easier. "Sometimes it helps to have support from others. It is often easier to take a risk when we are not alone. Can anyone think of a time when having someone to support you made it easier to act?"

After the students have shared a few such experiences, the teacher tells them that all people have courage. "Courage is a natural ability of people, like speaking and dreaming. Some people can call up courage easily. Some do not have much practice in doing this." She tells them that famous people, even movie stars, sometimes get anxious in public. "But they are usually good at calling up their courage and getting out in public anyhow." She asks, "Did any of you once feel it would be risky to do something, and then you called up your courage and did it anyhow?"

Following the students' responses, the teacher tells them it is also easier for people to take a risk if they are willing to accept the possibility that they won't succeed. "Sometimes it seems so important that we win, or come out on top, or get everything to turn out just right. It makes us nervous before we even begin. A part of us does not even want to begin. We forget the simple fact that things do not always turn out the way we like." She continues, "But if we can remember that people sometimes win and sometimes lose, we won't worry so much about sometimes losing. If we lose, well, we can try again another time. It's usually not the worst thing in the world." She asks the students, "How many of you are sometimes afraid of not winning? Do any of you back off and stop trying in such situations? How many would agree that when people can accept winning or losing, however things turn out, they will be less nervous, and if they are not so nervous might even be more likely to win?"

The teacher reaffirms the truth of the risk sign's message and tells the students she hopes they will be willing to take risks in her class. She asks the students to repeat the words of the sign, and then again. "Now say it like you mean it!"

Approaching the end of the lesson, the teacher tells the students that the signs will remain posted as reminders and that from time to time the class will talk about them again. She asks the students to look again at the five signs.

People seldom improve when they have no model to copy but themselves.

—*Anonymous*

"Which ones do you feel good about? Which do you think might help you do good learning in this class?" Pointing to one sign, she asks, "How many feel good about this one?" Acknowledging the raised hands of about 10 students, she continues. "How about this sign?" She voices an approximate count for each sign, to acknowledge the students who raise their hands.

In conclusion, the teacher asks the students to write down something they got from the lesson. She suggests that they write endings to one or more Outcome Sentences (Strategy 21-1) and points to list of sentence stems: *I learned . . . , I was surprised . . . , I'm beginning to wonder . . . , I rediscovered . . . , I feel . . . , I promise . . .*

Other Ways to Use Truth Signs

The five truth signs highlighted in the sample lesson are adapted from Grace Pilon (1996), who calls them "philosophy signs." Some teachers do not post all the signs at one time but, as the teacher above did, others post them all at once.

As the sample lesson suggests, when discussing the risk sign, it is useful to distinguish between a smart risk and a foolish risk. A smart risk is one that, all things considered, would be good to take. A foolish risk might be dangerous, or hurtful, or in some way not good for oneself or for others. Some teachers ask students to create a chart of smart and foolish risks, and they report that students enjoy doing so.

With older students, a discussion about foolish and wise risks can also be part of a discussion about smoking, drinking, or sex. "Can you think of a time," we might ask, "when it takes more courage to say no rather than yes?" We might then have students role-play situations, aiming to solidify the relationship between risk taking and intelligent choosing in ways that are meaningful to them.

It is preferable to use no more than six or seven signs in one classroom. Posting more than that might dilute the signs' power. Some additional possibilities for Truth Signs:

- We do our best work when we activate our best selves.
- We must each live our own lives. No one else can do it for us.

▲ TEACHER COMMENT

I have a son, age 7, in 2nd grade, and a daughter, just turned 5, in preschool. Often at dinner we share information about our days, in particular, "What we learned in school." I have discussed the Truth Signs you taught us with the children and tried to incorporate them into everyday living. One day last week my children were in the kitchen and I was in another room. I heard my son become exasperated with himself over something he had not done correctly. I then heard my daughter say, "Jed, it's OK to make mistakes. That is how we learn." Out of the mouths of babes.

—*Patrice Bain, Middle School Social Studies Teacher*

- Life happens one step at a time, one day at a time.
- If it happened, it happened. Let's go on.
- We can be a community—sometimes all for one, one for all, sometimes live and let live.
- We can accept and support one another. No one needs to be all alone.
- There is no "best" in the world of humans.

Such signs communicate important life truths. It is easy for us to forget these truths. It is often heartening and reassuring to be reminded of them. (See research cited by Caine and Caine, 1991; Hart, 1983; and Marzano, 1992.) The next strategy, Cushioning Questions, provides a meaningful way to keep such truths fresh throughout the year.

Strategy 4-2: Cushioning Questions

Purpose: To cushion student anxiety about learning and to expand student willingness to participate fully.

Description: Before asking students to demonstrate how much they learned, reinforcing basic truths about learning by asking such questions as "Is it OK if someone gives us a wrong answer today? Why?"

Posting a Truth Sign that says it's all right to make mistakes doesn't guarantee that students will not feel anxious about making a mistake. Many students need a long time to accept that making mistakes while learning is fully acceptable. Posting Truth Signs is a wise first step in the process of reducing learning anxieties and increasing learner confidence. However, a steady offering of reminders and support is almost always necessary. Pilon (1996) calls her strategy for doing this "cushioning."

Sample Lessons

The following dialogues show how one teacher, Mr. Jones, uses cushioning questions with his class.

Day 1

Mr. Jones: Class, before I ask my review questions today, I would like you to guess why I do not care if someone makes a mistake. Can you guess why that would not bother me?

Adam:	Because you want to know how much we know. Mistakes show what we don't know.
Mr. Jones:	Yes, you could say that. Anyone else?
Ashley:	As the sign up there says, "It's OK to make mistakes; that is the way we learn."
Mr. Jones:	Yes, that is true. Anyone else?
Frank:	It shows we're trying, risking it, even if we don't know for sure that we are right. And we learn more when we're willing to take a risk.
Mr. Jones:	Yes, all that is true. Our signs remind us of those truths. Now let's get to the review questions.

Mr. Jones's intent in this dialogue is to *cushion* student anxieties that might pop up during the lesson so students can relax and learn with confidence. Cushioning has a longer-range intent as well: to help students plant deeply inside themselves the truth about mistakes—that mistakes are a natural part of the learning process, that they are certainly acceptable, and that we can reduce our fears of making mistakes by reminding ourselves of this truth, thus learning an important life-management skill. As a result, this strategy can serve not only good classroom learning but healthful, productive long-term living as well.

Notice that Mr. Jones used cushioning *before* the lesson. This is significant. Imagine if he had waited until after a student made a mistake and then asked the class if it was all right to make mistakes. The class might agree that it is all right, but the student who just made the error might well be embarrassed and sorry about being the cause of such a discussion. Besides, if Mr. Jones had skipped the cushioning questions, the lesson might have proceeded with some students feeling unnecessarily anxious about making mistakes. The point: Cushioning is most potent before lessons begin.

Day 2

Mr. Jones:	Before we begin this lesson, I want to remind you that no one needs to learn this material perfectly today. Why do you think I say that?
Bill:	Because it is new material.
Mr. Jones:	Well, it is new. But I would say that even about old material. Why is it OK if someone has not learned something perfectly on any particular day?
Sue:	Because we all learn in our own ways, by our own time clocks. It might not be time for us to get something.
Mr. Jones:	Is that true, class?
Class:	Yes.
Mr. Jones:	Fine. So go as far as you can. It won't help you to feel bad if you fail to get it all today. Now to our lesson.

For every person who wants to teach there are approximately thirty people who don't want to learn—much.

—*W. C. Sellar and R. J. Yeatman*

Day 3

Mr. Jones:	Bob, before you give your answer, let me ask you, is it OK with you if I say no, the correct answer is a different year?
Bob:	Yes, I guess so, though I wouldn't like it!
Mr. Jones:	I can understand that. But it's OK if you make a mistake, even if you're not entirely happy about it?
Bob:	Yes, sure.
Mr. Jones:	Can anyone tell us why it would be fine if Bob's answer turns out not to be the correct answer?
Nicole:	Because it's OK to make mistakes. As the sign says, that's the way we learn.
Mr. Jones:	Thanks, Nicole. Sorry for the delay, Bob. Now let me repeat the question and hear your answer.

Day 4

Mr. Jones:	Class, before we begin today, let me ask, is it OK for some of you to fully understand this material and some to still be totally confused?
Class:	Yes.
Mr. Jones:	Why is that OK?
Sue:	We all need time to think and learn. Some of us didn't have as much time as we need.
Mr. Jones:	Thank you, Sue. Anyone else?
Cliff:	Some of us might not be very interested in this.
Mr. Jones:	Thank you, Cliff. Anyone else?
Jim:	We all learn in our own ways, by our own time clocks.
Mr. Jones:	Yes, and how does that truth free us from feeling bad if we don't get this material? How does it make it OK for some of us to know it and some not to know it?
Tom:	Maybe it wasn't our time to learn it yet.
Mr. Jones:	Right. It is also possible that you didn't yet have a way of learning it that worked well for you. So no one should feel superior if they learned this already, and no one should feel inferior or bad if they haven't learned it yet. In any case, let's go at today's work with an accepting, open mind, helping one another as best we can.

Day 5

Mr. Jones:	Today I'd like to start off by asking why you think it's smart to ask a friend for help if you are confused. Anyone?
Mary:	We can't all ask you all the time.
Denise:	Sometimes it makes me feel good when someone asks me for help.
Michael:	I'd say because we all learn more when we help one another.
Mr. Jones:	Fine. Those are all good answers. Just remember the sign. Let's read it all together again: "It's intelligent to ask for help. No one needs to do it all alone."

What is a classroom? A place for students and teachers. Students struggle, succeed, fail, give up, try again. Teachers struggle, succeed, fail, give up, try again.

—*Esther Wright*

Steps and Options for Using Cushioning Questions

As the above sample lessons suggest, cushioning involves the following three steps.

1. *Bringing a truth to awareness.* It starts with a question, not a statement. "Why would it be OK to make a mistake in today's lesson?" Such a Cushioning Question asks students to recall the truth involved: Mistakes are all right because that is the way we learn. But the goal is more than reassurance for today's lesson. The goal is to promote lifelong reassurance. By repeatedly recalling the statement that summarizes the truth, we help students deeply internalize that truth.

2. *Inviting participation.* Inviting students to respond to our question often results in students simply calling out one of the posted truth signs. We might, however, probe for a sign we want to emphasize: "Does the sign about risks touch on this issue?" Generally, we accept all student comments.

3. *Moving ahead.* A concluding comment might be valuable, but more often it's advisable to simply move promptly into the lesson. Cushioning Questions are not intended to take more than a minute or so. Pilon (1996), the creator of this strategy, recommends keeping cushioning brief and using it often.

Students who need reassurance will appreciate a moment of cushioning at least once every day. Even those who don't need such reassurance seem not to tire of the strategy. Varying the openings helps keep the process interesting. Some sample questions for opening a cushioning discussion:

- Does everyone have to know everything today? Why not?
- Does everyone have to get every answer right? Why not?
- I'd say it's OK if someone forgot what we learned last week. Why might I say that?
- Some of us expect too much of ourselves. How many of you sometimes feel like that in school? Do any of our signs help us with that?
- It might be unfortunate, but is it OK for someone to have forgotten to bring a notebook today? Why?
- What if some people know a lot about something and others know only a little? That might be OK because maybe some people aren't quite ready to know as much. And they can ask for help from those who know more. That's good for everyone. Which signs talk about this?
- I'd say that having the right answer is not as important as being willing to risk thinking and offering an answer. Can you guess why I'd say that?

• What is the best way to handle a failure? What would be the smart way to react?

• It takes courage to be willing to take a risk when you are not sure of the outcome. But it's often smart to do so. Can you guess why I believe that?

• No one can ever be me, and I cannot be anyone else. What does that say about how we can best learn?

• My worth as a person does not depend on how much I know. Why do you think I say that?

• It sometimes takes courage to say "I don't know." But sometimes that is the honest answer to a question. Why does it sometimes take courage to be honest in this way?

Another way to keep the Cushioning Questions strategy fresh and interesting is to vary the conclusion of the discussion. Here are some options:

• No one knows everything. No one ever will. So relax and get as much as you can from this lesson.

• We are each intelligent, but each of us is intelligent about different things. You will find your own intelligence as time goes by.

• No one has to know everything. Instead, we help one another. Our job is to live together as one cooperative community.

• All human beings make mistakes. So, if you are a human, what will you make? Mistakes!

• It's not mistakes that are important. It's what we do *after* we make mistakes that is important, right?

• Failing at a task is not as bad as many seem to think. Can you imagine what would happen if people were always afraid of failing? So let's just forget about failing and get into today's lesson.

• I'd like you to relax and to be fully aware. Be a confident learner. Don't worry. Risk jumping in wholeheartedly, thinking only of what you are thinking about. Trust that the outcome will be OK.

The Cushioning Questions strategy reminds students that it is all right to be human, to be oneself. It provides a practical way to help students digest that truth and thereby accept themselves—blemishes, tempers, and all. It is a good example of the old saying that the truth will set us free—in this case, free to approach academic lessons without hesitation and with confidence.

Strategy 4-3: Risk Language

Purpose: To help less confident students move beyond their apprehensions and participate fully and to remind all students how risk taking serves learning.

Description: When soliciting responses from students, using wording that encourages participation, as by saying, "Who is willing to risk an answer?"

One of the most helpful Truth Signs focuses on risk taking: "We can do more and learn more when we are willing to take a risk." But it can be difficult for many students to internalize that truth. Accordingly, it is useful to remind students of the value of reaching beyond a comfort zone, calling up courage and moving toward experiences that may be difficult. Risk Language, another strategy adapted from Pilon (1996), serves this purpose for us. It calls on us simply to use the word *risk* more often.

For example, when the lesson ahead may be challenging to students, we might ask, "How many are up for a risk today? How many are ready to do some good thinking? We have a tricky lesson today, an important lesson, so I want us to be ready. Can you stretch yourself for it?"

We can also use Risk Language in discussions. Rather than saying, "Who would be willing to give an answer?" we might say, "How many would be willing to risk giving an answer?" The former question tends to get a response from the usual volunteers, whereas the latter encourages more students to reach out into more active learning.

Compare the following two teacher-student dialogues:

Teacher A: Who knows the capital of Spain? Yes, Billy?
Billy: Rome.
Teacher A: No, not Rome. Who else has an answer?
Sean: Madrid.
Teacher A: Right. Who knows the capital of Ireland?

Teacher B: How many will risk telling us the capital of Spain? Yes, Billy?
Billy: Rome.
Teacher B: Good risk, Billy. However, Rome is the capital of Italy. The capital of Spain is Madrid. How many will risk telling us the capital of Ireland?

It is preferable to say "how many" rather than "who" because "how many" tends to encourage more students to volunteer. And saying "risk giving an answer" is preferable to "give an answer" because it reminds students that open-minded thinking and full participation often involve risk taking—risking the possibility that we might be wrong.

The trouble is, if you don't risk anything, you risk even more.

—*Erica Jong*

Far too many students are reluctant to speak out because they fear being wrong or appearing foolish. They participate far more actively when such fears are respected and they are encouraged to step beyond their apprehensions, to accept the risks involved and to speak out anyhow. Risk Language gives us a simple strategy for providing that assistance.

The advantages of using Risk Language also apply when speaking to one student. Consider this example: "Juan, are you willing to risk giving an answer?" If Juan hesitates or says no, a suitable reply might be this: "Fine. It's good to know our own limits. Perhaps you'll be willing to take a risk another time."

We might also add Cushioning Questions to the exchange, to call up the wording of one of our Truth Signs. For example, we might ask, "Would it be OK if some choose not to risk sharing right now?" "Sure," students might say. "We each have our own ways and time clocks. Besides, some of us may need more time to think."

If, then, we want to inspire students to do their best work, it's important to champion risk taking. Risk Language provides a convenient tool for doing so.

Strategy 4-4: Intelligence Call-up

Purpose: To advance responsible self-management.
Description: Reminding students frequently that they are intelligent beings, each with the capacity to stop and think and to make responsible choices.

In her book *Workshop Way* (1996), Grace Pilon discusses the value of repeatedly reminding students that they are smart enough to solve problems on their own. Here are some examples of teachers using the Intelligence Call-up strategy in various situations.

1. A teacher explains that thoughtful problem solving will be the preferred approach in her classroom:

> When things are not flowing smoothly in this class, I want you to pause and ask yourself, "What would be the intelligent thing to do?" So, for example, if papers are not being piled neatly, or a crowd is forming at the door, I might say, "What would be the smart, thoughtful way to handle this? Think about this and then go ahead and do what you think would be best."
>
> Let's use our brains. We want this to be a class in which we all learn how to think for ourselves. Call up your intelligence. I'll remind you to do that from time to time. If you were not a human with a human brain, you might not know what is best to do. But you have an amazing brain. You can think for yourself. So when things are not going right, pause and ask yourself, "What is the smart thing to do now?" Learn to reason things out for yourself. Humans can do that like no other

animal. Can anyone give an example of when something was not going smoothly, and you stopped and thought about what was best to do, and you did it?

2. A teacher addresses the problem of students' failure to clean up on time:

Class, we're having difficulty getting everything cleaned up on time. How can we handle this problem? Let's brainstorm a list of ideas on the board. We are smart enough to find a way to solve this problem that will be good for us all. After we brainstorm, we'll see what we think is best.

3. A teacher notices that some students are left out when he asks the class to work in pairs:

Class, I've had to use extra time to pair up everyone when I call for Sharing Pairs. I can understand that you want to sit with your good friends, but getting everyone paired is taking too much time. Besides, I want us to learn to get along with everyone here. From now on, please reach out to all students, even those not near you. Be generous and kind. You will know when it would be a good idea to do that. Make sure everyone gets a partner quickly.

4. A teacher prepares a class for the arrival of new students:

Here is a chance to exercise our brain power. I've been told that we will get new students next week. What would be the best way to get them into the flow of our classroom? We could talk it over now and use all our creativity. Or would it be better to ask a committee to think it through and give us a recommendation or two? Or is there a better choice yet? What do you think is best?

5. A teacher responds to a student who asks for guidance about a nonvital issue: "You decide." This is said with a tone that conveys the message "I trust you to exercise your self-management abilities wisely."

6. A teacher responds to two students who come to her complaining about each other:

Please talk it over yourselves. If necessary, write down your options for handling this and then agree on what would be the best choice. Use your creative intelligence. You two are smart enough to solve the issue.

In short, the Intelligence Call-up strategy has us often saying, "What would be the smart thing to do? Stop and think and you will know what is best." And we persist in talking that way, trusting that all students will eventually know we really mean it, all will come to believe it, and the intelligent way of handling situations will become second nature. We thereby hold high expectations and enlist the power of such expectations.

Some students, of course, do not believe they are intelligent. Perhaps their parents do not listen to them respectfully, or their parents confuse grades with

Risk! Risk anything! Care no more for the opinion of others, for those voices. Do the hardest thing on earth for you. Act for yourself. Face the truth.

—*Katherine Mansfield*

intelligence, or they compare one child unfavorably with another. Or perhaps earlier class experiences did not fit the students' learning styles. Such experiences lead many students to assume that they cannot think and live intelligently. Those students benefit from reassurance that all humans have a remarkable intelligence, a brain power that is not necessarily reflected in school grades. Here is how one teacher provides such reassurance:

> What does it mean to be intelligent? It is certainly not a matter of being able to remember facts or solve school problems. Some of you can do that better than others. But all humans can do much more. All humans are aware. And all humans can manage that awareness. Look at that window. Now look at the ceiling. That is managing your awareness. You are directing your attention where you want it. When you think about what to do next, you are simply managing your awareness, focusing your awareness on the options ahead. That is being intelligent.
>
> In this class I would encourage you to practice using your intelligence in this way. Try to become more aware of what is going on around you and inside you, including inside your head, where, if you are patient enough, you will find many good ideas. And including the world around you, where, if you listen and observe closely, you will notice many interesting events.
>
> Try to become better at managing your awareness, focusing it for longer periods of time on one thing, looking more closely at details and looking more widely at the scene around you. Practice that and you will learn how to use more of your native intelligence.
>
> In class, when unsure of what is best to do, pause and become more aware of what is going on. Then reach for all the ideas you can dream up. Perhaps ask others for ideas, too. As our sign says, "It's intelligent to ask for help." After you get ideas about what can be done, imagine what will happen if this is done or that is done. That is what it means to think ahead. Think like that and you will exercise your natural smartness, which will help you to live an intelligent life.

Strategy 4-5: Check-Yourself Message

Purpose: To remind students to practice managing themselves.
Description: Directing students to check what they have done, with the expectation that they will then notice corrections needed.

Moorman and Moorman (1989) recommend a Check-Yourself Message when students need a reminder. Simple statements such as "Check to see if the words are lined up properly on your paper" or "Check to see if your notebook contains all five items" fall into this category. The intention is to avoid criticism and to imply confidence that when students check, they will see what to do; they are smart enough. Communicating such messages helps build intelligent self-reliance.

Strategy 4-6: Confidence Builders

Purpose: To provide reassurance for students who are anxious about learning.
Description: Before asking students to engage in lessons, making a reassuring statement, such as "We'll go over this again, so don't worry if you don't grasp it right now."

Like Cushioning Questions, Confidence Builders relieve student anxieties. Confidence Builders are usually brief statements and can be injected into teaching whenever we sense apprehension about new or challenging material. No dialogue is expected. We simply make a statement that tells students we understand the pressures they may feel while learning. Some examples:

• We'll go over this several times, so you can relax and know you'll learn it eventually.

• Don't worry about making mistakes while you're learning this. We all make mistakes sometimes.

• Because this is important to learn, we'll make sure you get all the help you'll need. So don't worry if you seem to be having trouble at first.

• Today we'll be working with some new material. I might call upon you to try something you've never done before. Remember, it takes courage to risk, and we often learn more by doing so.

• I know that some of you already know this material. But some of us do not—which is natural. We all learn some things faster, some things slower. So do not feel superior if you already know this, and do not feel inferior if you did not yet learn it. We will all learn it eventually.

Other reassuring statements that increase active learning:

• You can do it.
• This is a smart group.
• You are an intelligent human being.
• I know you will remember this class as bringing out your very best.
• Remember that it's OK to make mistakes.
• I admire your risk taking.
• I trust you.
• You can do it in your own way, according to your own time clock.
• You handled that intelligently.

The ideal of using the present simply to get ready for the future contradicts itself. . . . We always live at the time we live and not at some other time, and only by extracting at each present time the full meaning of each present experience are we prepared for doing the same thing in the future.

—*John Dewey*

Strategy 4-7: Encouragement

Purpose: To support students who are low achievers or have a poor self-image.
Description: Offering verbal encouragement to students who struggle academically or personally or both.

Encouragement can be a powerful tool. A few well-placed comments to struggling students can mean the difference between them giving up and persisting. We don't want inflated compliments or empty praise here, simply honest, direct words that communicate the message "I want you to succeed, and I know you can do it." Some examples:

- Don't give up.
- Keep trying. I know you'll get it eventually.
- You've come a long way—don't stop now!
- Great effort! Keep it up.
- You're showing a lot of dedication to this work. Good for you!
- I'm here for you if you need help.
- I believe in you.
- Believe in yourself. You can do it.

Alson (2002/2003) reports that such encouraging comments are especially valuable for members of minority groups who experience discrimination, which would include special education students.

One teacher in our field tests attempted to make this strategy more personal to students by asking them to each create a list of actions and comments they would find personally encouraging and to keep that list handy, referring to it when they felt in need of a boost.

Strategy 4-8: Learning Challenges

Purpose: To inspire high-energy work.
Description: Posing an assignment not as a responsibility or chore, but as a challenging opportunity.

Young people nowadays can be said to have it too easy. Many could use more challenges. A challenge, as we use the term, is not another chore or burden. It's meant to be an exciting, adventurous, stretching opportunity, a chance to be brave and reach and conquer.

Appropriate challenges enliven students (Tomlinson, 2001). Consider these comments, made by a 5th grade teacher intending to add energy into a particularly lethargic group of students:

How many of you faced a really tough challenge and overcame it? Maybe trying something new, or working hard at something, or resisting doing something you really wanted to do but you knew was not smart to do. Anyone willing to tell us about a time you succeeded at something that was a real challenge to you, even though it might not have been a challenge to other people?

Of those who overcame their challenges, how many found it invigorating, good for you? How many found it good for you even when you were not able to succeed, just because you accepted the challenge?

Yes, we usually enjoy challenges, if they are appropriate for us. I would like to invite you to undertake more challenges in this class. Look at the next unit we will study, the one we introduced yesterday. I'd like to see if some of you feel up to a challenge with that unit.

One challenge, for example, would be to target a number of items to master that are not easy for you and then to really go for it. Perhaps challenge yourself to master your items by a certain date, if that will add zest to your challenge.

Another challenge might be to create something related to that material, not items to master but, perhaps, something to build or dramatize. And then do a masterful job with your creative project.

Or you might challenge yourself to study the standard material but do it in a new, challenging way, maybe with someone you do not ordinarily work with.

Anyone think of other challenges we could mention? Perhaps we can dream up more.

Some of you will not feel up to such a challenge right now. If a challenge is not right for you, or if the time is not right for you, then I would say it's smart not to undertake the challenge. Can anyone guess why I say this?

Yet we can all participate in this. In this next unit, the job of those of us without a challenge will be to act as cheerleaders to the others. So take some time and think about whether you can find a challenge for yourself in the unit ahead, or whether you prefer to be a cheerleader supporting and encouraging the challengers.

If you do undertake a challenge, I challenge you fully to strive and accept. Strive fully, really go for it, give it your all. Then whatever the outcome, accept it fully, take what you get, without regrets. We all win some and lose some. That's life!

After introducing a Learning Challenge, some teachers find it valuable to organize their class into groups of perhaps four students who then sit together for a month or more to support one another. Students without challenges, then, can be the cheerleaders for the group members who have accepted challenges. They can ask about progress, even phone them at home to inject spot doses of encouragement.

Consider, too, leading a discussion on the importance of people having cheerleaders in their lives, on how much easier it is to persist through difficulties

> Most learning is not the result of instruction. It is rather the result of unhampered participation in a meaningful setting.
>
> —Ivan Illich

when we do not go it alone, how much more we can accomplish when we are cheered on, and what kind of cheering works best for people.

What makes for an appropriate challenge? Some important factors:

- *The timing is right for that particular person.* Sometimes the last thing a person needs is another challenge.
- *The level of the challenge is right.* The possibility of success must not be too high or too low, with "high" and "low" defined for and, preferably, by the person involved.
- *The challenge is freely accepted.* A challenge unwillingly accepted will likely be a burden and a chore. An appropriate challenge requires willing, personal commitment.
- *The acceptance is invigorating, empowering.* An appropriate challenge ignites new motivation, new energy, yet does not overwhelm. One is proud of it, glad to have it.

One challenge that is almost always appropriate, to all of us, is the challenge to be our best selves, the selves that deep down we know we want to be.

Who reaps the rewards of classroom challenges? Everyone. On completion, it is beneficial to applaud everyone, not only those who succeeded at their challenges. Public appreciation for only the winners slights, even depreciates, the students who did not make it. Similarly, recognizing only the students who undertook a challenge can diminish those who chose "not now," those who may have wisely opted out. Applause should be for all, for the class community: "Let's give ourselves a hand for the way we helped one another with those challenges!"

Notice how this 2nd grade teacher reviews challenges with her class, using four rounds of applause:

> Let's see how our challenge went. First of all, how many are still working on their challenges, are not ready to call it off? Our job, of course, will be to continue cheering these folks on. Please stand, persisters! Let's give these folks a hand for their persistence!
>
> How many were brave enough to undertake a challenge that was not easy for you, whether or not you have been successful so far? Please stand and show us your courageous eyes. Let's give those folks a round of applause!
>
> How many were smart enough not to choose a challenge this time, because it didn't seem to be the right time or the right challenge for you? Please stand and show us your wise eyes. Let's give those folks a rousing round of applause!
>
> How many of you either enjoyed getting cheered on by others or did some cheering or at least thought about it? Everyone please stand. Let's stand tall and cheerful and give ourselves a super hand! I'd say we all did a good job.

If you wait until you're really sure, you'll never take off the training wheels.

—Cynthia Copeland Lewis

Strategy 4-9: Let Them Be

Purpose: To avoid discouraging students by expecting more than they can produce at the time.

Description: When we suspect students have not learned because they are not yet ready to learn, letting them be, not attempting to force something before its time.

Most of us have had the experience of being asked to learn something when, for one reason or another, it was not the time for us to learn it. We might have been asked to tell time, or to sing on key, or to grasp calculus. Unable to learn what was requested, and especially if our peers were quite able to learn it or if we wanted to please our teacher, we might have felt defeated, weak, stupid. Those are not feelings that lead us to become confident learners.

We do well to be alert for such occasions. In our zeal to get students to learn, we don't want to overlook the possibility that, from the student's perspective, we may be asking more than the student is then able to produce. Strategy 3-2 described the advantage of teaching in layers, not lumps. That strategy is a reminder to us that we can return to a topic another time, perhaps in another way, thereby avoiding pushing students too hard at any one time.

It is also helpful to remember that when in doubt, it may be wise to let students be, even if we cannot come back to the topic. There is wisdom in not discouraging students. More fundamentally, there is wisdom in communicating respect for students even when they cannot learn. Modeling such behavior is a fine way to teach students how they can accept their less capable neighbors, a primary skill in healthy community life.

Strategy 4-10: Ability Salute

Purpose: To acknowledge effort, regardless of how much was accomplished.

Description: Telling groups we appreciate how much effort they are putting into learning.

We might try making one of these statements the next time we finish a lesson that seemed particularly difficult for students:

- I salute your ability to work hard. No one could ask for more.
- I appreciate how much effort you all put into this.
- This is a group that gives its best! Congratulations!

There is a grave defect in the school where the playground suggests happy and the classroom disagreeable thoughts.

—John Spalding

• You all played hard at this game of learning. In my book, that makes you all winners.

• No group I've had gave as much as you did.

• You gave it your all, and I appreciate that.

• That was not easy. When I was your age, I probably would not have done nearly as well.

• I'm sending a note to the principal about the special work you all did on this project.

• You all really rose to this challenge.

The Ability Salute lets students know we recognize their efforts, no matter how much they accomplished. It is not meant for individual praise, although it also can be used that way. It is rather meant to give encouragement to all students, especially those whose efforts do not usually merit individual praise and who therefore may be most in need of praise. When weak students feel they are full members of a strong group, they tend to internalize that strength.

Establishing a Climate That Inspires High Cooperation

The strategies in this chapter are especially useful for building feelings of cooperation among students. Many of these strategies use "we" language. They suggest saying "we want" instead of "I want" to create a feeling that "we" all are in this together, that "our" class is one cooperative community. The first three strategies are each marked with an arrow to indicate they are recommended for your first consideration.

⤷ Strategy 5-1: Student Procedure Mastery

Purpose: To motivate students to cooperate and follow classroom procedures smoothly and willingly.

Description: Spending enough time teaching classroom procedures early on so they become comfortable, automatic routines for students.

It is tempting to assume that students will understand and follow simple procedures: "Pick a partner and talk over last night's homework." "When you replace your folder on the shelf, replace it in alphabetical order." But if you have taught school for more than one hour, you probably noticed that some students will neither comprehend nor follow directions carefully.

The remedy? Demonstrate that procedures are important by overteaching them, not underteaching them. Early on, announce that you care that things be done properly. Then aim for all students to reach absolute mastery of all key procedures and to feel good about having that mastery. It's often wise to walk students through each procedure, giving explicit instructions, as does this teacher:

> When I say, "Get a partner," first look around and make eye contact with someone. You can sit with someone nearby or not, as you choose. But if I ask you to

pick someone with whom you have not recently worked, you might have to walk elsewhere to make that eye contact. Then sit close enough to that person so you can talk quietly. Let's try that. Pick a partner with whom you have not recently worked and sit together. Please do that now.

After the students have found partners, the teacher reviews what happened:

Let's talk about how we did. Maybe some of you felt anxious about being left out, and felt it was risky to get partners. I see that some of you were, in fact, left out, and it was tempting to form a trio instead of a pair, or to sit by yourself, or to come and ask me what to do. Please go back to your original seats, and let's try again.

The teacher then gives more detailed instructions:

This time, when I say "Go," take a risk and do not rush to sit with the first person you see. If most others are paired up and you are still without a partner, look around to see if anyone else is available. A person might have been unwilling to risk today, so you may find someone sitting alone. Look carefully, like a detective looking for someone. If you have done that and still find no one without a partner, please make one trio. Ask a pair if you might join them. Let's try it again. Please get a partner with whom you have not recently worked. Go.

Like "pick a partner," an instruction to "talk over last night's homework" invites confusion, which invites noncompliance, which invites discipline problems. One teacher posts the following chart to specify what this instruction means:

Homework Groups

- Compare answers.
- Talk through disagreements.
- Help one another understand.
- Check with another group if unsure.
- Support one another in mastering the content.

Another teacher has a chart for checking homework that involves writing clearly:

For Homework in Writing

1. Exchange papers.
2. Read thoughtfully.
3. Make helpful feedback notes for the writer.
4. If time permits, talk over your reactions.

Note that it is generally best to teach and, if necessary, to reteach a procedure when it is first needed. Keep in mind, though, that it is also advisable not to introduce too many procedures at one time. The point: Spend enough time early on to make procedures perfectly clear and acceptable to all. And help students appreciate and enjoy their ability to perform procedures masterfully. Doing so not only eventually saves time, it also teaches students the importance of the little things in life. And mastery of classroom procedures provides all students, including the slowest learners, the opportunity to experience masterful success.

 ## Strategy 5-2: Class Agreement

Purpose: To communicate teacher respect for student thinking and to cultivate a climate of cooperation.

Description: Announcing a topic or problem and asking for students' input and agreement on the best way to deal with it.

Few of us react positively to bossy people. When people push us, our instinct is to push back or to resent their behavior. On the other hand, when people invite us to *join* in an activity, when they ask if we are *willing* to participate, we are likely to be nonresistant, ready at least to consider cooperating. This very human reaction underlies the wisdom of occasionally asking students to agree to our proposed plans.

For example, we might say to our students, "Rather than touch on all the topics in the book, I would like us to handle a few topics with depth and care. Here are the topics I recommend . . . Any reactions to that suggestion? Can we agree at least to start off in this way?" Such an invitation does not eliminate our authority. We still are responsible for deciding what plan to implement. Even after hearing students' thoughts, we can conclude that our initial plan is best. But inviting students' ideas has the effect of inspiring them to cooperate. Besides, it sometimes provides new ideas to consider, which can only improve our teaching plans.

In some cases it is wise to involve students in the construction of the plan. For example, we might say, "How shall we handle this next unit? Let's brainstorm and make a list of some options. Then let's see if we can agree on how best to proceed." If everyone can agree, the resulting plan will likely provide a high level of student commitment and motivation. Even if everyone does not end up agreeing, students will likely appreciate being respected enough to have their thoughts considered.

We might also ask the class to cooperate on solving a problem. We might, for example, say, "Let's brainstorm a list of ways we might do better at handing in all

Always make speeches shorter than anybody dared hope.

—*Lord Reading*

our papers on time. How about two volunteers write on the board all the ideas we can come up with. Later we'll sift through the list and see if we can agree on something worth trying." For more on this procedure, see Strategy 8-9, Whole-Class Problem Solving.

In general, this strategy recommends that we often invite students to participate with us in making classroom decisions, a step that almost always improves student cooperation.

Strategy 5-3: Ask a Friend

Purpose: To have students get their questions answered efficiently and to nurture a classroom feeling of mutual support.

Description: Encouraging students who need help to ask a friend.

When a student asks what page the class is on, or asks that the homework directions be repeated, or is unsure of how to complete a worksheet, a good response is usually "Please ask a friend." The comment serves us in several ways. It eases our load; many students can easily get the help they need from peers. It generates mutual respect and appreciation among students and builds a healthy, interdependent class community. And it communicates that we assume others in the class can be "friends" if only they are seen as such.

Grace Pilon (1996) notes that some students seem to create confusion for themselves so they can ask a teacher for help, perhaps because they thirst for attention. For such students, asking one friend may not be enough. Moorman and Moorman (1989) offer the phrase "Ask three then me." We might announce to a class, "Whenever you are working at individual tasks and need assistance, please ask three others before asking me." If a student approaches us, we can then simply inquire, "Did you ask three before me?"

▲ **TEACHER COMMENT**

At first, some of the children found asking a friend difficult because they wanted an immediate answer from the teacher—they weren't sure they could trust all their peers for the correct answer. After the third time of Ask a Friend, the students became more trusting of each other.

—*Miriam Harmon, 1st Grade Teacher*

Strategy 5-4: Once Principle

Purpose: To teach students both to listen and to live self-responsibly.

Description: Announcing that from now on directions will be given only once and that students not hearing directions are to use a dignified, intelligent way to catch up.

Pilon (1996) suggests that teachers introduce this strategy by saying something like this:

> Please, everyone look at me. From now on, I will say things only once. Page numbers. Directions. Anything like that. So please practice keeping yourself aware. If you miss what I say, find a way to catch up. Perhaps whisper to a friend, or watch and see what others are doing, or later quietly ask a friend what you missed. Call on your good intelligence. You will know the best thing to do. Now let's get started on today's lesson

Note that the teacher said this only once. She did not say, "Any questions?" That might well have led to a repetition of the same announcement.

Note, too, that the teacher began by asking all students to look at her. If a direction is to be given only once, it is fair to call for attention and insert an appropriate beat of silence so all students have a fair chance of hearing it.

Imagine, then, when students later ask, "When was that due?" or "What did you say the page was?" that the teacher simply smiles warmly and says, "Ask a friend," not "I told you" or "I say things only once." Eventually the teacher need say nothing at all to communicate to students that they are smart enough to see a teacher smile as an unspoken answer to their question.

Will this strategy work? Many teachers report that it works just fine. In our experience, if we have confidence that students will learn the Once Principle, they will. It is often more difficult for the teacher to stick to the Once Principle than it is for students to learn how to live with it.

Strategy 5-5: Class Meeting

Purpose: To establish a standard procedure for discussions of class concerns.
Description: Teaching students when and how class issues can be regularly and thoughtfully considered in a class meeting.

One of the best ways to build and strengthen student community is through regular class meetings. Consider the following steps:

• *Focusing awareness.* Begin class meetings by having students write Thought/Feel Cards (Strategy 21-7). For this, each student might use a three-by-five-inch index card. We might introduce the activity by saying something like this: "On one side of your card, please note some thoughts currently on your mind. These could be about anything. Do not worry about what you write—you will not need to share this with anybody if you don't want to." After a pause, we might say, "When you are done, please turn your cards over and write some feelings you

Everybody is ignorant, only on different subjects.
—Will Rogers

have inside yourself right now. Again, do not be concerned about what you write—you will always have the option to keep your feelings private."

• *Sharing.* We initiate a group Whip Around, Pass Option (Strategy 16-4), inviting each student to share a thought or feeling or to simply say, "I pass."

• *Choosing a topic.* The Whip Around sometimes reveals potential topics for a class discussion. If so, we might list on the board one or two that we think are appropriate and then ask for volunteers to propose other issues to discuss or problems to address. Students could then raise hands to show which issues they would like addressed; the issue with the most votes wins. Other topics might be saved for future meetings. Note that if a meeting has been called for a particular purpose, we could simply present that topic and ask for class agreement. (See Class Agreement, Strategy 5-2.)

• *Addressing the topic.* The Brainstorm/Sort strategy is a good way to address the topic. Students brainstorm options for handling an issue and then work together to sort the options, seeking the best. For example, students might brainstorm how to handle annoying behavior, cliques, teasing, a messy room, stealing. Or, if there is no issue to be addressed, students might brainstorm how the class can live and work together more productively. See Brainstorm/Sort (Strategy 16-8) for a more detailed discussion of the process.

• *Practicing.* When Brainstorm/Sort has resulted in proposals for new behaviors, we might give students time to role-play these behaviors, if that is practical. Students might best do this in pairs or small groups.

• *Concluding.* Ending on a positive note is key—especially when a difficult topic has been addressed. One way to do this is by closing with a moment of appreciation. We begin by stating something we appreciate about how the group handled that day's meeting—for instance, "I appreciate the way everyone tried hard not to interrupt while others were speaking" or "I appreciate how open-minded we were during our brainstorming." Then we give students a moment to reflect on what they appreciate and invite any who are willing to complete the phrase "I appreciate . . ." aloud.

Of course, as we become familiar with the needs of our class, we might adjust the meeting procedure and hold meetings more or less frequently. However, in general, it is preferable for class meetings to be as student-centered as possible, which might mean allowing students to propose meetings when they deem them necessary. It might also mean choosing one or two students to chair each meeting, perhaps by rotating through the class list. Or, if we use Class Leaders (Strategy 5-6), the leaders for that day could assume the job. Once students are

> Personally I'm always ready to learn, although I do not always like being taught.
>
> —*Winston Churchill*

comfortable with the Class Meeting procedure, we can give most of the responsibility for running meetings to such student leaders.

Many students appreciate structured time in which they can freely voice opinions and concerns—as do their teachers. In general, most of their opinions—positive and negative—are well received because of the dignifying format of the Class Meeting strategy. Individual self-management skills and awareness levels are increased as each student decides what to contribute. And because everyone is part of the process, it is usually an energizing experience for all.

Strategy 5-6: Class Leaders

Purpose: To give students some of the responsibility for managing the class.
Description: Choosing daily class leaders for special responsibilities.

The Class Leaders strategy provides a way to share responsibilities with students. It also helps the class run smoothly and builds student self-esteem. Here is one teacher introducing this structure to a class:

> From now on, two of you will act as class leaders each day. You will all have a chance to do this. Class leaders will have certain fixed responsibilities each day. For example, I will ask you to make an absence and tardy list for me, to lead the line into the cafeteria, to remind a student who disrupts class work to control himself or herself, to pick the class leaders for the next day, and to coach the next day's class leaders if they have any questions or need any help. The job list is posted alongside the door, and later we'll talk about how, exactly, to do each job.

That teacher had all the students write their initials on a wooden bead, which they put into a large plastic container. After fastening the lid, the teacher gave the container a good shake. She asked one student to hold the container while another student picked two beads. "That," the teacher explained, "is the way the two current class leaders are to pick the next day's leaders." The teacher then asked:

> What should we do if one or both of the beads of the *current* leaders are selected? We could let them be leaders two days in a row. But I'd rather they be given the responsibility of choosing someone else. Who? Someone who has not been a leader for a long time. Here is the way we'll handle that. Take one of the calendars from the piles I made on the windowsill. Write your name on the front and keep the calendar in your desk. When you are a leader for the day, write a big capital L in that day's box. If you are not a leader, write a number. Write 1 if it's the first day you were not chosen, 2 if it's the second day, and so on. Then when a current leader's bead is chosen, that current leader will ask all those who have the highest numbers on their calendars to stand. They will be the ones who were not leaders for the longest time. And the current leader will choose one of those, anyone he or she thinks should be one of the leaders the next day.

Later, in discussing how she had introduced the strategy to her students, the teacher said, "That bead-selecting process adds a nice touch of drama and fun to the day. Students like it." She continued:

It was important to role-play how to do all the leader's tasks and talk about potential problems. Students always want to know how two leaders are to do single tasks, and I say, "Use your intelligence and decide what is best. You might take turns or find a way to do a task together. For example, for the class absence list, one person might check the seating chart and another do the writing. Or one person could do it all and the second could check the list for accuracy."

I spend the most time having students practice offering colleagues what I call "polite reminders." They learn that when they are leaders they are to go to anyone who is a disturbance and to politely say, "Please control yourself." In that way the students take some of the responsibility for maintaining discipline. I find students listen to each other fairly well, perhaps because they know that when they are leaders of the day they will want to be listened to as well.

We each, of course, will need to shape our use of Class Leaders to suit our situation. Many teachers, for example, prefer using one class leader, not a pair; using a simple rotation system to choose leaders, not a random system; or not giving leaders the task of speaking to students who disturb the class.

Strategy 5-7: Getting-to-Know-You Activities

Purpose: To help students know and appreciate one another.
Description: Providing time for activities that involve personal sharing.

Getting-to-Know-You Activities help lay the groundwork for positive peer relationships throughout the year. Some possibilities, which we might use during the first month of school or to welcome a new student midyear:

Name Cards for the Teacher

Ask students to fill out a four-by-six-inch index card with information that helps you get to know each of them better. Tell them you will keep the information private. Students might begin by writing their name, address, and phone number. You might then ask students to write, for example, some things they love to do, are proud of, are good at, or sometimes worry about, or any other questions that might be of interest to you. You then collect those cards. They can be especially valuable for giving you insights into students who are not easy to relate to.

Student Name Tags

You might ask students to create name tags, perhaps again using index cards. In the center of the card, students might write their names along with three things they like about themselves. They might also include other personal information, such as their favorite food, entertainer, sport, or hobby. After the students have decorated their cards, we might ask them to walk about, observing one another's name tags. If time permits, we might use the Whip Around, Pass Option (Strategy 16-4) as a way for students to introduce themselves to the class; each student has the option to share or to simply say, "I pass." Perhaps conclude by challenging students to see how many names they can remember.

Personal Questions to Share

Pose a question such as "What is something you like or hate to do?" or "What is something in your home that you are proud of?" Then give students a moment to write a response (see Strategy 16-3, Question, All Write). There are several options for proceeding. Students might pair up to briefly share answers, rotating partners when they finish, which gives each person a chance to share notes with a few others (see Strategy 7-3, Rotating Pairs). Or you could initiate a whole-group Whip Around, Pass Option (Strategy 16-4), with each student choosing to share or pass.

Stand and Appreciate

This activity, from veteran teacher coach Lou Emge, is fun any time. It has an air of suspense and provides a bit of physical exercise. Each student will need a three-by-five-inch index card on which to write three lines. On the first line, ask students to write something they have in common with *many* people in the room, but probably not everyone. For example, "I'm taller than 5 feet, 8 inches." "I'm male." "I'm wearing something blue." "I have no sisters." On the second line, ask them to write something they have in common with *some* people in the room, but probably not many. For instance, "I moved to this area just this year." "We have two dogs." "I hate math." "I love baseball." Finally, on the third line, ask students to write something that is unique to them. It might be something they once did that was unusual, or some special talent they have, or something they have at home that no one else in the room probably has, or something very funny that once happened to them. For example, "I was once in a real igloo in Alaska." "One time, a horse bit me." "My birthday was yesterday."

Every man must do his own growing, no matter how tall his grandfather was.

—*Laurence Peters*

After collecting and shuffling the cards, ask all students to stand. Pick one card and read the first line aloud. Tell the students that if what you just read applies to them, they remain standing; otherwise, they should sit down. So if the first line is "I'm male," all the males remain standing and all the females sit. Continue until you have read all three lines. After you read the third line, only one person will probably remain standing and will even more probably feel special. You might then invite all students to applaud for the person who is "the only person who . . . " (Read that third line again.)

If there is time for another card or two, read those line by line, as before. You can save the rest of the cards for future use. If new students enter the class midyear, perhaps have them fill out a card and add it to the top of the pile. You might then welcome them to the class with a quick round of Stand and Appreciate. As you will see, it's a fun way to welcome newcomers and for everyone to experience a moment in the spotlight.

What's in the Sack?

For this activity you will need a copy of the poem "What's in the Sack?" by Shel Silverstein. In this humorous selection, Silverstein describes a mysterious character who carries a large sack with him wherever he goes. Onlookers repeatedly beg to find out what is in the sack, which only results in the man's increasing irritation. Sadly, people seem more interested in knowing what's in the sack than they are in knowing him. Here is how one of us, Melanie, used this poem in a 4th grade class during the first week of school:

After reading the poem aloud with much drama, I'd take out a laundry bag containing items that, I explained, somehow connected to my life. I'd then make quite a production of asking the class if they wanted to see what was in my sack. When they were sufficiently curious, I'd give each of them a copy of the poem, telling them we'd now read it together to see if they could convince me to show them what's in my sack. Their job, I'd explain, was to chime in every time the poem's words were "What's in the sack?" Without fail, they'd enthusiastically accept their duty. Sometimes, just for the fun of it, we'd go through it a third time—which they loved even more than the first two! Finally, with much ceremony, I'd reveal each item, odd and random things—a book I was reading, a running shoe, a saucepot, a rollerblade, a marble notebook, a seashell. Always, no matter what I pulled out, they were amused. I'd then tell them it was time to be detectives. I'd pair up students and ask them to use these clues to figure out as much as they could about me.

Afterward, each pair would be given a chance to share one conclusion they'd made, and I'd tell them whether or not it was on target. Finally, each student was given a paper lunch bag and told that for homework they were to fill these mini-sacks with items that revealed something about them. Items that could not fit in the sack could be represented by a drawing. The next day it was detective time again; pairs were formed and students tried to learn more about their partners by what was contained in the sacks. Later on, a few each day, students would introduce their partners by telling a few things they had learned about them. This was a favorite activity for my students. Nothing builds a community feeling like having fun together!

Strategy 5-8: Community Living Lessons

Purpose: To advance appreciation of what a cooperative classroom community requires.

Description: Occasionally presenting lessons and activities that help students appreciate what is involved in living as a cooperative classroom community.

Many students have no experience living in a healthy, cooperative community. It can be valuable, then, to make that possibility vivid and real for them.

Instilling Community Living into the Classroom

How might we weave the principles of community living into a classroom? Here are some possibilities:

• We might refer to the Truth Sign (see Strategy 4-1) that says "It's intelligent to ask for help. No one needs to do it all alone." We might tell students that the sign's message is part of living happily together. We might also remind them what a typical neighborhood looks like. One person drives a bus; another paints a house; a third walks home carrying groceries. Each person is doing different things, yet all are part of the same cooperative community.

• We might consider posting two new Truth Signs:

> We can aim to be a group that is all for one and one for all.

> We can accept and support one another. We need not ignore or reject anyone.

• We might connect this issue to principles that are associated with the history of the United States: democratic government; authority resting in the people; collective decision making; government of the people, by the people, for the people; no arbitrary laws or cruel punishments; laws based on open-minded discussions; a balance of powers to limit misuse of power; each citizen sharing in group responsibilities; respect for the common good; one nation with liberty and justice for all; freedom to speak one's mind; the right to life, liberty, and the pursuit of happiness; equal opportunity; the Declaration of Independence; the Bill of Rights.

These principles are advanced, of course, when they are practiced in the classroom. Such practice also prepares students for roles as mature citizens. We can remind students of some of these principles, perhaps concluding with a challenge such as this:

> Let's learn how we can live and learn well together here, each with the right to manage his or her own work, each with the responsibility to avoid interfering with others' rights, and each with the opportunity and responsibility to play a respected part in the group as a whole.

• To communicate the meaning of a healthful community, we might have students wear name tags the first week so everyone gets to know one another more quickly. One teacher who did this also talked about teamwork in sports and in factories. He said he wanted his class to learn to work together as a "great team." This particular class decided to give itself a class name, to exchange phone numbers so people could call if they needed help with homework, to set up a hospitality committee to welcome new class members, and to have occasional class outings on weekends.

• We might begin the school year with an inspirational motto. One teacher began the school year with the phrase "One for all and all for one," challenging her class to be tenacious enough to keep working for that class spirit, even when it was tough to do so. Later on she used two quotes, the first from Virginia Driving Hawk Sneve and the second from Edwin Markham, to start a discussion on what a community classroom might be like:

> The circle is a sacred symbol of life. . . . Individual parts within the circle connect with every other. What happens to one, or what one part does, affects all within the circle.

> He drew a circle to shut me out.
> Heretic, rebel, a thing to flout.
> But love and I had the wit to win.
> We drew a circle that took him in.

The man who makes no mistakes does not usually make anything.
—Bishop W. C. Magee

In some way, then, perhaps using images of a smoothly functioning family, a friendly neighborhood, effective teamwork, or basic principles of society, we might aim to inspire students to become a mutually supportive and respectful community of learners. Because this is not a familiar goal for many students, from time to time we do well to remind them of this ideal.

Fitting Class Rules into the Community Living Strategy

We do well to remember our purpose. We care about advancing both current academic learning and long-term dignified living. Our priority is not to control everything students do. Our aim is not to prevent behavior problems from ever coming up. We do not, of course, want unnecessary problems, and we certainly do not want to generate misbehavior. But some problems can be valuable for teaching students what is involved in living cooperatively in the real world.

The Intelligence Call-up (Strategy 4-4) reduces the need for a set of class rules. Using this strategy, rather than relying on rules, involves reminding students that they are intelligent beings, smart enough to make informed, appropriate choices in school, just as they do every day at home and on the street. It involves frequently reminding students to think through the situations they face and asking, "What are all your options? What would be the smart thing to do? What comes to you when you use your brain power?" It involves reassuring students that they are capable of figuring out what is best and what makes the most sense, and encouraging them to live together as one supportive, intelligent community. The intent is to teach students how they can handle problems, because they will need to handle them as mature citizens.

Some teachers, however, still feel the need for specific rules or, as we prefer to call them, behavior guidelines. If so, we recommend the second of these two approaches:

Example 1. We will need certain rules of behavior in our class if we are to work effectively—perhaps rules about speaking out or disturbing others or getting work in on time. What rules do you think we will need here? Let's discuss this and brainstorm a list. [The class brainstorms a list.] Which rules on our list are most important? How shall we handle those who violate rules? What would be appropriate consequences for such violations? How will we remember these rules and their consequences?

Example 2. I want us to get along well together. I want us to live and learn together much like a healthy community or family, with respectful give and take. I want us to help one another when that is appropriate, and to leave others alone when we judge that is the wise thing to do. Some guidelines might help us become such a community. One guideline might be this: "Honestly yet respectfully let someone know when he or she is bothering you." One guideline I personally need is "Do not leave the room without a hall pass." What other guidelines might we consider? [The class discusses ideas.] How can we keep to these guidelines and avoid ignoring them? How should we react when people make mistakes, as all humans do?

Both of the above approaches might end up with behavior guidelines, such as "Raise your hand before speaking," "No hitting or running," and so on. But the second is likely to elicit more goodness and cooperation from students. And because cultivating goodness and cooperation is one of our concerns, we can use our discipline plan to further this purpose. A discipline plan, then, need not be an unfortunate necessity. It can be a valuable tool both to prevent problems and to advance mature living. (For details, see Strategy 8-11, Discipline Plan.) Even in classes where rules are advisable, we recommend announcing early on that the intent is for the class to learn to live together as a productive, happy community, using words much like those of the second teacher.

Strategy 5-9: Dignifying Acts

Purpose: To demonstrate underlying care for students in a way that grows a positive, personal class climate.
Description: Doing little things that show we value students as persons, not only as learners.

Almost all students appreciate personal attention from teachers. For some students, it's the key to getting them to invest themselves fully in learning (Combs, 1982; McCombs & Whisler, 1997). How can we communicate a personal interest in students? Some ideas:

• Learn students' names quickly and use them often. By the way, if we have many groups of students, learning names quickly can be eased by taking photographs of the students during the first day or two of school.
• During lessons, make direct, friendly eye contact with individual students, strolling about if necessary so you can eventually look at all students, and if they don't look your way at least be near them for a brief moment.
• Chat with students informally before and after class. Ask about their interests, their preferences, and their hobbies. And share your hobbies, interests, and concerns. Perhaps mention the movies and TV programs you saw recently and ask if they saw them, too.

- Remember students who made contributions and give them credit later by saying something such as, "Juan's comment adds to the suggestion Nel gave us earlier."

- Make a note to remind yourself which students were absent, and welcome them back warmly when they return.

- Keep a log of birthdays and ask each birthday person to stand for a moment while classmates tap their fingers on their desks or otherwise acknowledge the day.

- Look for something you can turn into a small, private compliment. You can then bend close to a student as you walk by and softly say something like, "I like that blue shirt," or "I like how you spoke up today," or "That is a great doodle!"

- Visit the lunchroom, perhaps once a week, and chat with a few students, taking care to sometimes include the quiet students and the loners. Perhaps even occasionally eat lunch with students.

- Engage in some playground or gym activity with students (which might also demonstrate that people can do their best even when their best is dreadful).

- Mention a student's special talent or accomplishment to the whole class. Perhaps invite students to tell you privately when they have something that might be suitable for such a public announcement.

- Send a personal note to every student's home early in the year saying why you appreciate having that student in class. (See Strategy 27-9, Positive Parent Schedule.)

The more you do of what you've done, the more you'll have of what you've got.

—Anonymous

Strategy 5-10: Family Introductory Letter

Purpose: To generate positive expectations in your students' families.
Description: Sending an upbeat message to students' families early in the year.

Especially for teachers new to the profession or new to a school, reaching out to parents early in the year gains much support and respect. The Family Introductory Letter offers one simple way to do this. We might say that we are happy to have the family's student in our class, that we fully expect the student to work hard and to show improvement, and that we welcome any suggestions or questions at any time. We might even send a letter before the first day, if possible, to introduce ourselves and to let families know we are looking forward to a year of working together to help their children. In either case, it's valuable to get the families of our students on our side and, generally, to treat parents as valued members of the class community.

Structuring Class Time Efficiently

No one can learn the multiplication table for someone else. That is, learning, like eating, is an individual matter. We can do it *with* others, but we must do it *by* ourselves. Staying productively engaged is also an individual matter. In any group activity—a discussion, say, or a lecture—the aim is always to engage all *individuals* in the group, not merely the group as a whole.

One of best ways to respect that reality is to make generous use of individualized learning tasks. That helps us manage class time efficiently. We can ask students to work on individual learning tasks when, for example, we need to take attendance or handle other administrative chores, or when we want to work with a small group of students. This chapter presents six strategies that illustrate how we can take advantage of such opportunities. The first five strategies are each marked with an arrow and are recommended for first consideration.

 ## Strategy 6-1: Do Now

Purpose: To engage students productively as soon as they enter the room.
Description: Providing independent work for students to handle as soon as they arrive.

Rather than delaying teaching until all students have arrived and we are ready to teach, we can establish a standing instruction that informs students they are to handle an announced task as soon as they enter the room. Some possibilities include asking students to

- Write thoughts about a posted quote or question of the day.
- Solve a problem written on the board or overhead and then create a new problem in the same style.

• Draw something to illustrate a math concept or a line from a poem or an idea from social studies.

• Time themselves and in one minute see how many ways they can produce a sum of 25, write words that rhyme with "slay," list states or rivers, or perform any such task.

• Write a personal self-management goal for the day. (See Strategy 26-3, Self-Management Goals.)

The idea is to create a brief initial task so students waste no time and lose no energy waiting for activities to get underway. It also gives us time to prepare lesson materials, take attendance, or consult with individual students.

What do students do after finishing the Do Now task? It is helpful to have a catch-all activity available. If students have homework to be checked, they might proceed to a homework review; see Structure 1 in Strategy 3-4. Or students might move on to other independent tasks, such as those suggested by other strategies in this chapter.

It is often useful to begin class by randomly sampling one or two of the students' Do Now responses. That can add a bit of fun and intrigue to the activity, as students wonder, "Will I be called on today?"

Strategy 6-2: Learning Centers

Purpose: To provide students with ongoing self-directed learning experiences.
Description: Setting up activity or task centers in the classroom in which students can work on their own.

Learning Centers provide an efficient way to organize independent work. Some possibilities:

• A library center where students read independently or with a partner and, perhaps, record the number of pages they read or write their thoughts in a personal reading log.

• A writing center consisting of sentence starters, topic cards, or interesting photos for students to write about.

• An arts and crafts center with simple project ideas, perhaps involving collage materials, toothpicks to glue into structures, papers to fold or cut, or drawings to make.

• A relaxing center, perhaps with earphones for music listening or space for simple stretching or bending exercises.

Every blade of grass has its angel that bends over it and whispers, "Grow, grow."

—*The Talmud*

- A science center, perhaps with simple experiments to do, models to create, or objects to manipulate.
- A listening center where students can listen to poetry or books on tape and record their impressions in listening journals.
- A computer center linked to Internet sites that contain tutorials, interactive tools, practice problems, or enrichment materials.
- A preview center stocked with materials that preview a topic to be studied later.
- A review center where students do a puzzle or fill in a chart that refreshes earlier learnings.
- A spelling/vocabulary center in which students use Study Cards (Strategy 6-3), write definitions, create sentences, illustrate favorite words, or pair up and test each other.

Students might work at a learning center as soon as they enter the room. And they might also do so later on—for example, when they finish a worksheet we assigned. Or they might visit centers while we work with a group of other students or whenever they have nothing else to do. Or we might set up a schedule to rotate all students through all centers during independent work time. And to encourage all students to use learning-center time responsibly, we can ask them to log, say, one or two things they did or learned from each visit to a center. Although it takes some time to set up learning centers, the initial investment pays off, especially because we can reuse our centers year after year, improving them as we go.

Strategy 6-3: Study Cards

Purpose: To help students commit basic information to memory and to develop independent study skills.

Description: Asking students to create and study a set of cards containing material to be memorized.

Students often need to memorize math facts, spelling words, scientific formulas, definitions of key terms, and the like. Study Cards have proven to be valuable for this task. A possible sequence for using this strategy:

1. *Creating cards.* Students create a set of cards for themselves in class or as homework, perhaps using three-by-five-inch index cards, with each card having one item to be memorized. The front of a card might have a vocabulary word, for

example; the back might contain a sample sentence and a definition and, if the student chooses, a picture. Students might also decorate their cards.

2. *Categorizing cards.* Students then separate their cards into two categories, those with information they already know and those needing more attention. Students might store cards in two separate envelopes, perhaps marked "Know" and "Not yet."

3. *Studying cards.* Students then study on their own. Perhaps brainstorm with the class different times and ways students might study the cards—first thing in the morning, before going to sleep, drilling with a partner, and so on. And perhaps provide a few minutes in class for students to study cards in any way they choose. Instruct students to move cards from the "Not yet" envelope to the "Know" envelope whenever they feel confident to do so.

4. *Checking progress.* Regularly assess student progress, perhaps by having students meet weekly in pairs to test each other on the cards in their "Know" envelopes. You might also ask students to occasionally turn in their "Know" envelopes, with a note signed by partners verifying that the enclosed items were mastered.

5. *Appreciating progress.* To help students monitor their progress and appreciate their success, consider asking them to keep a private chart of how many cards they mastered each week. You might also offer special recognition when students show they mastered a certain number of items in a certain time period, with each student's threshold set individually, so the challenge is fair for all. (To define the challenge, after they are familiar with the process ask students to identify how many cards they learned each week for three weeks. Average those three numbers and that number becomes each student's "base" rate. The challenge is to meet or beat the base rate each week thereafter.)

The Study Card strategy is highly flexible and self-managing. It allows each student to pursue independent learning geared to individual pace and style. Students who learn quickly are not bored or held back, and those requiring more time need not feel either pressured or inadequate.

◆▶ Strategy 6-4: Independent Learning Assignments

Purpose: To provide independent assignments that develop self-responsible learning skills.

Description: Guiding students through steps that help them successfully design and complete independent learning projects on topics of their choice.

One way to initiate independent learning projects is to ask students to take a few moments to scan the textbook and, as they do so, to make a note of any question or topic that might be of special interest to them. After a minute or two, we might ask students if anyone is willing to share something he or she wrote. We might then continue by saying something such as this:

> One of my goals is to help you become effective independent learners—people who can enjoy learning on their own. In that regard, I'd like each of you to become an *expert* in one or more topics of special interest to you. It will be up to you to choose your topic, to choose how you will learn more about it, and also to choose how much time to spend on it. The list you just made might contain some ideas. And as we proceed in the class you may find other topics or questions that hold special interest for you.
>
> Starting today, be on the lookout for such items. When you find one, make a note and perhaps jot down some ways you might learn more about it. Before too long, I'll ask each of you to choose a topic for your first Independent Learning Assignment.

After a few days, then, we might ask for volunteers to share possible topics. This could be an occasion to discuss further steps for the project, such as the following:

1. Choose a topic or question of special interest.
2. Create a learning goal based on that topic or question.
3. Create a plan telling the steps you will take to achieve your goal.

As for learning goals, students might aim, for example, to explain why a historical figure was important and how that figure is relevant to life today, or to demonstrate speed in solving a particular math problem accurately, or to write a one-act play that illustrates an understanding. The point is to help students choose goals that are specific enough to guide their study and define their success.

As for steps to reach the goal, we might ask students to make a provisional plan, to ask a friend or two to read it for completeness and clarity, and then to revise it and turn it in to us for approval. If a classroom is set up with Learning Centers (Strategy 6-2) or a Task Workshop (Strategy 6-5) or some other activity that keeps students productively engaged while we meet with individuals, we could discuss plans with students one-on-one.

Independent Learning Assignments typically conclude with each student reviewing the learning process and reporting learning results. A Like/Might Review (Strategy 21-2) offers an effective way for students to review the process (first, students write what they *liked* about how they handled the assignment and, second, what they *might* do differently another time).

As for reporting results, this might be accomplished by having two presentations made each day to the whole class; or, more efficiently, by having students make presentations to one another in small groups, perhaps with parents invited; or, if appropriate, by having students display portfolios or posters of their work.

This Independent Learning Assignment strategy offers a valuable way to individualize instruction. As Sagor (2003) writes, "When we . . . assist our knowledge workers to set meaningful goals and help them to track their own progress, we create a feedback loop that builds powerful feelings of competence" (p. 40). That is especially beneficial to students who struggle academically, for they can experience success at whatever level is appropriate. For accelerated learners, such assignments present a chance to reach for new, higher levels of competence.

Strategy 6-5: Task Workshop

Purpose: To free up teacher time and to inspire self-responsible student work habits.

Description: Providing a standing set of sequential learning tasks and asking students to work independently at those tasks during class time.

Grace Pilon (1996) crafted a special format for using class time efficiently, which we call a Task Workshop. The workshop is made up of a series of 10 to 30 minitasks, each readily manageable by students working alone or, sometimes, with a partner.

One of us, Melanie, used tasks for spelling and math in her 4th grade class. For the spelling task, she posted a list of words for the week. Students knew that each day they had to do something different. Monday: Write all the words. Tuesday: Choose some words you are unsure of and write their definitions. Wednesday: Write some sentences using as many of the spelling words as you can. Thursday: Have a partner test you and rewrite misspelled words. Friday: Study the words in any way you choose.

For one of the math tasks, Melanie posted a different word problem each day. Students had to (1) solve the problem and (2) write the steps they took to solve it, explaining their reasons. A student might write, for example, "First, I rounded all the numbers because the problem asked me to estimate the answer. Next, I knew I had to subtract because of the clue words *more than*."

Pilon's research group has prepared sets of such tasks for most subject areas and grade levels, usually far more tasks than any teacher will need. (To sample the range of tasks available, see http://workshopway.com.)

We can learn something new anytime we believe we can.

—*Virginia Satir*

In the Pilon approach, students go to the Task Workshop as soon as they enter the room, while the teacher takes care of administrative chores and then meets with a reading group. For the first 30 minutes, students engage the tasks at their own pace, going sequentially from one to the other when they are ready to do so. However, the tasks are arranged in a certain order, so all students are certain to complete the more important tasks. Later in the day, when the teacher wants to work with a different reading group, students are again sent to the Task Workshop.

Students are never expected to finish the whole set of tasks in one day, however. Each does as many as time permits. As a consequence, students always have work to do, and except for those times when they are in whole-class lessons or teacher-led small groups, it is the students' own work. This steadily drives growth in self-responsible work habits and student dignity. It also conveniently creates teacher time for small-group work and individual consultations.

Maria Montessori (1964) similarly made great use of individualized learning materials. Many of her materials are both self-correcting (if a student tries to use materials incorrectly, things just do not fit properly) and diagnostic (when the teacher observes, she can tell when a student is ready for the next level of challenge). For more about available Montessori materials, see http://www.montessori-namta.org.

The general principle is straightforward: When we present a set of learning tasks that students can engage by themselves or, perhaps, with one or two others, and provide time for students to regularly engage those tasks, students are productively engaged whenever we need to be free to work with individuals or subgroups.

Strategy 6-6: Background Music

Purpose: To settle students and start a class in a positive atmosphere.

Description: Playing music that is soothing or refreshing to students as they enter the room or work independently.

Consider experimenting with Background Music at the start of your day or when students engage in independent tasks. Perhaps ask students to help you select and play music. You might also ask students to compare their experiences working with and without music.

For one of us, Melanie, playing music in the classroom brought some unexpected results. She thought that playing music would be a distraction to students but found the opposite to be true. Melanie notes:

My students were quite capable of listening to music and working simultaneously. In fact, it often seemed as if they worked better when music was playing—as if the music blocked out other distractions, including the impulse of some students to be disruptive. As a result, I observed many students working with increased focus and concentration.

At first I worried students might not be interested in music other than what was considered popular. Again, I was proved wrong. Instrumental pieces worked well and nature sounds were also a hit. I was pleasantly surprised by how receptive my students were to various kinds of music.

7 | Using Small Groups Efficiently

A group of five students is asked to discuss a film. The students are slow to get started, quick to slide off the topic. Two students do most of the talking; three pay little attention. And the discussion as a whole is strikingly devoid of active learning. This is an inefficient way to use student groups. Happily, there are far better ways, including those described in the strategies in this chapter. These strategies also help students work with dignity, self-management, and feelings of community. The first two strategies are designated for first attention. Each is marked with an arrow for easy identification.

Strategy 7-1: Sharing Pairs

Purpose: To provide a simple way for students to voice their ideas and hear the ideas of others.

Description: Asking students to pair up and briefly share thoughts on a question or topic.

Students are most active when they talk in pairs. In pairs, each person is either a talker or a listener. No one is left out. This Sharing Pairs strategy not only invites active involvement, it also encourages students to put ideas that may yet be unclear to them into words, thus clarifying their thinking. It also meets students' basic needs for social contact and freedom of expression. Sharing Pairs can be used often and in many situations, including the following:

• *To allow students to put ideas into their own words and thereby extract more understandings from a lecture.* For example, "Pair up and take two minutes to share your thoughts or your understanding about what I've just said."

• *To quickly share opinions.* For example, "Many people disagree about X. Before we discuss this as a group, please pair up and exchange your thoughts or your questions with one person. You'll have just a few moments for this." Note that the Quick Pace approach (Strategy 3-3) used here prompts students to start quickly and stay on topic.

   • *To exchange understandings,* as when students share their Outcome Sentences (Strategy 21-1) on the day's lesson or share what they did on homework assignments.

   • *To express ideas or talk through confusion* in the midst of a discussion.

   • *To share responses to a question,* such as after use of Question, All Write (Strategy 16-3). "Please share your thoughts with a partner, and then we'll get together and see what we all think."

   • *To add energy into the room,* for example, when most students have been working alone for a while or have been mainly listening to others. "Take a few minutes and share your thoughts or your work with one other person."

    Sharing Pairs might be used as needed by the students themselves. Consider how one teacher organizes this:

    You will now have time to work independently on . . . Periodically you may want to take a break from working alone and share with one other. You might simply report your progress on the assignment or share some questions that have come up for you. If you have no questions, perhaps share a comment or two about something you found particularly interesting or challenging.

    When you feel ready to share, simply stand up and scan the room to see if someone else is also ready. When you spot someone who is standing, form a pair. Take as much time as you need for both of you to share. Afterward, return to your independent work and continue until you feel ready to share again.

    What happens if you're ready to share but no one else is? Just resume your work and try again later. Stay alert, and when you see someone standing, stand and join him or her.

    You may wonder how many times or how long you can do this sharing. You'll have to judge that for yourself, but it's important to keep in mind that you have a job to do. You have to finish your independent work. So you'll want to use your time wisely. Now let's give it a try.

▲ TEACHER COMMENT

I tried Sharing Pairs when working with prepositional phrases in my slower English classes. We had been working with prepositions for a few days, and homework was going slowly. Instead of having students take work home, I asked them to choose a partner and do sentences together. Students were pleasantly surprised at the progress they made when they helped each other. This was a very productive class for everyone.

—*Cathy McGarrahan*
Middle School English Teacher

Strategy 7-2: Learning Pairs

Purpose: To review and strengthen learnings and to build interdependence.
Description: Asking students in pairs to help each other learn something new or to drill each other on past learnings.

Pairs can be used for more than a sharing of ideas. For example, students might drill each other on material to be memorized, by using flash cards of math facts or words from spelling lists. Or, using an outline of material or questions from a text, students might explain their understandings of the material to each other and teach each other parts not well understood.

Sometimes a pair of students will have a task they are unable to handle by themselves. In such cases, we can instruct the pair to ask another pair for help. It is advisable to give that instruction at the outset rather than waiting for the problem to arise. "Whenever you are working in groups, always feel free to ask another group for help," we might say. "I want us all to be friendly and helpful to one another." Soon students will know that whenever they get stuck they can always ask others for assistance. They need not come to us. If Class Tutors (Strategy 17-12) were identified beforehand, pairs might also be invited to call upon those assistants.

It is useful to distinguish Learning Pairs from Sharing Pairs. The task of Sharing Pairs is simply to compare and share ideas, as when students share completed homework or brainstorm ideas for a problem. Learning often results from Sharing Pairs activities, but students are not charged with the responsibility to produce it. Producing learning, however, is a responsibility of Learning Pairs, as when we ask students to compare homework answers and, if their partner does not understand a point fully, to explain or otherwise assist the partner the best they can.

Usually we can let students choose their own partners for Learning Pairs, intervening only when a particular pair isn't working well. However, we might provide an appropriate partner for some students, such as those who are difficult to help. See also the related strategy Underexplain and Learning Pairs (Strategy 14-2).

> Let people know what you stand for— and what you won't stand for.
> —*H. Jackson Brown Jr.*

Strategy 7-3: Rotating Pairs

Purpose: To give us an efficient process for re-forming student pairs, so all students can quickly work with new partners.
Description: Asking student pairs to share ideas or to work together briefly, and then to rotate partners, so each student can compare thoughts with yet other students.

Students might have thoughts about a question we've raised. Or perhaps they have written some Outcome Sentences (Strategy 21-1) based on a lesson or discussion. Or they have their homework responses in hand. Or they have listed some things they each know or would like to know about a topic. We might then say, "Please pair up with someone nearby. Take just two or three minutes to share your thoughts. Go."

We might then ask the students to choose an A and a B in each pair, and then say, "A's, in a moment I will ask you to walk around and sit with a different B. The B's will stay seated." You might suggest that the B's hold up their hands until they get a partner, so the A's know who is available. "When you get into your new pairs, again share your thoughts. You can even include thoughts you picked up from your first pair. OK, A's, get ready to find a new partner. Go."

We might rotate again, by next saying something like this: "Now it will be time for the B's to find a new partner. A's, stay seated and raise your hand until you get a new partner, to help others find you. When your new pair is formed, again share your ideas. B's, please move now."

We can continue this rotating procedure with as many pairings as seem appropriate. The general aim is to give students the experience of sharing thoughts with many others easily and efficiently.

Strategy 7-4: Practice Pairs

Purpose: To blend practice with peer instruction.
Description: Giving practice problems to students sitting in pairs, so they can help each other master the material.

When we want students to practice solving challenging problems, it is very valuable to group them in pairs, pose a problem, and ask them to help each other solve it. While students are working, we might put the correct work on the board or show it on an overhead projector. Students can then check to see if they solved the problem correctly.

We recommend keeping the pace moving quickly during this process, so there is little wait time. For example, when students have a question, we try to answer it quickly and choose our next problem so it provides a review of what we just explained. In this way, little by little, students' understandings get shaped. We don't need to do a lot of explaining and we don't risk boring students who already understand.

Reading what people write on desks can teach you a lot.
—*Tiffany, age 13*

Sometimes it is advisable to shift pairs around to improve chances that slower students will learn. To pep up the energy level, we might even ask all pairs who got the correct answer to stand for a moment, raise hands, or exchange high-fives. See also Underexplain and Learning Pairs (Strategy 14-2).

Strategy 7-5: Selecting Group Size

Purpose: To maximize active learning.
Description: Selecting the smallest group size feasible for learning, preferably pairs.

When forming groups, smaller is usually better. Use pairs whenever possible. When an odd number of students are involved, form one trio. Why? Pairs maximize participation. Each person is either talking or being talked to. No one remains unengaged. And pairs help students feel connected with others, thereby decreasing the loneliness some students feel in school. When students sit in groups of three or four, in contrast, it's easy for some students to feel left out, which serves neither dignity nor community. Pairs are also less noisy than larger groupings. Two students can sit close together and hear easily. Pairs are also best for making eye contact, which facilitates honest communication and develops respectful relationships.

Pairs are not always the best group size, however. When a task calls for much creativity or many different perspectives or the solution to a hard problem, two students may not have enough resources. In such cases it is often better to use groups of three or four. Because the goal is to maximize student involvement, however, groups of three are preferable to groups of four. Groups larger than four almost always lead to much passive participation; even if discussion time is shared equally, which is rarely the case, most students must remain quiet most of the time, and active learning drops significantly.

Strategy 7-6: Selecting Members for Groups

Purpose: To form groups efficiently and to grow student self-responsibility.
Description: Asking students to select their own group members and assisting them in doing so only as necessary.

In terms of efficiency and providing students with opportunities for learning self-management, self-selection is the preferred mode for forming groups. We can simply say, "Pair up with someone near you. Go." Sometimes, to encourage students to sit with new partners, we might say, "Pair up this time with someone with whom you have not worked recently."

Self-selection has many advantages. It is efficient. Once students learn how to handle it, they form groups quickly, and we need be involved only occasionally, as when one person remains without a group.

Self-selection also helps students learn how to take initiative in social situations. "We all need to learn how to start relationships," we might say. "Choosing our own group members will give us practice in doing this. Although reaching out to others may feel risky at first, practice will probably make it easier."

Although self-selection is the preferred procedure, it has its problems. Common issues can be handled in a variety of ways, as the following examples illustrate.

Issue 1

Everyone keeps choosing the same friends. Cliques are beginning to form.

Try telling the class that you want students to get to know and work with more than just a few others. At the same time, acknowledge the anxiety that some people feel when they are asked to reach out to someone new. You might say, "Today please practice calling up your courage. Risk asking a new friend if he or she is willing to work with you."

Occasionally go to some groups and tell them not to sit together again for, say, the next two weeks. Explain that you want all students to get to know and appreciate one another. Do not be too quick to say this, however. Be willing to allow time for a secure, cooperative class climate to build. If we invest enough in climate-building strategies, we will find that before too long almost everyone is willing to work with anyone else. If we rush this process and push students to reach out too early, we will find that it slows the development of this community climate.

Nevertheless, it is often advisable to give students a structure for group formation, in part to mix students and in part for the fun that variety provides (Marzano, Pickering, & Pollock, 2001). Some examples of procedures to use for forming groups:

• *Pair up within categories.* Here is one way to explain this approach: "When I say, 'Go!' I want you to walk around and pair up. But pair up within colors. If you are wearing red, I want you to sit with someone who is also wearing red. If you are not wearing red, sit with someone not wearing red. Go!" Other categories you

> Calming down a noisy, rebellious group of adolescents is a lot like defusing a bomb. Careful, premeditated, calm responses are crucial to success.
>
> —*James Nehring*

can use for this procedure include hair that touches the shoulders or doesn't, wearing a belt or not. You might also say, "Hold up two fingers if you were born in an even-numbered month, one finger if you were born in an odd-numbered month, and pair up with someone in the same category."

• *Count-off procedure.* The count-off procedure is an old favorite. If groups of four are needed, for example, divide the number of people present by four. That gives you the count-off number. In a class of 32 students, for example, the count-off number would be 8, and students would count off by 8's. Then the four 1's could be told to sit in a particular place in the room, the four 2's in another place, and so on.

• *Playing card procedure.* Take a deck of cards and, to form student pairs, for example, make as many card pairs as the class needs. Distribute the cards randomly among the class and then ask students to find the person with the card that has the same value and color as their own, so the two red jacks sit together, the two black fours, and so on.

• *Chalkboard procedure.* Try the "chalkboard" (or whiteboard) procedure when students finish individual work at different times and need to form small groups. Sample instructions for forming trios:

> When you finish your individual work and are ready to work in a trio, write your name on the left side of the board. If someone has already written a name, write your name under it. If two names are already there, erase both names, find the two people, sit together, and begin your trio work. The next person ready would, of course, see no names and write his or her name to begin a new trio group.

Issue 2

No one wants to sit with Roberto. Several times you have had to intervene to get him into a group.

You might try speaking to a few of the more good-natured students privately, the ones likely to be gracious. Tell them that you notice that not all students are readily being accepted by others when groups are formed. Ask them to go out of their way, please, to look for students being left out and to choose them, modeling for the class the supportive community spirit you want. Chances are you will find students willing to do such good turns. You may or may not mention Roberto by name, depending on how much you trust the students with such sensitive information.

Alternatively, you might face the issue directly with the whole class and afterward wait, allowing time to do its work:

Our aim is to discipline for activity, for work, for good, not for immobility, not for passivity, not for obedience.
—Maria Montessori

I've noticed over the last few days that some students are not chosen as quickly as others. Because we want to learn to get along with everyone and be kind to everyone, I would like you all to go out of your way to make sure everyone has a partner. We do not want anyone here to feel left out. I know you like to be with your good friends, but we want all students to feel that they are worthwhile members of the class. Please keep on the lookout for classmates needing help or needing partners. Practice giving a hand to those in need. Let's build a caring, cooperative community here.

Issue 3

Some students react to your calls for goodwill by never refusing to help those who ask for it. They feel they must always say yes, even when someone asks for help far too often or in an unkind way.

Look for an appropriate time to talk to the class about the wisdom of not trying to please all the people all the time, about the wisdom of learning how to occasionally say no politely and respectfully, about the wisdom of respecting one's own need to sometimes help others and sometimes not help others. You might say something like this:

So say, "No, thank you," if you think that is best, all things considered. We all have to maintain our own limits, or we will not be very good for others very long. And if someone says, "Sorry, not now," to you, respect their right to live their own lives in their own ways. Do not ask them why and do not fret about it. We all have our own ways. You would probably not want to be quizzed about all the choices you make. Let's respect one another's rights here.

Issue 4

The boys by the window keep gossiping and hardly do any work in their groups.

Do not complain, scold, or threaten, for that is likely to be counterproductive in the long run, making it harder for you to establish an active, cooperative learning classroom. It would probably be wise to do nothing the first time you notice those boys. But soon after the second time, you might simply say, without rancor, "I need you to get right down to work."

If that simple authority statement does not work, the next time you might inform those boys that, because you want everyone to use learning time productively, you want them to choose other students to work with for the next two weeks. Skip the warning step you might be tempted to issue, such as, "I'll change your groups if you do not settle down to work," for students usually interpret that as a threat, which is usually counterproductive.

Issue 5

Slower students sit together and cannot do some of the academic work even when they try.

Although sometimes you might ask such students to pick different partners in the future, you might simply instruct them to ask other groups for help whenever they feel stuck. The quicker students usually feel honored with such requests for help. You may find, too, that the issue tends to vanish as the group climate grows more secure and cooperative. Eventually, then, slower students do not restrict themselves to choosing just their slower peers.

Some teachers prefer forming groups themselves, so they can mix student ability within each group or at least get some capable students in every group. And some teachers prefer to connect grades to group work, to motivate serious work. We find both of these approaches unnecessary. Concerning grades, we find that a combination of Quick Pace (Strategy 3-3), small-size groups, and appropriate task assignments eventually motivates productive group work just as well as rewards and punishments, and it produces far fewer difficulties.

Strategy 7-7: Grouping Students for Instruction

Purpose: To group students for instruction.
Description: Considering the options for grouping students and choosing those that best suit us and our classes.

Consider four ways to group students for instruction:

• *Ability groups.* Many primary school classrooms contain three reading groups, with students grouped according to their current level of reading ability. Older students can similarly be grouped by levels of competency. This procedure helps us tailor instruction to the level of student understanding. One downside: It labels slower learners and, as a result, complicates the problem of developing high expectations in those students.

• *Learning style groups.* An alternative is to group students by learning styles. Students who learn best with close adult supervision, for example, might be in Group A. Students who work well alone could be in Group B. And students who work well in small groups could be in Groups C, D, and E. Students could then be given assignments appropriate to their learning style, with Group A getting the most direct instruction. Or Group A could be the abstract thinkers, B those who learn best by manipulating materials, C the creative students, and so on. Such grouping by learning style can help us address learning needs effectively, and as long as different learning styles are viewed merely as different, not better or worse, it avoids labeling some students as inferior.

• *Mixed groups.* A third option is to mix all abilities in each group. For example, we could form trios or quartets, aiming to include in each group at least one student who learns well or has leadership ability, with the other students representing a mixture of learning abilities. We might then instruct the groups to cooperate and help one another learn. This procedure minimizes the problem of labeling some students as inferior and maximizes the development of cooperative skills. It also efficiently keeps all students productively engaged, for the quicker learners help those having difficulty, and—because we all learn by teaching others—all learn well together.

• *Random groups.* In the first three formats, group membership remains stable. We could also use groups that are more randomly assembled. For example, we might say, "Pair up with someone. Now two pairs form a quartet." In that way, students would work with different students at different times, a process that injects variety into the proceedings and tends to foster feelings that the classroom is one cooperative community. Additional suggestions for forming random groups can be found in Strategy 7-6, Selecting Members for Groups.

In general, if your goal is to bring out the best in students, it is best to avoid ability groups, for they have a significant downside. As for the other three kinds of groups, neither research nor the experience of the many teachers with whom we have worked provides a clear recommendation, which suggests you can use whichever ones most suit your needs and the needs of your particular students.

Strategy 7-8: Support Groups

Purpose: To ensure that all students feel they belong and have access to peer support.

Description: Forming stable student groups, usually groups of four, and giving them the assignment to support one another.

Support Groups are groups of students who sit together and support one another over a period of weeks or months. Such groups provide a secure base for students. Group members might exchange phone numbers to help one another when questions come up about homework or to catch up when they are absent. Members might also read one another's portfolios and suggest improvements.

The acorn is not a deficient fully grown oak, nor is the sapling an incomplete tree. . . . You are in this moment exactly what you are. You do not lack anything, nor is there anything broken or missing. You have all the power and potential you need for further growth.

—*Don Havis*

They might share personal problems and help one another talk through solutions. Each group could also have a class task: taking attendance, passing out books, and so on. Also, one person in each group could be responsible for, say, collecting support group papers for the teacher, handling group lunch money, or marking absences for the group.

Fours are a good size for Support Groups. We generally recommend they be formed by some random method, so students learn to get along with all sorts of people. Before disbanding and forming new groups, we could ask students to exchange Honest I Appreciates (Strategy 20-7), as in this example:

> Write your name on a card and pass it around in your group. When you get a card from one of your support group members, write one or more things you honestly appreciate about the person—something he or she once said, once did, once wore to class; the way you were once helped; anything at all, anything you can say that you honestly appreciate about the person. Afterward, you each can take out your card anytime you feel low. It will give you a nice reminder of some aspects of your goodness.

Although Support Groups can be used for instructional purposes, we recommend treating them less as task groups and more as family groups, a stable home base within a class community.

Strategy 7-9: Group Challenge

Purpose: To inspire students to work creatively and cooperatively at a learning task.
Description: Challenging small groups to find ways to help one another learn something.

Here is how a 3rd grade teacher implements this strategy:

> OK, you're now sitting in fours. Your challenge will be to find a way to help all members of your group learn the multiplication table. I'll give you about 10 minutes in class each day to work on this. During that time you might pair up and drill each other with flashcards. Or you might make a game to give practice to those who need it most. Or you might gather in fours to share memory tricks that worked for you. Or you might say to those in your group who are having trouble, "How can we help you, in or out of school?" You can even call each other after school, if you like.
>
> Create your own best ways to help each other. I'll go around and offer any suggestions I have, and I'll check you all from time to time. But the challenge will be for your group to come up with a system that works for those in the group. The challenge: Help one another master the multiplication table. Go to it!

In addition to using this strategy to help students learn facts, such as the multiplication table or vocabulary words, we can challenge students to help one another learn skills, such as how to handle job interviews skillfully, how to manage their time so they can complete their daily homework, or how to write clear, well-organized paragraphs.

The idea is to enlist the creativity and responsibility of students by posing the challenge in a way that is likely to inspire their full, productive aliveness. After the students work a bit, we might invite groups who are having success to share their methods with the whole class. And we may want to talk a bit about leadership and ways to get started promptly and to budget time efficiently. We may occasionally find it best to shift a student from one group to another. But for the most part, we want to trust the groups. Teachers who issue such learning challenges more than once or twice report that most students come to master the process well enough on their own.

This group challenge strategy works for many topics and for many age groups. It puts the teacher on the side, to serve as a facilitator. And it inspires student self-responsibility, cooperation, appreciation of individual differences, and, of course, active learning. There are few better ways to learn something well than to create a way to teach it to others.

Strategy 7-10: Group Role Sheet

Purpose: To eliminate confusion during group work and to increase productivity.
Description: Before starting group work, familiarizing students with the roles and responsibilities they can expect.

Establishing clear expectations about group work can substantially reduce problems later on. A Group Role Sheet does this nicely. We can use such a sheet to introduce group work or, if groups are not running smoothly, to review expectations. Some steps to consider:

1. *Carefully establish and define group roles.* With older students we might brainstorm a list of common roles and responsibilities. With younger students it is usually best to simply explain the roles expected. Some possibilities:
   • The Reporter: Makes notes to share with the teacher, other groups, or the whole class. May also use notes later for a class newsletter or to create charts or summaries.

- The Cheerleader: Praises, encourages, thanks group members when they participate.
- The Agreement Checker: When there are choices to be made or understandings for the group to reach, makes sure all agree, as by asking, "Does anyone not fully agree? Does anyone disagree?"
- The Taskmaster: Notices when the group stalls or gets off task and helps the group to refocus.
- The Dignity Scout: Watches to make sure all have chances to participate and there are no put-downs or bullying.

2. *Discuss the rules and conduct some role-playing of them.* One way to launch a discussion is by posing questions such as these:

- What qualities are important for the Reporter?
- How might the Cheerleader encourage others in the group? What might he say?
- What are some ways the Agreement Checker might handle a disagreement?
- What might the Taskmaster say if the group has lost focus?
- How might the Dignity Scout protect the feelings of those in the group?

3. *Give each student a copy of the Group Role Sheet and post it.*

4. *Decide how roles will be rotated.* Groups can, for example, remain intact until all students have performed each role. Or we can assign each student a role for a certain period of time or students can select them anew each time a group meets. Having students write Outcome Sentences (Strategy 21-1) about their experience with each role can help them discover more about their social skills and, perhaps, which role or roles suit them.

Children have never been very good at listening to their elders, but they have never failed to imitate them.

—*James Baldwin*

Preventing Discipline Problems from Arising

8

The best way to handle misbehavior, of course, is to prevent it. And the best way to prevent it is to (1) craft lessons and organize students and time so active engagement is attractive and satisfying; (2) establish a class climate that minimizes anxiety, so full participation is easy for students; and (3) establish a class climate that generates cooperation, so students want to get along with others. Earlier chapters dealt with those tasks. This chapter contains more specific strategies for problem prevention. Later chapters, Chapters 33 and 34, contain strategies for dealing with discipline problems that have not been prevented. Of the 11 prevention strategies in this chapter, our field tests suggest that the first four strategies deserve first attention.

Strategy 8-1: Setting Procedures and Expectations

Purpose: To set behavior expectations in a way that inspires students to abide by them.

Description: Establishing very clear classroom expectations without mentioning consequences for misbehavior.

Beginning teachers are often told to engage their students in a discussion at the start of the school year about classroom rules and the consequences students can expect for rule violations. Over the years, however, we have found that most teachers do better when they avoid mentioning rules and instead manage students with a combination of clear procedures and positive expectations (Curwin & Mendler, 1988; Slicker, 1998). How can we do this? Some suggestions:

- *Make class procedures absolutely clear to all.* We set the basis for many class procedures when we use Truth Signs (Strategy 4-1), as discussed earlier. Yet many students will want to know, for example, what to do if they need to use a washroom or if they finish their work while others are still working. Clarity about such routines both helps students feel secure and contributes to a problem-free classroom. We can announce initial classroom procedures or develop them collaboratively with students, however we choose, but it is important that all students understand very specifically how such procedures are to work, as discussed in Strategy 5-1, Student Procedure Mastery.

- *Consider announcing a Code of Conduct.* In some situations, some students will come to school dressed inappropriately or will frequently use inappropriate language, especially among themselves. In such cases, we might choose to announce a Code of Conduct that covers those matters and any others deemed important. We do not usually recommend trying to develop a Code of Conduct collaboratively with students, for such a code flows from adult standards, at least some of which young people are unlikely to fully appreciate. Our recommendation: Avoid mentioning penalties for violations of the code; just state what is unacceptable, aiming to communicate that you expect all students to follow the code.

- *Expect students to comply.* When we expect good behavior, we are much more likely to get it. And when we expect bad behavior, we tend to get that, too. Expectations make a difference. It's smart, then, to expect students to give us their best—that is, to make reasonable and intelligent choices about classroom behavior and to respect the class as a community in which everyone wants to get along. Some teachers find it useful to explicitly communicate such expectations: "I know all of you are intelligent enough to see the advantage of our class procedures and to adjust your behavior accordingly, and I fully expect you to do so." Other teachers find such a statement unnecessary, for, in fact, students can almost always sense when the teacher holds such positive expectations confidently and certainly.

- *Avoid talking about rules and punishments.* With a combination of clear procedures and positive expectations, buttressed by wise responses to students who do misbehave (discussed in later chapters), we find rules are generally unnecessary and usually counterproductive. How are they counterproductive? The saying "Rules are meant to be broken" suggests part of the problem. Some students, especially those with contrary tendencies and those for whom personal freedom is particularly important, will feel an urge to push against even the most reasonable rules. It can be a way of proving themselves or asserting their egos or showing off to peers. More generally, whenever we set rules, and especially when

A good leader inspires people to have confidence in the leader; a great leader inspires people to have confidence in themselves.

—Anonymous

we talk about consequences, also known as punishments, we communicate that we believe all students will not make reasonable and intelligent choices. Why else would we even think rules and punishments are necessary? That is, rules and punishments communicate a negative expectation—which is noteworthy because, again, we tend to get what we expect.

Therefore, we recommend, if you want a smooth-running classroom with minimum misbehavior, rely on clear procedures and positive expectations. Restrict your use of rules and consequences to later, for students who seem to need rules and consequences to learn self-control. Some may need that, but some will not. Is it fair, you may wonder, to have rules for some students and not for others? Absolutely. Just as younger children have specific bedtimes and older ones have no rule about bedtimes, it is advisable to treat all students in ways that are best for them. Being fair is not giving all students the same treatment. It is giving all students what they need for healthy development.

> ▲ **TEACHER COMMENT**
>
> I never liked classroom rules. It got me judging behavior mechanically and arbitrarily and led to lots of arguments with students who felt they had a good reason to break a rule. Yet I didn't want to be wishy-washy or act as if any behavior was OK. So I translated my rules into "guidelines" that I expected students to use intelligently, and it's working much better. Of course, I still have behavior problems, and I deal with them individually, not mechanically or arbitrarily. It's a more dignifying approach for us all.
>
> —*Nikki Colodny, Middle School Science Teacher*

 ## Strategy 8-2: Communicating Confident Authority

Purpose: To motivate students who are likely to act disruptively to exercise self-control.

Description: Exuding a confidence that we can handle whatever discipline problems arise.

Mr. Rainez was sitting at his desk, close to tears. His students had just left, and Mr. Rainez, in his first weeks as a teacher, concluded he could not possibly stop the disruptions that were wrecking his classroom. He felt totally disrespected—not an uncommon experience for new teachers. After all, many classrooms harbor students with pent-up hostilities, students who themselves may have suffered from hostility. When such students see a teacher seemingly vulnerable to attack, perhaps a teacher communicating uncertainty or an ambivalence about authority, or a new teacher apparently unskilled in exerting control, the temptations to create trouble are strong.

How can we avoid this situation? Exude enough confidence in our ability to handle discipline problems so students are not so readily tempted to act out. The problem, however, is that we may not *feel* confidence in our ability to handle all discipline problems. How, then, can we exude confidence? Do it the way plumbers cut their first pipe and surgeons their first bone. Step past lingering hesitations and just do what we have to do to get started. Behave as if we feel confident until we get enough experience to feel it in fact.

If you feel a lack of confidence, try this. Pick a lesson you might typically teach and imagine yourself teaching it to a class that contains potential troublemakers. Then imagine carrying out the following five-step process. Practice it many times, perhaps standing in front of a mirror or with a friend observing and giving you feedback. You want to make this practice as real for you as you can. Repeat the role-playing as many times as you need to, much like an actor practicing again and again to master a role.

Step 1: Being aware of students. Continually scan the room as you teach, so you are constantly aware of what students are doing. You want students to see you as someone who is unquestionably in touch with classroom realities, not someone who is likely to be easily fooled. Therefore, practice looking about alertly as you teach, making direct eye contact with students, perhaps even walking about the classroom. Develop the distinct feeling of being a teacher who remains constantly on top of the classroom situation.

Step 2: Signaling disapproval. Then imagine a student giving a first hint that he may soon create a disturbance. He might talk too long to a neighbor, close his book too loudly, or stand up inappropriately. Imagine yourself responding immediately, without hesitation, yet *without communicating any distress*. Without interrupting the lesson, you might simply catch the student's eye and hold out a hand, palm down, as if to signal "cool down," much as you might signal a friend in a restaurant who may be losing his composure. Direct, clear eye contact indicates confidence. Or you might signal by giving a small shake of your head. Or you might simply walk near the student and teach for a bit from that nearby position, so the student senses your presence. The key is not to hesitate. When in doubt, it's better to be overly sensitive and signal students too quickly. You can later communicate more tolerance and balance, but at the outset you want to model someone who has full confidence in his ability to take charge. Note that you do not want to communicate an impression of someone who is distressed. Confident people are not easily distressed. For now all you want to communicate is an impression of someone who is concerned that the classroom runs smoothly and who sends out mild signals to forestall possible disruptions.

Step 3: Inviting private talk. Assume the signal does not work and the student repeats the behavior. Do not repeat your initial response. Do not signal again.

An endeavor to please elders is at the bottom of high marks and mediocre careers.

—*John Chapman*

Rather, walk toward the student, face him with square shoulders, make direct eye contact, and say quietly, directly, calmly, even pleasantly, "Please see me after class. I'd like to talk privately for a moment." Do not reply if the student asks why or claims innocence. Just make the request and return to the lesson, communicating that you fully assume the student will, as you requested, talk later. Be as unemotional as if you were asking a post office clerk for a roll of stamps. Just make a clear request. This step communicates to the class, including the student in question, that you are indeed ready to face classroom problems. Again, as you play this part, note that you do not want to communicate any distress, just a readiness to be in charge.

Step 4: Making authority statements in private. Now imagine that it is after class, and you and the student are speaking privately. Your task now is to elaborate on your initial signal, not to warn or to scold the student. Squarely face the student and look directly in his eyes, sending a message of confidence, not submissiveness. "Pat," you might say, "I do not want even minor distractions or disruptions in our lessons. I'm not blaming you for anything you did. I just want to make it clear that I care very much that we become a cooperative class, doing our best to help one another to learn well, and I need you to do your share. Thank you. Please go now and join the rest of the students." The content of your little speech is unimportant. What is important is that it does not blame or otherwise incite guilt or anger in the student and that it *does* communicate an unhesitant willingness to use your authority for the benefit of the class. (For more on the Authority Statement, see the next strategy.)

Step 5: Making authority statements in public. Sometimes the first four steps will still not settle the student down. Assume the student again acts inappropriately. You now want to be prepared to square off and face him promptly and, this time, publicly. More specifically, imagine that the very next time he acts inappropriately you walk over to him, face him directly, and with a firm but still undistressed voice tell him exactly what behavior you want, such as, "I need you to stop talking to neighbors. It's time to control that. Thank you." Do not focus on what is wrong, but focus on what behavior you want to see. If the student complains or talks back, do not argue. Simply repeat your statement verbatim: "I need you to stop talking to neighbors. It's time to control that." (See Strategy 33-1, Broken Record, for more on such repeated statements.) While practicing this step, you may want to try several levels of intensity, aiming to be ready to use whatever level you need at any particular time, taking care, again, not to communicate an impression of someone who is distressed. It is someone who is confidently in charge that you want to model.

When I am working in class and the teacher is looking over my shoulder, I get nervous.

—*Tina, age 17*

Practice this five-step process until you feel fully confident in your authority. Know that the more confidence this practice generates inside you, the less often you will need to use it—or any other discipline strategy. Students have an uncanny knack for identifying teachers who are willing to assert their authority. Most of them will control themselves quite well when faced with such teachers (Brophy, 1998).

 ## Strategy 8-3: Authority Statement

Purpose: To use authority respectfully.
Description: Making a simple, direct statement of our authority as teachers.

There is no doubt about it—teachers have both the authority and the responsibility to keep student behavior within bounds. And that sometimes requires that we disapprove of what students are doing. The trick is to deliver such disapproval in ways respectful of human dignity—both our students' and our own. We want to employ our responsibilities easily, comfortably, firmly, never harshly. Consider the following examples:

- When you say, "We do not do that here," you do not want the student to feel chastised, just informed. You do not want to stir up resentment, just communicate clearly. You do not want the student to think you're really saying "You should have known better than that." It is preferable that the student hears your statement as "You just did not know this, so I'm giving you the information."

- When you say, "That is just too much for me," you do not want to sound apologetic or weak. And you do not want the student to think you're saying "You should not want to act the way you are acting." You simply intend to say that you have limits. You, too, are a human being. Too much talk or noise or whatever is going on is, in fact, too much for you right now. Furthermore, you want the student to hear in your tone, "I know you are willing to make a reasonable adjustment to meet my needs, for that is what people do when they live together as a cooperative community."

- When you say, "No, you may not leave now," you do not want the student to hear "You should know better than to ask" or "What a silly question" or "Do not bother me with such questions." You do not want the student to feel stupid or slighted or put down. You want the student to hear your statement simply as a fact; the responsible adult's position is no, you may not leave now.

- When you say to a student who is arguing with you angrily, "I'll be happy to speak about this, but not now; let's do it when we can speak calmly," you do not want to further infuriate the student. You want to acknowledge that disagreements arise and it's good to talk them over, but it's important to do so in a frame of mind that makes talking useful. You want the student to conclude, "I guess it's no use trying to argue with the teacher now. I might as well wait until I simmer down." Incidentally, in this situation, you might well need to repeat your statement a few times (as in Strategy 33-1, Broken Record), before angry students can hear the intended message.

- When you put a finger to your lips to signal someone to shush, you do not want the student to feel guilty or bad or irresponsible. You want the student simply to think, "Oops, I should stop talking. The teacher is reminding me of what I simply forgot."

- When you say, "Sit down this very minute and turn to page 25. Please take control of those impulses," you do not want the student to feel that you are being hostile and punitive or that the student is a defective or uncontrollable person. You want the student simply to notice that you are taking charge at a time when self-control has temporarily failed, that you are doing what is necessary to protect the welfare of all. You want the student to feel that you are on the side of safety and learning, not against her or anyone else.

- When you say, "Please sit over there for now," you do not want the student to think you are against him. You want him to know that you object to the behavior, not the person. You want him to sense that you make your request simply to end a class distraction.

- When you say, "Will you do that for me?" you want to communicate a warm confidence that the student, at heart, will want to go along with you. You do not want to leave the impression that you are unwilling to insist if need be. You rather want to leave the impression that you care that students choose to behave well. (By the way, when students answer such a question affirmatively, they have, in effect, given their word, which adds to their motivation to follow through.)

The Authority Statement is similar to what Ginott (1972) calls a "sane authority message." Ginott says that it would be insane for a teacher to belittle a student who has lost self-control or to suggest that a student should not be feeling what he or she is in fact feeling. Here are examples of "insane" messages and their "sane" counterparts:

Insane: Stop talking. You have no consideration for those who are working.
Sane: This is a quiet time. We need it to be absolutely quiet.

> You have to be either critically loving or a loving critic, but you should never be indifferent.
>
> —*John Gardner*

Insane: You have no right to be angry. You know what to do. You must wait
              your turn.

Sane: I know you are upset. We can all get upset sometimes. But now I
              really need you to wait your turn.

Three Guidelines for Authority Statements

1. *No hostility.* In general, disapproving statements should be emotionally neutral, like a red traffic light. A red light does not communicate criticism or malice. It does not blame or sting. It just gives a signal to stop. We recommend that Authority Statements be similarly straight and simple, similarly unemotional, noncritical. They are to stir up no antagonism. Sometimes we can even exert our authority with a playful touch, as in these examples:

   ○ When a student is fussing about in a way that is too distracting, you might simply pause for a split second and glance her way, with a wink or a smile.

   ○ Try a joke: "Let me finish this, please. I've been waiting all week end to give this speech."

   ○ Simply keep talking and walk near the student and touch him warmly on the shoulder—not a sting, but a touch of care.

2. *No hesitancy.* It is best to make Authority Statements promptly and cleanly, not hesitantly or apologetically. You want students to see you as strong enough to speak forthrightly, not needing to apologize for your responsibilities. And you want students to see themselves as strong, too. Facing students directly and looking in their eyes conveys both a lack of submissiveness on your part and a respect for their ability to handle whatever you have to say. In general, you want each student sensing, "He clearly sees me as strong and smart enough to take straight talk."

3. *No excessive intervention.* Some teachers voice disapproval more often than is necessary. A girl may be walking aimlessly about the classroom and that quickly triggers a disapproval reaction in those teachers. But saying nothing might have been the better choice. The girl might soon get back to work. Or she might not be disturbing others more than they can easily handle. Even if it is not easy for other students, it might be better to remain quiet. The other students might then practice calling up extra concentration power, or some of their conflict-resolution skills. There is some advantage to giving students the opportunity to stretch in these ways. When we too quickly solve the problems of healthy community living in the classroom, it sends a signal that we do not trust students to handle such events on their own. This assumption sets up dependency expectations. Students might then expect us to handle all group behavior problems,

The greatest opportunity is where you are. Do not despise your own place and hour. Every place is under the stars, every place is the center of the world.
—*John Burroughs*

probably slowing the development of self-responsibility. For all these reasons, it is advisable to avoid intervening unnecessarily.

More Tips on Making Authority Statements

• *Use body language.* We can use body language to make a simple Authority Statement. Here is an example suggested by Fredric Jones (adapted from Charles, 1996, p. 84):

> Sam and Jim are talking while the teacher explains fractions to the class. The teacher makes eye contact, pauses momentarily, and then continues with the explanation.
>
> If Sam and Jim continue to talk, the teacher pauses again, makes eye contact, and shakes his or her head slightly but emphatically, perhaps giving a fleeting palm-out signal.
>
> If Sam and Jim continue talking, the teacher calmly walks over and stands near Sam and Jim while explaining, and perhaps increases the invitation for productive engagement by saying, "Now all work this problem on your scrap paper."
>
> If Sam and Jim still keep talking to each other, the teacher makes eye contact with each and calmly says, "Jim, Sam, I need you to stop talking right now" or "Speak with me before lunch."

• *Provide a brief explanation.* Many teachers find it wise to include a brief explanation with a request for different behavior. For instance, "Please do not touch that material now, Dennis. I'll need it later for my demonstration" or "I want no teasing in this room. I'm the kind of teacher who gets very upset when others are being put down or made fun of." A brief explanation highlights the reasonableness of Authority Statements. It makes them sound less arbitrary, therefore easier to accept. Avoid long explanations, however. Long explanations suggest we do not trust students to understand or do not expect them to accept our authority.

• *Personalize explanations.* Explanations are most effective when they are personal. Compare these two comments:

> Teacher A: Everyone must have work in by Wednesday at 3:00 p.m. I cannot get my evaluations in on time if any work comes in after that.
>
> Teacher B: Everyone must have work in by Wednesday at 3:00 p.m. It is difficult for me to handle the papers and budget my time if work comes in after that.

Teacher B's authority is likely to be easier to accept. Students are more likely to believe that it is "difficult" to handle the paperwork than to believe that it "cannot" be done. Here is another example in which Teacher B's words are likely to be more effective, more likely to lead students to conclude that the teacher is on their side, not unsympathetic and certainly not against them:

Teacher A: No running in the halls. People who run in halls get hurt.
Teacher B: No running in the halls. I do not want to see you or anyone else get hurt.

> Children need love,
> especially when they
> do not deserve it.
>
> *—Harold Hulbert*

• *Activate your care for students before speaking.* You may have noticed that some very strict teachers are fully respected by students, and some very lenient teachers are very respected by students. On the other hand, some teachers who are very strict are not respected at all, and might even be highly resented and resisted. Similarly, some teachers who are very lenient are not respected, and might even be teased by students. It's relatively unimportant whether a teacher runs a tight ship or leads a loose community. What is important is that students perceive the teacher as someone who sincerely cares for their welfare and who will act to serve that welfare. And that perception rests largely on whether or not they perceive the teacher as behaving reasonably, respectfully, and fairly.

Explanations can clear up potential misunderstandings about this. If students see our limits as too restrictive for them, for example, an explanation can make it clear that, say, we really need the limits so we can teach effectively, or they need the limits even though they may not currently appreciate it. Similarly, if students feel a need for more security or more guidance, an explanation can communicate, for example, that we do not feel comfortable being more controlling than we are now, or that they may feel insecure but they need to eventually learn to manage their own lives and this freedom can help them do it. The message in both cases is simple: I am doing the best I can to care for you.

Motives, then, are critical. Authority tends to be accepted, indeed appreciated, when students know the intention is to do what is best for them, that we are, in effect, on their side. A caution, however: It is not enough to say, "This hurts me more than you." Words are not enough. If it isn't honestly hurting, students will sense that fact and will learn not to trust what we say. Similarly, it is not enough to say, "I'm doing this for your own good." Unless we can feel that, we are not entitled to say it. Truth, after all, also matters. (Also see Strategy 3-5, Personal Inspiring Power.)

 ## Strategy 8-4: Procedures That Energize

Purpose: To prevent student restlessness.
Description: Using classroom procedures that help keep minds and bodies active.

When restlessness grows among students, misbehavior may not be far behind. One of the easiest ways to prevent restlessness is to give students plenty of chances to use their energy healthfully and productively. The prime way to do this, of course, is to conduct active-learning lessons, lessons in which all students can stay comfortably, actively engaged. But we can also intersperse additional energizing activities into the classroom. Some examples:

- Instead of passing out papers, place three piles around the room and ask students to stand up and get their own paper, perhaps twisting and stretching as they walk.
- When using Sharing Pairs (Strategy 7-1), invite the pairs to stand while they talk, even to move about, as long as they do not bother anyone.
- When asking Voting Questions (Strategy 9-3), such as "How many of you agree?" or "How many are ready to move on?" or "How many had a good weekend?" sometimes ask students to vote by standing. Or ask students who have a question to stand. Or ask students who do *not* have a question to stand.
- During quiet reading, encourage students to stand or even to stroll about while they read. Interestingly, some of our field teachers report students read better and remember more when they do this.
- Tell the class, "Whenever you feel the need to stretch your muscles, please stand for a moment at the back of the room." One teacher designates a special area in the room for this activity, calling it the "stretch-and-bend area." And perhaps ask three or four students to role-play moving to that area without bothering anyone, and then stretching while you continue teaching.
- After someone takes a risk, or after group presentations, or after a class activity is completed, ask students to give themselves a round of applause or a quiet standing wave for the good work done so far.

Strategy 8-5: Clock Focus

Purpose: To settle restless energy and develop students' power of concentration.
Description: Having students stand and watch the second hand of a clock circle one, two, or three times, as they choose, then sit to resume work.

Sometimes an elementary school class will get restless or too edgy, especially during long stretches of individual work. At such times, we might announce, "Clock Focus, please." This strategy from Pilon (1996) helps students learn to manage their energies and focus their attention while also settling the class. In addition, it helps students develop concentration power. Students probably like it for another reason—it gives them a chance to stand and stretch and take a break from brain work.

Here is a teacher explaining this procedure on the first day of school:

When I say, "Clock Focus," here is what you do. You all stand, relax, and then watch the second hand on the wall clock. Watch closely as the second hand moves around the circle. Practice your focus power. You can watch for one full circle, or two or three full circles, depending on how much focus power you want to practice. This will develop your ability to concentrate. It's also useful for settling yourself. Incidentally, you can do this any time, whenever you want to settle your energies, in school or at home.

Let's try it all together now. Please stand. Now do a Clock Focus for at least one full circle, and then, whenever you are ready, sit and resume your individual work. We will practice this again later, but let's do it now and afterward talk about how it went.

Strategy 8-6: Special Energizing Activities

Purpose: To maintain student vitality.

Description: Inserting energizing activities into the classroom when a slump or restlessness emerges.

In many Asian elementary schools, students have 10- or 15-minute breaks for vigorous play every 45 minutes or so, compared to the usual once-a-day recess in the United States. The difference may help explain why Asian students maintain better focus in school than do American students. We can approximate some of the benefits by inserting energizing activities into our lessons. Such activities are especially valuable when we notice the classroom energy slumping or student restlessness rising. Some possibilities:

• *Stretch, wiggle, relax.* "Stand up now and stretch your body like this . . . Now wiggle part of your body, like this . . . Now do a few stretch-wiggle-relaxes on your own, easily or vigorously, whichever feels best. Then sit down and relax while I get ready for the next activity. Go!"

• *Palms over eyes.* Have students rub their palms together until warm, then cross their arms and cover their eyes. While palms are on eyes, ask students to take two deep breaths and then to relax and feel good all over. Reports Mike Bentley, an education professor, "It's my favorite class energizer."

• *Music.* Ask students to stand and sway to recorded music being played. Perhaps ask students to bring in their favorite music for this. You could even have a list of music masters of the day—the students whose job is to play a bit of music any time you call for it. For extra energy, have students dance, jump, or skip rope to the music.

- *The DESCA stretch.* Ask students to stand up and lift their hands over their head and to stretch upward as far as they can. "You're reaching for the highest DESCA level you can achieve in our classroom. Now reach even higher . . . Stretch . . . That's it. That's where we want the DESCA level in our classroom to be. Now everybody tell one another, 'We can do it!'"

- *30-second scramble.* When you announce the 30-second scramble, all students rise and walk around the room quietly for 30 seconds, without talking, and then take their seats. One student—the helper of the day or a volunteer with a watch—might signal when time is up. Resume teaching promptly at the end of 30 seconds, even if some students have not yet reseated themselves. To vary this activity, on some days call for a special kind of walking: tiptoe walking, twisting walking, shoulder-waves walking, backward walking, hands-on-head walking, hands-high-behind-the-back walking. Or ask students to walk like they are walking in water, or to walk taking only baby steps, or to walk in a silly way, or to walk on their tippy-tiptoes.

- *Simon Says.* "Simon says, please stand up now. Simon says, put your hand on your shoulders like this . . . From now on, don't do it if I don't say, 'Simon says.' I'll try to trick you. Keep track of how many times I do trick you. If you make a wrong move, it's OK. Keep going and try to do better next time. At the end we'll see how many got fooled only once or twice or not at all!"

- *Plastic-bag juggling.* This activity, from our colleague Neil Rothman, requires preparation. Ask each student to bring in three or more plastic grocery bags and to keep them in their desks or backpacks. Or you can bring in enough bags for the class. Then demonstrate these steps for students to follow: (1) Hold two bags in one hand and one in the other. Hold them down at your sides. With an underhand motion, toss up one bag from the two-bag hand, to about head height. Allow it to come down, and catch it with the other hand, so that hand now has two bags. (2) Practice this until you can do it with either hand. (3) Then start tossing two bags. Start by first throwing one bag up from the two-bag hand and then throwing the single bag from the other hand before catching the first. From there it's a small step—at least for some people!—to smoothly juggling the three bags and to experimenting with variations on the theme.

- *Rock, Paper, Scissors.* Instruct students to stand, pair up with someone they haven't worked with recently, count 1-2-3, and then extend their hand out with a fist for rock, a flat hand for paper, or two fingers making a cutting motion for scissors. Scissors cut paper. Paper covers rock. Rock breaks scissors. The goal is to see who has the most wins when the timer you set chimes, which is the signal for all to sit and be ready for lessons to resume.

The Sufis advise us to speak only after our words have managed to pass through three gates. At the first gate, we ask ourselves, "Are these words true?" If so, we let them pass on; if not, back they go. At the second gate we ask, "Are they necessary?" At the last gate, we ask, "Are they kind?"

—*Eknath Easwaran*

• *Student-created energizers.* Ask groups of students to create an energizer for the class and have it ready for the next time the class needs an injection of energy. One person from each group might lead the activity. Tell students you want the energizers to be safe for all. If you feel it's wise, ask groups to check with you before they finalize an activity. Then, next time you want an energizer, call on a group to lead it. As a variation, have each group write its activity and give the written description to you. You then choose which to use. Afterward, ask the group to stand and receive a standing round of applause.

Strategy 8-7: Think Time Sheet

Purpose: To help students take responsibility for classroom management.
Description: Asking students to think about how a behavior problem might best be handled.

Imagine this: Early in the school year, when a problem arises (students are interrupting, the room is left messy, two students fight) the teacher gives every student in the class a sheet of paper with the heading "Think Time." It lists four questions:

1. What would you say is the problem?
2. How might the problem be avoided in the future?
3. What can you do to help?
4. What can I do to help?

"It seems to me we have a problem here," the teacher says. "Let's all look at the problem. Please use this sheet to write some notes about your thinking." Afterward, the teacher might ask students to pair up and share their thoughts. A brief discussion might follow that.

The aim here is not for the class to agree on a solution to the problem, although that sometimes happens. This strategy has two other aims: (1) to emphasize that the teacher and the students are all responsible for the class welfare, and it will serve everyone well to share ideas about what to do; and (2) to introduce the Think Time Sheet to the class so, later, the teacher can use it with individual misbehaving students.

Let's say Tanya keeps acting out and nothing much has helped. The next time Tanya acts out, the teacher might say, "Please take a Think Time Sheet from the pile on the shelf, sit by yourself, and fill it out. You can write or draw anything you wish on the back first, if you want, perhaps to vent your feelings. But be sure to think and make notes about the four questions, because I'd like you and me to find a better way for us to work together." A follow-up discussion with Tanya might lead to a Self-Management Contract (Strategy 34-2). If the student is too young to write answers, we can ask the student to draw something for each question and, later, to talk to us about the drawings.

This strategy (adapted from Nelson and Carr, 1999) gives teachers a constructive alternative to what is often called "time out." In effect, "time out" is turned into "think time." If a school has a detention or time-out room, the teacher in charge might even ask every student to complete a Think Time Sheet for each visit, which might lead to useful group discussions in the room.

Strategy 8-8: Self-Discipline Lesson

Purpose: To help students master the art of self-control.

Description: Teaching a lesson about making wise choices in stressful situations, how important it is to do so, and how we can help one another do it.

Some students profit from a lesson that helps them understand they can always make a choice not to disturb the class, although that choice is sometimes very hard to make (Sagor, 2003). Such a lesson might start with an example, something like this:

> Josh asked his buddy what page the work was on. Because Josh sometimes talked to his buddy unnecessarily and because that kind of talk usually bothered the teacher, she got angry and snapped at Josh. "I told you to be quiet," she called out. "I was only trying to find the right page," Josh started to say, but the teacher was out of patience and interrupted him. "I don't care what you were saying. Just keep quiet." Josh, however, persisted. "I wanted to do the work but I didn't know the page." "Go to the principal's office," ordered the teacher.

After presenting the example, you might ask such questions as "Can you imagine this situation? Was it necessary for Josh to get into trouble? At what points could he have chosen to act in a way that would have kept him out of trouble? What could he have done? Can you imagine how hard it might have been for Josh to actually do that?"

The point to emphasize is that although sometimes emotions catch us up, we can always notice we are getting emotional and pause and do nothing that will make matters worse. And although it can be a real challenge to do that, it is a valuable ability for everyone to master, an ability that most successful people, including athletes, *must* master to be successful. Perhaps give an example from your own life. You might then do one of the following:

There's nothing wrong with teenagers that reasoning with them won't aggravate.

—*Anonymous*

• Ask students for examples of times they were punished for misbehavior. Ask them if, at the time of the incident, it would have been difficult for them to have made a better choice than the one they made. Students could also discuss such questions in small groups, which might be appropriate for those who most need to learn this lesson.

• Mention that there is no one way to control one's impulses to act out. Perhaps ask the class for examples of how they personally control, say, impulses to call out answers in class, or to yell at someone who has angered them, or to leave clutter at their desks. You might then make a list of these self-control methods and suggest that other students try some of them, "so we all find our own ways of controlling unproductive impulses."

• Suggest that students with behavior problems practice praising themselves when they do well. A student trying to control impulses to call out answers, for example, might practice holding back and, for each success, say to herself, "See, I can wait. Good for me!"

• Invite students to remind one another to cool down when they get too emotional and risk making poor choices. Good friends come to one another's aid that way.

• Finally, for more difficult cases, consider the following three-step process. (1) Tell a student you will give him a daily rating on how well he behaved himself and you will reward all high-rated days with a token prize, which you then do. This step often sensitizes students to their behavior patterns and encourages self-control. (2) Tell the student that now you want him to guess at the daily rating he earned before you tell him. This step tends to make students even more aware of their own behavior. (3) Gradually discontinue the prize and, finally, discontinue the daily rating. According to Drabman, Spitalnik, and O'Leary (1973), this three-stage procedure teaches students to regulate their own behavior in a way that has lasting results. For a related strategy, see Rights, Responsibilities, Rewards (Strategy 26-4).

Strategy 8-9: Whole-Class Problem Solving

Purpose: To get maximum input for solutions to a class problem and maximum commitment to chosen actions.

Description: Asking students to brainstorm a list of possible solutions to a class problem and then seeking agreement on what options are best for all concerned.

Consider some typical whole-class issues: too many students arriving late to class; cliques that dampen class spirit; bickering that often escalates to fighting; students

I love to teach as a painter loves to paint, as a musician loves to play, as a strong man rejoices to run a race. Teaching is an art—an art so great and so difficult to master that a man or woman can spend a long life at it without realizing much more than his limitations and mistakes and his distance from the ideal.

—William Phelps

who are falling behind. Here is an example of how a teacher might begin a Whole-Class Problem-Solving episode:

> Class, before we get started today I'd like to talk about the problem we've been having with class supplies. As I once mentioned, I do not like the waste that I often see. I wonder if we could brainstorm possible ways we could do better. Can I get two volunteers to write ideas on the board? OK, you two, take turns writing all the ideas we come up with. Later we'll go through the list. I'll see which ones I can live with, and we'll see which ones all of you can live with. Our goal will be to create something that works for all of us. But now let's be imaginative and see how many possible ideas, oddball or serious, we can list that might help us avoid wasting class supplies.

Here is another example, one which includes role-play of some of the best suggestions. The teacher begins:

> I have heard reports of bullying after school. That, of course, is something we cannot tolerate. Let's first list some things on the board that an observer might do when he or she sees someone being bullied, either by a group or by one person.

After the brainstorming session, the teacher continues:

> Now let's role-play some of the options on our list that we agree have possibilities, to get the feel of them. Who would be willing to play one of the bullies? Let's have two more volunteer bullies, so we have a group. Fine, now who would play a victim for us? Who will play an observer? OK, you three bullies, do something to bully our volunteer victim, and, after a while, you, Miss Observer, try making the first response we want to look at. We can role-play this a few times if we like . . .

The role-play can be repeated for several observer responses, if appropriate. The teacher then continues:

> Now let's consider what the victim of bullying might do in the situation. First we'll brainstorm a list of possibilities. Then we'll role play a few, to see which we would recommend. After that we'll create a list of what one or all the bullies might do, either when one of them first feels an urge to bully someone, or once they all get into it and want to stop, or after they finish bullying someone. We'll make a list first and then role-play some of the actions, so we can get the feel of them.

This Whole-Class Problem Solving strategy serves many purposes. It tends to uncover more solutions than a teacher alone can dream up. It elicits student cooperation in the solution of the problem. It strengthens the feeling of the class as a community. It models an intelligent way to solve social problems. And when it includes role-playing, as in the bullying example, it starts a process of helping students internalize healthy behaviors. You might even want to extend the process by organizing all students into small role-playing groups, so all students practice healthy behaviors.

Strategy 8-10: Parent Aides

Purpose: To strengthen the adult presence in a classroom and increase school-parent cooperation.

Description: Inviting parents and other adults to visit often and, perhaps, to serve as teacher aides.

Many students who would readily misbehave with one adult in the room rarely do so when two adults are present. Perhaps it is the extra pair of eyes, or the lack of a single focus for their resentments against authority figures, or the additional mature presence in the room. Whatever the reason, having other adults in a room often reduces behavior problems significantly.

But there are other reasons to welcome parents, grandparents, or any adult visitor. Such visits are good publicity for good education; much public criticism of schooling might vanish if more adults saw how hard it is for teachers to do their jobs. Also, when parents visit and share in their children's daily experiences, they are often in a better position to help their children with homework. Perhaps most important, parents can see a model of an adult interacting respectfully and productively with children, a model that might well inform some parents.

Besides, adults can be valuable aides. One teacher regularly sends a letter home to parents inviting them to visit any time without making prior arrangements. She also sends an announcement to nearby service clubs soliciting volunteer aides. Whenever an adult shows up, a student monitor is instructed to give the visitor a sheet of Visitor Guidelines. The sheet is simply a note of welcome and a suggested list of ways to help (for example, just sit and enjoy watching the children, offer to assist individual students, join in at cleanup time, offer to run errands), and suggested things to avoid (for example, giving special attention to your own child, assisting students who would do better to solve problems on their own).

Strategy 8-11: Discipline Plan

Purpose: To be able to teach with a confidence that we can handle whatever discipline problems arise.

Description: Taking the time to make a plan for handling the situations we are likely to face.

It is likely that, despite all our best efforts, some students will still upset us occasionally. We may be in a situation in which *groups* of students will upset us. It is wise to be prepared to handle such events. The best way to do that is to think through in advance what we want to do, what actions will best serve our long-term interests, so we will be most likely to avoid impulsive actions that are counterproductive. In short, make a plan.

Steps for Creating a Discipline Plan

Step 1: Start a personal collection of discipline strategies. Aim to gather a toolkit of discipline strategies that feel right to you and are likely to be consistent with the inspiring approach of this book. That is, aim to gather strategies that are likely to bring out the *best* in students, in particular their cooperativeness and self-control, not the *worst*, in particular their resentments and hostility. You might start by reviewing the strategies in this chapter. They illustrate the kind of discipline strategies that draw students to your side. But consider looking elsewhere, too, including into Part IX of this book.

Step 2: Check to make sure you're looking at the big picture. It's easy to lose sight of the big picture. It can be tempting to use discipline strategies that are familiar but that do not elicit students' best traits. Some familiar strategies even bring out the very worst from students (Charles, 1996; Kohn, 1993; Wolfgang, 1995). Let's say Bobby's talking is bothering you. You could threaten Bobby with a punishment ("One more time, young man, and I will . . ."). Or you could embarrass him with a nasty reprimand ("Is your head so dense I must tell you again?"). Such acts might get Bobby to stop talking. But too often they will also prompt him to resent you, even to want to retaliate at the first opportunity he can safely do so. Or they could prompt him to withdraw from your lessons, at least until the sting of your comment subsides. And if Bobby is acting out to compensate for doubts about his basic worth, which is not uncommon, those doubts will likely be intensified, which is not something that will serve either him or you. Besides, it's not particularly pleasant to spend your days threatening and humiliating students. Some discipline strategies bring out the worst in students and in us, too.

Alternatively, you could respond more calmly to Bobby's disturbances, perhaps by saying nothing and simply writing Bobby's name on the board, as a reminder to him and others that you noticed his disturbance and that a punishment is now in order. But even that action has significant side effects, especially because it suggests that Bobby's problem was getting caught and possibly being punished, not failing to curb his disturbing impulses. That suggestion, repeated often enough, devalues the kind of self-responsible behavior we aim to produce (Brophy, 1996).

Fortunately, strategies exist that allow you to handle such problems without these unfortunate side effects (Borg & Ascione, 1982; Emmer & Evertson, 1981).

Unless one has taught . . . it is hard to imagine the extent of the demands made on a teacher's attention.

—*Charles E. Silberman*

For example, without interrupting the lesson, you might catch Bobby's eye and put your finger on your lips, as a signal. Or use a shake of your head as a signal. Or you might walk over to Bobby and stand near him while the lesson continues. You might even lean on his desk until he stops talking. Or, using Intelligence Call-up (Strategy 4-4), you might lean over and quietly say, "Try to control that side talk, Bobby. You're smart enough to do that." Or you might, using an Authority Statement (Strategy 8-3), say without any negative tone whatsoever, "I need you to be quiet now, Bobby." Another strategy, Redirecting Student Energy (Strategy 33-11), would have you redirect Bobby's attention: "Bobby, would you read the next problem aloud to the class?" On another tack altogether, you might look within yourself and conclude that Bobby's talking is not a classroom problem—he and those around him are still fully engaged in the lesson—but is your personal problem, perhaps an unreasonable need on your part for complete control.

Note that effective classroom managers give students what they individually need in order to learn self-management; some will need encouragement, some a gentle reminder, some a not-so-gentle demand, some an appropriate punishment. Ineffective managers tend to treat all students the same (Marzano, 2003).

Teachers must, of course, control class disturbances, and each must do it in ways that feel right, but some ways of doing so are far better than others. In line with this book's inspiring approach, the goal is to use strategies that will inspire students to develop their ability to live with full dignity and intelligent self-management. That is the big picture to keep in mind as you create and review your personal toolkit of discipline strategies.

Step 3: Use rewards and punishments wisely. Although we don't recommend that anyone rely on rewards and punishments, you certainly can use them—as long as you don't contradict the big picture. In the situation above with Bobby, for example, you might, in fact, punish him. But if you did so you would want Bobby to know that you are punishing him not for you—because you are angry or because you need quiet—but because of him, because you care about him and his future, because you trust he can grow toward more self-responsible maturity and you believe a punishment is your best current choice for promoting such growth, and perhaps because it is the only action that is likely to grab and hold his attention.

Approaching this issue more conceptually, one might say it is inadvisable to rely on extrinsic motivations. The purpose is to ignite and develop students' healthful intrinsic motives. This doesn't negate our ability to use extrinsic motivators, such as rewards and punishments. But it does require we use them only as tools for larger purposes. It also requires we reject any punishment that is cruel

> It is a mystery why adults expect perfection from children. Few grownups can get through a whole day without making a mistake.
>
> —*Marcelene Cox*

and any reward that is unfair. The research is clear about this. Only mild punishments are effective (Bear, 1998). And the only rewards that are effective are those that do not engender corrosive envy in other students (Kohn, 1993). In this regard, you might consider Praise and Rewards for All (Strategy 20-4).

Step 4: Avoid a radical change. If you are an experienced teacher and plan to improve your discipline style, it might be better to change gradually and not immediately discard all your current discipline procedures. You do not want students who are ready to test your authority to get out of hand. It is far easier to improve yourself in an orderly classroom than a chaotic classroom. Indeed, you may want to start by changing your strategies of instruction so you get more students actively, constructively involved in lessons, thereby reducing student frustrations and increasing student good will. Doing so will make it a lot easier to adjust your approach to discipline.

Step 5: Make a preliminary plan of action. When it comes to handling discipline, it's unwise to wing it. You do not want to vacillate and backtrack. Doing so complicates matters substantially. Perhaps start your plan by listing the kinds of problems you might face. Then group those problems, and for each category, list strategies you would be willing to try. Or write out your general approach and what will be your first course of action, your second, and so on. If you take the time to be specific and clear, you will be able to act with maximum confidence, and, significantly, confidence is one of your best tools (Emmer, Evertson, & Worsham, 2002). You can always revise your plan. In fact, it would be foolish not to. One cannot go too far toward mastering the art of teaching without trying and adjusting, living and learning.

Step 6: Stand tall and be flexible. Stay in charge. Students do not want a wishy-washy teacher. But they will resist a teacher who they sense is uncaring. Students want a teacher who is with them, not unconcerned, and certainly not against them (Brophy, 1996). So stand tall and be caring. And be willing to revise your plan as you live and learn. Be flexible and seek to handle problems creatively, not mechanically. Throughout, never lose sight of human dignity—yours or your students'. Said differently, aim to use your best abilities to bring out the best abilities of each of your students. You can then move ahead with integrity, certain you will find your own best way to run an inspiring classroom.

Final Thoughts

- Please do not push yourself too hard or too fast if this inspiration approach is new for you. Furthermore, create your own path forward. Stay true to yourself. We all learn in our own ways, by our own time clocks.

Teaching is painful, continual, and difficult work to be done by kindness, by watching, and by praise, but above all by example.

—*John Ruskin*

• Please do not get discouraged at errors or failings. It's all right to make mistakes. That is, of course, the way we learn. We try this and that and sometimes make mistakes. Mistakes can also be valuable by providing us with an opportunity to apologize to students—an act that often serves remarkably well to bring students to our side.

• Here is a special warning if you are a beginner and find yourself in one of those angry schools in which students show new teachers no mercy (see the first 10 pages of Bel Kaufman's [1964] novel *Up the Down Staircase* for an accurate description of such a school): Don't be surprised if your initial lessons are a complete bust. Some teachers are greeted by students who bang books, create arguments, speak insolently, and generally create mayhem. If that happens, sometimes the best you can do is maintain your dignity and wait until those frolics subside. Deep down students much prefer a well-managed classroom to a chaotic one, and they will eventually simmer down enough for you to begin to take charge. If you stand proud through their best (worst?) shots, you will have gained much admiration and respect and be in a position to start bringing students to your side.

• Finally, consider a memory exercise. Recall times when you could not go outside without an adult, or could not read a whole sentence, or did not know how to drive a car, or were not able to do something else important to you, and then, after you grew a bit more, or after someone showed you how, you were able to do what you wanted. What was impossible became second nature. You might also recall some anxiety about letting go of the old and moving on to the new. Risks often show up when new opportunities arise. Those memories may remind you that when you are willing, you can move past risks and in time move up to a bright new level of effectiveness. Go for it!

▲ TEACHER COMMENT

I planned a series of escalating responses to problems. First I would give a nonverbal signal. If that didn't work, I would use an Authority Statement. A conference with the student would be my third response. From there it would depend on the student and the situation. That was my plan, and it is working well so far, although I find myself often sending the toughest cases to my partner's room across the hall to fill out a Think Time Sheet. If I were to revise my plan I would include that strategy in the plan, for it works well for me. I never announced this plan to my students. I don't want them to see it as a series of threats, like a series of escalating punishments they have to worry about. Sometimes I use a punishment, if you can call sending a student to the office "a punishment," but that is only when I sense it is the only way for the student to think seriously about what he is doing.

—*Joanne Goldberg, Middle School Teacher*

PART III

Strategies for Starting
Classes Efficiently

The beginning of a class session typically involves several tasks. This part of the book presents strategies for three such tasks: gathering students' attention, handling completed homework, and providing quick reviews of past learnings.

The language we use as we handle these tasks makes a difference. What wording inspires students to do their best work and be their most cooperative? Consider these three comments and the messages they send to students:

Least inspiring: "Please take out your homework."

In between: "How many have their homework ready for today? How many found the homework difficult?"

Most inspiring: "How many of you are having a good day so far today? How many are ready for a good day here in our class? Anything we need to handle before we go over our homework?"

Gathering the Attention of Students

9

It is often necessary to gather the attention of students, especially at the beginning of class and when students are working in groups. What is the best way to do that—and do it in a way that dignifies and energizes students and encourages self-management, community, and awareness as well? The strategies of this chapter illustrate ways we might do that. The first four strategies are recommended for first consideration.

◆ Strategy 9-1: Hand-Raising Signal

Purpose: To gather the attention of students who have been working individually or in groups.

Description: Silently raising a hand as a signal that it's time to discontinue individual work or small-group discussions.

Imagine a teacher explaining this strategy to a class. Here is what he might say:

> When I raise my hand during group time or individual work time, it signals it's time to end those activities. Whenever you see my hand go up, please raise your hand. When you raise your hand, people who cannot see me will see hands go up and raise their hands. If you are talking when hands go up, please finish the sentence you have already started, but do not start a new sentence. If you are working alone at something, listen up so I can speak to you all.
>
> If something important is interrupted, which will sometimes happen, please remember what it was. You can always later return to it, if necessary during lunch or after school.

▲ TEACHER COMMENT

I use the Hand-Raising Signal on the playground. When I need students to come inside, I raise my hand, students who see me raise theirs, and soon all the hands are waving in the air. The students somehow enjoy going through the process, and I do not have to yell or complain. They just do it, and I wave them in. Works wonderfully well.

—*Clara Bowles, 2nd Grade Teacher*

Perhaps this hand-raising signal works so well because it gives all students some-thing to do—raise their hands—rather than focusing on what students should stop doing—talking or reading or whatever. The strategy is active and constructive.

 ## Strategy 9-2: One-Minute Warning

Purpose: To maintain active student participation.
Description: Allowing students to continue working only as long as they are actively engaged.

Often students are working independently or with a few others. When it is time to reconvene the entire class, it is helpful to give students a One-Minute Warning. We can simply call out, "One more moment, please," as a signal for students to wind down whatever they are working on.

It can be also useful to announce a time limit on such work, as by saying at the outset, "You will have only five minutes." Many students work with more enthusiasm when they know time is limited. Note, however, the wisdom of being willing to adjust any announced time limit. When we see all students remaining actively engaged, we might consider letting them continue without calling time. And when we notice participation waning before the time limit is reached, we might well call out, "One more minute," to alert the group that we will soon move on. Students rarely complain when we gather them *before* the announced time has expired, probably because they would rather be highly involved than bored.

 ## Strategy 9-3: Voting Questions

Purpose: To gather the attention of students and to help them appreciate one another.
Description: Asking general-interest questions to which students can respond by raising hands.

We can gather the attention of students by asking questions that they can answer quickly, simply by raising their hands. Some examples:

- How many of you are completely finished with the work I assigned?
- How many still have a bit to go?
- How many need a lot more time?

Think about how hard it is to change yourself. Then you will understand how hard it is to change others.
—Anonymous

Voting Questions of a personal nature are especially useful at the start of a class. Some examples:

- How many of you had a birthday this month?
- How many like to play soccer? Baseball? Basketball?
- How many of you have been on an airplane? A boat? A submarine?
- How many here have younger siblings? Older siblings? Is anyone an only child?

Because questions such as these naturally capture student interest, we naturally get the attention of students and are then in a position to direct their attention to the lesson ahead or to whatever else we wish to talk about. Voting Questions of a personal nature also help students get to know one another and, often, appreciate one another. Voting Questions might address general student interests, such as music, hobbies, families, sports, TV programs, money, friends, hopes, dreams, travels, or clothes. However, questions might also lead into subject matter lessons, like the following introduction to a lesson on heat:

- How many of you like summer?
- How many of you find extreme heat more uncomfortable than extreme cold?
- How many of you know what heat is and could define it?

Responses to Voting Questions, of course, are meant to be voluntary, not mandatory. Students may raise their hands or abstain as they wish. No count of the votes is ever taken.

▲ **TEACHER COMMENT**

We used the Voting Questions strategy several times last week. One example was in a science lesson. We were discussing properties of matter, specifically, sinking or floating. Each child tested one object by placing it in a tub of water. Before doing so, the class voted on whether the object would sink or float. This kept everyone involved and interested in the activity, which was rather lengthy. Second graders love to vote on anything!

—Ginny Beatty, 2nd Grade Teacher

Strategy 9-4: New or Goods

Purpose: To gather student attention and build a healthy community climate.
Description: Asking students if anything is new or good in their lives.

This strategy from Jackins (1974) starts the class with the question "Who can tell us something new or good in your life?" The first time we use this strategy with a group, it's useful to give some prompts, so as to clarify the question. We might say,

"Anything new or good in your lives? Anyone get a new compliment or a new car? Anything good happen lately at home or school?" Whatever students mention in response, then, we are to accept, usually by simply saying, "Thank you for sharing that" or "I can sure appreciate that." After a few moments, we can move into the day's lesson.

The intent here is not to raise issues for discussion, although it is sometimes wise to allow a discussion to follow, as when a student comment raises an issue that is important for many others. The intent rather is to give students a few moments to share the happy or sad events in their lives. It allows those who may not shine in academic areas to announce good news in other areas of their lives—being on a winning baseball team, for example. It allows students anguishing over an event—the death of a pet, for example—to express feelings of distress. In many ways it brings a class together in deeper and more expansive appreciation of one another. Besides, it opens a class with a positive, personal touch and usually brings student attention fully into the classroom.

Strategy 9-5: Lesson Agreement

Purpose: To maximize student cooperation.
Description: Announcing our general plans for the lesson ahead and inviting student agreement.

Asking students for their agreement to the outline for the day's lesson might go something like this:

> Today I plan to start with our homework. Then I thought we would begin our discussion on France. After that, there will be time for your group project work. And if time remains we can do some map work. OK?

Or, if classes are usually structured in a particular way, we might use this time to announce any changes in routines, for instance:

> Today, I'd like you to have some extra time for your Independent Learning Assignments. Instead of doing our usual lesson together, I'd like you to work independently while I call individuals to meet with me to report on their progress. Is everyone OK with this change?

Some students might have alternative suggestions, of course. Some suggestions might even be worth a change of our plans. We each have the final say, however. The intent here is not to expect all students to agree. It is rather to take a moment to demonstrate respect for students' perspective and intelligence, to invite collaboration and hear suggestions, so everyone moves ahead with maximum cooperation.

We can present a class outline orally or by writing it on the board. For older students, the outline might extend for a week or more. This Lesson Agreement strategy is similar to what Madeline Hunter (1984) called an "anticipatory set." Both strategies get students looking forward to the lesson ahead. However, the Lesson Agreement strategy includes an invitation to accept the plan. When we ask, "Is that OK with you?" we are, of course, encouraging students to be *willing* to participate in the work ahead.

Strategy 9-6: Relaxation Exercise

Purpose: To channel and settle scattered student energies.
Description: Providing a mini-exercise that prepares students to do their best work.

Sometimes students become agitated or distracted or overactive, and it is useful to relax and refocus their energies. A gentle physical activity can serve that purpose. Possibilities include (1) standing and taking four slow, deep breaths; (2) standing and slowly stretching and bending, perhaps to music; and (3) leading students in one or two simple yoga postures. For a particularly valuable source of healthful exercises, see www.braingym.org. Also see the strategies in Chapter 8.

Guided visualizations can also be effective. We might, for example, say something such as this, pausing between statements to convey a relaxed frame of mind:

> Let's all take a few minutes to get relaxed and focused. Find a comfortable position and breathe deeply. You might even want to close your eyes—whatever feels good to you. Now let's create a picture in our minds. Picture a place that is very relaxing—perhaps a forest or a beach, a mountain or a meadow, maybe a special place you once visited. Wherever it is, try to get a very clear picture of it in your mind. Notice the colors and shapes. Notice any sounds or smells. Picture yourself being there and take a few moments to relax and enjoy your surroundings. When you feel ready, slowly open your eyes.

We can use a similar process to help students reflect on a particular issue or problem. Here is an example (again, pausing frequently enhances the relaxation effect):

Those who can, teach. Those who can't, go into some less significant line of work.

—*Anonymous*

I'd like us to take a minute to think about what happened. Find a comfortable position and take a few deep breaths. Think about the problem we experienced. How did it make you feel? How do you think it made other people in our class feel? Is there anything you'd like to say to someone sometime about what happened? Take a few moments to reflect. When you feel you are finished, slowly open your eyes.

Strategy 9-7: Brain Drain

Purpose: To help students clear their minds and be ready for new work.
Description: Giving students a few minutes to vent their thoughts in writing.

When we sense that students are overwhelmed, distracted, upset, or otherwise not ready to handle the lesson ahead, we can have them take out a piece of paper while we say something like this:

> I sense we have so much going on in our brains right now it might be difficult to concentrate. Please take whatever is clogging your brain right now and put it on that piece of paper. I'm going to set the timer for two minutes, and when I say "Go!" write whatever comes to mind. The only rule: You can't stop writing until the timer goes off. Even if you have to write "I don't know what to write," keep writing—eventually something will come to you. Ready? Go!

As students become comfortable with the procedure, we might want to extend the writing time. Afterward, we can hear from a few volunteers, especially if students are anxious to share some of their thoughts. When sharing is not practical, we might give students the option of either throwing away their papers or handing them in to you, with or without their names, as they choose. It's usually best not to return the papers and rather let the experience slip into the past, although occasionally you might want to speak privately to someone about what he or she wrote.

Handling Completed Homework

10

For some students, completing daily homework can be a challenge. It can also be a challenge for teachers to handle the homework that students complete. How, for example, do we handle one student's questions about yesterday's homework without boring all the students who already understand the material? The strategies in this chapter offer suggestions for this and other issues consistent with the goal of helping students make good use of their natural motivations to live and work with dignity, energy, self-management, community, and awareness. We suggest giving first attention to the first two strategies, each marked with an arrow, for our field tests show they are particularly effective for handling completed homework.

◀•) Strategy 10-1: Homework Sharing Pairs

Purpose: To maximize academic learning and advance self-responsibility.
Description: Asking students to pair up and share completed homework.

We could simply ask students to pair up in class and compare their homework. If the homework involved right/wrong answers, those could be posted or read aloud at the outset. We might tell students they are to teach each other when one person in the pair understands more than the other, and when both are unsure, they are to ask another pair for help. We might also tell students that if they finish and time still remains, they are to create new questions for each other or to review past content in some appropriate way. Some variations of this strategy:

• *Sharing Outcome Sentences.* One history teacher asks students to come to class each day with one or more Outcome Sentences (Strategy 21-1) written in response to the homework reading assignment. Often, but not every class period, she then asks students to sit in fours and take turns reporting at least one of their Outcome Sentences and, after each has had a turn, to informally discuss what they learned from the reading. The teacher reports: "Students work more seriously and learn more when they have a few minutes to tell others what they learned. They also hear others' perceptions, which are often different from their own. They hear about ideas they never thought about."

• *Reading aloud to a partner.* For homework, a 2nd grade teacher asks students to prepare to read aloud, with feeling and meaning, a 25-to-50-word selection. In class, then, she tells students to find a partner they have not read with recently and to take turns presenting their reading. Partners are to listen and, afterward, to comment on how well they heard and understood. The teacher reports:

> I recommend students read from a storybook but allow them to read from anything. Some even pick a comic book. One always reads from the daily newspaper! I want them to get in the habit of reading whatever is meaningful to them. Some need to practice reading aloud many times at home in order to do well in class, and I send letters home that tell parents how to help. Mainly, I say, Do not push the child. Do not even remind the child of the homework. Offer to help once or twice, but then allow the child to ask for help when it's needed. I want children to learn responsible initiative. If requested, help the child read the words until he or she feels comfortable and ready for the next day's presentation. Do not tell a child when he or she is ready. I want children to learn to judge that for themselves.

• *Critiquing each other's writings.* A high school English teacher has students give one another feedback on their homework writing samples. All students pile homework up front when they come in the room and then take a paper from the stack and write a critique in the margins. They are to do as many papers as time allows, which is usually 8 to 10 minutes. Some homework papers get more than one critique. As preparation, this teacher includes lessons on how to offer constructive feedback and distributes a form with specific hints. The teacher reports: "Many students learn more from the critiquing process than they ever do from the writing process, and the class as a whole gets much more feedback than I ever have time to give, and they get it more promptly, too."

• *Teaching something that was learned.* A college teacher asks students to prepare mini-lessons based on their homework reading. In class, students form random trios, a timer is set, and each person has five minutes to give his or her mini-lesson to two peers. Homework readings contain many ideas, so each mini-lesson is almost always unique. The two listeners are to respect the time of the speaker and are not to interrupt with their own thoughts. When the timer rings, the next person is the presenter. After all three have spoken, the timer is set for an extra five minutes, so all trios can discuss their ideas informally.

Nothing in the world can take the place of persistence. Talent will not; nothing is more common than unsuccessful men with talent. Genius will not; the world is full of educated derelicts. The slogan "press on" has solved and always will solve the problems of the human race.

—Calvin Coolidge

Students often benefit from occasional discussions of the homework sharing process: "How did the groups go today? How can we do better next time?" Students might write Like/Might Review notes (Strategy 21-2): *Today I liked the way I* ... and *Next time I might* ...

Note that no teacher evaluation of homework is included in this strategy. Learning takes place quite naturally, without any need for teacher involvement other than, perhaps, the teacher roaming the room and assisting as appropriate. The natural desires of students to understand and succeed and to share their work advances student knowledge. The emphasis of the strategy is on having the class review homework seriously and cooperatively, not on how well students did the homework. This emphasis, we find, tends to bring out the best in students and thereby maximize learning. It clearly honors and protects student dignity. Because all are actively involved, energy is high. The students also exercise much self-management. Community feelings naturally grow. And as students hear one another's ideas and assist one another in learning, they continually stretch and refine their awareness.

Strategy 10-2: Homework Self-Correcting

Purpose: To check right/wrong answers efficiently.
Description: Asking students to check homework against an answer key with little or no teacher involvement.

When homework involves right/wrong answers, we can efficiently handle completed work by having students correct their own work. We might do this by posting answer keys in a designated area, writing correct answers on the board or an overhead, or by reading (or having designated students read) the correct answers aloud. Alternatively, students might exchange papers with a classmate.

In either case, no explanation of the answers may be necessary. Because explanations for a few students are often boring to others, it's usually wise to help students with questions another way. We might say to a class, for example, "If you find you got some answers wrong and want some explanation, ask a neighbor for help. If there is no time to do that at the moment, follow up and take responsibility to seek help later. Just so you know that many of your friends would be happy to explain things they understand and you do not, let me ask, 'How many would be happy to take a few moments to help a classmate who has a homework question?'"

We might also follow Homework Self-Correcting with a reteaching or review strategy that actively engages the whole class. Or use Clear-to-Muddy Groups

(Strategy 17-1), in which students are grouped for a follow-up activity according to their levels of understanding. (For additional strategy options see Chapters 11 and 16.)

To acknowledge student work and to gauge the level of class understanding of the material, so we know how much reteaching is necessary, we can follow with Voting Questions to Assess Understanding (Strategy 16-6). Sample questions:

- How many of you did work that shows excellent understanding of the material?
- How many feel you need some more practice?
- How many feel you need more help before you can fully understand?

Strategy 10-3: Homework Hearing Time

Purpose: To advance self-responsible work habits and give each student a moment of our personal attention.

Description: Meeting briefly with individual students to hear about their completed homework.

This strategy, adapted from Pilon (1996), gives each student a moment or two to report work directly to the teacher. Here is how a high school biology teacher explained this to a class:

> As you know, part of the time each Friday you will be in a work group. During that group time, I will take turns visiting each of your groups. When I join yours, please stop your work temporarily. I'd like each of you to read me something from your homework journal. You can read any one or two of your recent learnings or tell me about a question you have. Others will just listen in as you give me this report. This procedure will give me a few moments, each week, to visit with each of you personally on your homework. It will help me keep up with how you are doing.

An elementary school teacher uses a different system:

> Each day you will have some time for individual work, as when you are working on your individual study tasks. During that time I will call students to my table, a few at a time, in alphabetical order. When you get here, you will have a chance to read me the words you mastered for homework.
>
> Here is the way it will work. I will be sitting at one side of this table. Opposite will be five chairs for five of you to sit in, starting with the five of you who are at the head of the alphabetical order. You know by now where your place in the order is. I will hear the words from the student in the first chair. When that student

is finished, he or she simply goes back to individual work. When that happens, the other four students slide over. In that way, the last of the five chairs gets to be empty. Keep aware of when your name is coming up, and if you are next in the alphabet, come over and sit in that empty chair.

Have your homework with you, for when you eventually slide into the first chair, your job will be to read aloud, with as much confidence as you can muster, the words you worked on for homework. Let's walk through this procedure now to be sure we can handle it smoothly.

Note that with this strategy the teacher speaks to one student at a time while others sit nearby. This allows other students to listen in and, perhaps, to learn something from the conversations. It also helps some students feel less intimidated than they might feel if they had to meet with a teacher alone. From the point of view of efficiency, this also reduces time between student reports. Teachers typically find they can go through a class of 30 students in 30 minutes.

Of course, it is not always possible or profitable to meet with every student during each Homework Hearing Time. We might, for example, call only one row or table each day. Or start at the beginning of the alphabet and hear from as many students as we have time for, picking up where we left off the next time.

How might we respond to each student in this procedure? Some recommendations:

- *Use friendly eye contact.* When a student is ready to report to you, aim to look relaxed and accepting, inviting whatever eye contact the student is willing to offer. We need say nothing. Just look at the student warmly. We want each student to be clear that he or she has inviolable self-worth, an essential value, one that need not be earned. Allow the student to initiate his or her report.

- *Provide supportive responses.* When a student gives a report, aim to respond in some way that does not highlight praise or rewards, as by simply saying, "Thank you. I very much liked that report," and then signaling for the next student to slide into the reporter's chair. In terms of generating healthy, responsible work habits, we want to respond to students in ways suggested by the strategies in Chapter 20, which include Plain Corrects, Plain Incorrects, Incorrects with Appreciation, Honest I Appreciates, I'm with You's, DESCA Inspirations, and Spontaneous Delights.

- *Ask Cushioning Questions.* It is occasionally useful to use Cushioning Questions (Strategy 4-2) during Homework Hearing Time, especially when a student who is reporting (or one who is sitting nearby listening) needs a confidence boost. It also inoculates students against learning anxieties and continues the process of deepening learner confidence. Some examples:

> Be confident, for the stars are of the same stuff as you.
> —*Nicholai Velimirovic*

Before you begin, Rosa, tell me, would it be all right if you made mistakes in your homework? [The teacher continues after Rosa responds.] Why would that be all right?

Matthew, before you start, tell me if you think it would be OK if you or anyone else did not understand a thing about the homework assignment—not one single thing. [The teacher continues after Matthew responds.] Why would that be OK?

Sometimes Cushioning Questions can incorporate reminders to students of the messages contained in the Truth Signs (Strategy 4-1) posted in the classroom:

You have no homework to show me today, Terry. Well, we each have our own ways and time clocks, so that sometimes happens. Do you remember what the sign about that says? [The teacher continues after Terry responds.] Can you handle having your homework ready for tomorrow?

Before we talk, I want to ask, Josh, what if someone did not have time to learn this material yet? Can you think of a sign we have posted that would explain why that sometimes happens? [The teacher continues after Josh responds.] Thank you. Now please tell me about your work for today.

• *Use self-management stimulators.* Some teachers report that it's valuable to use Homework Hearing Time as an opportunity to stimulate attention to good work habits. Some examples:

You did more than the minimum required. Do you feel good about yourself for having done that much? [The teacher might continue after the student responds.] Thanks, Ellen. I was just wondering.

It seems to me you did your work very carefully. Did you deliberately choose to work very carefully this time?

You have nothing to report for homework. That sometimes happens. I wonder how you feel about not having work today and if you feel OK about it.

You have no homework to show me. Please take a moment and ask yourself if you are willing to do what it takes to have tomorrow's homework completed.

You do your homework very well every day. Is it hard for you to say no to temptations that might distract you from your work?

You have not done very much. I wonder if you could use some hints or more support for managing your time or for saying no to distracting impulses. Can I, or one of your classmates, help in some way?

▲ TEACHER COMMENT

I changed my approach to homework. I decided I wanted all students to know they were not less worthy if and when they did not do homework. Since, in Spanish, homework is very important, this was a very risky experiment for me. But I did it, and guess what? Eventually students started doing more—not less—homework. They also did it more willingly. I no longer struggle with students about homework, although I still find myself slipping. I must learn patience with students even as I am beginning to appreciate how I can teach them to be more patient with themselves. Giving each student a chance once a week to show me what they learned without worrying that I will judge the work or correct it or in any way be critical has changed something important for us all. Now students like to show me their stuff.

—*High School Spanish Teacher*

Such self-management stimulators call for a creative touch. If possible, work with other teachers for practice and feedback until you feel comfortable with them. Note, however, that you need not use self-management stimulators to extract large benefits from the Homework Hearing Time strategy. The stimulators simply add an extra nourishing element.

Finally, remember that the focus of Homework Hearing Time is not on grading students' work, although you might well make mental notes of which students need extra help or what learnings need extra review. The focus is rather on demonstrating that you respect the value of the homework students do.

This strategy gives each student a minute or two of personal, fully respectful attention. For some students, a regular dose of such attention from an authority figure can make the difference between essential self-esteem and persisting self-doubt.

Strategy 10-4: Credit for Completing Homework

Purpose: To reduce homework-related stress and inspire homework self-management.

Description: Checking homework assignments but not grading homework or penalizing students for not completing it.

It is sometimes useful to give credit for completing homework, so as to motivate such completion and give students a chance to improve their overall grades. For this purpose, credit for completion is usually enough; it is not necessary to grade the quality of the homework.

However, we might want to dispense entirely with credit for homework. We do want to *give* homework, ideally to every student every day, to provide review practice and to develop self-managed learning skills. And we do want to check on homework and encourage students to do the best they can with it. It's also important to expect good effort and to offer positive feedback when students show such effort. Our experience suggests, however, that it's unwise to withhold credit or penalize students who do not complete homework. Doing so often discourages the students who most need encouragement, including those with chaotic home situations and poor work habits. Besides, not tying credit to homework reduces the negative feelings that students often associate with homework, which in turn tends to increase student dignity, to promote self-responsibility and

We should not only use the brains we have, but all that we can borrow.

—Woodrow Wilson

good work habits, to help preserve positive teacher-student relationships and, not insignificantly, to reduce our record-keeping chores. The bottom line: Many teachers report that giving and checking homework is sufficient; they lose more than they gain by also grading homework.

What should we do, then, when a student does not do homework? If it's a pattern, we recommend privately asking the student why homework is not being completed and reacting accordingly, depending on what is best for all concerned. Chapter 33 has more specific strategies for handling such routine misbehavior problems. If, however, many students are not doing homework, Whole-Class Problem Solving (Strategy 8-9) might be in order. It might also be an occasion to review our homework assignments and see if they are as effective as they could be. See Chapter 22 for discussions of effective homework assignments.

Providing for a Quick Review of Completed Content

11

In Chapter 3 we discussed the strategy of Teaching in Layers, Not Lumps (Strategy 3-2). The strategy involves returning to material many times, in many ways, helping students to gradually master it. But how can we provide such reviews without being repetitious, even boring? The strategies of this chapter suggest some possibilities. We recommend the first three strategies for your first attention; each is marked with an arrow.

Strategy 11-1: Review Test

Purpose: To keep all students involved in reviewing subject matter with many experiences of success.

Description: Posing a set of review questions and having students (1) write answers and (2) immediately check their work against the provided correct answer.

The Review Test covers material previously introduced in class. The "test" is for the students alone. Their challenge: To answer as many correctly as they can.

An Example in Spelling

The teacher asks students to write on scrap paper, first, the correct spelling of the word *generosity*. As the students begin to write, the teacher turns to the board and writes:

1. generosity

When students finish writing, they look up and check their work and, if necessary, erase and correct their writing, so each has the word spelled correctly.

Without much delay, the teacher then says, "Next word, *classic*. The book was a classic. Classic." Students begin to write the word. As they do so, the teacher writes on the board:

2. classic

The students check their work; the teacher says the next word. The process continues for 10 spelling words. To avoid any student inactivity, the pace is brisk. The teacher expects students to speed up to his pace rather than ask him to slow down to theirs.

At the end of the lesson, the teacher might use some Voting Questions to Assess Understanding (Strategy 16-6). For example,

- How many had all 10 words correct?
- How many had 8 or 9 correct?
- How many have 1 or more words you need to add to your list of spelling practice words?

An Example in Math

"Problem 1," says the teacher, writing on the board:

1. $(a + 4)(a + 5) =$

As the students begin to work the problem, the teacher works the problem on the board. When students finish their own work, they look up and see that the teacher has written

1. $(a + 4)(a + 5) = a^2 + 4a + 5a + 20 = a^2 + 9a + 20$

Students check their work and make corrections if necessary.

The teacher notices that two or three students are confused, so she makes the next problem similar to the first one, expecting that the model for the first problem, which remains on the board, will help those students. "Problem 2," she says, as she writes:

2. $(b + 6)(b + 3) =$

And again, as students begin to work, the teacher works the problem out correctly on the board. The process continues for several problems, all without much discussion.

Uses of the Review Test

Review Tests can be an everyday routine. They can include one or two questions from very old material to refresh memories. They can then move into recent material covered, to deepen understandings and, as students correct their work, clear up misunderstandings.

As an option, we might announce, "We'll use a special process today for the even-numbered questions. After I give the correct answer, I'd like all those who had written that answer correctly to stand up for a second. If nothing else, that will give you some exercise!"

A Review Test is an efficient way to get students practicing and clarifying learnings. Students enjoy the strategy. With every Review Test, each student sees how much content has already been learned. Even for content not quite mastered, each student gets a chance to try answering questions without feeling threatened.

We can check class understanding in a general way by scanning the room and getting a sense of how well students understand. However, the intent is not to assess learning. It is to have students review and clarify prior content and obtain immediate feedback on both right and wrong answers (Bangert-Downs, Kulik, Kulik, & Morgan, 1991).

One of us, Merrill, uses a variety of Review Test questions in his graduate classes for teachers. His first two or three questions might be factual—for example, "What is the name of the psychologist who wrote about a hierarchy of human needs?" When the class members start writing their answers, he writes the correct answer, Abraham Maslow, on the board. Without discussion, he poses the next question. However, after everyone gets into the rhythm of the strategy, he might ask more complex questions, such as "What are some purposes served by the Outcome Sentence strategy?" For such a question, he does not write an answer on the board. Rather, he simply waits until teachers have made some notes and then asks for several volunteers to share one of their ideas. In this way, he can intersperse simple right/wrong questions with questions involving many correct answers. As usual, the intent is to give participants a chance to review and refresh prior knowledge and, no small matter, feel good about having already learned something, all in a nonthreatening format.

▲ **TEACHER COMMENT**

A slight variation of the Review Test strategy I tried is using the Review Test with Sharing Pairs. I have students work with a friend to try to get the solution to the problem before I put the answer on the board. This method is effective because it creates a lot of aliveness and cooperation in the classroom.

—*Cindy Huels, Middle School Math Teacher*

⏩ Strategy 11-2: Choral Work

Purpose: To get students to memorize material effortlessly and heighten class energy.

Description: Flashing a series of cards to which a class responds in unison.

Teachers of young children often have had students chanting material together, such as numbers, letters, or math facts. We've now found that this strategy is effective at all grade levels. When one of us, Merrill, taught junior high school math, for example, the strategy involved preparing a set of 10 to 20 cards, each card containing on one side a multiplication fact ($9 \times 7 =$) and on the other side its product (63). He gave these instructions to the class:

> I'll hold up a stack of cards like this, each showing a problem. Then we all say it aloud together: "9 times 7." Then we pause a beat, I turn over the card showing the product on the other side, and we all then say that together, "63." OK, let's go through all these cards. Call out now with as much power as you can.

He then led the class through his set of cards, occasionally saying "A little more power, please," to energize participation. He also sometimes said "Good rhythm," to encourage students to stay with the rhythm of the card turning. The first time he did this, the class was a bit uncertain. But he simply persisted with full confidence. On the second day, participation was higher. By the third day, most students were into it with zest. As the days went on, he removed the easier cards and added cards with newer material—for example, a card that had on one side, "Area of a parallelogram," and on the other, "$A = b \times h$."

What were the benefits of this kind of choral work? His students rarely made errors in calculations. They knew their facts cold. In addition, class spirit increased. Chanting brought students together, much the way group singing can. And no one was embarrassed because of slow learning. Those who knew the answers called them out with assurance. Those who were unsure might have looked at the revealed answer on the back of each card before speaking out. But all were full-fledged members of the chorus.

We can use Choral Work with any material we want students to memorize effortlessly: chemical symbols (sodium fluoride/NaF), geography facts (New York/Albany), definitions (noun/person, place, or thing). Some suggestions for using the strategy successfully:

A teacher asks Tommy what two plus two equals. "Four," he says. "Very good, Tommy." "Very good?" says Tommy indignantly. "It's perfect!"

—Quoted by Richard Kehl

• *From time to time, reintroduce old cards to reactivate and deepen prior knowledge.* To recall information readily, most students must encounter it frequently and then, afterward, be reminded of it occasionally (Nuthall, 1999).

• *Keep the cards turning.* Don't worry if some students do not know the information or say it incorrectly. Repeating the same cards on many days will produce mastery. Likewise, don't worry if some students already know the information. If the pace is quick, all will enjoy being part of the group.

• *Maintain group energy.* Generating group energy is an important benefit of Choral Work. To maintain that energy, it's often useful to occasionally say, "Say it with power," "Speak up as if you mean it," "A little more energy please," or "With more gusto."

• *Distinguish energy from loudness.* When the noise level needs to be modulated, demonstrate the difference between a soft, powerful voice and a weak, thin voice. Show students that it's possible to even whisper with high energy. Then you can request softer voices with power.

• *Vary the volume.* Some teachers ask students to speak more or less loudly depending on how high the cards are being held at the moment. When the teacher holds the cards shoulder height, it means speak with normal volume. Waist high means speak strongly but in a whisper.

• *Use visuals and color.* Pictures and color facilitate memory for many students. Consider adding simple sketches on cards or using different-colored markers on different cards.

▲ **TEACHER COMMENT**

I tried Choral Work with my Essentials of Algebra/Geometry class. We were studying the names of the polygons. I would say, "A 10-sided polygon is called . . . ?" The class would say, "Decagon." I went through all of them from 3 sides to 10 sides, 12 sides, and 15 sides, slowly. Then we went faster and faster through all the polygons. This was a great way for the students to memorize the polygons and to participate as a whole class.

—*Cindy Huels, Middle School Math Teacher*

 ## Strategy 11-3: I Say Review

Purpose: To review and strengthen learnings and increase student cooperation.
Description: Asking pairs of students to share what they would say about certain subject matter.

Some students become anxious when asked to explain a theory or procedure. *Do I understand it well enough? Can I explain it well enough?* And that anxiety, of course, impedes their ability to learn to do better. To avoid raising such anxiety, instead of asking students to explain something, we can simply request that they say what they can about that theory or procedure, with no expectation that what they say will be complete, correct, or clear. For example, an English teacher could pair up students and ask them to take turns telling their partners what they would say about each of the words on a vocabulary list. The teacher might continue explaining in this way:

> One person starts by saying what he would say about the first word, *osmosis*. If the partner would like to add something or suggest a different definition, he or she does that. If not, go on to the second word. You could take turns starting. Or one person could talk about the first four or five words and the partner could talk about the next batch. Go back and forth in some way you find good for you.
>
> Your aim in this activity is not to produce a perfect definition. The aim is for each of you to say whatever you know about each word. By taking turns and hearing what your partner knows about a word, you should learn more about it. If you disagree or are unsure of any aspect of the definition, look it up.

Asking pairs to share what each person would say about a word, rather than asking them to give the correct definition, usually produces a relaxed, thoughtful exchange. Students quite naturally talk about what is the correct definition, without the anxiety often associated with being correct.

Of course, we can use the I Say Review with many types of content, such as a list of formulas, people, important events, places, or scientific principles. We can also use it with lists of key review questions: What makes a good paragraph? Estimate 250 times 9. What factors often cause wars?

Strategy 11-4: One Say, All Say

Purpose: To get a whole class to review subject matter with lots of energy and awareness.

Description: Having one volunteer read something aloud and then having the whole class repeat what was read.

If we wanted students to improve their language usage, to give one example of this strategy, we could start by preparing a set of cards. Each card would hold a grammatical phrase, such as "she and I are," "it isn't," "between him and me," or "to whom shall I give it?" We would select phrases that students are likely *not* to use properly in normal conversation. And we would write each phrase in large letters on heavy paper or cardboard.

The One Say, All Say procedure is straightforward: We hold up a card. All students willing to read it aloud raise their hands. We select one reader, perhaps by

"Come to the edge,"
he said. They said,
"We are afraid."
"Come to the edge,"
he said. They came.
He pushed them . . .
and they flew.

—*Guillaume Apollinaire*

looking at the person and nodding. That student then reads the card aloud. We say, "Everyone," and all repeat what the reader just said. We then turn to the next card and repeat the process.

When we repeat that activity often enough, say each day of the week for five minutes or so, students effortlessly absorb our correct language, and that usage tends to replace any incorrect usage (for example, "it ain't") that students absorbed when they were infants and, ever since, have had difficulty escaping. The One Say, All Say strategy, then, gives us a handy way to reinforce learnings for a whole class.

Here's another way to use the One Say, All Say strategy, in this case without cards:

Teacher: What is the definition of a noun?
Jacob: A person, place, or thing.
Teacher: Yes, a noun is a person, place, or thing. All together, class.
All students: A noun is a person, place, or thing.

This approach can reinforce any special content. For example, a science teacher might say, "It is important to see the environment as one whole system. Together, please say with me, 'The environment is one whole system.'" After the students recite the statement, the teacher might ask them to "say it again, with more power." After the second recitation, the teacher might reinforce the point and begin elaborating by saying, "Yes, it is important to see that the environment is one whole, interdependent, active system that . . ."

Strategy 11-5: Sketching to Review

Purpose: To involve all students in a quick creative review of a topic.
Description: Before reviewing a topic, asking students to draw part of what they remember.

A teacher wanted to summarize the events of the Civil War before moving to the next unit but, first, asked students to take a moment and sketch something they each remembered from that war. Then students paired up and briefly shared their sketches with each other, explaining what it was that they tried to depict. The teacher then made his summary—to students whose memories were now jogged and, presumably, who were more motivated to hear what he would say. Incidentally, we might sometimes ask students to sketch something *prior* to teaching it, as a means of motivating interest in a new topic.

Strategy 11-6: Pass the Q&A

Purpose: To involve all students in a quick, safe review of a concept.

Description: After announcing a question and an answer, having students pass them along down the rows or around their tables.

First grade teacher Janet McCann once addressed her class by saying, "The question today is, *Is this Black History Month? And the answer is, Yes, this is Black History Month.*" She then stooped and, eye-level with the boy in the first seat in the first row, said, "Is this Black History Month?" The boy replied, "Yes, this is Black History Month." The boy promptly turned to the girl behind him and asked, "Is this Black History Month?" The girl replied, "Yes, this is Black History Month," and she then turned to the student behind her and asked the same question. And so it went. Each student in turn asked the question and heard the answer, down the first row, passing along the Q&A.

Meanwhile, Janet had started the same process with the first student in the second row, the third row, and the remaining rows. As a result, within two or three minutes, every student had said aloud the question and the answer and had heard both several times.

▲ TEACHER COMMENTS

I use the Pass the Q&A strategy almost every day to get students to internalize proper language usage. Many of them were brought up in families where proper usage was uncommon. The kids love it somehow. I use such Q&A's as, "Did he and I go? Yes, he and I went." And, "May I have permission? Yes, you may." I also use it to help them memorize authors, such as, "Who wrote *Moby Dick*? Herman Melville wrote *Moby Dick*." I think they like the idea of never being wrong. They hear the question and answer from me, and all they need to do is remember it for two minutes. Actually, I find most of them remembering it long after! Repetition is the mother of remembering, or something like that.

— *Alanzo Cruz, Junior High School English Teacher*

I sometimes use the Pass the Q&A strategy without an answer. I'll say in Spanish, "Turn to page 122," and have each student turn and pass the phrase down the line. I do sometimes use it with answers, to help them practice their speaking and to memorize vocabulary. For example, in Spanish I say, "If today is Monday, what is the next day? The next day is Tuesday." Then they pass that question and answer down the line."

—*Martina Pugh, 9th Grade Spanish Teacher*

When the last student in each row answered, Janet said, "Everyone together now, 'Is this Black History Month?'" You might guess how the class responded. What is good about this strategy?

- It raises the energy level of the class.
- It gets even restless, inattentive students to focus on a concept.
- It gives students a chance to practice looking others in the eyes and exercising their personal power.

This strategy originated with Grace Pilon (1996). Some teachers use it to review an old concept before going on to something new, to insert a bit of worthwhile content that is not part of the curriculum, and simply as a way to increase the energy level of students who have been passive a bit too long.

Strategy 11-7: Reteach Review

Purpose: To avoid discouraging students who did not understand prior lessons.
Description: Overlapping lessons by briefly reteaching prior material before introducing new material.

Let's say we taught a lesson yesterday and today we want to introduce new material. To clarify any confusion about yesterday's material, we might be tempted to begin by asking, "Are there any questions about yesterday's lesson?" But it's usually wise to resist that temptation. Inviting such questions is not likely to be very helpful to students who are too shy or confused to ask a good question, and it is even less helpful to those who were absent or mentally dozing yesterday.

Alternatively, we can remind students of yesterday's material before asking for questions. We might say, "Yesterday I talked about how magnets can generate an electric current, and I demonstrated a simple machine that uses that principle. Any questions about any of that?" But that's not often the best approach either. It is also unlikely to help the shy or confused student or the ones who were either absent or asleep yesterday.

It would be better to very briefly reteach yesterday's lesson, as if we had never taught it before. We might use different words or examples or a different approach, and we would use a small fraction of the time we used earlier, but it would be fresh reteaching of the material. The intention is to provide a quick review statement for those who understood and a new chance to learn for those who did not. Because the reteaching is brief, few students are likely to be bored.

It may be too late already, but it's not as much too late now as it will be later.

—*C. H. Weisert*

And because it is a coherent presentation of the material, however brief, slower learners will have a second chance to learn it.

What might you do after the reteaching? Typically we'd still not recommend asking for questions, unless you had reason to expect that the resulting Q&A would keep the whole class actively involved, which is not always the case. Instead, if you wanted students to digest the prior material before going on, you might use a Review Test (Strategy 11-1) or Sharing Pairs or Learning Pairs (Strategies 7-1 and 7-2). And if you wanted students to digest the material and also wanted to know what they understood and misunderstood, you might use Outcome Sentences (Strategy 21-1) and a brief Whip Around, Pass Option (Strategy 16-4).

And if you preferred to move ahead into the new material, perhaps because you predicted that the new material would help many students better understand the old material, which is often the case, you could simply follow your brief Reteach Review with a statement such as "Let's now learn something new about this."

I had a rough marriage. My wife was an immature woman. See if this is not immature to you: I would be at home in the bathroom taking a bath and my wife would walk in whenever she felt like it and sink my boats.

—*Woody Allen*

PART IV

Strategies for Presenting New Content

This part of the book deals with the presentation of new material. Our first task is often to motivate students to be interested in such material. Our next move might be to give a lecture on the material. Or we might use a discovery approach. We might also want to use written materials to facilitate the learning of that material. Part IV contains chapters of sample strategies for each of those tasks.

The language we choose as we handle such tasks makes a difference. What wording activates the best motives students carry within them? Consider these three comments and the messages they send to students:

Least inspiring: "If one or two of you have questions, I'd like to hear them now."

In between: "Any questions?"

Most inspiring: "Some of you probably have questions. Who would be willing to share one?"

Motivating Interest in New Content

12

How should we deal with our unmotivated students, the ones who might be tempted to doodle, look out the window, or look for mischief—the ones not particularly eager to learn what we have to offer? Some basic guidelines for increasing student motivation:

- *Maximize success experiences.* Success is especially important for the weakest students. Students who keep failing tend to give up entirely, falling into a mindset that says, "I can't keep up with others. No sense trying. Maybe I'll go through the motions so as not to get in trouble, but that is about it."
- *Minimize anxiety.* It is difficult to do excellent work when we are anxious, our minds frozen because, for example, we are fearful of making a mistake or we feel we must learn it right now. The same is true of students.
- *Allow students to personalize the process.* If we can do something our way, we are more likely to do it and do it well than if we must do it the way someone else demands. The same is true of students.
- *Respect students' personal time clocks.* If we can do the job in our own time, when the time is right for us, we are more likely to do it and do it well than if we must do it too fast or too slow for our time clocks, or before we are ready to do it.
- *Take advantage of the power of teamwork.* Students can be brought to excellence by the energy of a group they're in. It's the power of teamwork.
- *Do not rely on rewards.* Rewards and recognition are usually better for improving production of the good workers than for inspiring the unmotivated.
- *Avoid penalties for poor performance.* Penalties or the fear of penalties rarely bring out people's best efforts, especially over the long run. Few students commit themselves to personal standards of excellence as a result of a scolding or a punishment.

• *Craft lessons that are intrinsically satisfying.* The most successful lessons give all students plenty of opportunities to express their healthy motives, such as their desire to engage life with personal dignity, natural energy, appropriate self-management, feelings of community, and satisfying awareness.

The seven strategies of this chapter take advantage of these principles. On the basis of our field reports from teachers, we recommend the first four strategies for your first attention. Each is marked with an arrow for easy identification.

 ## Strategy 12-1: Motivational Question

Purpose: To heighten student interest in a lesson.
Description: Asking a question, both to focus attention on a topic and to start the process of student thinking.

Questions can generate thinking and attention for the lesson ahead, as in these examples:

- What would be an example of an antonym?
- What do you know about the reasons for the Civil War?
- Can anyone estimate how much faster a dime falls than a nickel?

Sometimes a Motivational Question can refer back to an earlier lesson:

- What were the key points of yesterday's discussion?
- What did we say last time about a good diet?

Note, too, that a Motivational Question has more punch when we ask the question and then have students risk giving answers, as by saying, "Jot down some notes for yourself as you think about that question." That is the Question, All Write strategy (Strategy 16-3).

 ## Strategy 12-2: Know and Want to Know

Purpose: To build a unit on students' knowledge and questions.
Description: Starting a lesson by asking students to note what they already know or might want to know about the topic.

We do not recall teachers ever asking us what we personally wanted to learn about a topic. Had we been asked, we might have thought about it and uncovered

English spelling is weird . . . or is it wierd?

—*Irwin Hill*

a curiosity or two. And if we heard what our classmates were curious about, we might have found something we, too, wanted to learn. As it was, teachers did not ask and our curiosities lay fallow.

Carr and Ogle (1987) recommend that we do ask students what they know and want to know, and ask systematically. Here's an illustration of a teacher using their approach:

> We will begin a unit on the Congress today. What are some things you already know about the U.S. Congress? Let's brainstorm. I'd like two writers to come up and take turns writing down all the ideas that come up, true or otherwise, on sheets of newsprint. Who will start us off? We want a list of things you already know about the U.S. Congress.

When the class seems ready to move on, the teacher continues:

> We'll leave that list posted for a bit. Now let's start another list. What are some things you would like to know about the U.S. Congress? What are some things you are curious about or concerned about? Be creative and open-minded. Who will start our brainstorming?

If the teacher anticipates few responses, prudence recommends priming the pump with comments such as these:

> For example, you may wonder how to meet with your congressional representative, or how you can become one, or how much it costs to get elected. Or you may wonder if representatives really read citizen letters, or if it makes any difference, or why we have so many representatives in Congress. Or you may wonder about scandals, or what adults in town think of the present Congress and what the Congress should do. Do any of those questions interest anyone here?

The particular questions students list at the outset do not limit the learnings that will eventually result. We can add any content deemed necessary. The lists are simply a starting point to open students' minds to the unit ahead.

Once the lists are formed, we have several options.

• *Option 1: Leave the lists posted for future reference.* We could simply proceed with instruction as usual, taking advantage of the fact that some students will now probably be more motivated to dig into the unit. We would also have the advantage of being aware of what the class already knows and what interests them, which might help in planning instruction. At the end of the unit, then, we might refer back to the lists, as in this example:

> Looking back on our study, I'd like you to take some time and answer four questions. (1) Did you find that something you originally thought was true turned out to be not exactly as you first understood it? If so, write that down. (2) Did you

If at first you don't succeed, you're probably just like the teacher in the next classroom.

—Mary Shanley

learn anything new? If so, write that down. (3) What now would you say are the three or four most important things you now know about the U.S. Congress? Write a list of those things. (4) Do you now have some questions you still wonder about? Write them down. Later we'll share your ideas in pairs and then use a Whip Around to sample the whole group's ideas.

• *Option 2: Update the lists as the unit proceeds.* Gradually the lists could be revised and augmented so that, at the end of the unit, they represent what is then known by the class and what is now of interest to at least some class members. One 4th grade teacher asked a committee to reproduce the original two lists and the final two lists and then invited students to take them home, to show families the kinds of learnings that occurred.

• *Option 3: Turn the lists into an individual or group learning activity.* We could have students with overlapping interests get together and study further, using some form of cooperative learning or, in the words of Sharan and Sharan (1989/1990), using the "group investigation model." Or students could design individual study projects. (For possible strategies, see Chapters 17 and 18.) Here is one teacher's approach:

> I'd like you to design your own study now, based on what interests you. Although you could work alone, I'd rather you work with one or two others. I prefer that no group have more than three people because it is hard to keep active and involved when there are four or more people in one group. Let's see if we have any common interests. Who can say something they would like to investigate? Speak up if you have an idea, and then we'll see who might be interested in that same general idea.

Alternatively, we could develop a chart on which students sign up for topics. Or we could form new groups, each of which would develop a topic. An example:

> I'd like you to get into trios now, sitting with people with whom you have not worked recently. Get to know some new friends better . . . Now, before I tell you about deadlines and what product I'd like each group to produce, I'd like you to talk over some possibilities for your group investigation. What might be fun or important to do or learn more about?

 ## Strategy 12-3: Make a Prediction

Purpose: To motivate student interest in a topic and to exercise students' ability to think ahead.
Description: Asking students to make predictions.

We might ask students to predict any number of things: the best way to solve a new math problem; what the chapter is about; how the film will end; what Edison did when he kept failing; what happened because the United States dropped atomic bombs on Japan. We can then expect that if we taught something connected to the prediction, students would be fairly motivated to see how prophetic they were.

We can also ask students to make predictions as a way of summarizing lessons or seeking applications from lessons we taught, as in these examples:

> We talked about several ways of . . . [increasing awareness of world events, insulating old homes, publishing a class newsletter, and so on]. Which would you say has the best chance of working? Next best chance? Please list the ways we discussed in the order of your personal preference.
>
> Consider what might happen if . . . [the UN had the world's strongest military force, no candy were allowed in school, we all wrote our personal letters in poetry, and so on]. List the possible consequences of such an act. Then number them in order, from the one that is most likely to occur to the one that is least likely to occur. Finally, star the two consequences you personally would most like to occur, even if they are not very likely.

It is often useful to ask students to explain their reasoning: What led you to predict that? What information supports your prediction? How certain are you?

Strategy 12-4: Challenge Opener

Purpose: To motivate student interest in a reading or presentation.
Description: Posing a problem that generates many student questions, confusions, or frustrations and only then presenting the information we want students to learn.

Too often people give us answers when we don't have questions. When that happens in school, the result is low levels of attentiveness. One antidote is to challenge students with a problem or question that leaves them with questions, confusions, perhaps even frustrations, and only then presenting the information we want them to consider. Some examples:

• A teacher asked each student to rank three proposed causes of the Civil War in terms of importance. She tallied the votes on the board. She then had students read a chapter that explained that a different, fourth cause was really the most important. "That led to delightful discussion," reports the teacher. "The students seemed to enjoy being surprised."

• A teacher had pairs of students puzzling over the best way to convert inches to centimeters. All the students then shared their ideas. The teacher then explained one simple way to do it.

• A teacher asked students to list the foods they usually eat. For homework, she then challenged them to find a way to judge the adequacy of their diets. The next day the class discussed their various suggestions. Only then did she offer standard criteria for assessing one's diet.

Strategy 12-5: Experience Before Concept

Purpose: To produce learnings in a context that enhances understanding.
Description: Giving students a meaningful experience of a concept before discussing it abstractly.

A teacher once announced that students with blue eyes in the class would thereafter get special privileges: they could sit in the best seats, go to lunch before everyone else, run all the errands. Brown-eyed students would get no such privileges, said the teacher. And for several hours the teacher did, in fact, follow that rule.

After students experienced the dramatic, often distressing reality of living as superior and inferior citizens, the teacher announced it was all an experiment and then led a discussion of the experience. What, she asked, can that experiment teach us about discrimination, prejudice, and the effect of group labels? The students leaped into the discussion with passion. They were deeply moved and involved in learning profound lessons.

The teacher's approach is a striking example of the strategy Experience Before Concept. The strategy involves giving students an experience before talking about it abstractly. Here are more examples:

• A social studies teacher tells a story about George Washington with which students can emotionally identify. The teacher then talks about Washington's problems in more general terms.

• A teacher asks students to pick an issue they have strong feelings about and to write a letter about it to an official. That leads to a lesson on letter writing form and style.

• A teacher tells some students to pretend to be Southern whites before the Civil War; she tells others to pretend to be Southern blacks, Northern whites, and Northern blacks. She asks the students to debate what should be done about the

Few things help an individual more than to place responsibility upon him, and to let him know that you trust him.

—Booker T. Washington

increased tensions in the country during the prewar years. And only then does she present details about what actually happened.

• Students role-play various communication problems: a person who frequently interrupts, a person who obviously is not listening to someone speaking, a person without any empathy for someone who is suffering. The class then role-plays and practices more effective communication skills.

• A teacher asks some students to play the role of prisoners and others to play the role of prison guards and to act out several daily prison routines. A discussion follows on the role of punishment in society and on prison reform.

What is good about helping students experience a concept before talking about it abstractly?

• It naturally draws students into a topic, making learning more interesting.
• It leads to richer, more complete understandings and more lasting learnings.
• It meets the needs of students who learn better from emotional or concrete experiences than they do from abstractions.
• It counteracts feelings that school is irrelevant. It makes schooling real (Dewey, 1938).

Note that many of the Discovery Lesson examples (Strategy 14-1) can also be adapted to begin a lesson in this style. A related strategy for ending a lesson, Application Projects (Strategy 18-2), asks students to apply a concept *after* they have learned about it.

Strategy 12-6: Clear Learning Target

Purpose: To heighten student motivation and increase self-responsibility for learning.
Description: Providing a clear learning target for students.

Motivation is often highest when students know exactly what they want to accomplish. It's valuable, therefore, to give students a clear learning target. Do we, for example, want all students to do the best they can with the next unit? That could be one of the prime targets. Do we want them to understand certain concepts and definitions? Or aim to get a high score on a final test? Or cooperate effectively in small-group work? Or produce papers that will make us, each student, and each student's parents proud? These are questions worth taking time to think through.

It is often unwise, however, to announce detailed, specific objectives for a unit. Research shows that doing so often causes students to focus narrowly, as in learning just for the test, and they consequently end up learning less than they would if they had engaged in lessons with more general goals in mind (Fraser, Walberg, Welch, & Hattie, 1987; Walberg, 1999). Some examples of more general goal statements:

- I'd like you to understand what caused the Revolutionary War well enough to be able to explain it either orally or in writing.
- Your goal is to write a report comparing the use of active and passive verbs.
- Our aim is to master the use of the drill press.

In terms of motivation, it's especially useful for students themselves to choose their targets. Consider the following possibilities:

- *Ask students to discuss what might be of interest to them in the general area being studied.* Perhaps ask individuals to write endings to such sentence stems as these: *I'd especially like to know . . . , I want to be able to . . . , I'm curious about . . . , I wonder why . . .* In one 4th grade class, for example, for a unit on the human body, the teacher explained that her goal was for students to understand how each of the main organs works individually, as well as how the organs work together as a system. Based on these broad goals, one student wrote: "*I want to know more about* the kidneys and how they work. My grandpa is having a kidney replaced soon. *I know that* the heart pumps blood through the body, but *I want to know* how a heart attack happens. *I want to know if* the intestines are really four miles long" (from Marzano, Pickering, & Pollock, 2001, p. 95).
- *Pose several questions about a general topic.* You might say something like, "Although I want you all to be able to answer all questions, some of you may want to become expert in a few. Or you may have some other questions that are especially interesting to you. List those questions now." Students might then share questions, and if they hear new questions that interest them, they might add those to individual lists.
- *Outline a general area or skill along with several levels of accomplishment, from minimal to expert.* You might ask individuals to choose a level of accomplishment each is willing to aim for.
- *Help students identify skill targets for the unit, as well as learning targets.* They might, for instance, increase their ability to listen to others, practice a new note-taking procedure, do a longer or neater report, or extend their persistence, their ability to work through boredom or difficulty.

I was successful because you believed in me.

—Ulysses S. Grant (to Abraham Lincoln)

Strategy 12-7: Specific Levels of Excellence

Purpose: To communicate teaching goals clearly and provide a means of giving students feedback on performance.

Description: Before giving an assignment, reviewing with students a written rubric with characteristics of good and poor work.

To help students understand exactly what is required to reach certain levels of achievement, we might announce that written work will be judged according to a rubric like the one shown in Figure 9. We recommend presenting such a rubric before students begin, so they know more precisely what their goal should be.

It is also useful to give written samples of work at various levels of excellence, to help students grasp the meaning of the rubric's elements. When such a procedure is used, students' first efforts tend to be better. Furthermore, when feedback on their work is based on a rubric, students learn more from their mistakes than when work is merely graded *A*, *B*, *C*, and so on (Crooks, 1988; Wilburn & Felps, 1983). This procedure has an even greater effect when students practice using rubrics to judge their own work and that of others.

Figure 9
Rubric for a Written Assignment

Criteria	Levels of Achievement		
	3	2	1
Mechanics	Free of grammar and spelling errors	One or two minor errors	Three or more errors
Clarity	Very clear to the reader	Careful reading required	Difficult to understand
Quality of expression	Language artistic or eloquent	Interesting to read	Not at all interesting

13

Explaining and Lecturing Effectively

You may have noticed that it's possible for someone to explain something to you without you understanding much at all. That is especially likely to happen when the explanation is in the form of an extended lecture, for then you may be wondering about points C and D while the speaker has moved to points K and L, until you finally give up. Yet when we teach we must often explain things at length. How can we maximize the likelihood that such a presentation will be productive? This chapter offers some practical suggestions. The first three strategies are recommended for first consideration.

 ## Strategy 13-1: Attentive Lecture

Purpose: To keep all students attentive in lectures.
Description: Watching students while lecturing and changing either content or procedure before attention slips.

Some educators would eliminate lectures. Lectures, they note, restrict learning to a passive process. We disagree. We have known teachers whose lectures keep students actively involved for long periods of time. Most of us, unfortunately, cannot do that. If we talk too long, some students begin to tune out. However, almost all of us can lecture well enough for short periods. The key to success is to make all lectures *attentive* lectures, that is, lectures that stop as soon as student attention begins to drift. How can this be done? No single formula applies, but there are a number of options.

Lecture Options

• *The micro-lecture.* One option, recommended by our colleague Neil Rothman, is to lecture only in portions students are likely to find easy to handle.

Perhaps speak for two to five minutes and then, before moving on, pause to give students a brief opportunity to digest information. During the pause, perhaps ask students to write a summary of what they heard, or to write about how they would connect what they heard to concepts or issues presented earlier. Or ask students to apply the information to a problem or question, or to draw something to illustrate what they heard. If appropriate, you could then move on and offer another micro-lecture. After a series of such experiences, it's often valuable to invite students to write Outcome Sentences (Strategy 21-1) and then to share those sentences in a Whip Around, Pass Option (Strategy 16-4).

• *The write-share insert.* When you sense that students are beginning to squirm and lose focus during a lecture, you might insert a write-share element into the proceedings. First, ask students to make notes on what they heard so far: "Perhaps write the main points, or your questions, or your personal reactions." When you see that one or two are finished making notes, to keep the pace brisk, say, "One moment more." Then ask all students to sit with a partner and share thoughts. While they do that, consider what might be the best thing to do next. A discussion is often appropriate. Or you might resume the lecture. And occasionally you may find it best to put the topic aside and come back fresh another time.

• *The quick review and out.* You might just quickly review what was so far covered and tell students the class will pick up the material another time. Or you might ask a few students to restate one of the points they remember. Or you might say, "Before we turn to something new, please take a moment and review for yourself what we covered, perhaps noting questions that remain for you."

• *The mind-settling pause.* For very young children, those for whom writing is not possible or easy, you might say, "When I pause, you may write or draw something, if you like, or just sit quietly and see what goes on in your mind as you think back over what I said. Think it over for yourself." You might then resume speaking, or move on, as soon as you sense students are no longer thinking about what you said.

• *The lecture with feeling.* Abstractions, names, and dates touch people only slightly and slip from memory easily. In contrast, gripping stories, stunning images, and emotional events touch them deeply and linger longer. Therefore, if you can center lecture material around stories, images, and events—or at least include them—students are more likely to grasp and recall your material.

More Tips and Reminders for Using Attentive Lecture

• *Start with questions that get students wondering.* Perhaps ask students to write notes about their preliminary thinking. Your lecture then might answer the questions students are wondering about.

In teaching the greatest sin is to be boring.

—*J. F. Herbart*

- *Start with an overview statement.* For example, a physical education teacher might say, "Today I'll outline the main rules of basketball. Then I'll demonstrate a violation of each rule and ask you to identify the rule broken." An overview helps students see the whole of a lesson. Otherwise some tend to see each statement as a disconnected idea.

- *Use handouts such as a printed list of key words, principles, or definitions.* Or perhaps distribute a printed outline for students to fill in as you proceed.

- *Ask a series of questions that provoke students' thinking and gradually lead them to discover new understandings.*

- *End with an activity that gets students using the material presented.* Possibilities include summarizing the material, applying it, explaining it to a partner, or answering questions about it. Use whatever works to avoid boring students. Students enjoy boredom no more than we do.

The moral behind this strategy is straightforward: Lecture only as long as attention is high. Quit speaking when you sense student attention is slipping. Do something else.

Strategy 13-2: Presentation for Task

Purpose: To encourage purposeful listening.
Description: Assigning a task and then presenting the information needed to complete it.

If you want to clean mildew from inside a wall, you're likely to read up on the topic or ask around and try to understand what is involved. If, on the other hand, you had no mildew problem and someone offered you information about mildew and how to handle it, you'd very likely not pay much attention. The point: If we want students to pay attention, it's wise to give them a problem before we provide information. Consider the following lesson introductions:

Weaker: I'm now going to talk about the events leading up to the Emancipation Proclamation.

Stronger: Your task is to prepare a summary of the events leading up to the Emancipation Proclamation and post it on the side wall. I'm now going to talk about those events a bit.

Weaker: We'll now discuss the function of plant cells.

Stronger: Working in pairs, your job will be to create some kind of visual that shows the function of plant cells and turn it in to me before lunch. I'm now going to tell you more about plant cells.

Some tasks we might assign before presenting information:

- Create a list of questions and answers about the material.
- Make a graphic organizer.
- Write a list of possible applications or uses of material covered.
- Categorize elements in a way that makes sense.
- Write a song about the material.
- Prepare a skit based on the material.
- Prepare a chart of good and poor examples, or right and wrong uses.
- Prepare a cartoon.
- Plan a poster or model.
- Write a newspaper ad or news story or a feature story.
- Make up a story or write a poem that is inspired by the material.

Here is an example of a lesson using the Presentation for Task strategy:

1. *Motivational Question/Question, All Write (Strategies 12-1 and 16-3), 1 minute.* Pose a question such as "How might we define capitalism?" Then ask students to write some notes about their ideas.

2. *Brainstorming/Risk Language (Strategies 19-9 and 4-3), 3–5 minutes.* Write a few of the students' ideas on the board. "Who's willing to risk giving us one idea?"

3. *Voting Questions (Strategy 9-3), 1–2 minutes.* After six to eight items have been listed, point to each idea and say, for example, "How many think this one should be an important part of the definition?" As the class votes on each idea, assess the number of hands raised and put an L, H, or S next to the idea, depending on whether the proportion of students raising their hands was large, about half, or small.

4. *Presentation for Task (Strategy 13-2), 5–10 minutes.* Lead into the lecture by saying something such as this: "Let me now tell you some things about capitalism. Take notes as I go along, because afterward I'll ask you to use what I say and what is on the board to write your own more complete definition on a card, sign your name, and turn it in to me."

Strategy 13-3: Explanation Back-off

Purpose: To avoid turning off students who are having trouble understanding an explanation.

Description: When continuing an explanation would turn off more students than it would help, backing off and doing something else.

> The world could use more vision and less television.
>
> —*Anonymous*

Imagine the scene: A teacher has explained a concept twice already. Some students still just don't get it. Yet other students understand very well and are starting to get restless, ready for something else. The teacher pauses, wondering how she could explain that concept better, or at least differently, and then it occurs to her: Maybe it would be better to stop explaining.

Good thought, we'd say. The tendency is to keep explaining too long, which has two hazards: (1) boring those students who must sit and wait while we keep at it, and (2) raising the level of confusion or anxiety of those students who, for one reason or another, are not then understanding, making it even harder for them to grasp it.

Some options for handling such situations:

• Pair up all students, aiming to ensure that those who do not understand sit with someone who has at least some understanding. (Perhaps say, "All those who would like more help please pick someone to sit with who might help you understand better. Now the rest of you pair up any way you like.") Then ask all students to discuss the concept or to work on sample problems.

• Turn to another topic and make a mental note to do something later to help the students who don't understand (perhaps by a mode other than direct instruction from you, such as through learning materials, peer instruction, computers, or a homework assignment).

• Divide the class into two groups, giving those who understand something else to do (reading, computer work, small-group work, a challenge question) while you keep working with those who don't understand.

• Embed the concept in future whole-class lessons, as in your review statements or in Review Tests (Strategy 11-1), so the concept is touched on at least briefly again—perhaps at a time when those who didn't understand earlier are more ready and able to learn it.

• At another time, teach the concept to the class as if you never taught it before. The freshness will keep those who already understand involved—it might even make them feel smart—and will give those who didn't understand earlier a new opportunity to get it.

Strategy 13-4: Visual Aids and Graphic Organizers

Purpose: To help students keep their attention focused.
Description: Using visual aids and graphic organizers to enhance presentations.

When you are dissatisfied and would like to go back to youth, think of Algebra.
—*Will Rogers*

We can use visual aids during presentations in several ways. Some suggestions:

• Outline key points, perhaps using an overhead projector and revealing the points one at a time as you speak, or simply by writing key phrases on the board as you go along.

• Give students handouts with outlines, perhaps with space for them to make notes as you explain.

• Display large charts, perhaps filling in key information as you speak.

• Show relevant graphs, photos, or even physical objects. Perhaps even pass such items around the class.

Graphic organizers can be especially useful. We might even introduce graphic organizers to the class and later ask students to use them to organize information for themselves. Here, a teacher introduces two basic graphic organizers to her class:

Graphic organizers are one way to show the relationship between wholes and parts. [Teacher points to Figure 10.] Can anyone identify one of the relationships this graphic organizer is showing?

Some graphic organizers show more complex relationships, like this one. [Teacher points to Figure 11.] Who can guess what some part of this graphic organizer is showing?

Figure 10
Concept Pattern Organizer

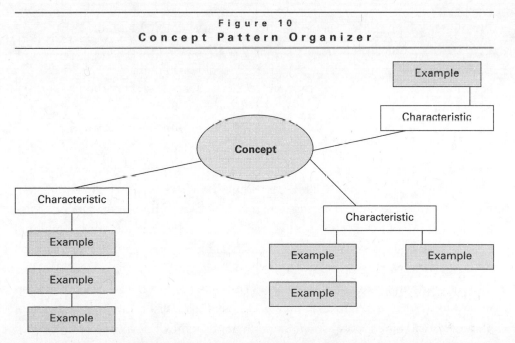

From Marzano, Pickering, and Pollock, 2001, p. 78. Copyright 2001 by McREL. Reprinted with permission.

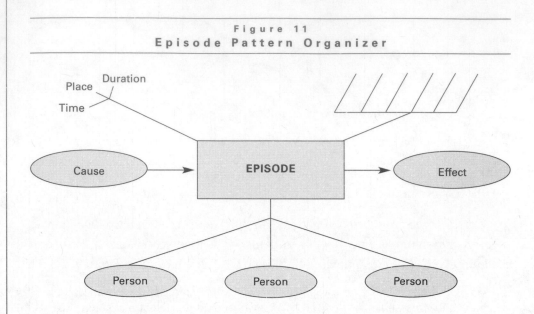

Figure 11
Episode Pattern Organizer

From Marzano, Pickering, and Pollock, 2001, p. 77. Copyright 2001 by McREL. Reprinted with permission.

Strategy 13-5: Lingering Board Notes

Purpose: To help students keep perspective on the whole of a topic.
Description: Not erasing important board notes.

Stigler and Hiebert (1999) report that teachers in Japanese classrooms typically write concepts and examples on the board and then, as they move ahead in their lessons, do not erase what was written but rather write new notes in different places. They often start at the left side of the board and then keep adding notes, moving left to right. Earlier notes then linger in full view for students. In contrast, teachers in the United States often erase what they wrote on the board earlier, perhaps to keep student focus on the new notes. Many teachers in the United States also use overhead projectors, which requires them to remove earlier material before showing new material. Teachers in Japan rarely use overhead projectors.

Is this a trivial difference? We think not. Leaving all notes visible serves at least three important purposes. First, it allows students to scan back and refresh their memories of earlier points they may have lost; thus a visual summary of sorts is always available for students to look at. Second, it provides a way for us to offer summaries at the end of lessons. We can scan the notes as we review the lesson, and students can do the same, thereby getting both an oral and a visual review—something especially valuable for the visual learners. And third, allowing board notes to remain throughout a lesson often adds coherence to lessons. It makes it less likely that students will experience a lesson as a set of disconnected elements. It makes the whole of the lesson easier to grasp.

We recommend, then, that you avoid erasing board notes unless they are trivial. Likewise we recommend not using overhead projectors, other than for pictures and other visuals not easily presented otherwise. A practical option, when board space is limited, is to make notes on large sheets of newsprint. When full, a sheet can then be posted on the side of the room. If sheets contain basic information, you might well leave them posted for multiple days so they can serve as long-range reminders to students. Such sheets also help students who were absent to catch up on material missed.

Strategy 13-6: Concept Charts

Purpose: To keep key concepts fresh and alive.
Description: Creating and maintaining a classroom chart of important concepts studied.

Imagine walking into a classroom and seeing this alert on the wall:

> Equality of opportunity
> Loyalty
> Kindness
> Self-control of impulses
> Integrity
> Striving and accepting
> Candor
> Supportive behavior

You ask about it, and the teacher explains that it's something called a Concept Chart. "Whenever an important idea comes up in class, I write it on the chart. It stays posted sometimes for months," the teacher says. "I refer back to those ideas from time to time, when they naturally come up in class. I sometimes include important names, even symbols I want students to remember. It helps me keep key ideas fresh and active."

You should be careful around those younger than you. It is surprising how much of an impact a word or action can make on them.

—*Sarah, age 12*

We can use Concept Charts to post many different kinds of material, including the following:

- Key formulas covered in class so far
- Special vocabulary words
- Historical events of note
- Authors studied
- Phrases that illustrate correct language usage
- Tricky spelling words

Concept Charts provide handy reminders for everyone and facilitate learning in layers, not lumps (D'Arcangelo, 2000). This strategy works especially well with visual learners.

Strategy 13-7: Note-Taking Template

Purpose: To keep students engaged in the content as it is presented.
Description: Using a sheet of paper to help focus, organize, and engage awareness during a lesson.

A Note-Taking Template is a simple device. One teacher introduced such a template as she began a class discussion about the Reformation. She asked her students to take out a sheet of paper and fold it in half vertically. On the left side of the fold, the students were to write or draw something that they already knew about the Reformation. "If you do not know anything about this topic, perhaps write one or two things you'd like know about it," the teacher suggested. After giving the class a few moments, she asked if any students would like to share one thing they wrote. She then told the students that she was going to share information with them. "If you hear something that you find interesting, make a note on the right side of your fold. Or perhaps you might think of a question and jot that down. Feel free to write as many things as you like."

At the end of her presentation, the teacher asked the students to take a minute to look over their notes. "As you do so, write a *U* next to those points that you are sure you understand," she said. Then, after a moment or two, she continued. "Now look only at the points that have been marked with a *U*. From those, choose three you would be able to explain to another person." She concluded by asking the students to find a partner and take turns explaining the three points that they had just chosen.

As that example illustrates, the Note-Taking Template strategy often involves four steps:

1. *Preparing the paper.* The key to this part is that everyone can do it. General awareness is engaged by a nonintellectual task. We might ask students to fold their papers vertically, horizontally, or in three parts. Or we might ask students to draw a circle, labeling the area inside the circle "old information" and the area outside the circle "new information."

2. *Stating the known and the unknown.* Awareness is engaged as students recall and make notes about what they know or what they want to know about the topic. This prepares students to listen more thoughtfully to the discussion ahead.

3. *Recording new information.* As we present information, students are asked to make notes in certain places on the paper. We might have places for key facts, questions, Outcome Sentences (Strategy 21-1), or anything students find interesting. Or we can have students record information in pairs—for example, writing spelling words on the left, definitions on the right; or historical names on the left, identification information on the right.

4. *Processing information.* Students review what they have written and, perhaps, choose something to share. Pairs might then work together to share and teach each other what was learned.

Strategy 13-8: Signal for the Big Picture

Purpose: To help students distinguish a general principle from its supporting details.

Description: Doing something special to call students' attention to a big idea or a general principle.

Many students have difficulty distinguishing the forest from the trees, the general idea from the subsidiary facts. They get lost in the details. They fail to appreciate the main purpose or the core meaning. Using a special visual signal when speaking about the big picture can help. One such signal, which we learned from educational leader Terri Bianco, is to gesture as if you are outlining a picture frame around your head, with your face in the middle. We explain to students that the gesture signals that we are now talking about the big picture, a particularly noteworthy idea. The big picture for this book, for example, concerns bringing out the best in all students. Each of the strategies is but an example of a practical way to do that.

We are so accustomed to wearing a disguise before others that eventually we are unable to recognize ourselves.

—La Rochefoucauld

We might even bring into the classroom an empty picture frame that will fit around a face and use it the first time we offer a big-picture idea. Then afterward, for convenience, we simply use the square-around-the-head gesture.

As noted by Thornburg (2002), the ability to view things in context has become increasingly important in today's world, and this strategy may help students develop that ability.

Strategy 13-9: Finger Feedback

Purpose: To help prepare and conduct high-involvement lectures.

Description: Preparing lectures that include questions to which students respond by holding up fingers.

Imagine a teacher speaking to the class:

> Today I'd like to teach you a new way of participating in lectures. I will present material as usual, doing it as interestingly as I can. But every once in a while I'll pose a question. I'd like you to answer by holding up fingers. For example, I might say, "True or false: I'm talking now about a new way of participating in lectures." If you think that is true, when I say "Go," hold up one finger. If false, hold up two fingers. Go!

The teacher pauses and looks around the room, and then congratulates the students for responding correctly. She tells them that when she asks a true/false question, one finger will always indicate that they think it's true, two fingers will always indicate that they think it's false.

She asks the students to try another true/false question: "This is a procedure that I'll sometimes use during lectures. Go!" After looking over the raised fingers, she continues:

> Good again. You're getting the idea. I might also ask an opinion question, perhaps in the form of "agree" or "disagree." In that case, one finger will indicate agree; two fingers, disagree. Try this one. Agree or disagree: I want only those who are sure of their answer to raise fingers. Go!

The teacher pauses to observe raised fingers before continuing:

> Disagree is correct. I want everyone to raise fingers after I say "Go" even if you are not absolutely certain. It's OK to make mistakes while you're learning. When everyone raises fingers, I can tell how well I am delivering the material I want you to understand. By participating in this way, I'm hoping you will all stay actively involved in the lecture and end up learning more.
>
> Try this. True or false: There is no need to listen carefully. You can wait until others raise fingers, look around, and then put up the number of fingers most of the others show. Go!

The trouble with facts is that there are so many of them.

—*Samuel Crothers*

The teacher scans the room and tells the students, "The two-finger people are right. It's smarter to stay involved and think for yourself and not waste your opportunities to learn."

The teacher then explains a slightly more complicated version of the strategy, in which she gives three choices. For example, in a discussion about Abraham Lincoln's childhood, students could be told to raise one finger if they think he was born in New York, two fingers for Kentucky, and three fingers for Illinois. She continues:

> There may sometimes be more than one answer to a question I ask. In that case use both hands, one for each correct answer. Here is a question like that. What is Lincoln famous for? One, the Gettysburg Address; two, handling the War of 1812; three, ending slavery. Go!

The teacher congratulates those students who held up one finger on one hand and three fingers on the other hand. Then she asks how many students had correct answers for all the "finger tests" and praises them for a job well done.

The Finger Feedback strategy serves two key purposes: (1) it helps keep all students actively involved in lectures, and (2) it provides useful feedback on how material is being received, which helps us make adjustments as we go.

Some suggestions for getting the most out of this strategy:

• Prepare questions in advance and build presentations around them, at least at the outset, until the process becomes second nature to you.

• If necessary, remind students that you want all to participate so you know how well they are understanding the material.

• To add suspense, ask questions about what students predict will happen. For example, "One, you predict the water will boil; two, you predict it will not." "One, you predict the Supreme Court voted for it; two, against it." "One, you predict the answer will be more than six; two, you predict it will be less than six."

• Ask students to keep score of how many times they were correct. You can then ask those who answered all—or perhaps all but one—correctly to stand "so we can all give ourselves a hand for today's good work." Or you might have daily or weekly contests among teams or rows.

• Place questions on an overhead transparency or a computer and reveal them one at a time, a procedure that helps visual students grasp the procedure.

• Ask the same question more than once, perhaps to reinforce an important point.

▲ **TEACHER COMMENT**

When I prepare for a class now, I don't think so much about what to tell students as I do about what I am going to ask them to do. What am I going to encourage to have happen in their heads—that is what matters. And I've found that it fundamentally changes how I teach.

—*Chris Jernstedt, Dartmouth College Professor*

Strategy 13-10: Partner Restatement

Purpose: To insert active-learning episodes into long presentations.

Description: Pausing during a presentation and asking students to pair up and restate points that were made.

To use Partner Restatement, pause during a presentation and instruct students to turn to a person nearby and restate, in their own words, the points last made. If time remains, students might also exchange thoughts about those points. A minute or two usually is all that is needed. To keep the pace moving quickly, as soon as most students have had a turn to speak, simply say, "Just finish the sentence you're on" and quickly resume your presentation.

Strategy 13-11: Checklist for Effective Lectures

Purpose: To prepare engaging lectures.

Description: When planning lectures, keeping in mind the importance of (1) generating initial interest, (2) maintaining student engagement, and (3) helping students construct learnings.

Do you want your lectures to be winners? Take the time to ensure that you can satisfactorily answer these three questions:

1. *How will I generate and focus students' attention?* It might be enough simply to say, "I'd like today to continue our discussion of Henry James." But you can probably do better. You may need to start with a question that stimulates curiosity, or a challenge that prods students to recall what they already know. Or you might use one or more of the motivation strategies in Chapter 12. In any case, your first task is finding a way to catch and focus the attention of students.

2. *How will I maintain student engagement?* You do not want students' initial interest to soon devolve into dreaming and doodling. To ensure that doesn't happen, plan a way to keep students actively engaged. You might, for example, frequently ask students to write something about what you just said, to talk to a partner about it, or to invent an example of it. Rarely is it sufficient to occasionally say "Any questions?" Contrast the "Any questions" approach with a teacher who points to a label on a diagram of the parts of a plant cell and says, "This part is the vacuole. Say that word aloud with me, class: *vacuole.* Once again, *vacuole.* Now write the word a time or two on scrap paper, to get more familiar with it. And

now turn to a partner and take turns saying aloud all the parts of the plant cell we've identified so far." It's those kinds of specific directions that put the most life in lectures. For more suggestions, see the strategies in this chapter and two other strategies, Choral Work and Voting Questions to Assess Understanding (Strategies 11-2 and 16-6).

3. *How will I conclude the presentation?* Winning lectures feel satisfying to students. Students take something from them. The information presented makes sense to them, is meaningful, is useful, and is clearly part of a larger whole. To maximize the likelihood that students find meaning in your lectures, you might conclude with Sharing Pairs; Practice Pairs; Whip Around, Pass Option; Brainstorm/ Sort; Summarizing; or Outcome Sentences (Strategies 7-1, 7-4, 16-4, 16-8, 19-6, 21-1). Or you might have your lectures be a jumping-off point for an Independent Learning Assignment, a Mini-task, or Project Work (Strategies 6-4, 17-2, 18-1). It's often valuable to find some way for students to put the content presented to some use, conceptually or practically. What, after all, would be the point of the lecture if they didn't?

Education should include knowledge of what to do with it.

—*Anonymous*

14 Providing Discovery-Type Experiences

One of the best ways to inspire active learning is to enlist puzzlement, suspense, and the human need to know how things turn out. You can do so by means of discovery-type lessons. This chapter presents five practical strategies for facilitating discovery. Field tests indicate that the first four deserve first attention. Relevant, too, are the strategies in Chapter 18 (on student projects) and in Chapter 19 (on generating higher-level thinking).

 ## Strategy 14-1: Discovery Lesson

Purpose: To generate a curiosity that will motivate serious study.
Description: Posing a problem and allowing students to puzzle on it before providing an answer.

Here is a question: Why would you guess we label the following four lessons "discovery lessons"?

Science. The teacher has students observe and notice what happens when she adds a certain chemical to water. She does not explain, but asks, "Why do you think the water bubbled as it did? Write some thoughts and then let's talk about it."

Mathematics. The teacher draws several polygons on the board. He asks students to create a way to find the sum of the interior angles on any polygon. Students are told to puzzle on it alone at first. After a bit, the teacher invites students to pair up and work in groups if they like. The teacher then asks for volunteers to explain their proposed solutions. Finally the class votes to see which solutions they judge to be the best. Throughout, the teacher offers no helpful hints or corrections and makes no judgments.

History. The teacher sets up a mock political convention in the classroom. Some students play parts of Northern whites during the Civil War. Some play Southern whites. A few act as black men, some free and some slaves. No one acts as a woman. The convention's purpose is to debate what is to be done about slavery. The teacher's aim is to help students understand those times.

Art. The teacher gives students a new painting tool and asks them to experiment and see what they can do with it.

Why label these "discovery lessons"? Clearly, the teacher does not start off by giving information. Rather, lessons begin by getting students to think things through for themselves. When we begin by stimulating thinking that way, student energy and awareness are almost always higher than when we begin by presenting information.

The basic sequence is this: Pose a question or problem. Provide time for students to ponder on their own or, perhaps, with one or two others. Then provide an answer, or, for even more thinking and deeper understanding, guide students until they can resolve the issue for themselves (Piaget, 1970).

Action Flow Lesson 1 in Chapter 3 illustrates a Discovery Lesson, as do the science, math, and art lessons described above. As for the history teacher discussing the Civil War, that is a more complex version of a Discovery Lesson, closer to what might be called a simulation. Here are more examples, in this case examples of how teachers changed from a presentation approach to a discovery approach:

Before: There are several guidelines for identifying effective poetry. First . . .
After: Make a note of what you think makes for good poetry.

Before: There are three basic types of moths . . .
After: From what we've discussed about moths, how many different
             types would you say there are?

Before: Jefferson wrote this about democracy . . .
After: Make some notes about what you think defines a democracy.

Before: Let me show you how to add fractions like these . . .
After: See if you can invent a method for adding fractions like these,
             working alone or, if you prefer, in pairs.

Interestingly, the typical mathematics lesson in Japan and China has students discovering the day's concept or skill. In contrast, the typical math lesson in the United States starts with teachers explaining a concept or skill (Stigler & Hiebert, 1999). The difference might help explain the superior test scores of the Japanese and Chinese students.

Life is like playing a violin in public and learning the instrument as one goes on.

—*Samuel Butler*

Strategy 14-2: Underexplain and Learning Pairs

Purpose: To maximize thoughtful involvement and minimize student frustration.
Description: Explaining material briefly, so only some students understand it, then asking pairs to work together to help each other more fully understand.

We can often generate high involvement by doing a minimum of explaining. Imagine the following math lesson:

1. *Whole class.* The teacher begins by saying, "To find 40 percent of a number, we can simply multiply the number by .40. For example, 40 percent of 200 could be done this way." The teacher then writes on the board:

$$\begin{array}{r} 200 \\ \times\ .40 \\ \hline 80.00 \end{array}$$

> The secret of education is respecting the pupil.
> —Ralph Waldo Emerson

2. *Working alone.* The teacher continues by asking students to try a similar problem by themselves: "See what you think 40 percent of 120 would be."

3. *Whole class and Learning Pairs.* "How many got *48*?" the teacher asks. She tells the students that while they were working on the problem, she worked it on the board. "How many did it somewhat like I did? How many found another way to get *48*?" She avoids a long discussion, to keep a quick pace. She then writes three more problems on the board and asks the students to first work on them alone, then with a partner. "Compare answers and help each other understand," she tells them. "If both of you understand, try creating a new problem for each other—maybe a harder one. Go!" As the students begin to work, the teacher also starts working the problems on the board, so anyone can get help whenever it's needed.

The teacher scans students' work, answering most questions by saying "Ask another pair for help." When about half the pairs seem finished, she announces, "Just a few more seconds." To maintain a pace that keeps everyone involved, she does not wait for everyone to finish. She uses later lessons for necessary reteaching and review.

4. *Whole class and Learning Pairs.* The teacher winds down the lesson by noting that most of the students produced something similar to her examples. Then she writes three somewhat more difficult problems on the board, to advance student practice a bit further. "Again, work these problems alone and then compare

with your partner. If you both understand, you might challenge each other with something more difficult. Or write out a word problem I can use someday and put it on my desk. Go!"

Note that the teacher in this example underexplained the calculation procedure. Many teachers do the opposite. They overexplain. They might explain something, ask "Any questions?" and then explain again. Or they might notice some students obviously puzzled and then explain again or explain the procedure in another way. After two or three such explanations, three results are likely:

• Boredom sets in for students who understood the first explanation or who understood before the lesson even began. Energy slumps. Awareness dulls.

• Boredom sets in for the students who cannot concentrate on one topic too long, some of whom are known as "slow" students.

• Boredom sets in for students who do not learn well from any teacher explanation, the ones who need to discover things for themselves, often from hands-on experiences.

To avoid such outcomes, this teacher used an underexplain approach and put students into pairs to work it out together, or to teach each other, or to check each other's ideas and correctness. With this strategy, after students work alone a bit, we say something like, "Take your time, but whenever you feel ready, find a partner and share your thinking." Or if pairs are already set, "Whenever you see that you and your partner are both finished, get together and share your thinking."

Guidelines for Effective Use

• *Explain until only about half the students understand.* Then put students into pairs to check and teach each other, or to create new problems for each other. Leave students in these pairs for a fairly brief time—not so long that confused students feel stuck in their confusion and students who understand feel bored. Then bring the class together and repeat the cycle, raising the level of challenge if students are ready for that.

• *Don't prod students who are slow to get started.* It's usually counterproductive in the long run. Instead, move the lesson along quickly and give enough easy examples so students can experience success and will naturally want to be involved.

• *Let students select their own partners.* Doing so helps students develop self-responsibility. Help only those students who do not find partners by themselves. But you might also let them work alone or talk to them later, encouraging them

Before I got married, I had six theories about bringing up children. Now I have six children and no theories.

—John Wilmot

to practice more initiative in risking to reach out to others. For each student, consider what would be best in the long run.

- *Adapt discovery-type lessons.* You can apply the Underexplain and Learning Pairs strategy to discovery-type lessons simply by giving a bit of explanation, but not too much. In a math lesson, you might show students two or three correct examples of something and two or three incorrect examples. Then ask students to see if they can write a rule for this and come up with additional pairs of correct and incorrect examples. (This is similar to the concept attainment strategy; see Joyce and Weil, 1991.) In a science lesson, you might demonstrate a scientific principle, such as how a candle flame reacts to insufficient air, and offer a brief explanation. Then ask students to write a useful application of the principle illustrated.

- *Use the power of expectations.* A hidden strength of this strategy flows from the expectations it communicates. The more it is used, the more students will likely appreciate the fact that one responsible adult, the teacher, fully expects them to be able to think and learn on their own and fully expects them to be able to support and help one another. Even if students never need the subject matter acquired, they may well believe more firmly that each of them is a capable, positive person.

An additional example of the Underexplain and Learning Pairs strategy can be found in Action Flow Lesson 3 in Strategy 3-1. Note that this strategy is similar to Arthur Whimbey's (Whimbey & Lochhead, 1986) paired problem solving and Stanley Pogrow's (2004) controlled floundering. See also work on inductive teaching as discussed, for example, by Jerome Bruner (Bruner & Kenny, 1966).

 ## Strategy 14-3: Think Aloud

Purpose: To give students a model of how they might think through a problem and to demonstrate that thinking is not always linear.

Description: Talking aloud while working out a problem so students hear how we think.

Students often misunderstand what is involved in thinking through a problem. Many assume that answers should come quickly and easily. When that does not happen to them, many lose confidence in their ability to think. We can, however, teach students that problem solving is often slow and messy, rarely quick and easy. Perhaps the best way to teach it is to model it. As an example, consider this teacher thinking aloud as she works a problem on the board:

> Let's see here . . . I could divide 6 into the 50. Wait a minute. Would that help me find my answer? What was the problem again? Find one-sixth of 50. Dividing feels right. Let me try and see if I get something that at least looks approximately correct. Now, let's see, 6 goes into 50 . . . hmm . . . 6 times 5 is 30 . . . 6 times 7 is, uh, 42. That will fit. And 6 times 8 is . . . 48, which is more like it. Seems like 6 times 9 is bound to be too much, 48 is just 2 less than 50. So I'll write 8 here, 2 here and . . .

Consider another teacher, who is demonstrating one way to handle a real-life communication problem:

> Now, how am I going to argue with him when I'm really frightened? I'm not sure what will happen. I want to tell him how I feel but . . . I don't know . . . All I know is that I'm scared. What are some phrases I can use? I think I'll make some notes; that might help me keep my mind on this issue. But to start, what is my purpose? My main purpose is . . . [The teacher writes on the board: "Tell him how I really feel."] But I'm not sure. Maybe I'll ask Jean if she has ideas . . . I'd rather forget the whole thing. Yet I want him to know how I feel . . .

The Think Aloud strategy, which some consider a metacognitive strategy, involves talking in ways that reflect real searching, with errors, correction of errors, and whatever else goes on in the mind of someone engaged in thinking. It is an effective way to teach both an intellectual skill, like math problem solving, and the reality that learning is not always tidy and straightforward. This is often reassuring to students who are reluctant to admit that they are often confused and all too ready to avoid thinking altogether. Think Aloud is also valuable in peer teaching, as when one student thinks aloud as she performs a task, showing other students, for example, how to focus a microscope, balance a scale, or use a certain computer program.

▲ TEACHER COMMENT

To show my special ed students how to read a new word, I use the Think Aloud strategy like this: "I know the story is about birds. And this word begins with an R. Maybe it's a kind of bird. Could it be a robin?" I find that with prodding my special ed students can think that way. Perhaps it is just that they cannot figure out how to think that way. After I show them how, they do just fine.

—Bruce Maskow
Special Education Elementary School Teacher

···◆▶ Strategy 14-4: Guided Discovery

Purpose: To involve all students in practicing and mastering subject matter.
Description: Leading students through a set of practices that help them circle in on mastery.

We can explain a process to a student. But it is often more effective to pose questions that, little by little, lead students from easy or familiar examples to a new understanding or an advanced skill. The following are two examples of this strategy in practice, one in language arts and the other in math.

Language Arts. Using Question, All Write (Strategy 16-3), the teacher asks all students to write the plural of *fox*, a plural they already know. As soon as students begin writing, the teacher writes *foxes* on the board, so students can see the correct answer soon after they finish writing. Students check and correct their own work. Discussion is avoided at this point.

The teacher then calls out the next word, another easy word or perhaps one that may be less familiar or that may lead to a new rule for making plurals. Students bend over their desks to write the plural of that word, and when they do so, the teacher writes the correct plural on the board. "If you didn't get this one, don't worry. The next one may follow the same rule," the teacher might say, aiming to reassure students and keep them alert to discovering new understandings.

The process continues at a fairly brisk pace, without extended discussions. The emphasis is on students learning by practicing and observing and thinking. While students are working, the teacher glances about, getting a sense of how well they understand. If understanding is low, the teacher may insert extra explanatory comments or, better yet, strive to make subsequent words easy enough so students do come to understand.

Mathematics. The teacher poses a problem, and all students work at their desks to solve it. While they do so, the teacher works out the problem correctly on the board. Students then check their work. Extended discussions are avoided so as not to bore students who already understand and to keep the lesson focused on learning from practicing. The teacher then poses the next problem, and, as before, correct work is displayed so students can check themselves. The aim is to get students practicing familiar work and then to gradually introduce new work. The teacher might have on hand a list of problems that range from easy to hard, so examples are readily available to lead the students forward. The teacher might even have on hand sheets of problems correctly worked out, either prepared in print large enough to be seen by all or prepared for an overhead projector.

In some cases, students who cannot grasp the correct procedure from the teacher's examples might be told they can ask a friend, or raise a hand for someone who understands to come over and assist them. The teacher might reassure students: "It will take some time and practice for everyone to get this perfectly. I'll try to give examples that show you how to handle key points. Take your time and you will get it." Or the teacher might find it better to shift, temporarily or completely, from this self-checking practice to a strategy that involves more direct

They are able because they think they are able.

—Virgil

instruction, such as Underexplain and Learning Pairs (Strategy 14-2) or Think Aloud (Strategy 14-3).

The Guided Discovery strategy is essentially a method of teaching by discovery, with students led forward in appropriately small steps. As long as students see the strategy as one of learning something new, not one that tests prior learnings, this self-checking practice is naturally motivating. It elicits students' natural desires to understand and do well. Furthermore, it not only teaches subject matter but neatly exercises thinking skills and grows self-responsibility (Feuerstein, 1980).

Strategy 14-5: VAK Attack

Purpose: To engage multiple senses while learning.
Description: Providing visual, auditory, and kinesthetic learning experiences.

If someone offers you driving directions and you're left feeling confused, it may be because you're a nonauditory learner. Oral instructions alone do not do it for you. You need to be able to *visualize* the route, either by seeing a map or imagining the details of the pathway. For you and others like you, verbal explanations often produce little understanding. Far better is a demonstration or an illustration. Better still is a presentation that interweaves illustration and explanation and direct experience (Rose & Nicholl, 1997). This, of course, suggests the wisdom of creating lessons that respect the needs of visual, auditory, and kinesthetic learners, lessons that use what we call the VAK Attack.

Consider how a 1st grade teacher might use this strategy for a math lesson. The teacher writes the problem 4 + 3 on the board and asks for a volunteer to read it aloud. "Thank you, Barry. Now let's all read that problem together, with power," she says, using Strategy 11-4, One Say, All Say. She then continues, "When I see a plus sign, I know that means I'm going to add. How can we put 4 and 3 together? Well, I can count four fingers on one hand and three fingers on the other and see how many I have in all. Let's all do that." Next the teacher draws a set of three circles and a set of four circles and leads the class in counting them aloud. "When we add 4 + 3, the answer is 7. Now let's read our solved problem together." The teacher guides the class through another problem, instructing them each to draw their own picture to help them solve the problem. She then says, "Please form pairs and explain your picture to your partner."

In this way, students are given many opportunities to grasp the skill, by seeing, hearing, and doing. The teacher could easily incorporate the use of manipulatives,

In our differences we grow; in our sameness we connect.

—Virginia Satir

perhaps asking students to count crayons or other objects in the room. Or the teacher could ask students themselves to form groups of seven, then guiding them to form sets of four and three, five and two, and so on.

Here is another way to give students an integrated visual-auditory-kinesthetic (VAK) experience (adapted from Rose & Nicholl, 1997). Assign a reading, telling students that as they read, they should think about how, working with a partner, they might act out something based on that reading. "You can use words in your presentation, maybe simply give a summary, or you can act out a skit without words, pantomime style. Each presentation must be done in a minute or two, so you'll have to make it punchy." Afterward, give students a few minutes to sit in pairs and plan their presentations, using a quick pace so students don't dawdle. Then join three pairs and say, "Each pair will now have about two minutes to stand and make its presentation to the other two pairs. Proceed in any order you choose. Go!"

In this way, students visualize while they are reading and while they plan their presentations with a partner; they have auditory experiences while they plan and, if their skits use words, during the presentations; and they have kinesthetic experiences when they stand and make their presentations.

For a simpler, working-alone VAK Attack, instruct students to choose one of these three options:

• *Visual:* Read and visualize the material as you read it. Perhaps draw it.

• *Auditory:* Create questions and answers from the reading and say the questions and answers aloud to yourself. Perhaps speak aloud with feeling.

• *Kinesthetic:* Write the major points on index cards and arrange them in some way useful to you. Perhaps draw a summary or a Learning Map. (See Strategy 17-3.)

Several other strategies can help students with diverse learning styles, especially Visual Aids and Graphic Organizers (Strategy 13-4) and Models and Manipulatives (Strategy 16-13).

▲ TEACHER COMMENT

My students love the VAK Attack procedure. And I love it, too, not only because it is fun for all but because students remember the material they attack with VAK very well. I like to have students do it in pairs, for that adds yet another dimension: the social. Most all of them learn more when they have a chance to talk about it with a neighbor. When I use pairs, I tend to keep pairs together for a long time. That makes the procedure go more quickly, and students learn to appreciate how other people learn differently than they learn and are better able to help one another.

—*Maria Lopez, Middle School English Teacher*

Using Written Material to Present New Content

15

We can use written material to provide instruction in class, but if it is to be maximally effective, we must take care to use it in a way that produces *active* learning. That is not easy, for written material often leads to passive reading. This chapter presents 10 strategies that produce more *active* engagement. We recommend giving first attention to the first five strategies.

 ## Strategy 15-1: Paired Reading

Purpose: To structure high-involvement reading.
Description: Asking pairs of students to take turns reading to each other.

"Pair up with someone," says Mr. Franz, "and take turns reading the next section to each other. One person volunteer to start. Read aloud for a bit. Then give the other person a turn. In that way, take turns, back and forth, reading through the selection. Switch readers whenever you like. If you come to something hard for you to read, just ask your partner for help."

Teachers report that students usually enjoy Paired Reading. Compared with what is sometimes called round-robin reading, when one person in a whole class reads aloud while all others sit and listen, it is far more engaging. Students rarely tune out during Paired Reading, for they are either reading or staying ready for their turn.

When using this strategy, aim to give minimum directions, partly to allow for maximum self-direction and partly to allow for individual variation in ability. Students usually know when it's best for them to change readers and how to assist a partner who needs help. But do give directions about what students are to do when the reading is completed. You might, for example, tell students that when they finish the reading they are to

- Talk over the reading and see what you each think. Then, each of you, write in your journal some Outcome Sentences [Strategy 21-1] based on the reading.
- Identify some things you liked or found interesting in the reading. Perhaps make notes for yourself so each of you is ready to report to us all later on.
- Think of something in your own life that the reading reminds you of. Or think of something about you that is like a person in the reading. Share that with one another.
- Thank your partner and write a summary or an outline of the reading or prepare a graphic organizer of it. Later on, I may pair you up with a new partner and ask you to use your work to summarize the reading to that classmate.
- Write about what you disagree with. Or what you would have done differently.
- In your own words, rewrite the part headed . . . , for I want you to consider that part carefully.
- Begin some of your other individual work.

You might also

- Give students the option to "read and say something" while they do the reading. That is, if a thought or comment comes up as they read, they can pause to share it with one another before continuing to read.
- Instruct students to note key issues or questions that emerge as they read, perhaps items they would like you to address later. Or students might note new words or parts of the reading that, even after they talk them over, are still unclear to them.

Strategy 15-2: Reading for Task

Purpose: To help students read more purposefully.
Description: Giving students a task that requires them to read thoughtfully.

"Read the next chapter for tomorrow" is a weak assignment. "Read the chapter and write a one-paragraph summary of it for tomorrow" is far stronger. It reflects the distinction between purposeful behavior and aimless behavior. Accordingly, we are likely to inspire higher engagement with reading material if we ensure that

> A teacher is one that makes himself progressively unnecessary.
>
> —*Thomas Carruthers*

students have a clear purpose for the reading. We might tell students, for example, that their task is to read and to

- Write a summary.
- Illustrate the turning point.
- List main characters and give traits for each.
- Create a time line of key events.
- Construct an outline.
- Write Outcome Sentences. (See Strategy 21-1.)
- Write definitions for key terms.
- Answer the review questions.
- Create a list of questions and answers about the material.
- Make a graphic organizer.
- Write a list of possible applications or uses of the material covered.
- Categorize elements in a way that makes sense to you.
- Write a song about the material.
- Prepare a skit based on the material.
- Prepare a chart of good and poor examples, or right and wrong uses.
- Draw a cartoon.
- Plan a poster or model.
- Write a newspaper ad, a news story, or a feature story.
- Make up a story or write a poem sparked by the material.

We might also consider providing time for students to share their work in Sharing Pairs or Rotating Pairs (Strategies 7-1 and 7-3), or asking them to write all such work in a reading log, which we could review periodically to assess student learning.

 ## Strategy 15-3: Reciprocal Teaching

Purpose: To help students learn from text material.
Description: Asking students to take turns reading aloud in a small group and then to take turns leading a group discussion of the reading.

For Reciprocal Teaching, we ask students to sit in small groups, three or four to a group. Rotating around the group, each student has a turn being the Student Teacher. Each group completes the following steps (adapted from Palincsar & Brown, 1984, 1985):

> If people knew how hard I worked to get my mastery, it wouldn't seem so wonderful after all.
> —*Michelangelo*

Step 1: Reading. Students take turns reading aloud a few passages of a text to one another. The Student Teacher chooses who starts reading. Each reader then chooses when to pass the reading to the next student. The Student Teacher decides when the group has read enough and is ready for the next step, a summarization.

Step 2: Summarizing. The Student Teacher either gives a summary of the section just read or chooses someone else to offer a summary. Others can then chip in to improve the summary, perhaps adding missing elements or voicing thoughts on the passage.

Step 3: Clarifying. If the Student Teacher is unclear about something or does not fully understand, she asks the group to help her. The group does its best to help. Then the Student Teacher invites others to voice individual confusions or questions, which the group then addresses. If nothing needs clarification, the group moves to Step 4.

Step 4: Stating outcomes. The Student Teacher reflects back on the reading, seeking some learning outcomes for herself. She might do this by completing one of the phrases on a posted Outcome Sentences chart (Strategy 21-1): *I learned . . . , I was surprised . . . , I'm beginning to wonder . . . , I rediscovered . . .* One at a time, then, other students take a turn adding what outcomes they can find for themselves.

The group then advances to the next passage to be read, and the four-step process is repeated, with the next student becoming the Student Teacher.

Some other possibilities for organizing Reciprocal Teaching:

- Designate one chair to be the Student Teacher chair. Then, after each round, all students shift chairs, with a new student taking the teacher's chair—and all getting a chance to stretch muscles.
- Instead of the Student Teacher deciding how much of a text is to be read before each summary step, you might announce the text divisions in advance.
- Because groups will finish at different times, provide a catch-all activity. For example, students might write Outcome Sentences (Strategy 21-1) for the entire reading in their personal Learning Logs (Strategy 21-3), or engage in some enrichment activities, or start homework. (For other suggestions, see Chapter 6.)

Reciprocal Teaching takes advantage of research showing that students who need explanations often get them more quickly and clearly from peers; that students who explain to others strengthen their own understandings; that students work harder when they have many chances to talk, take initiative, and make choices; and, generally, that student-directed learning experiences contribute to responsible lifelong learning habits (Rosenshine & Meister, 1994; Vygotsky, 1978).

Bringing the student's world into the classroom is the most relevant act a teacher can perform.
—*Marc Robert*

⟨⟩ Strategy 15-4: Cooperative Reading Groups

Purpose: To inspire students to study readings cooperatively and supportively.

Description: Teaching students a structure for discussing a reading in small groups, with each student taking turns playing a different role in the group's discussion.

In this strategy (adapted from Daniels, 1994), each student reads the material assigned to the class. In a process similar to Daniels's Literature Circle, students then work together in small groups, usually fours, to help one another process and digest the material. During the group work, each student has a distinctive role to play—Leader, Summarizer, Connector, and Quizmaster—each of which is outlined on a handout they receive (Figure 12 on p. 194).

Tips for Success

- It's usually advisable to use the same group at least four times, so that students have an opportunity to rotate through the roles and play all four.

- Go over roles with students before the first round, emphasizing that all are to cooperate and assist one another in the performance of individual roles. It is to be a cooperative learning experience, not a competitive one. Inform the class that Leaders are to improvise the role of any student who is absent with, of course, the assistance of other group members. If there are five students in one group, two people can be Summarizers.

- Though it is tempting to intervene, Cooperative Reading Groups often work best with minimal teacher involvement. You may, however, choose to sit in on each group for a few minutes.

- All reading assignments are to be done by students independently, in or out of class. Readings could be based on a textbook, novel, article, or handout. If reading is done in class, make sure fast readers have something to do while waiting for the slower readers to finish.

- If a long reading is involved, specify which parts are to be read by certain deadlines and when groups will meet. Teachers report that it's effective for Cooperative Reading Groups to meet twice a week, for 20 to 30 minutes.

- If students are reading a novel, you might keep groups together for the time it takes to go through the whole book.

- When it's time to shuffle group membership, consider the playing card procedure: prepare a set of cards and then pass cards out, having, say, four jacks sit together, four 10's sit together, and so on.

Figure 12
Handout for Cooperative Reading Groups

Leader: Keeps group on task. The leader is responsible for . . .

- Starting meetings promptly.
- Keeping track of time during meetings.
- Calling on students, so all have a chance to play their roles.
- Reminding students that they should support one another, that criticism is out of place.
- Improvising the role of any absent group member.
- Making sure all know the reading and their individual roles for next time, if a long reading is involved.
- Conducting a Like/Might Review on the group's work when each meeting is finished, if the teacher assigned it.

Summarizer: Starts the group's work by offering a summary of the reading. This summary might include the use of . . .

- An outline.
- A chart.
- Pictures.
- A dramatization of part of the material.

- A review of important, interesting, or unusual sentences.
- Any combination of the above.

Connector: Notes connections to other material, such as . . .

- Previous lessons.
- The outside world.
- Personal experiences, feelings, or thoughts.
- Other people, places, events.
- Any combination of the above.

Quizmaster: Creates 5 to 10 questions based on the reading and conducts a brief oral quiz. This quiz might include . . .

- True/false questions.
- Multiple-choice questions.
- Fill-in-the-blank questions.
- Flashcards with words to define, characters to identify, or events to sequence.
- Opinion questions that fuel a group discussion.
- Any combination of the above.

Other Possibilities to Consider

• Allow each group to work with a different reading, so students have a choice in what they read.

• Have each group work with a different reading by the same author, which can lead to displayed reports as part of an author study.

• After each group meeting, have students write Like/Might Reviews (Strategy 21-2) or Outcome Sentences (Strategy 21-1) for evaluation purposes.

• Conclude group meetings with a Review Test (Strategy 11-1), so you can highlight parts of the reading you want to emphasize, or a Productive Discussion (Strategy 16-2), so you can conveniently add your thoughts on the reading.

 ## Strategy 15-5: I Start, You Finish

Purpose: To involve all class members in a reading activity.
Description: Reading the first part of a sentence aloud, then pausing to let the whole class read the remainder of the sentence in unison.

Do you want students to read something with high attentiveness? Consider the I Start, You Finish strategy. Here is how one teacher uses it:

> Before we start our activity, I want to be sure you all know what the directions are. Please find the directions at the top of your handout. I'm going to start reading the first sentence. I might read just the first few words, or most of the words. Then I'm going to stop, and that is when it will be your turn. When I stop, you all continue, out loud, all together, from where I left off. Keep your place while I'm reading so you know where to come in. Then when you reach the end of the sentence, it will be my turn again. We'll continue this way until we've read all the directions. Ready? I start, you finish.

The teacher reads for a short time, making it easy for all students to follow along. The group then reads in unison, hopefully with spirit, so weak readers go unnoticed. In that way, classroom dignity, energy, community, self-management, and awareness are all well served.

Once students become familiar with this strategy, no instructions are necessary. You can simply direct students to the page to be read and state, "I start, you finish." Alternatively, you can ask for volunteers to start and let the rest of the class finish. In either case, you might also want to remind students to read aloud "with power, as if you really mean it!"

We can use this strategy as a variation of Paired Reading (Strategy 15-1). It is also useful for introducing important definitions or concepts.

Strategy 15-6: Directed Reading

Purpose: To keep students highly engaged and focused on reading material.
Description: Actively guiding students through a reading, frequently requesting student responses, offering comments when appropriate.

A man who finds no satisfaction in himself seeks for it in vain elsewhere.

—*La Rochefoucauld*

Rather than asking students to read material and rather than presenting the information to them orally, we can intersperse the reading and oral discussion in a way that produces high-participation lessons. This is especially useful for poor readers and poor listeners.

Consider this segment from a science lesson. The teacher begins by asking the students to find a particular page in their science text. "What is the heading of that section?" she asks. "Susan, please read it for us." After Susan reads the heading, the teacher continues. "Thank you. Today we will be learning about warm-blooded animals. I'd like you to now scan the first paragraph and find the definition of *warm-blooded*."

After a pause, she asks a different student to read the definition. Then she invites the class to read the definition in unison with her. "Again, please, but this time read it like you mean it!" The teacher asks the students to look at the next paragraph and find three examples of warm-blooded animals. "Who can tell us the first? The second? The last?" She writes each example on the board as volunteers respond. "Based on these examples, who can think of some other animals that would be classified as warm-blooded?" She adds to the list on the board as students offer examples. "Now I'd like you to silently read page 214 to find out . . ."

Note how the teacher intersperses scanning, reading, questions, and comments. From time to time she writes key points on the board. In addition, she occasionally asks students to write a response and share it with a partner. And sometimes she presents a mini-lecture about the material.

This style of Directed Reading can be used with fiction as well as nonfiction. For example, imagine a teacher dramatically reading aloud the first page of a story and then saying something like this:

> Think about what you know so far. On scrap paper, write a prediction telling two things you think might happen in this story. Then read the next paragraph to find out what time of year it is . . . Let's vote: How many think it is winter? Spring? Summer? Fall? The correct answer is spring. What words gave you a clue it was spring? Now please continue reading until you find out the name of . . .

Strategy 15-7: Timed Reading

Purpose: To activate student energy and provide a quick exposure to content.
Description: Giving students two to three minutes to read, scan, or simply turn pages of some text.

It's not what you look at that matters, it's what you see.
—Henry David Thoreau

"I'd like you all to turn to Chapter 5," says the teacher. "Now scan that chapter or simply turn the pages and look at each page. I'll give you just a few minutes for this."

The teacher might then give an Attentive Lecture (Strategy 13-1) to elaborate the content of Chapter 5. In this case, the Timed Reading strategy served as an introduction and, perhaps, a question motivator.

If the class had already studied Chapter 5, the teacher might skip the Attentive Lecture and introduce material from another chapter. In this case, Timed Reading would have served as a review of prior learnings. Or, again using Timed Reading as a review of Chapter 5, the teacher might conduct a Review Test (Strategy 11-1) or ask for Outcome Sentences (Strategy 21-1) on the chapter.

Timed Reading, then, is a strategy to motivate students to dip briefly into a reading without pressure or a particular purpose. Teachers report that it makes reading feel less onerous to many students and thereby helps them appreciate what reading has to offer. Fast pace is one key to its success. Saying something like "See how much you can get from the reading in these few minutes" is one way to challenge students to attack the task with high spirit.

Strategy 15-8: Learning Sheets

Purpose: To enrich and individualize the learnings students obtain from reading material.

Description: Helping students to engage a reading by providing a question sheet that guides and stimulates their learning.

Learning Sheets lead students through written material in a way that almost always enriches the experience. Learning Sheets can be long or short, depending on student maturity. Figure 13 on p. 198 is an example of a short one.

Once Learning Sheets are distributed, students are free to work by themselves or in pairs or, perhaps, trios. We might walk around to help, or ask students with questions to come to our desk. We might also post a list of students who we know will be good helpers to serve as Class Tutors (Strategy 17-12). When students finish a Learning Sheet, they might check their names off a posted progress chart and begin the next sheet in the series. Or they might move to a totally different project or activity. Usually all answers to Learning Sheets are to be written on separate papers, which allows us to reuse those Learning Sheets with other classes.

Figure 13
Learning Sheet

Find-Out Questions (required)

1. True or false? Abraham Lincoln was born in Kentucky.
2. Lincoln is known by the nickname (a) "Old Abe" (b) "Honest Abe" (c) "Big Abe."
3. In his entire life, Lincoln was only able to go to school for a total of _____ year(s).
4. Abraham Lincoln was elected the _____ president of the United States in the year _____ .

Larger Questions (required)

1. Name two government positions Lincoln held before becoming president.
2. Think of three ways Lincoln's life was different from the lives of other presidents you know.

Challenge Questions (optional)

1. In 1858 Lincoln said, "A house divided against itself cannot stand." In what ways might that apply to the world today?
2. What can you say about Lincoln's political philosophy?
3. Lincoln defended many unpopular viewpoints during his political career. Have you ever defended an unpopular point of view? Explain.

The Benefits of Learning Sheets

What is so special about Learning Sheets? Consider the sets of questions:

• *Find-Out Questions* focus student attention on the basic data in the reading and pace the students comfortably through the reading. Find-Out Questions are simple to answer, especially if they are listed in the order that answers appear in the text. This ensures that even the slowest student can answer Find-Out Questions correctly. For extremely slow learners, and to give frequent reinforcement, we might have one Find-Out Question for every sentence or two of the text. Rarely do students complain that a Learning Sheet contains too many easy questions.

• *Larger Questions,* which are addressed after the reading is completed and the Find-Out Questions are finished, direct more thoughtful attention to the reading. The trick here is to provide questions that exercise thoughtfulness without frustrating students who read poorly or think slowly. We recommend that questions in this part be easy enough so most students can experience success with all of them. Some examples of questions that are easy yet require more than merely copying answers:

○ How many different cities are mentioned in the reading?

○ Name at least one way in which iron and steel are the same.

○ List some key points.

○ Write some summary sentences.

○ How is X in the reading the same as or different from something you know?

○ How might X be useful to you or relate to your life?

○ What does X make you think of?

○ What idea or person do you most like, dislike?

○ What would you predict will happen next?

○ What would you like to see happen?

• *Challenge Questions* challenge even the best students to think harder and more broadly. This section is designed to be optional. Although many students will rise to the challenge, some will skip it and, it is hoped, will not feel inadequate because they did so. One way to encourage engagement is to include Challenge Questions such as these, used for a reading on magnets: "What kind of people attract or repel you?" "Tell about a time you played with a magnet or used a magnet to find something." "What are some things a person could do if he found a super-strong magnet, one strong enough to make a bus fly in the sky?" Answering such personal and subjective questions can act as a reward or a change of pace from academic work. It can also help students clarify their values and express their feelings. Because these types of personal questions have no right or wrong answers, it's best not to attempt to evaluate students' answers.

Tips for Success

• Use plenty of Find-Out Questions. Find-Out Questions lead to easy, rapid rewards, generating feelings of success. For typical school texts, we advise using one Find-Out Question for every paragraph.

• Use questions that are already available. You do not need to create every question from scratch. Consider using questions already available in teacher's editions or workbooks. Also consider collaborating with other teachers in preparing sets of Learning Sheets. It's well worth the time. Once Learning Sheets are prepared, you can use them year after year as an efficient way to ease your preparation tasks and enhance student learning.

• Consider appointing student helpers. Helpers might have two jobs: assisting students who have trouble and, afterward, correcting the first two sections of completed Learning Sheets. That leaves only the Challenge Questions for you to review. To give all students an opportunity to be helpers, you might start at the top of the alphabet (or the bottom), pick two or three students, and brief them in

Do what you can, with what you have, where you are. What better can you do?

—*Theodore Roosevelt*

advance on the correct answers. You might even give them a copy of the text with numbers inserted to show where the answer to each question is located and provide an answer sheet illustrating reasonable answers to Larger Questions. Thus even the slowest students, perhaps *especially* the slowest students, can enjoy the experience of being a student helper. (See Strategy 17-12, Class Tutors, for more information on using student helpers.)

Strategy 15-9: Dramatic Reading

Purpose: To make readings more memorable.

Description: Modeling dramatic reading and then asking students to read important passages aloud with as much dramatic flair as they can manage.

Rose and Nicholl (1997) remind us that we tend to remember more than twice as much of what we say aloud than what we read silently. This suggests the advisability of frequently asking students to talk about what they are reading, as by using Directed Reading (Strategy 15-6). Vocalizing can be even more memorable when the words are spoken dramatically, with emotion. We can take advantage of this by, first, modeling for students how to read dramatically; we might demonstrate by reading an important definition or a key text passage. Then we ask a few students to read a sentence or two aloud dramatically, with as much feeling as they can generate. Finally, we might recommend that all students take any portion of a reading that they want to remember and say it dramatically, aloud or silently to themselves. And when we want to emphasize a key definition or idea in class, we can always invite a few students to read it aloud to the class, being as outrageously dramatic as they dare. Invite students to have fun with the strategy. And expect them to remember more of what they read. Teachers report it almost always works out that way.

Strategy 15-10: Jigsaw

Purpose: To give all students responsibilities for both learning and teaching.

Description: Asking quartets of students to each read or study part of a topic and then meet to share what they learned.

Especially with older students, teachers often face the problem of covering a large amount of reading in a short period of time. In such situations, the Jigsaw strategy (adapted from Aronson & Patnoe, 1997) can be both highly engaging and time efficient. Here is an example that uses four steps to implement the strategy:

1. *Divide a reading of nonsequential material into four parts.* You might use, for example, a reading on different animals, countries, people, functions of the government, or parts of a plant cell. These are the "pieces" of the jigsaw.

2. *Divide students into groups of four.* If necessary, create some groups with five members. In each group, have students count off—1, 2, 3, 4. All 1's then receive the first reading, all 2's the second reading, and so on. In groups of five, two students work on the same reading, perhaps the one that is most difficult.

3. *Provide time for students to individually read and study their segments.* When students read, ask them to make notes, such as the following, so they can explain their reading to others:
   - Listing main ideas and supporting details
   - Creating a web
   - Writing questions and answers
   - Outlining information by levels and sublevels
   - Preparing a chart of what they know, want to know, and have learned
   - Writing Outcome Sentences

4. *Re-form original groups and have students put the "pieces" together.* Each student then teaches his or her piece to the group, starting with the 1's. (If two students in a group have the same number, they can team teach or take turns presenting their segments.)

If time permits, you can set up "expert groups." These meet before students teach their segments to others. (Have all 1's get together, all 2's, and so on.) Then tell group members to help one another prepare for the teaching of their segment. Groups might review the content for one another, answer questions for one another, or create a chart or graphic organizer to use during their individual presentations. Although this step takes extra time, expert groups help ensure that the students will do their best to teach and learn the topic.

You could conclude the jigsaw activity with a Productive Discussion (Strategy 16-2) that addresses unanswered questions, or by having students write Like/Might Reviews (Strategy 21-2) or Outcome Sentences (Strategy 21-1) for sharing or evaluation purposes.

> Good teaching is one-fourth preparation and three-fourths theater.
>
> —*Gail Godwin*

PART V

Strategies for Helping
Students Master Content

It is obviously not sufficient to present material to students and leave it at that. We must help students move toward mastery of the material presented. How can we handle that very complex task? This part of the book offers strategies for promoting mastery of both new and old material. Included are chapters on facilitating mastery in whole-class, individual, and small-group formats; on managing project work; on generating higher-level thinking; and on responding effectively to the comments students make while learning.

The language we use as we handle these tasks makes a difference. What language activates the best motives students carry? Consider these three comments and the messages they send to students:

Least inspiring: "I hope you all remember what we did yesterday because it will be on Friday's test."

In between: "Let me summarize briefly what I said yesterday."

Most inspiring: "Everybody write down something you remember from yesterday's class. Let's have some volunteers report and see what we remember and if any misunderstandings show up. Before we begin, let me ask, Would it be all right if somebody reports something incorrectly?"

Helping Students Master Content in a Whole-Class Format

16

Let's say we've presented material to students, perhaps by asking them to read something for homework, or by explaining it in class. Can we now assume that students fully grasp it? Hardly. Almost always we must also help students think about the material, interact with it, practice it, digest it, make it their own. How might we do this, especially if our aim is to bring out the best our students have in them? Several strategies from earlier chapters are effective, especially Review Test, Choral Work, and Underexplain and Learning Pairs (Strategies 11-1, 11-2, 14-2). This chapter contains 15 additional strategies (the first 8 of which merit first attention), all appropriate for a whole-class format. Chapter 17 contains strategies for facilitating mastery in individual and small-group formats.

Strategy 16-1: Clarifying Questions

Purpose: To help students learn from presentations.
Description: Asking questions that get students to think about material presented.

Let's say students read something or we gave a lecture or showed a film. A useful next step is to ask questions designed to help students think more clearly about what they heard or saw. Some clarifying questions we might ask:

- What was new or interesting in it for you?
- Was anything surprising?
- What do you need to think more about?
- What can you learn from it?
- What or whom does it remind you of?
- What questions does it bring to mind?
- Was there something in it that was pleasing or displeasing to you?

- What does it make you wonder about?
- Does it stir any memories?
- Does it suggest any changes that are worth considering?

Using Question, All Write (Strategy 16-3), we might have all students make notes about one or more of these questions. We might then invite students to share some of their notes, which might lead into a discussion. Even if it doesn't, the sharing of ideas among students will likely stimulate some to ask themselves, "Is that true for me, too?" In this way, simply by asking questions and having students share responses, we stimulate reflection and clarify personal meanings.

Note that the questions in the list are all open-ended. They do not have right/wrong answers. Nor are they intended to direct students to a particular learning, as when we ask, "Why did the captain get so angry?" or "What do you think Freud would say to that idea?" Directive questions are sometimes valuable, of course. But for helping students think through material and extract personal meanings, open-ended, clarifying questions are usually better.

Strategy 16-2: Productive Discussion

Purpose: To keep all students involved in whole-class discussions.
Description: Continuing a class discussion only as long as all students are productively engaged.

Perhaps your students have read material for homework and written Outcome Sentences (Strategy 21-1). Or perhaps you have just concluded an Attentive Lecture (Strategy 13-1). Often at such times you begin a class discussion. "Would anyone like to comment or ask a question?" you might say. Unfortunately, often the discussion that follows does not engage all the students actively. The talkative ones talk, while many others wait passively for lunchtime. And that leads to our first rule for effective class discussions:

1. Continue discussions only as long as most students remain fully and actively engaged.

As soon as some students become inattentive, make a change. Do something else.

Before abandoning a discussion, however, consider aiming to re-engage students. Some examples of how that might be done:

- "How many of you basically agree with what Todd has been saying? How many disagree? Are unsure?" (This is Strategy 16-6, Voting Questions to Assess

Recently I went to a center for teenage girls where the teacher asked what they would like to discuss most. Human biology? Care for their infant? Physiology of childbirth? Family planning? The girls showed no interest. Then the teacher asked, "Would you like to discuss how to say no to your boyfriend without losing his love?" All hands shot up.

—*Eunice Kennedy Shriver*

Understanding.) We may then follow with, "How many people have something else to say? Let's hear from only four more people now. OK, Tom, and then Jane, and then Sue, and then Rick." This signals the class that the discussion will not go on endlessly. It also encourages some of the slow-to-volunteer speakers to get more involved. (This is Strategy 16-5, Set of Speakers.)

- "Please all take a moment to write or draw your ideas about this general topic. What do you think about it now?" (This is Strategy 16-3, Question, All Write.) This might lead to our saying, "Now turn to a neighbor and take a minute or two to share your thoughts" (Strategy 7-1, Sharing Pairs).

- "Let's use a class Whip Around. We'll start in this corner. When it is your turn, please say your ideas, even if it feels risky to you. This is a class in which we accept all thinking. Or, of course, you may always pass." (This is Strategy 16-4, Whip Around, Pass Option.)

- "Before we go on to something else, think back over the discussion and see if you can find some learnings or ideas for yourself. Write a few sentences, perhaps starting with phrases like *I learned, I rediscovered,* or *I'm beginning to wonder.* Let's sample a few and then decide if we want to talk more about this, now or in the future." (This is Strategy 21-1, Outcome Sentences.)

Our second rule is equally straightforward:

2. Do not assume that discussions stimulate thinking or advance understandings.

Discussions often do not serve either goal. Often all that is stimulated is opinion exchange and thoughtless chatter, and all that advances is the hour.

We have found that discussions almost always work best as a part of a more varied lesson, as in this sequence:

- First, students think about a topic and make notes of their preliminary ideas.
- Students then pair up and very briefly exchange thoughts.
- A brief whole-class discussion follows, with just a few volunteers speaking.
- The teacher offers new information or perspectives, aimed at advancing student understanding.
- All students think back over the topic and write Outcome Sentences, which may then be shared in a class Whip Around, discussed in Sharing Pairs, or placed in portfolios.

Discussions rarely produce as much learning as their popularity would suggest. Most students seem to experience a discussion much like they do a lecture: as a set of statements that do not add up to personal meaning. The bottom line:

> Do you realize if it weren't for Edison we'd be watching TV by candlelight?
>
> —Al Boliska

Be quick to discontinue a discussion that fails to keep students actively engaged. Our field tests consistently show that many discussions have limited effectiveness.

Ideas for Improving Discussions

• *Use discussions mainly as a brief transition or concluding strategy.* That is, use discussions between strategies that demand harder thinking, as times for students to relax their minds a bit, or to give you feedback about how much they learned. You might also use discussion to give your talkative students a brief opportunity to vent their pent-up pressures to talk. Or you can use discussions mainly as a concluding activity, as a time for students to summarize and share their current understandings.

• *Create a list of provocative topics.* Some discussion topics are far more engaging and productive than others. Especially effective are questions and issues that touch the students personally or emotionally. "What would you be proud to tell someone about that?" "What would you never do about that?" "What would get you standing up and objecting?" "What can you actually *do* about it? Will you do it? When?" (See Chapter 24 for other suggestions.) Consider creating a handy list of such questions or issues that you might sometimes use.

• *Appoint a student discussion leader.* Perhaps ask a student to lead some discussions. It's often easier to notice when a discussion is about to slide toward restlessness or boredom when you observe from the sidelines.

• *Use visuals.* Write key words, ideas, or numbers on the board during a discussion to help students maintain focus. Many students hear better when they also see, and most students benefit when more than one of their senses is active.

• *Appoint board writers.* Ask students to make notes on the board of key points. This is especially useful when the class is generating a list of ideas, as during brainstorming. Perhaps ask two recorders to take turns writing, so one can begin writing an idea while the other is finishing the previous one. In the case of rambling student comments, you can suggest what phrase the student should write on the board.

• *Give Nods of Recognition.* To get people other than the usual talkers into discussions, tell students that you'll ask for volunteers to answer a question, but that you might just look at a volunteer and nod to indicate that you are waiting until more people are willing to say something. See Strategy 16-7 for more about this technique.

• *Maximize eye contact.* Many students on the edges of a group or in the back of a room feel they are not noticed, not part of class discussions. To minimize this problem, make frequent eye contact with those students. And perhaps

One of the advantages of being young is that you don't let common sense get in the way of doing things everybody else knows are impossible.

—*Anonymous*

walk about the room during the discussion, to draw student attention to that area. Perhaps also occasionally change student seats.

- *Move to circle seating.* If feasible, ask students to sit in a circle or a two- or three-row semicircle for discussions. The more that students face each other and the closer they are to the center of the action, the more they are likely to stay involved.

- *Use small groups instead of the whole-class format.* The easiest way to maximize student involvement in discussions is not to use the whole-class format too long, for that makes it too easy for some students to remain passive. Instead, switch to small groups, using strategies such as Sharing Pairs and Rotating Pairs (Strategies 7-1 and 7-3).

Strategy 16-3: Question, All Write

Purpose: To maximize the number of students who actively think about a question we ask.

Description: Asking all students to write an answer to a question before calling on someone to reply.

When dealing with groups of students, it's useful to insert a pause between asking a question and calling on someone to respond. That pause, or wait time, as Mary Budd Rowe (1974) calls it, is designed to give all students a chance to frame an answer in their minds. Without wait time, more students are likely to sit passively, waiting for the students who are always ready to give correct answers to speak up.

However, it's difficult to continue inserting those pauses. Our instinct is to keep the class busy, and wait time can feel like an invitation to restlessness. Furthermore, many students fail to use the pause to frame answers for themselves.

An alternative is to ask students to jot down an answer to a question before calling on one student. "What was the name of the person who shot President Lincoln?" we might say, adding, "Please write your answer on scrap paper." We pause while the students write, and then ask, "Who would be willing to read what they wrote?" With this strategy, involvement tends to be high and thought tends to be precise.

As a variation, some teachers ask a question and have students write an answer on a personal slate and then hold up the slate for the teacher to see. This procedure has some advantages. We can then tell how well the class understands the topic. We can personally acknowledge students who have the correct answer. And we can also spot students who are working carelessly or not at all. The procedure has disadvantages as well. Some students might be embarrassed at having to show imperfect work to us. The pace of the lesson is usually substantially slowed. And the emphasis of the strategy shifts from activating self-responsible involvement among students to checking on student work. Inasmuch as our basic purpose is to inspire students to do the very best they can with schoolwork, we rarely recommend this variation.

Strategy 16-4: Whip Around, Pass Option

Purpose: To increase the number of students who share their thoughts and to promote responsible self-management.

Description: Asking students to speak one at a time, in turn, on an issue or, if they prefer, to pass.

Sometimes we want to hear from many students, not just a few volunteers. In such situations, we could say, "Let's whip down the row of students by the window. When it comes your turn, either tell us your thoughts on the topic or say, 'I pass.'"

We can use the Whip Around, Pass Option with all or part of a class. It's especially useful when different people are likely to have different views on the issue being addressed. It's an efficient way to inspire high participation and hear from many students, including those who tend not to speak up. Here are two examples of teachers using this strategy:

> We all have our own ideas about the new policy. Let's start with Bob and whip around the whole class, giving each person a chance to share one idea. You can always pass, if you prefer. OK, Bob, please start us off.

> Look over the Outcome Sentences you wrote about that chapter. I'd like to whip around at least part of the class and ask you to read just one of your sentences; or if you like, say "I pass." Let's start today with Jose.

The Whip Around, Pass Option not only gives all students a chance to voice their ideas; it also tends to raise the energy and interest level of a class. Students often listen very closely to how others respond to an issue to which they also have a response. And the strategy offers a dignified way to inspire shy students to express their thoughts. In addition, it poses a valuable self-managing choice to students: Should I risk speaking up or risk saying "I pass"? In some situations, to risk saying "I pass" might call for greater

▲ TEACHER COMMENT

I discovered that the Whip Around, Pass Option strategy makes students more responsible. I've used it quite a lot and have noticed lately that the students who passed because that was the "cool" thing to do are now participating. It has been really great to see the progression of these boys from everyone wanting to pass to 99 percent participation. It took a while, but the wait was worth it.

—Linda Prater
High School Special Education Teacher

courage. In either case, the procedure provides students with practice in managing their lives wisely and responsibly.

Strategy 16-5: Set of Speakers

Purpose: To select speakers efficiently.

Description: Requesting volunteers to speak and, then, from all volunteers, choosing a set that will take turns speaking.

Rather than calling on one student at a time during discussions, we can occasionally select a set of students to speak. "How many would be willing to share ideas?" we might ask. As hands go up, we point to some students: "Let's hear from five people today. You be first. You be second." And we continue until we have identified a set of five. We then ask the first person to speak. All students then tend to relax and pay attention. The speakers know their turns are coming up, and they know the order in which they will speak. The rest of the class knows the next bit of time is organized, and they need not worry about whether or not to volunteer.

Set of Speakers makes it easier to avoid calling repeatedly on the same students and to notice the more tentative hand-raising of students who are almost ready to respond. We can often prompt more volunteers by saying something like, "How about some volunteers from those who have not spoken lately?" Or "Simpson, I see you might be willing to be one of the speakers. Are you?" It's easier for the reserved student to volunteer to be part of a set of speakers than to be a solo speaker.

Strategy 16-6: Voting Questions to Assess Understanding

Purpose: To efficiently assess the readiness of a class to move ahead.

Description: Rather than asking "Any questions?" asking "How many of you have questions?" or "How many would like to move on and come back to this topic another time?"

Have you ever concluded a presentation by asking "Any questions?" only to be answered by a sea of blank stares? Perhaps the students did not know enough to know what to ask. Or perhaps they were reluctant to admit their confusion. If you suspect this might be the case, you might instead try asking what we call a voting question, which is a question that usually starts with the words, "How many . . . ?"

In this case, you might ask, "How many of you would like me to explain this again?" This usually gives you a more accurate sense of the class understanding.

Alternatively, have you ever asked "Any questions?" and received more questions than you wanted to take the time to answer? Or have you ever become stuck in a round of questions and answers with only a few individuals while many others tuned out? Try asking instead, "How many want to spend more time on this now?" Or "How many now feel ready to move on?" The show of hands then helps you choose whether it's better to move ahead or to stick with the topic.

In terms of keeping student involvement high, Voting Questions to Assess Understanding has two major advantages. It avoids inviting individual student comments that can slow class progress, and it makes it easy for all students to participate in the vote, so all feel involved in class proceedings.

We can also use a voting procedure that allows students to give more complex responses. Here are two possibilities:

- *Degrees of agreement.* "If you agree, raise your hand all the way. If you half-agree, raise it halfway. If you disagree, point thumbs down."
- *Readiness to respond.* "Hold up one finger if you have an idea but do not want me to call on you, just so I know who has some idea. Hold up two fingers if you are willing to respond aloud but are really not all that sure. Hold up three fingers if you are fairly sure and are willing to respond. Otherwise hold up a fist, so I'll know how many really have no idea. I'll call on only those holding up two or three fingers.

Strategy 16-7: Nod of Recognition

Purpose: To maximize the number of students who will have time to speak up in class.

Description: Nodding to a student who has just volunteered to speak so as to communicate that we noticed the offer, yet looking about so as to give more time for others to consider volunteering.

Usually a few bright students quickly volunteer to answer questions. To avoid calling on those few students all the time, we can use the Nod of Recognition. We might explain it to the class this way:

> Sometimes I'll ask for volunteers to answer a question, you will raise your hand, and I will not call on you or anyone else for a moment or two. I might just look at you and nod. That means I noticed you were willing to volunteer, so you can

put down your hand. I simply want to wait a bit before calling on someone, to give more time for people to think about the question and to consider if they also are willing to risk an answer.

If that strategy does elicit additional volunteers, we need not neglect the early volunteers; we can call on all who volunteered, time permitting. We can even call on them in the order in which they volunteered. But we might well want to start with a late volunteer, saying something like, "We haven't heard much from Maria recently, so let's hear from her first." Or saying, "We'll not have time to hear from everyone right now, and because we haven't heard much from Maria, I'd like to call on her."

 ## Strategy 16-8: Brainstorm/Sort

Purpose: To get students to think about an issue open-mindedly and comprehensively.
Description: Asking students to brainstorm options for handling an issue and then to sort the options, seeking the best.

Many students are not in the habit of thinking through the issues in their lives carefully and making choices wisely. We can help them develop that habit and, at the same time, spur them to think carefully about a school issue by using the Brainstorm/Sort strategy. The steps are straightforward:

1. *State a problem.* We might do this by asking a question; for example, How might the character in the story handle her current plight? How can erosion be prevented? How might poverty be reduced? What are some ways to keep our classroom materials more orderly? What can be done about racial prejudice?

2. *Brainstorm a list of options.* To stimulate thinking, we then lead the whole group in brainstorming options. Or we might start the brainstorming with the whole class and then direct small groups to continue the brainstorming and make their own more complete list. In either case, standard brainstorming rules apply: Everyone tosses out ideas creatively and open-mindedly. The more ideas, the better. No idea gets evaluated during brainstorming. Reasonable and unreasonable ideas are equally welcomed. One person or, often better, two people take turns recording all the options presented.

3. *Sort options by desirability.* To help students develop the habit of distinguishing the better choices from the quick fixes or the merely popular choices, we then do well to stimulate thinking about long-term consequences. We might have students work alone or in groups, saying something such as this:

> When I give a lecture, I accept that people look at their watches, but what I do not tolerate is when they look at it and raise it to their ear to find out if it's stopped.
>
> —*Marcel Archard*

I'd like each of you to now copy the list and, as you do so, consider each item. Think about what each option will probably lead to, in the short and long run. Then assign a code to each item. If you think the option will result in a positive long-term solution or benefit, mark it with a plus sign. If you think the option will result in a negative or only a temporary solution, or will do more harm than good, mark it with a minus sign. If you are unsure whether the option is positive or negative, mark it with a zero.

4. *Examine the top group in a search for the very best choices.* To see which options received the most pluses, we might use some Voting Questions (Strategy 9-3), asking, "How many put a plus by this first option? The next option? The next . . . ?" We could then initiate a Productive Discussion (Strategy 16-2), asking students to consider which among those highly rated options we might agree is the very best choice. Or we could ask small groups to make their own tallies and talk through the issue and then report their preferred choice to the whole class. The purpose of this last step is to encourage broad, long-range thinking and a deeper understanding of the issue.

▲ **TEACHER COMMENT**

My students turned Brainstorm/Sort into the "BS strategy," but I don't mind because it's so good for them. I see it cutting through their either-or thinking and growing the habit of not jumping to conclusions, but saying, wait a minute, let's think about this some more. I think it also opens up their time frame and gets them thinking beyond immediate gratification. I know most of them get into the process and enjoy it.

—*Laurie Hopp, 5th Grade Teacher*

Strategy 16-9: Mastery Learning Game

Purpose: To encourage risk taking and teamwork without inviting unhealthy competition.

Description: Asking review questions in a gamelike setting without keeping score.

Games can be powerful motivators. They can increase enthusiasm, participation, and teamwork. Games can also breed unhealthy competition and stoke feelings of inferiority. How can we harness the benefits of games without generating negative side effects? Consider the Mastery Learning Game, a game students enjoy that focuses on risking rather than winning. It begins with students sitting in small teams; pairs or trios work best. Once the students are organized, we follow these four steps:

1. *We pose a question.* Each student, working alone, then writes an answer, as in Question, All Write (Strategy 16-3).

2. *Teams choose an answer.* Students collaborate within their teams to choose what they believe is the best answer. This gives some students an opportunity to

learn the material. It gives all students opportunities to relate productively with peers and build community.

3. *We give a warning signal.* We might call out, "Five seconds, please," to alert students that collaboration time is ending.

4. *We randomly call on one person.* "Mary," we might say, "are you willing to risk an answer?" The student can pass or respond. If the student gives the correct answer—"Brazil," for example—we might offer the group, not the individual, some positive feedback: "Good job, group." If the student gives an incorrect answer, we might say, "No, Cuba is not correct. The correct answer is Brazil. How many knew it was Brazil? Now, the next question is . . ." and simply continue the game by asking the next question. If the student passes, we simply announce the correct answer and move to the next question.

Some suggestions for using this strategy effectively:

- Keep the pace quick to heighten the sense of fun.
- Prepare the game questions yourself, or have student teams work together to prepare questions, in which case it is helpful to review the criteria for a "good question," encouraging students to go beyond questions that require simple memorization when possible.
- Perhaps encourage camaraderie by asking teams to create names for themselves or to identify themselves by wearing special hats, pins, ribbons, and the like.
- Avoid excessive competition. The goal is to gain satisfaction not from doing better than other groups, but from playing the game well.
- Consider having someone keep score for each group, yet downplay the importance of winning.
- Perhaps have a mini-celebration at the end of the game by leading a round of applause for everyone, a desk tap for all, or high-fives all around.

Strategy 16-10: Face-off Game

Purpose: To energize students for a review of material.
Description: Asking questions to students sitting in pairs, with each person in the pair representing a different team.

Low engagement is a serious problem with spelling bees or other games in which students must wait a long time before having a turn to answer a question.

When you reach for the stars, you may not quite get one, but you won't come up with a handful of mud either.

—Leo Burnett

Like the Learning Mastery Game, the Face-off Game is a better choice. Here are the steps:

1. *Create pairs.* Each pair should consist of students of roughly the same ability. Designate one person in each pair as representing Team A, the other Team B. Post a list of pairs or tell all students who their partners are. Ask students to sit in those pairs during Face-off Games, so each will have someone with whom to "face off."

2. *Establish team identities.* Have the A's and B's meet separately to choose their own team names and, perhaps, a team color, badge, or hat to wear during games. Aim to foster camaraderie within the two teams.

3. *Play the game.* Pose a question that has one right answer, such as a math problem, a spelling or vocabulary word, or a geography or science fact. After posing the question, ask all students to write an answer. Give the correct answer and have the pairs quickly check the answers they both wrote.

4. *Score and tally points.* If one person in a pair wrote the correct answer and the other did not, a point is given to the team of the correct student. If both students are correct or both are incorrect, it's called a "draw" and no points are scored. After each question, call out, "People scoring points for Team A [or whatever the team is called], please stand [or please raise a hand]." Those students are counted, perhaps by two students whom you designated as the "counters" of the day, one counting the boys and the other the girls. Team A's points are recorded, and the same procedure is used to record points for Team B.

5. *Acknowledge the winners.* At the end of the game, give the winning team some sort of simple recognition, such as "Today's winner is the Red Team. Now let's all give ourselves a hand for a game well played!" Keep the pace quick throughout, with the emphasis on reviewing subject matter, not on tallying points.

We can keep pairs and teams stable over time, although we might make occasional adjustments to maintain fair competition. If discipline is an issue, we might want to award bonus points for good behavior. We might, for example, award extra points after every five questions or so, saying something like, "The Blue Team has shown excellent self-control recently. No one called out or disturbed opponents. Extra point for the Blue Team."

▲ TEACHER COMMENT

To keep competition close and suspense high, I make a set of three-by-five cards, each including something like "Five extra points," "Two extra points," "Ten extra points." Then before the last question, I have a student pick a card from the pack and announce the extra points selected. Those points apply to that last question. Students then know that the team lagging in points might win the day's contest at the last minute. I find that keeps student interest high throughout the game.

—*Nick Carrocci, Middle School English and Social Studies Teacher*

Strategy 16-11: Avoiding Re-explanation

Purpose: To avoid wasting time by trying to re-explain something when it would be wiser to move on.

Description: Limiting the number of times we re-explain and, instead, reassuring students that no one needs to understand everything right now.

Piano lessons can make fifteen minutes feel like an hour.
—*Jack, age 9*

"I don't understand," whines the student, still unable to grasp the point of the lesson. It's a situation we often face. And often we respond by trying to explain again and—sometimes—again and again. But, alas, such re-explanations often do not settle the issue. Why? Perhaps because when students are confused and frustrated, their minds are too unsettled to learn; and sometimes because the re-explanation raises new questions for other students, including those who were ready to move on; and sometimes simply because some students are not yet able to learn the lesson.

It is often wiser to relieve the frustration of confused students by saying something like, "It's OK not to understand for now. You'll have a chance to learn more about this another time, and, when you do, you will understand." We might continue by reminding students that we each learn in our own ways, by our own time clocks. "So it might be best to relax now, come back to this another time, and give ourselves all the time we need to learn." By avoiding lots of re-explanations, we avoid boring many students and wasting valuable teaching time. (See also Strategy 13-3, Explanation Back-off.)

Strategy 16-12: Think Time

Purpose: To increase learning and ensure dignity for slow learners.

Description: After posing a question, allowing time for all students to formulate an answer for themselves before inviting students to share ideas.

Keeping a quick pace has many benefits. More students stay actively engaged. There is less time for boredom or restlessness. And the class energy remains high. But what about students who think more slowly and, for example, cannot readily formulate answers to our questions? How can we accommodate fast and slow learners without losing our quick pace? We can build Think Time into lessons. Some options:

• *Use Question, All Write.* We have all students write their answer before asking for volunteers (Strategy 16-3).

• *Use the Nod of Recognition.* We nod to indicate we have noticed a student who has volunteered to answer but we want to wait a bit, to give more time for others to think (Strategy 16-7).

• *Signal to students when we're ready for volunteers.* We might say, "We all have our own time clocks for learning, and that means we won't all have our answers ready at the same time. I want us to respect that reality by giving time for everyone to think before calling on volunteers to answer. So we'll use a signal here. I'll raise my hand like this when it's time for you to raise your hands to volunteer. Please do not raise your hand before I give the signal. That might be distracting to those who are still thinking."

• *Use group responses.* When asking closed-ended questions, to indicate we want everyone to answer together we might consider another signal, choral style: a countdown. One of us, Melanie, noticed that when she used multiplication flashcards, the students who really needed the practice never had a chance to answer. So she started holding the card in one hand and putting up three fingers on the other. In the beginning, she'd count out loud, "3, 2, 1," as she put each finger down. Then she'd point at the students and say "Go!" Eventually she simply put her fingers down one at a time and pointed when it was time to answer. She found then that more students were willing to join in the choral work.

Strategy 16-13: Models and Manipulatives

Purpose: To include concrete objects into the learning process.
Description: Enhancing learning by using models and manipulatives.

We do well to keep on the lookout for opportunities to use models and manipulatives in our lessons. For example, we might have students

• Learn math by handling tokens or objects.
• Write facts on three-by-five-inch cards and use the cards to memorize the facts. (See Strategy 6-3, Study Cards.)
• Create a clay model of a scene or a scientific principle.
• Use paper and tape to create a model.

• Use blocks, sand, or other materials as a free-time option.

• Use clay or pipe cleaners to create a physical representation of an idea, or, with young children, to model letters or numbers.

If materials are limited or students need close supervision for such activities, we can have the bulk of the class working at Learning Centers or a Task Workshop (Strategies 6-2 and 6-5) while we work with a subset of the class.

> ▲ **TEACHER COMMENT**
>
> I have all my students keep in their desks a lump of plastic clay, the kind that doesn't dry up. I can then easily ask them to model a concept or number or almost anything. Although their models are rarely good, it works well as a change of pace, especially healthy for those who like to use their hands. Some like to play with the clay during down time, too, and I find that's also good for them.
>
> — *Janica Cusitus, 2nd Grade Teacher*

Strategy 16-14: Parking Lot

Purpose: To provide a dignifying way to defer some student questions.
Description: Writing on the board student questions that are best deferred, as a reminder to us to return to them later.

Sometimes a student will ask a question that we would prefer not to answer at that moment. Our answer might take the discussion too far off track, or our answer might unwisely slow the development of the lesson, or it might be boring to those not interested in the question. What to do? Education consultant Frank Siccone suggests setting up a Parking Lot for such questions. We might, for example, say, "That is a good question, Terry. But I don't want to take the time to answer it right now. Let's set aside this part of the board for that question and any others that come up that would be best dealt with later." While we're saying that, we write "Parking Lot" on a section of the board, and under that heading write the student's question, perhaps adding the student's name. This strategy reminds us to handle such deferred questions, assures students that their questions will not be forgotten, and, of course, helps us to keep our lessons flowing with active involvement.

Strategy 16-15: Physical Movement

Purpose: To insert physical movement into lessons.
Description: Enhancing learning by providing opportunities for students to move their bodies.

Minds and bodies are not disconnected. Sitting too long results in sluggish minds. It's valuable, then, to create ways students can move about from time to time. Some possibilities to consider:

Some parents could do more for their children by not doing so much for them.

—Anonymous

• When using Sharing Pairs and Learning Pairs (Strategies 7-1 and 7-2), have students stand while they work.

• Allow students to stand or even walk about during silent reading.

• Ask groups of students to pair up and act out a story or a historical event for one another.

• Have students portray statues that illustrate various moods or events.

• Put students in pairs and ask them to try to pantomime words from a vocabulary list.

• Have students create a dance that represents a story or an event.

• Instead of passing papers to students, distribute three or four piles of papers around the room and ask students to each come up and take one.

Strategies 8-4, 8-5, and 8-6 provide additional ideas for getting students moving.

Helping Students Master Content in Individual and Small-Group Formats

17

Assisting students to master the subject matter that was presented to them is, of course, always a challenging task, one of the most challenging tasks teachers face. How many of us, after all, when we were students, mastered all the content presented to us?

The preceding chapter offered strategies for handling that task with the class sitting as one whole group. This chapter offers strategies for handling the task via small-group work and independent study, two formats that turn out to promote mastery much more effectively. It is, after all, difficult to respect individual learning differences when students are treated as one whole group.

Several strategies already discussed use small-group or independent work to help students digest and master subject matter, including Learning Centers and Independent Learning Assignments (Strategies 6-2 and 6-4). In fact, any strategy that has students handling subject matter thoughtfully can be said to serve student learning.

Because this task is so central to our mission as teachers, we've included an unusually large number of the strategies that our field teachers have found to be both practical and effective. We recommend that you look over at least the first nine, each of which is marked with an arrow.

Strategy 17-1: Clear-to-Muddy Groups

Purpose: To give students help at the level they need.
Description: Asking students to put themselves in one of three groups—clear, buggy, or muddy—depending on how clear their present understanding is.

After we introduce new material, it is often crystal clear to some students, hazy to others, and totally unclear to a few. How might we then proceed? Consider the following discussion:

Teacher: Think about the windshield of a car. What would the glass look like right after going through a car wash?

Jerry: It would be clean.

Teacher: Yes. When the windshield is clean, we can see clearly through it. And sometimes a topic is very clear to us. Now then, how many of you would say you're very clear about the topic we just studied? Just raise your hand so I can get an idea.

The teacher scans the room and then returns to the windshield image:

Teacher: Did you ever go for a drive that got bugs on the glass? What does the windshield look like then?

Mike: It looks dirty.

Teacher: Yes, it does look dirty, but can you still see through it?

Mike: Sure.

Teacher: That is right. We might say it's buggy. When we partly understand something, but some things are still unclear, we could say that we're "buggy" about that topic. How many of you would say you're buggy about what we just did in our lesson?

Again, the teacher scans the room and then asks students to imagine they have driven through a big, muddy puddle that splashed over the windshield:

Teacher: Do you think we'd be able to see well then?

Class: No!

Teacher: So when we're really unclear about something and it doesn't make much sense to us, we can say we're "muddy" about that topic. How many of you would say you're muddy about our last topic?

Following such an introduction, we would be able to readily divide students into three groups for further study. We start by identifying how many would say they are clear about the topic just studied, how many would say they are buggy—understand it somewhat but not very clearly—and how many would say they are muddy—far from clear about it. We might, then, ask each person in the "clear" group to pair up with one of the "buggies" and to help them with a review sheet, or to move on to a challenge activity, or to proceed to some other independent work. Or those in the "buggy" group might pair up to help each other with a review sheet, perhaps using the I Say Review (Strategy 11-3); or they might work together to create a Review Test (Strategy 11-1) for the material. Once the "clear" and "buggy" groups are actively engaged, we would be free to meet with the "muddy" group to personally reteach and review with them. (This strategy is adapted from Brimijoin, Marquisse, and Tomlinson, 2003.)

 ## Strategy 17-2: Mini-task

Purpose: To engage students in review tasks likely to be personally satisfying.

Description: Assigning a task that students can complete within one session that is likely to give them a feeling of satisfying accomplishment.

A Mini-task is a task that students can comfortably complete within one session, either working alone or with a partner. The best are those likely to give students a feeling of satisfying accomplishment. Some examples:

• Read pages 14 through 16 and write a 30-to-40-word summary of the material. Then pair up and read each other's summary. If your partner's summary is not completely clear to you, help your partner revise it. When finished, sign each other's project as the "checker."

• With a partner, brainstorm a list of possible solutions to the problem on the board. Then rank your solutions, putting a 1 by the item you think is best, 2 by the one you think is second best, and so on. Each of you should then make a copy of your list, because we may want to discuss the solutions later.

• Create a diagram, chart, or picture illustrating the topic. Put your name on your work and post it for others to study.

• Complete the review problems on the worksheet. Then compare answers with someone who is also finished and, if necessary, correct your work. If you both are stuck, ask any friend for help.

Productive Mini-tasks might include:

• Reading and summarizing
• Listening and listing
• Making charts and diagrams
• Brainstorming and sorting
• Creating applications
• Making an outline
• Completing worksheets

• Writing Outcome Sentences (Strategy 21-1)
• Interviewing other students
• Writing questions
• Solving problems
• Working on Study Cards (Strategy 6-3)

These Mini-tasks are meant to help students engage subject matter in a way that doesn't raise fear of failure. Students have specific, limited tasks to complete that are very doable. Student satisfaction therefore is high in classrooms that use lots of such Mini-tasks.

The most satisfying of tasks are reasonably difficult—not too easy, not too hard. Tasks that are too easy are often boring. Those that are too hard are often frustrating. Reasonably difficult tasks are fun, like games that are winnable but still offer challenges. Because what is reasonably difficult for one student will not be for another, we do well to offer tasks that can be handled at various levels of excellence or to ask students to adjust how they handle a task so it becomes a "just-right" challenge. We might make a poster like the one in Figure 14, which gives students ideas for how to make tasks more fun.

Some Mini-tasks are automatically self-adjusting. Students naturally self-manage how challenging to make the task. Some examples of self-adjusting Mini-tasks:

- Write something you learned.
- Tell what you remember.
- Do as many as you can.
- Look at the answers whenever that will help you.
- Work with someone if you need to.
- Say how you felt about it.

When we create and assign Mini-tasks, then, students have a satisfying way to engage subject matter and, presumably, to increasingly understand it. And we

---

Figure 14
Poster for Mini-Tasks

To make an easy task more fun, try . . .	To make a hard task more fun, try . . .
• Doing it fast. Give yourself a time limit. • Doing it better. Aim to do it better than last time; perhaps keep a score card. • Challenging a friend; see who does it best or first. • Doing it creatively, in a way unique to you.	• Asking a friend to help when you feel stuck. • Doing only part of it. • Asking the teacher for something easier or different. • Doing it with a classmate. • Doing it creatively, in a way unique to you.

obtain a classroom structure that makes it easy for us to work with individuals or small groups as needed.

Some students typically zip through our Mini-tasks, finishing while others are still working. Those students can then become a distraction to those still working. They can also become distractions to us. And even if they wait very patiently, they are losing valuable learning time. How to avoid that problem? One remedy is to make our practice tasks meaty, rich, offering many engagement opportunities, many ways to keep busy. Examples:

More meaty tasks	Less meaty tasks
• Write some easy, medium, and hard problems, so we can later exchange them and give one another more practice.	• Practice doing these problems.
• Write some silly or serious sentences containing adjectives (or any part of speech).	• Circle the adjectives in the sentences on the worksheet.
• Write some Outcome Sentences about what we did so far.	• Do the review quiz on page 84.

In general, a more meaty task is rich enough to keep all students busy. A less meaty task tempts students to do it and quit.

Hint: An easy way to make tasks more meaty is to add an optional activity:

• If you have time, illustrate your notes.
• When you finish, make up some new examples.
• If time remains, find someone who is also finished and share your work.

If our classrooms include Learning Centers, a library, computers, or a Class Workshop, we can sometimes use that as the option, as by saying, "When you finish, please work at one of the Learning Centers." If students have ongoing personal projects, such as journals to keep, that can also be the option, as by saying, "When you have done as good a job as you can with that task, work on your personal project."

Strategy 17-3: Learning Map

Purpose: To review the relationships between concepts and ideas.
Description: Helping students develop a method of taking notes that integrates words, symbols, pictures, and other images connected to a central topic.

Our brains have the ability to be aware of generalizations, pictures, scenarios, colors, sound, and music. Yet schooling often reduces learning to abstract, disconnected facts. Research shows that does not fit well with students' complexity of

A mediocre idea that generates enthusiasm will go farther than a great idea that inspires no one.

—Mary Kay Ash

thought (Rose & Nicholl, 1997). One way to engage student awareness more fully and help students more fully understand topics is to use a Learning Map. Instructions for creating a Learning Map might go something like this:

1. *Choose a topic.* Write the core idea in the middle of the page.

2. *Branch out.* Work outward from your core idea by adding several related "branches."

3. *Incorporate key words.* Add relevant verbs and nouns to each branch. Aim to use as few words as possible, selecting those that are most likely to trigger recall of the lesson.

4. *Add symbols, colors, pictures, and other elements.* Combine a variety of styles to make your learning map more memorable. Perhaps vary the size of the words, writing some in bold, others in all capitals. Or add simple symbols like check marks, question marks, exclamation points, stick figures, shapes, or anything else that is likely to trigger recall of important points.

5. *Consider these hints:*
   - Leave plenty of empty space to help information stand out.
   - Use bold print, vivid colors, highlighted words, and a unique style to help you remember important information.
   - Redraw a Learning Map so you can clarify ideas and remember details.

The instructions can also be incorporated into an eye-catching poster like the one shown in Figure 15. Visual learners will appreciate having the instructions conveyed in this way.

Strategy 17-4: Paper Exchange

Purpose: To arrange for students to help one another improve written work.
Description: Asking students to read one another's papers and to write feedback notes.

To introduce this strategy, we ask students to take a paper they wrote and pass it to someone else. Students are to keep the papers face down, not looking at them until we tell them to do so. When we give them the go-ahead, students are to look over the papers they have received and to provide some written feedback—things they liked about the paper, suggestions for improvement, questions, or anything else that would be constructive. We remind students that the goal is to help the person do even better than he or she already did. We might ask, "Does this mean you cannot be critical or cannot mention errors? Wouldn't that be constructive?

Our mistakes and failures are always the first to strike us and outweigh in our imagination what we have accomplished and attained.

—*Goethe*

Figure 15
How to Make a Learning Map

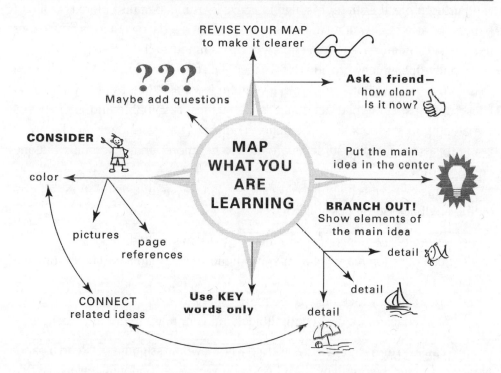

Would you like someone to note errors on your paper so you could correct them before you turned it in? I think you probably would." Finally, we might tell the students they may sign their comments, so the original writers can ask for more feedback if they wish, but signing is optional.

We then conclude our instructions this way:

> You will notice a pile of papers here on my desk; right now that pile has a few papers some of you wrote before. After you finish with your paper, come up to the desk and put your completed paper on the bottom of this pile. Then take a new paper off the top of the pile and, as before, read it and give the writer some constructive feedback. Continue on that way, putting papers you finish on the bottom, taking a new paper off the top. You will have time to read over several papers, so no need to rush. After we're all through, I'll return your papers to you, so you can see the feedback your papers received.

What is good about this process? First, it gets all students looking over others' work. Most will notice that some work is done better than theirs, and almost all will get ideas for improving their work. In that way, students keep sharpening and expanding their awareness. They may also be reading the feedback notes others had written, which often helps students see things of which they were unaware.

Furthermore, the strategy is high in active learning. Because there is a pile of papers on your desk waiting to be read, no student needs to wait for a new paper to read. All students are reading and writing comments all the time.

Finally, this strategy provides lots of feedback to students very efficiently. One reason we read students' work is to give them feedback. Yet, as peer instruction keeps demonstrating, peer feedback is sometimes as valuable and is often less threatening to students than is teacher feedback (Bangert-Downs et al., 1991). Using this strategy, then, students are able to get more feedback than we alone could provide.

In some cases, it is helpful to give students more specific instructions for providing feedback. Some possibilities:

- Underline all the words you think might be misspelled.
- Put a question mark in the margin whenever you read a part that is unclear to you.
- Draw a smiley face next to the parts you really like.
- Put a check mark over every subject and verb that are not in agreement.

We can also turn Paper Exchange into a homework assignment: "Read a paper at home and make comments." And we can use it as an optional activity: "When you finish the work you are now doing, take a paper from the top of the Paper Exchange pile, make your comments, and replace it on the bottom of the pile."

Strategy 17-5: Question Exchange

Purpose: To provide a quick review of a completed reading or lesson.
Description: Asking students to write questions about material that was studied and then to discuss each question with others.

As a review, we might ask students to write some questions about the material they have been working with: "What questions do you still have about that material? Or what questions, if they came up on a test, would not be entirely easy for you to answer? Write as many questions as you can in the next few minutes." We might then ask students to find a partner and take turns asking each other their questions. "One person asks; the other gives his or her best answer. You can further discuss and seek the best answer for a question, if you like. If you finish all your questions and I have still not called time, continue asking each other new questions."

> What is more wonderful than the delight which the mind feels when it knows? This delight is not for anything beyond the knowing, but it is the act of knowing. It is the satisfaction of a primary instinct.
>
> —*Mark Rutherford*

Afterward, we might reconvene with some Voting Questions to Assess Understanding (Strategy 16-6):

- How many of you found one or two questions that were interesting to you?
- How many found some questions challenging?
- How many feel they need more practice with this material?

One teacher who uses this strategy regularly has her students write their questions on index cards so they can be collected and used again. In this way, students create questions throughout a unit of study and they can use the questions for a cumulative review. And several teachers report using Rotating Pairs (Strategy 7-3) to allow students to share questions and answers with more than one student.

▲ **TEACHER COMMENT**

The book we were reading led to lots of questions about divorce. So I used the Question Exchange. I had each student write two or three questions they had. I then told students to pair up and to ask each other their questions and to give their partners the best answer they had. After three or four minutes, I rotated partners and told students to ask their new partners the same questions. I then did another rotation so each student had a chance to discuss the questions he or she most wanted to discuss with three others. Students loved it! It also helped students talk through issues of real concern to them.

—*Clara Bowles, High School Teacher*

 ## Strategy 17-6: Student Question Writing

Purpose: To motivate students to think more deeply about a topic.
Description: Defining three levels of questions—recall, thinking, and personal—and then asking students to create questions on as many levels as they can.

We want our students to think beyond the level of factual recall. We can encourage their doing so by asking questions that deal with concepts and generalizations, applications, and personal values. We can also ask them to *create* such questions. We might begin by giving students a sheet that defines three levels of questions, for example:

- *Facts and details.* These are memory questions. All we need to do is recall the answer. Examples: "What were the main causes of World War II?" "At what temperature does water freeze?"
- *Concepts and generalizations.* These are more complex questions. We probably need to do some thinking on our own to get a correct answer. Examples: "In general, what factors contribute to the outbreak of war?" "What is known and not yet known about global warming?"
- *Personal.* These are questions about values issues and personal opinions. Only we know what the correct answer is for ourselves. Examples: "Are there any

conflicts that bother you, and is there anything you can do about them?" "What is your view on global warming?"

We might also discuss the definition of each level and create sample questions with the whole group. Then, before or during study of a topic, we can ask students to create questions on as many levels as they can for the topic. Although it is the question writing itself that motivates thinking, we might also find uses for the questions the students created. Some ideas:

- Have student pairs trade questions or work together to find answers.
- Collect and save questions for later use during active-learning games, such as the Mastery Learning Game or the Face-off Game (Strategies 16-9 and 16-10).
- Ask students to answer one or more questions during independent work time or for homework.
- Choose suitable questions, particularly those at the values level, as a starting point for a class discussion or a Learning Log entry (Strategy 21-3).
- Save questions for possible inclusion on Learning Sheets you create in the future (Strategy 15-8).

By learning you will teach; by teaching you will learn.

—Latin proverb

 Strategy 17-7: Teacher Role-Play

Purpose: To provide all students with the chance to teach part of the course content to others.

Description: Asking students to work individually to learn something and then to role-play being a teacher who teaches that material to others.

According to William Glasser (1990), we learn 10 percent of what we read, 20 percent of what we hear, 30 percent of what we see, 50 percent of what we both see and hear, 70 percent of what we discuss with others, 80 percent of what we experience personally, and 95 percent of what we teach someone else. Teaching is thus a powerful tool for learning. And when students are asked to learn something in preparation to teach it to someone else, they often attack the task with a special determination, which is one strength of the Teacher Role-Play strategy.

The strategy has two parts:

1. *All students are assigned the same reading.* They are told to learn the material well enough to teach it to another student.

2. *Students are then paired up.* All are then given, say, 10 minutes each to teach the material to their partners, who are to pretend that they have not yet studied it themselves—a role most students fully enjoy playing.

Here are some ways to implement this strategy:

- Use the strategy almost every day, perhaps to lead students through careful study of a textbook.
- Have only one student in each pair role-play being a teacher on any particular day. The second day the strategy is used, then, have the second student role-play being the teacher. To encourage all students to do the reading every day, even if they are not the teacher, you might ask all students to write Outcome Sentences (Strategy 21-1) on all the readings they have completed.
- Rather than announcing in advance who will be the teacher in the pair for the day, flip a coin each time you use the strategy, adding some suspense to the procedure.
- Conclude the class, or begin the next class, with a Review Test (Strategy 11-1) that covers the material just studied.

It's sometimes useful to give students help in preparing for their teaching time. For example, we could talk about

- Creating an outline.
- Writing summary statements for themselves.
- Preparing a visual organizer such as a web, chart, graph, or illustration.
- Noting connections to other ideas/learnings.
- Noting personal thoughts and practical applications.
- Preparing questions to ask their "students."

We might also discuss aspects of good teaching, such as

- Maintaining eye contact.
- Listening without interrupting.
- Asking questions politely.
- Complimenting their "students" for a job well done.

▲ TEACHER COMMENT

This is my favorite way of getting students to read our textbook. Students like it, too. I usually put students in threes or fours and have the "teacher" stand up when teaching, which I think helps the person stay in role. Although everyone must read the material, I have only one student being the teacher each day. All keep Reading Logs, however, which I check from time to time. And all have to pass the tests, of course, so they all read as much as they ever did. What I especially like is the built-in review it provides. Students read the material for homework. Then they hear someone else teach at least part of what they read. And then we have a class discussion of the material afterward. I think they learn a lot more than they ever did. I haven't given enough tests to be sure, however.

—*N. S. Cappi, High School Social Studies Teacher*

It is almost always useful to follow up a Teacher Role-Play event by giving your own perspectives on the reading or lesson of the day and discussing students' outstanding questions.

 ## Strategy 17-8: Boss/Secretary

Purpose: To promote active engagement in a review exercise.
Description: Asking student pairs to take turns dictating answers to a list of questions.

This strategy was written by Laurie Kagan for the Winter 2003 issue of the Kagan Online Magazine (http://www.KaganOnline.com/Newsletter/index.html). It involves giving students a list of questions to answer or a sheet of problems to solve, and then pairing them up for another kind of role-play—in this case, playing the roles of "boss" and "secretary." Here is how this might be introduced:

> Just as a boss might dictate a letter to a secretary, who then writes the letter, you will take turns being a boss and a secretary for this task. To start, A will play the role of a boss, B the role of a secretary. The boss is to look at the first question or problem and dictate an answer. The secretary either writes the answer or, if he or she thinks it's not correct, coaches the boss until the boss can dictate the correct answer. Then switch roles for the next question or problem. Continue until answers have been written to all the questions. Put both names on your answer sheet.

Laurie Kagan says students love this role-playing. We suspect many enjoy being a boss for a change.

 ## Strategy 17-9: Consult Time

Purpose: To give all students a moment of personal teacher attention.
Description: Organizing activities so there's time for each student to visit briefly with the teacher.

Consult Time is time for each student to sit with us and to consult or report briefly on, for example, homework just completed or progress with a personal project. We might make time for this by arranging for the class as a whole to work at individual or small-group learning tasks. Each student, then, takes a few moments away from these tasks to visit with us.

Students could take turns coming to where we sit. Or, if students are in small groups, we could travel from group to group to visit with individual students while others wait their turns. Meeting with students in a small-group setting offers some advantages. When students meet with us alone, they may feel more anxious than when peers are sitting alongside them. Also, students often learn something when they hear others talking with us.

What might students consult on? Some possibilities:

• Students can read one or more of the Outcome Sentences (Strategy 21-1) they wrote for homework. (See also Strategy 10-3, Homework Hearing Time.)

• Students can read or talk about an item from their personal journals or discuss progress on a personal project.

• If students are learning to read, each might read aloud from a story or reading sheet.

• If students need to memorize a list of terms or formulas, each might recite items recently mastered or ask to be quizzed on a few of them.

• If we simply want to get to know our students better, we can invite them to talk about anything of interest to them, in or out of school. For this option, we might want to make this Consult Time a choice for students, rather than a requirement.

Consult Time provides a time for us to connect personally and meaningfully with each student, which, of course, can also be an occasion to clarify each student's progress or to offer brief instruction or support. It is also a time when students can experience moments of personal, caring attention from a respected adult, something many students, especially those in fractured or stressed families, may rarely experience.

> I reckon there's as much human nature in some folks as there is in others, if not more.
>
> —*Edwards Noyes Westcott*

Strategy 17-10: Plan, Do, Review

Purpose: To help students become more self-responsible learners.
Description: Having students plan how they will handle an assignment and then, afterward, reviewing how well they did.

We often ask students to *be* more self-responsible, but we may not as often help students learn how to *become* more self-responsible. For this goal, consider the Plan, Do, Review strategy (adapted from Ilfeld, 1996). Here is one teacher using it in a math class:

Today I'd like you to work individually or in small groups on your multiplication facts. There are many different ways you might proceed. Some of you might prefer to study alone, some with a partner. Some of you might learn better by writing the multiplication facts, some may do better by reciting them aloud. Because we all learn in our own ways, the best way for you might not be the best way for someone else, right? What way might be best for you? Let's list some possible ways of learning the multiplication facts.

As the class brainstorms, the teacher records their ideas on the board. She then tells the students that their job has three parts: "First, plan how you personally will go about mastering more of your multiplication facts today. Make some notes about what steps you will take." She writes on the board:

1. Plan. Write steps you plan to take.

Then she tells them, "Next, I'll give you time to carry out your plan." She writes on the board:

2. Do. Carry out your plan.

She concludes by telling the students that when they finish the assignment, she will ask them to review how it went and to write what they liked about their plan and how they carried it out, and what they might do differently next time (Strategy 21-2, Like/Might Review). She writes on the board:

3. Review. Write Like/Mights.

The Plan, Do, Review works well for brief assignments, as in the example above, as well as long-range assignments. Here is the plan and review one student wrote for a project to learn more about Egypt:

My plan: Read at least three sources. Make notes. Write summary. Compare with Kate. Help each other to prepare a poster as a visual report.

My review: I like the way I started. I did all the reading and also made some good notes. Next time I might do better at writing a summary. I didn't really understand everything all that well, and then Kate and I got off track when we talked. But the poster we made was great, I thought.

Some other possibilities for this strategy:

• Use the Plan, Do, Review frequently with classes that have many students who need better self-management skills.

• Use the strategy for homework assignments to help all students improve self-management skills.

- Use the strategy for many or all independent work time assignments.
- Use the strategy instead of a penalty for students who fail to complete assignments.

For additional possibilities, see Vogel (2001).

Strategy 17-11: Student Self-Evaluation

Purpose: To help students monitor their own learning.
Description: Providing students with opportunities to evaluate their own work.

We can, of course, correct students' papers. However, when students are asked to evaluate their own work, they often see more clearly what they've learned and what they still need to work on. Here are three possibilities for employing such self-evaluations:

- *Answer keys.* For right/wrong answers, students might self-check their papers using an answer key, perhaps written on the board or posted somewhere in the classroom. Students might then work in pairs to help each other correct their wrong answers. When they are finished, all students can have the satisfaction of handing in "perfect" papers. See also Strategy 10-2, Homework Self-Correcting.
- *Rubrics.* We might provide all students with a rubric and a model by marking a sample paper with the whole class. Students could then work individually or with a partner to check their paper against the rubric provided. Afterward, we might ask students to rate how satisfied they are with their work, using a scale of 1 to 3, with 1 being not satisfied, 2 being moderately satisfied, and 3 being very satisfied. For more suggestions, see Rubrics (Strategy 31-7) and the related strategy, Specific Levels of Excellence (Strategy 12-7).
- *Criteria of excellence.* We might give all students an example of an excellent paper and ask them to read it for themselves and think about what makes it excellent. The whole class might then discuss what makes that paper so good. Students could then compare their own work with the model paper. We might conclude by asking students to write a Like/Might Review (Strategy 21-2), telling what they liked about their paper and what they might do differently next time. Or we could ask students to write a few Outcome Sentences about the experience (Strategy 21-1) and share those with a partner.

Strategy 17-12: Class Tutors

Purpose: To provide extra help to students efficiently.

Description: Establishing a procedure whereby students can readily be tutored by other students.

Peer teaching offers great advantages. It usually helps both the giver and the receiver. Furthermore, it helps not only with immediate learning, but also with the development of cooperative habits that have lifelong value. One way to take advantage of peer instruction is to set up a tutoring program. We might begin by addressing students like this:

> We all learn by our own time clocks and in our own ways, of course. As a result, some of us will learn some things more slowly, some more quickly. That is not good or bad, any more than it is good or bad that some plants grow more slowly than others. It is just the way life works.
>
> Another aspect of life is helping one another. People can do that. And in our class, I want us to do so. I want us to live as a cooperative, helpful community. So here is what I suggest.
>
> Those of you who understand a topic and are willing to be tutors for others on that topic, please sign the tutor sheet I have posted on the wall for the topic. Then, when any of you would like some help, you can look on that sheet and find someone you can ask. When you ask someone for help, consider arranging to work together after school, if you can, or during lunchtime. You might even do your tutoring on the phone or via e-mail, if you both agree. I say that because there may not be a lot of free class time to get the help you deserve to have.
>
> I might also use those tutor lists. If I notice a few students who I feel need extra help or practice, I might look to see what volunteer tutors I can pair the students with. If I do that, I may tell the tutor exactly what it is that I want covered.

When all students receive training in tutoring, many do better at both giving and receiving help and in developing the constructive habits that tutoring promotes. The next strategy suggests a way to provide such training.

Strategy 17-13: Tutor Training

Purpose: To improve the effectiveness of tutors.

Description: Teaching students skills for effectively giving and receiving help.

Students often need training if they are to be good tutors for one another. Such training also provides a good excuse to teach important life skills, such as how to listen to others, how to discipline urges to upstage others, and how to interact productively with others. Even without a tutoring program, if we often ask students to sit in pairs to help each other, we will find it valuable to include tutor training in our classes.

Part 1: Introducing Tutor Training

A possible plan for introducing tutor training to students:

1. *Teacher introduction to whole class, 1 minute.* Say that you will often ask students to help one another learn something, usually in pairs, and that some of them may also sign up to be special tutors for specific topics. Then ask, "What does it take to help someone learn?" Suggest that good listening is one essential skill. "If tutors are to do good jobs at helping others," you might say, "they will want first to listen and check what the other now knows."

2. *Whole class and teacher brainstorming, 5–12 minutes.* Lead the class in brainstorming a list of actions that distinguish good listeners from poor listeners. "How many of you know someone who listens really well? Does anyone know someone who is a terrible listener?" Ask the students to consider what good listeners do that terrible listeners do not do and have perhaps two students write the ideas on the board as other students offer them.

3. *Instructions and practice pairs, 4 minutes.* Tell the students that there are two key listening skills you would emphasize:
   ○ Looking at the speaker pleasantly (not looking out the window).
   ○ Giving the speaker plenty of time to think (not interrupting).

Tell the students that when you give the signal, they should find a partner, someone with whom they have not worked recently, and choose one to be A and the other to be B. The A in each pair will start. "A's job is to talk about someone he or she knows who is either a fairly good listener or a very poor listener. B's job is to be a good listener." Tell students that you will give them a signal when 90 seconds is up. "Until then, B's, do not take the focus from your A partner. B's will have a turn to talk later. Get in pairs now. And now, B's, start listening!"

4. *Review discussion, 3–5 minutes.* Ask the class, "How many A's had a B who did a great job listening, even though this was the first time we tried this? What problems came up? What did you all learn from this?"

5. *Second instructions and practice, 4 minutes.* Ask the students to reverse roles. The B's are to talk about listening—the experience they just had as a listener, people they know, or anything else that is relevant. The A's are to check for the two key listening skills. Remind the A's that they should not steal the focus from their B partner; rather, their job is to be as good a listener as they can be.

Tim was so learned that he could name a horse in nine languages. So ignorant, that he bought a cow to ride on.

—*Benjamin Franklin*

Tell them that they will again have 90 seconds, and launch the second practice by saying "Go!"

6. *Review discussion, 6–12 minutes.* Ask how many B's had an A partner who showed great listening ability. Then ask, "What can we say about this practice time? Was anything hard? New?" After a few minutes, wrap up the lesson. "That is enough for now. I just wanted to get us started on what I call tutor training." Then briefly explain your overall goal: "It's training so you can be better helpers for one another. Next time I ask you to help one another, stretch yourself toward excellent listening skills."

We recommend that you review the listening lesson after a day or so. You might simply have a whole-class discussion: "Has anyone become more aware of good and poor listening since we had our practice? Has anyone practiced becoming a more skillful listener? How many of the two good listening skills can you now list on scrap paper? How many listed one? How many listed two? Please continue practicing, here or out of school."

Or you might use a Like/Might Review (Strategy 21-2), as in this example:

Think back to times you listened to others in the last day or so, in this class, in other classes, at home, anywhere. As you think about the listening you did, write one or two things you might say: "*I liked the way I . . .*"

[Teacher resumes after a minute or two.] Now, as you think back to those listening experiences, see if you can write something that starts, "*Next time I might . . .*" You could write about doing things better, or differently, or anything else. This is not a promise; it's just a sentence about what you might do the next time a similar situation comes up for you.

You might then invite some students to share what they have written.

Part 2: A Second Round of Practice Pairs

After an appropriate time, you might conduct another set of practice pairs, this time focusing on disciplining urges to upstage others—that is, holding back one's own thoughts when others are speaking. You might say something like this:

A's, please pick a topic that you have pretty strong feelings about; for example, what parents, teachers, police, or the president should do or not do; what is wrong with this town or school; or your opinions on any controversial topic. Anything you like. Tell B your topic.

B's, your job is to pretend your opinions are very different from A's. I'll give you two or three minutes to tell that opinion to A. Speak as if you really mean it, with dignity and power, the best you can.

A's, your job is to practice good listening and to practice not upstaging the person who is speaking—not interrupting, not taking away that person's right to speak up, not showing disrespect to the person. Put your own ideas on the shelf and just listen. While B speaks (1) aim to look pleasantly at the person, (2) give your partner plenty of time to think about what to say, and (3) most important, do not interrupt. If you feel the need to say anything, say something like, "Yes, I think I understand how you feel." Or try a brief summary of an idea your partner expressed, like this: "As I hear it, you feel parents should never ground teenagers." Go!

A few days later, you might review as before, using a discussion or the Like/Might Review (Strategy 21-2):

> Did anyone become more aware of holding back thoughts when others were speaking? Did anyone become more aware of when others failed to do that? Did anyone risk practicing the self-discipline skill? Please keep aware of this skill and keep practicing, for it will help us be good tutors to one another in class.

Part 3: Further Training and Practice

As you continue Tutor Training, you might discuss further the various skills involved. Here is one approach.

1. *Introduction and pair/trio brainstorming, 3–5 minutes.* You might begin by noting that some people are skilled at tutoring. "What do they do?" you could ask. "They might ask the person they're tutoring how they can best help. They might also say, 'Am I going too fast?' or 'Do you need a break now or do you need some new practice problems?'" Then you might invite the students to sit with one or two others and write a list of what good tutors do, including the ideas you just mentioned and any others they can think of.

2. *Group reporting and class summary, 10–15 minutes.* Invite the students to see if they can agree on which, from all their lists, are the top four or five items. You might say something like this: "I want each group to start by giving one idea for our board list. Then we'll vote to see which we agree are important. Finally, I'll ask one or two of you to make a wall chart, so we can occasionally review our Guidelines for Good Tutoring."

Soon after training, if a real tutoring situation does not arise, you might invent a practice exercise for students to do in pairs, again designating an A and a B in each pair. You might, for example, ask students to pretend they are not sure how to do long division. The job of the B in each pair is to be a good tutor and help A learn how to do long division. You can suggest the pairs look at the Guidelines for Good Tutoring they helped to create earlier. After a few minutes, you might discuss the experience, and then ask students to reverse roles.

I am the master of everything I can explain.

—*Theodore Haecker*

It's important to pick subject matter that both students are likely to understand fairly well—how to add fractions, how to memorize three spelling words, how to remember what they read in a book. You can even ask them to tutor each other on how to get from the school to the post office.

After the practice session, you might review by asking each person to write some Outcome Sentences (Strategy 21-1), completing phrases such as "*I learned …, I was surprised …, I'm beginning to wonder …*" and then have students share them, allowing any student the option to pass. Finally, you might use Learning Challenges (Strategy 4-8), as in this example:

> I challenge you to keep stretching yourself toward tutoring excellence, and toward excellent communication outside of class, too. If you accept this challenge, keep track of how it goes, perhaps using Learning Logs. If you have a difficult communication situation to deal with, perhaps ask a friend to be one of your cheerleaders. And from time to time you may want to let us know what progress you are making.

Strategy 17-14: Best Choice Debate

Purpose: To promote open-minded consideration of controversial issues.

Description: Instructing students to pair up, consider one side of a controversial issue, and then share their thoughts with a pair that has considered the other side of that issue.

Students often carry misconceptions about complex ideas, such as the rule of law, truth in advertising, protecting the environment. Giving them more information improves understanding only slightly. Having students discuss what they know and believe improves understanding a bit more. And having students engage in a thoughtful debate can improve understanding even more (Guzzetti, Snyder, & Glass, 1993).

Organizing a Best Choice Debate

Here is an efficient way to organize such a debate, or, in the words of Johnson and Johnson (1987), "a thoughtful controversy." In this example, the teacher is preparing students for a debate on the issue "Should smoking be illegal?" He begins by discussing the *formation of pairs:*

> Please pair up with someone with whom you have not worked recently. I will arbitrarily assign half the pairs to take the "Yes" side of our question. The people in these pairs are to pretend that they strongly agree that smoking should be illegal. Half the pairs will be assigned the "No" position. They will strongly disagree.

The best things and the best people rise out of their separateness; I'm against a homogenized society because I want the cream to rise.

—*Robert Frost*

He then discusses *preparation time:*

We will start with preparation time. During this time you are to work with your partner to understand your side of the issue very thoroughly, with reason and evidence, and to prepare to face an opposing pair.

He proceeds with a detailed explanation of the actual *debate:*

When you face your opposing pair, you will be in fours and your job will be twofold. The first part of your job is to work together as a pair to get the other pair to fully appreciate your position. They may not clearly understand your position at the outset. In fact, because they were preparing the other side of the issue, they may be so committed to their side that they will have trouble listening to your reasons and evidence with an open mind. You will need, then, to practice a common life problem: getting people who think differently than you to understand your thinking. Note that your job will not be to convince them they are wrong and you are right. Your job, as a pair, is to make sure they understand your side of the issue.

The second part of your job is to pretend you do not now understand their position. If you did not do this, they would have no practice in communicating effectively, which is the first task. That does not mean you have to be stubborn or argumentative. Don't go to extremes. This is not a conflict, beat-the-opposition debate. It's really a search for expanded, balanced understandings. So even if you fully understand the thinking of the other pair, pretend you do not. If you think it will not be too upsetting, you can even show some disagreement with their ideas so they get practice in communicating with people who have different positions. That is something we all must do in real life.

The teacher moves on to the task of agreeing on a *best choice:*

Finally, at the end, I'd like each foursome to see if it can agree on the best choice for resolving the issue. The question to address is this: Now that you four understand more about both sides of the issue, what do you think, overall, is best for all concerned? Make smoking illegal? Leave it as is? Or perhaps your group can come up with a third choice. We do not want to get stuck in either-or thinking. Nor do we want to get stuck in selfish, what's-best-for-me thinking. We don't want to forget what is good for us personally. But we also want to consider what would be best for others and conclude by putting into words the best overall choice.

The teacher concludes by giving students some *hints for preparation time:*

During the debate, you may face problems. What do you do, for example, if you and your partner do not cooperate and even contradict each other, making it hard for the other pair to understand your position? What do you do if an argument breaks out and people stop listening to one another? It would be smart to use some of your preparation time to talk about how you will handle such problems. Do you want to talk now about options for handling the two problems I mentioned? Do you want to identify other problems that might come up before we form pairs, assign positions, and get into our planning time?

Suggested Issues for a Debate

Any controversial issue can provide the basis for an effective best choice debate. Some options:

- Should property and sales taxes be replaced by income taxes?
- Should children have an evening curfew?
- Should language in song lyrics that some people find offensive be prohibited?
- Should the minimum driving age be lowered?
- Should the metric system be required in the United States?
- Should all handguns be outlawed?
- Should the pay of top executives be limited to less than a hundred times the average wage of all other workers?
- Should children get an allowance?

This above all: To thine own self be true.

—William Shakespeare

Strategy 17-15: Task Group with Communication Practice

Purpose: To develop teamwork skills while reviewing material.

Description: Instructing small groups to work at a task and, while working, practice an interpersonal skill.

This strategy is a most powerful form of cooperative learning. It advances not only academic learning but also effective interpersonal skills. The strategy takes some time, however—usually a minimum of 45 minutes. Adapted from *A Guidebook for Cooperative Learning* by Dee Dishon and Pat Wilson O'Leary (1998), four steps are involved: (1) assigning individual tasks, (2) assigning a group product and choosing a teamwork skill for practice, (3) reviewing the teamwork skill, and (4) reviewing the task.

Assigning Individual Tasks

We might assign this step as homework. For example, each student could be asked to

- Find examples of a specified physics principle.
- Identify four or more new ideas from a text.
- Write down personal recommendations for preventing waste in school.
- Create a poem.
- Draft a letter to the editor on an issue each feels strongly about.
- Seek real-life applications for a math procedure.

Assigning a Group Product and Choosing a Teamwork Skill for Practice

For this step, we ask students to work together in groups of two to four to produce one specific, tangible product built around the earlier individual task, signed by all persons in the group. Some possibilities (in the order of the list in Step 1):

- A report summarizing the identified physics examples, augmented by any additional examples that emerged during the group interaction.
- A list of ideas from the text reading ranked by importance.
- A list of individual ideas for preventing waste ranked by estimated long-term effectiveness.
- An illustrated booklet of poems.
- An improved version of the original draft letters.
- A poster showing a real-life math problem with a clear, illustrated solution on an attached sheet.

We also tell students that while they work in their groups, they are to practice a particular communication skill, such as

- Listening closely to each person.
- Taking turns.
- Reacting to others' comments positively.
- Returning to the task when they notice they are off track.
- Disagreeing politely.
- Managing time.
- Asking for help.
- Being supportive.
- Sharing honest feelings.
- Keeping everyone involved.
- Paraphrasing.
- Helping without giving answers.
- Expressing honest appreciations.
- Listening with deep empathy to others.
- Restraining unproductive impulses.
- Making everyone feel important.
- Making eye contact.

It's best for the assigned teamwork skill to be defined with many examples, so students get specific guidance in how they might practice it. We might say, for example, something like this:

Some cause happiness wherever they go, others whenever they go.

—*Oscar Wilde*

While doing this task I'd like you to focus on being supportive to one another. Let's brainstorm some things a person might do or say that would suggest the person is being supportive, and some things a person might say or do that might be not supportive at all.

The class then brainstorms and produces a chart of items, such as this:

Being supportive	Not being supportive
• Nods.	• Does not listen.
• Smiles.	• Looks out window.
• Thanks others.	• Does not help out.
• Gives credit to others.	• Is slow to join in.

It's possible to invite students to select specific roles for their group work: someone to be the group coordinator, time watcher, recorder, keeper of materials, and the like. Some teachers do not use role assignments, however. They would rather keep groups small enough so that all quite naturally have important roles to play.

Reviewing the Teamwork Skill

After the groups have had enough time to do their task and practice their skill, it's usually best to gather the class and review the skill first, while the experience is fresh. Our aim here is to help students clarify what they learned about the skill. One effective procedure starts with students making Like/Might notes (Strategy 21-2, Like/Might Review). We first ask students to think back to the group time and to note what they liked about their own performance of the skill or about how someone else demonstrated the skill. Next we ask them to note what they might do next time they have an opportunity to practice the skill. Finally, we invite a few students to share something they noted, which often leads to a Productive Discussion (Strategy 16-2).

Reviewing the Task

The final step is to review the task, aiming to advance subject matter understandings. We might, for example,

• Lecture on the task and then draw out understandings from the group in a Productive Discussion.

• Have students post the results of their task groups, so they can view each other's work.

• Ask students to form Sharing Pairs (Strategy 7-1), each person sitting with someone not in their task group, and to discuss their experiences.

During my piano recital, I was on a stage and scared. I looked at all the people watching me and saw my daddy waving and smiling. He was the only one doing that. I wasn't scared anymore.

—*Cindy, age 8*

• Instruct students to write Outcome Sentences (Strategy 21-1) about the subject matter and then to share those in a Productive Discussion or by using the Whip Around, Pass Option (Strategy 16-4).

Strategy 17-16: Computers and the Internet

Purpose: To use Internet resources to help students master learnings.
Description: Tapping into appropriate programs available on the Internet.

A rich and growing selection of high-involvement projects is available on the Internet, many under the heading of "WebQuests." The field is changing too rapidly for us to cover it here, but examples and guidance are available from www.webquest.org. Computers can also be used to help students review material. Consider, for example, how one algebra teacher planned to do this:

> In my classroom we have six computers. I have set them up with links to Internet sites that contain tutorials, practice problems, and interactive tools for helping students who are having some difficulties and feel that they would benefit from additional practice or guided reviews. Additionally there is enrichment material available on these links for the more advanced students. These computers are ready to go, with the links available on the desktop. Those links are also available during student free periods in the library, and they are even available from the school intranet, so students can access the sites from home.

Strategy 17-17: Task Group, Share Group

Purpose: To maintain high involvement during group work.
Description: Instructing students to work together to complete a brief task and then to pair up and report results to each other.

Courtesy of McCarty and Siccone (2001), here is a highly involving, flexible small-group activity. It proceeds in two steps.

Step 1: Task group. Form small groups. Pairs usually produce the best results; the smaller the group, the larger each student's active role. Assign a task that each group can complete in a few minutes. Some examples:

• Make interesting sentences out of vocabulary [or spelling] words.
• List what you think is particularly interesting about . . . [China, the UN, rivers, and so on].

• Come up with three or four real-life applications of [a multiplication fact, a science idea, or any general principle].

• Rank in order of importance the government agencies we studied.

• Think of three or more alternative ways to handle a real-life problem.

• Create a set of problems with answers.

Specify the time for the task. Shorter is almost always better than longer. Being confined to a short time period motivates students to start promptly and move quickly. Inform students that when time is up, all will pair up with someone not in their task group and will report at least part of the group results. "Make notes, if you like, so you are each ready to do that."

Step 2: Share group. Use Sharing Pairs (Strategy 7-1) when task groups begin to lose high engagement, regardless of the number of minutes you might have originally announced. Ask students to find one person not in their task group and to take turns sharing task-group results. Assuming each task group had two students, for example, you might say something like this:

> Each pair, choose an A and a B. I'd like the A's to remain seated. B's, please go sit with a different A. You now have new pairs. In those pairs, B's, start by reporting what you did in your task group. Then, A's, you take your turn and tell what your task group did. There is not much time for this, so move quickly. Go!

As usual, to maintain high engagement and attentive listening, it is almost always better to keep sharing brief. A second or third set of Sharing Pairs is sometimes useful, as when a variety of important learnings are involved, or when quiet students could use more experience in speaking to peers. You might simply say, "Now, A's, please find another partner and share either what you did in your task group or, if you like, some ideas that came up in your first Sharing Pair." (See Rotating Pairs, Strategy 7-3.)

A whole-class discussion might follow, or students could write personal Outcome Sentences (Strategy 21-1), perhaps followed by the Whip Around, Pass Option (Strategy 16-4). Outcome Sentences could also be inserted in individual portfolios or Learning Logs (Strategy 21-3).

▲ **TEACHER COMMENT**

Students love to hear me read them stories. And I enjoy it, too. But lately I often use Task Group, Share Group. I ask students to pair up and take turns reading a part of a story to each other. "No one read too long, please, so both have turns. Yet read at least one sentence. Ask your partner for help with a word, if you like, or just guess. When you are done, take turns giving answers to the questions I posted." The poster says: What happened so far? What do you predict might happen next? Have you any reasons for your prediction? For Step 2, I say, "When I say 'Go,' find a new partner. Take turns telling what you or your former task partner guessed will happen next in the story. Just two minutes for this. Go." Somehow students really get up for this reading activity.

—Miriam Harmon, 2nd Grade Teacher

Strategy 17-18: Option Display

Purpose: To teach students a procedure for resolving complex problems open-mindedly and thoughtfully.

Description: Instructing groups to construct a display showing several options for solving a problem, the likely consequences of each option, and the group's preferred solution.

This strategy starts with an open-ended problem, as in these examples:

- *Language arts.* How can we get people to read newspapers and watch television more critically? How can we help the young students in our school who cannot read well? How can we best distribute the magazine the class produced? How can we make more use of poetry in our lives?
- *Math.* How can we remember all the geometry formulas? How can we keep track of the cost of a cart of groceries? How can we estimate the number of beans in a bottle?
- *Social studies.* What might reduce prejudice nowadays? How might we help the poor in our area? How can we get more people to vote in elections?
- *Science.* How can we measure temperature without a thermometer? How can we provide better health care for infants? What is the best way to dispose of garbage?

The problems students address could call for research or simply for creative thinking. We might offer one problem to all students or ask them to select a problem from a list. This leads us to the Option Display procedure:

- *Form small groups.* If the whole class works on one problem, groups can be formed in any way convenient. If students are offered more than one problem, individuals can select a problem that interests them; persons selecting the same problem can form pairs or larger groups. Alternatively, groups can form first and then jointly choose a problem. As usual, pairs are the preferred group size.
- *Explain the Option Display.* "By next Monday," we might say, "your team is to produce a wall chart containing four elements." Then describe the four elements and explain how each should appear on the chart:

   1. *Problem.* On the top of the chart, write a clear statement of the problem, in your own words.
   2. *Options.* On the left side of the chart, list three or more possible options for handling the problem. List as many reasonable ideas as you can identify by reading, thinking, or interviewing friends and relatives.

The best and deepest moral training is that which one gets by having to enter into proper relations with others. . . . Present educational systems, so far as they destroy or neglect this unity, render it difficult or impossible to get any genuine, regular moral training.

—*John Dewey*

Nobody is bored when he is trying to make something that is beautiful, or to discover something that is true.

—*William Inge*

3. *Advantages/Disadvantages.* On the right side, next to the option list, write the chief advantages and disadvantages of each option. Think ahead to the long-term difficulties and benefits that would likely result if each option were implemented.

4. *Recommendation.* On the bottom of your chart, write your team's overall recommendation. All in all, what would you think would be the best option for handling the problem? Sign your names to the chart. We will leave the charts on the wall for some time, so all have a chance to examine each other's ideas.

• *Review and conclude the activity.* The activity might well lead to a group discussion. "Did anyone get any new ideas from this activity? Did it change anyone's mind? Does the Option Display activity suggest steps you might take when you face a tough problem in your own life?"

Using Projects to Help
Students Master Content

18

Projects can provide a particularly rich experience for students and can be used both for reviewing prior learnings and for initiating new learnings. Project work is especially valuable for producing comprehensive and integrated understandings, not merely rote memorization, and for developing self-reliant, curious, independent learners (Donald, 1991; Hyerle, 1996; Woloshyn, Willoughby, Wood, & Pressley, 1990). What are effective ways of making use of such projects? The three strategies of this chapter offer suggestions. Based on our field tests, we suggest you give your first attention to the first strategy, which is marked with an arrow.

⋯◈▶ Strategy 18-1: Project Work

Purpose: To help students to engage long-term independent learning projects effectively.

Description: Helping students design independent learning projects, complete them successfully, and report their learnings appropriately.

Some classrooms thrive on a steady diet of independent student projects. The hardest part for us can be organizing the projects so they run smoothly and then giving up some of our control, trusting students to meet the challenge. The best part is usually the sustained energy and integrated, meaningful learnings that result. Here are some suggestions for successful project work.

Identifying the Project

Projects need a focus. Usually the focus is to prepare a report on a specified topic at a specified time. What kind of topic? It might be a *subject matter concept:* plant growth, world government, weights and measures, sonnets, harmony. Or it might feature an *interdisciplinary theme:* designing an ideal city; graphing the responses of citizens to interview questions; considering the health of senior citizens; studying kite building, peanuts and their products, the measurement of time.

Projects can serve as a *culminating activity,* to help students refine and solidify their learnings. And they can also be used *during a unit,* to enrich it and to inspire self-responsible learning. Most teachers have students work on projects in small teams, which has the additional benefit of inspiring growth in teamwork skills. Here is an example of a teacher introducing such a project:

> Our next unit is on rivers. I thought we could have one group studying the formation of rivers: How do they start? Where do they start? What is necessary for a river to continue to flow? Another group could study our local river: What can we discover about it? A third group might identify the major rivers of our country and their characteristics. A fourth group could investigate rivers as means of transportation. There are other ways to approach rivers: their contribution to the economy, the way they have been used by artists and writers, their connection to issues of ecology, the fish and vegetation commonly found in rivers. There are also other ways to focus a project on rivers.

Students might team up, then, on the basis of which focus most interests them. Rather than suggesting projects, we can start by having students brainstorm a list of what they already know about the topic, and then a list of what they might want to know. That can lead into a discussion of what issues might be explored further. Students might then team up with those interested in studying similar issues.

Project work can also be organized around *action projects,* which focus more on action than study. Groups could be formed, for example, to produce a monthly class magazine:

> Everyone can contribute writing and artwork. You can use parts of your journals, even your doodles. But we need groups to put the magazine together and get it out. We might, for instance, have a typing team, a proofreading team, a team that takes care of the duplication, and another team for publicity and distribution. Maybe a team for collecting material from parents and other classes, if we want that. I think we'll need people to manage the fund-raising. They could also take care of the bookkeeping. Each of you could be on more than one team, of course. And maybe we'll need other teams. What do you all think?

Some other examples of action projects:

• Implementing a tutoring program for younger students in the school.

• Testing alternative remedies for a problem in the cafeteria or in the community.

• Managing a program for finding adults to consult in the classroom or to accept students as temporary apprentices.

- Conducting public opinion polls on issues of interest to the group.
- Surveying expert opinion on drugs, health care, or any such topic.
- Constructing a greenhouse for the school.
- Creating exhibits showing past and future space exploration.
- Designing and preparing a model of an ideal home, car, or city.
- Preparing an assembly for the school.

Projects can also be based on *student interests:*

We will cover many topics in our class. But I would like you to practice learning on your own and become more skillful in an area or with a topic that interests you. You could work at this personalized project alone or with one or two others. If you work with others, I want to keep groups small, pairs or trios at the most, so all of you have important parts to play in your groups. Most of the time you will need to work outside of class. But you might be able to substitute some project work for some class work. Speak to me if you think such a substitution would serve your best interests.

What can you design such a project on? Almost anything you think would be fun or good for you and that you are serious about pursuing. Overcoming procrastination, perhaps. The history of bicycles. Chess. Secret codes. Mark Twain. Labor unions. Heroines in history. Scuba diving requirements. Computer art. The concept of generosity, or imagination, or pantomime, or discrimination. Modern music. Improving your sleep habits. Perhaps improving staying-awake habits.

Just check with me before you start. I'll ask you to draw up a provisional plan of action and turn in weekly progress cards. Then we'll go from there.

Setting Guidelines for Project Work

A few simple guidelines will help to ensure that students stay on track during the course of the project and that the process results in a meaningful outcome.

- *Group size.* If students do not work alone, it's best to keep project teams small. Pairs produce the highest level of engagement. When a team has more than two persons, it's easy for one or two students to do all the work, so others feel left out.
- *Clear time lines.* Specific deadlines are essential. If the project is long-term, take care not to allow so much time between progress reports that students are tempted to dawdle. Strategy 22-6 has ideas for helping students manage long-term projects.
- *Progress reports.* You might request, say, a weekly list of "What was accomplished" and "What specific plan do you have for next week?" Each group could have a rotating reporter who would submit that report, with the names of all group members included. Or each student could submit a card each Friday reporting on "What I did this week. What I promise to do next week."

Nothing in education is so astonishing as the amount of ignorance it accumulates in the form of inert facts.

—Henry Adams

- *Final product.* It's valuable for students to have a final product to produce and to have clarity about what that is to be—for example, a display; a collaborative written report; a collection of personal Outcome Sentences (Strategy 21-1); notes so each student can report the group's work to a classmate from a different group (as in Strategy 17-17, Task Group, Share Group); a chart of group ideas (as in Strategy 17-18, Option Display); a group assessment of the work, along with any "minority" viewpoints.

- *Avoiding copy work.* Avoid projects that invite routinely copying from a text or encyclopedia. Rather than having a team report on crime prevention, for example, suggest something more active: "Summarize the opinions of three experts and interview at least five adults to see what they think of that expert advice." Another example: "Design a plan for an ideal health center that includes programs for nutrition and illness prevention." Consider asking students to interview, compare opinions, make a model, design an ideal, find contrasting views, produce a mural, prepare an educational debate, or create a dramatic presentation for another class.

Reporting Completed Work

Many teachers assume that reports on projects should take the form of groups taking turns standing in front of the room and, one after the other, telling the class what they did. However, in terms of active learning, we find that is rarely time well spent. The same applies to book reports; students in the audience rarely are actively engaged in a series of such reports. There are better alternatives for reporting completed work:

- *Random daily reports.* Schedule only one report a day. And perhaps use a random method of choosing the report of the day. "To make it interesting, the group for each day will be chosen from a jar at random, so stay prepared!"

- *One-minute reports from individuals.* Ask individuals, not groups, to make reports. Ask each student to take a turn and give a one-minute report, perhaps on one aspect of the group's results, or on what he or she personally learned from the project work. "We'll set this timer for 60 seconds, and you will each have that much time, so do the best you can. If you prefer to pass, let me know privately and we'll see what else we might do for your report." You might plan three to five of these one-minute reports each day.

- *Creative reports.* If the report is to be given by a group, ask students to make their reports as interesting as possible and discuss some possibilities with them, as in the following examples of teacher directions.

People always told me that my natural ability and good eyesight were the reasons for my success as a hitter. They never talk about practice, practice, practice!

—*Ted Williams*

○ *Poster or model for viewing.* "Create a poster that somehow reflects the work you did. Or make a model you can bring to class. We'll walk around and view each person's poster or model on Friday."

○ *Group skit.* "Present a skit related to the material. Make it interesting, perhaps funny or dramatic. All members of your group must be involved in the presentation, so design it so you all have a part to play. We'll do two or three skits a day."

○ *History report.* "Every day next week, we'll start off with several of you playing the role of a person you studied. Your job will be to wear something—a hat, badge, or anything else—that shows us something about that person. We will then guess who you are. If we can't guess, say something that person might have said. You can even team up with a classmate and act out a skit showing something that person did."

○ *Pantomime or puppetry.* "I'd like the next reports to include either some pantomime or puppets." Or "Without words, act out a principle or key learning you took from your work."

○ *Compact disc cover.* "Think of some song titles that might be associated with your work and design a CD cover that might include those songs. We'll pass all the covers around on Monday."

○ *Dramatic reading.* "Read to us, and as you read, be fully into it. Read with feeling."

○ *Class activity.* "Each group is to get the rest of us to do something that might be fun and that relates to your topic. In the past, to give you some ideas, students have asked us to close our eyes and draw a pineapple, to stand up and wave like an old tree about to topple over in the wind, and to take a fun, five-minute quiz. The idea is to get us involved in your presentation in some way."

○ *Murals, designs, or collages.* "I'd like each trio to produce a mural." Or "Using only geometric figures and colors, create a design that communicates something about your project." Or "This project's report must be in the form of a collage. You could cut words or pictures from old magazines or newspapers. You could even paste on small objects. In some creative way, communicate images or learnings you took from your work."

○ *Short story.* "Write a short story, funny or dramatic, that tells what you did and learned or that tells about people you studied. Include one blank sheet at the end. Write all your names on the story and put it in the story box. Afterward, whenever you have free time, pick a story from the box to read. Note any reactions on the blank sheet and include your name."

The following two strategies are variations on project work. They also suggest additional ways students can report their completed work.

Strategy 18-2: Application Projects

Purpose: To make learning less abstract and more relevant and meaningful.
Description: Encouraging students to apply learnings to real-life situations.

We can sometimes make learning more relevant to students by asking them to take something learned and apply it in real life. Here are three examples of this approach.

Example 1. Students are studying the Bill of Rights, and the teacher says, "Take a few moments and jot down one or two rights you think are not well protected in our community. Perhaps also try to write some words for a law that would better protect those rights." When a few students finish writing, the teacher announces, "One minute more," then has a few students report their thinking. She concludes by saying, "Some of you may want to engage in an extra-credit project to promote your proposed law in town, or to do something else to better protect the rights of citizens in our area, young or old. You can work alone or with one or two others. Let me know if you would like to do this and I'll suggest how you can write up a plan."

Example 2. The teacher has talked about the wisdom of thinking before acting. The teacher then asks, "Is there someone in your life, perhaps a friend or relative, who you wish would do more thinking before acting? Or are there some situations outside of school in which you yourself might wisely do more thinking before acting?" Students make notes, with the caution from the teacher: "No need to share any of this. Keep private anything you care to." A brief discussion follows. The teacher then concludes by saying, "In all of life, now and later, perhaps especially when you are out of school, there are advantages in pausing to think before acting. You might want to practice building that into your life. If you do something about this, please let us know sometime. If I ask what is new or good in your life [New or Goods, Strategy 9-4], as I sometimes do at the beginning of a class, you can report your experiences. It would be interesting to hear about those experiences. We all might learn something from them."

Example 3. A unit has been completed and the teacher says, "Think back to something you learned. Can you imagine a practical use for what you learned?" The teacher might add, "Write or draw something that tells what applications you thought of. Work alone or together with a partner or two. Tomorrow we will share our ideas and see if some of you want to take some action on one of your ideas."

When we routinely ask students to apply what they have learned to reality, we promote the habit of connecting learning to living. For many students, that makes learning more exiting and living more thoughtful.

As soon as you trust yourself, you will know how to live.

—*Goethe*

Strategy 18-3: Service Projects

Purpose: To reinforce the value of learning and to cultivate healthy attitudes about citizenship.

Description: Encouraging students to engage in projects that provide service to others.

Like Application Projects, Service Projects connect learnings to real life. These projects, however, focus on providing service to persons who might need it. Such projects can range from simple to complex, as in these examples:

- Applying knowledge of measurement to cooking, students might bake cookies for senior citizens, soup kitchens, or other groups.
- After a unit on plants, students might collect money to buy seeds and plant them to beautify school or community grounds.
- After learning about natural disasters, students might donate food, money, or clothing to hurricane or flood victims or to poor countries.
- In conjunction with environmental studies, students might conduct recycling campaigns or make presentations to other classes to raise awareness of environmental concerns.
- Applying language skills to letter writing, students might write to hospitalized children, political leaders, or other individuals.
- Students might create "big books" to donate to younger classes, or write stories to be read to younger children, or write and present skits or puppet shows to younger children on character education or to institutionalized adults.
- Students might create portable birthday parties for children in homeless shelters or family abuse shelters, or make "cool" hats for children in hospitals.

To promote an attitude of community service, in our instructional units we might also seek to highlight persons who have dedicated their lives to service. In addition, we might call students' attention to examples of service found in newspapers or on television and encourage students to share with the class examples of service they participate in or hear about.

19

Stimulating Higher-Level Thinking

Research shows that "higher order" questions, those that go beyond recall, are critical to expanding awareness and producing deep learning (Marzano, Pickering, & Pollock, 2001; Pressley, Wood, Woloshyn, King, & Menke, 1992; Redfield & Rousseau, 1981; Ross, 1988). Thinking questions are even more effective with slower learners, who sometimes have difficulty with remembering abstract concepts but may have excellent creativity and intuition and unique experiences to bring to lessons (Hattie, Biggs, & Purdie, 1996). Suitable questions can even generate wisdom, for, as British historian and statesman James Bryce put it, "Wisdom grows out of the temper and heart of a man as well as out of his intellect."

How do we know when we have a good thinking question? A teacher in Japan had a simple explanation: "A good question can keep a whole class going for a long time; a bad one produces little more than a quick answer." Note that "whole class" is part of the criterion. It is not enough to stimulate the thinking of the students with high IQs. We want strategies that call up the ability of all students to learn and grow. This chapter contains strategies that do this well.

But first, a reminder of one of the most versatile of thinking generators, the strategy called Outcome Sentences (Strategy 21-1):

> After a discussion, lecture, reading, story, or any potential learning experience, we point to a posted chart showing sample phrases such as *I learned ...*, *I was surprised ...*, *I'm beginning to wonder ...*, *I rediscovered ...* We then say, "Think back over the experience. See what you can get for yourself from it. Write a few sentences, perhaps starting with words like those on the chart."

Here are 11 more strategies for generating valuable thinking. We suggest giving your first attention to the first five, marked with arrows.

Strategy 19-1: What's the Difference?

Purpose: To ask students to find distinguishing elements.
Description: Asking students in what ways two items are different.

This strategy, from Pilon (1996), asks students to consider two items and identify ways they are different. Some possibilities:

In language arts, what is the difference between . . .

- Colon and semicolon?
- Verb and adverb?
- Shakespeare and Hamlet?
- Preposition and proper name?
- Formal letter and informal note?
- Incomplete sentence and jail sentence?

In social studies, what is the difference between . . .

- Community and country?
- Leader and elected official?
- Legislation and legislator?
- Truce and peace?
- Ecology and environment?
- Free elections and secret ballot?

In general, what is the difference between . . .

- Surprise and delight?
- Clock and calendar?
- Home and house?
- Temperature and heat?
- Fraction and decimal?
- Request and question?
- Hills and valleys?
- Opinion and judgment and conclusion?
- Wish and hope?
- Elephant and box of cookies?
- Square and rectangle?
- Evaporation and perspiration?
- Inspiration and concentration?
- Poems and songs?

We can generate more precise thinking if the two items are very similar. For example, what's the difference between . . .

- Sad and sorrowful?
- Yard and meter?
- Boil and broil?
- Capitalism and free enterprise?
- Smart and intelligent?
- Wet and soaked?

The index of a textbook is a useful source of items for this strategy.

Our heads are round so that our thinking can change direction.

—*Francis Picabia*

Strategy 19-2: What's the Same?

Purpose: To ask students to find similar elements.
Description: Asking students what is similar about two items.

In this strategy, students are asked to compare two items and state ways in which they are the same. For example, What is the same about clouds and mist? Leaders and followers? Eating good food and hiking tall hills? Many of the examples in the preceding "What's the Difference" strategy can also be used for discovering similarities.

The strategy is most challenging and most fun when it involves items that are quite unlike each other. Try asking a group, for example, what is the same about . . .

- One tree and two zebras?
- A liter and a letter?
- Thursday and evaporation?
- George Washington and long division?

- Compound interest and electricity?
- Newspapers and kindness?

 ## Strategy 19-3: Comparing

Purpose: To advance skills of discrimination and perception.
Description: Asking students to compare two items and note both similarities and differences.

We might ask students, "In what ways are humans and mice the same and different?" That is a more complex task than asking for similarities or differences (Chen, 1999; Cole & McLeod, 1999). Perhaps ask students to make comparisons by using two overlapping circles (as in a Venn diagram), with similarities placed in the center section, differences in the two outer sections.

 ## Strategy 19-4: Sorting the Items

Purpose: To ask students to review content thoughtfully.
Description: Asking students to sort through items and place them in certain groups.

Using this strategy, we might give students an assortment of ideas, objects, or words and ask them to consider them and then sort them in some specified way, for instance:

- Divide the list of foods into two groups, those that are high in calories and those that are low.
- Divide the animals into carnivores and noncarnivores.
- Make a pile of blocks that are neither red nor yellow.

- Find pairs of synonyms in the word list.
- Star the prime numbers on page 34.
- Identify the metaphors in the story.
- Divide the assignments you completed into two piles, those you are very proud of and the others.

Pilon (1996) recommends turning subject matter into materials students can physically manipulate. Consider this example. The teacher prepares several envelopes, each containing several cards. The instructions to students are simple: "Select an envelope and lay out the pieces in it in any way that makes sense to you." Here is one result:

> A girl spreads the cards from her envelope on her desk. She notices that most cards are white and contain common phrases: "in the house," "John went out," "hardly noticed." Two cards, however, are blue. One reads, "prepositional phrase." Another, "not prepositional phrase." She puts those two cards at the top of her desk. One by one, she puts the other cards under one of those headings. When she is finished, she asks a boy nearby to check her work. The boy, following instructions given previously, randomly points to one of the cards and asks, "Did you have a reason for putting this one here?" The girl says, "*Under the tree* is a prepositional phrase." The boy says, "Thank you" and makes a check on the girl's record sheet, to indicate the girl completed that envelope. The boy returns to his desk and the girl then puts the pieces back into the envelope and files away both the envelope and her record sheet.

Notice that after sorting the items the girl was asked to explain the reason behind the placement of one card. Either another student or the teacher might ask such a question. Answering such questions, especially if done regularly, heightens students' awareness of their own thinking processes.

Pilon has created several sets of cards for such envelopes, and they are highly effective for different academic subjects and different grade levels. There are enough sets of cards, which she calls THINKERS, so each student can work with one each day of the school year. (See http://workshopway.com to obtain these cards.)

Strategy 19-5: What Might Explain?

Purpose: To ask students to use cause-and-effect thinking.

Description: Asking students to think back and consider what might explain an event.

Teaching should be such that what is offered is perceived as a valuable gift and not as a hard duty.

—*Albert Einstein*

When we ask students, "What happened before?" or "What might explain this event?" we motivate them to think about relationships between causes and effects. For example, we might ask: "What factors might have led to the water boiling in that situation?" "What might be major causes of our crowded highways?" "What might explain why Mark Twain is so popular?"

Note that many explanations will be incomplete, because often it is not possible to know all of what caused an event. For example, correct but incomplete answers to the question "What caused the water to boil?" might include "The heat under the pot," "Enough time for the heat to raise the water temperature," "My intention to boil water," and "The fact that I did not keep adding ice to the pot." The best answer to such questions, therefore, is often, "I'm not entirely sure, but I would include these factors . . ."

Incidentally, it is usually better not to ask "Why did it happen?" or "Why did Lincoln act as he did?" or, after a student misbehaved, "Why did you do that?" Asking a "why" question invites students to assume that the event *can* be explained fully. This assumption is probably untrue and is not one we want students to carry forth into their lives. It is preferable for students to remain open to new and ever more complete explanations. Accordingly, we recommend not asking simple "why" questions and instead posing more open-ended questions, such as "Do you have any explanations for . . . ?" "Can you think of reasons why . . . ?" "What are some of the factors that might explain . . . ?"

Strategy 19-6: Summarizing

Purpose: To encourage students to think comprehensively about a topic.
Description: Asking students to summarize information on a topic.

Summarizing automatically calls forth high-level thinking. It is not possible to summarize something effectively without both considering the whole of it and sorting out its significant elements (Anderson & Hidi, 1988/1989). We might ask students to

- Write the theme of a story in less than 30 words.
- Summarize Edison's approach in less than 50 words.
- Draw a sketch or diagram showing how something works.
- Create a chart or graph summarizing the important details of a chapter.
- Outline the arguments for and against slavery in 1850.
- Identify the main ideas covered.
- Summarize orally what has been learned so far.

> Children know how to learn in more ways than we know how to teach them.
> —*Ronald Edmonds*

Strategy 19-7: Creating Groupings

Purpose: To ask students to think about ways that elements of a topic are similar.
Description: Asking students to sort items into categories they themselves create.

This strategy asks students to create their own categories for sorting, rather than to place items into predetermined categories. We might, for example, ask students to list all the sports they can think of and then to divide their lists into groups, putting together the sports that are in some way similar. We might similarly ask students to create groupings for

- The states in the United States.
- The fractions written on the board.
- The words on page 202 of the index.
- The parts of a plant.
- The battles of the Civil War.

We might also ask students to apply categorizing skills to a physical set of objects: blocks, classroom supplies, books, math manipulatives. Asking students to create their own categories for classifying items provides an especially rich thinking experience (Taba, 1965).

Strategy 19-8: Solving a Problem

Purpose: To apply problem-solving skills to subject matter areas.
Description: Asking students to solve a problem that lacks an obvious solution.

To use this strategy, we might simply challenge students to solve some problem related to the content we are teaching. We can increase the difficulty of the problem and make it more like reality by giving more data than necessary, or less. Some examples:

- We provide a page listing the eating needs of three different dogs and the costs and nutritional values of four different dog foods. Then we ask, "What would be a good plan for feeding the three dogs at a cost of less than $100 a month? If you have reasons for your choices, tell what they are."
- We supply information about a person, real or fictional, who is trying to accomplish something, say, get a job (or save money, eat a healthy breakfast, stop smoking). We then might say, "What else would you want to know before

recommending a plan? Invent that information and then make a plan for that person. What problems do you predict might complicate your plan?"

• We pick a real-life problem: What might be the best way to distribute books in class? What might be a better way to take attendance? How can we keep work groups from losing track of time? What can be done about poverty in our community? What might we do about traffic congestion? What can we do to stop ourselves from watching too much television? How can we help reduce air pollution? How can we improve voter turnout at election time? We ask students to recommend a plan for dealing with the problem and, perhaps, to explain the reasons behind their choices or to predict possible complications and brainstorm ways to avoid them.

For a more systematic assignment built on such thinking, see Strategy 17-18, Option Display.

Strategy 19-9: Brainstorming

Purpose: To ask students to exercise creative thinking skills in a content area.
Description: Asking students to think open-mindedly about a topic and to generate a list of ideas without worrying if any idea is reasonable or not.

We might ask students, sitting in a small or large group, to create as long a list as possible of alternatives for, say, balancing the budget, choosing a story topic, finding an effective way to read a chapter, doing mental long division, heating a home, reducing TV violence. Three useful guidelines for using this strategy:

• *Accept all ideas without judgment.* An unrealistic idea may generate a new, valuable idea.
• *Write down all ideas as they are mentioned.* Do not attempt to evaluate each idea as it is offered. Rather, keep minds open during the brainstorm. Judgments are for later, when students look back over the written list.
• *Generate ideas quickly.* High energy and a quick pace often lead to the most creativity. If ideas come too fast for one person to write them, have two or more students take turns recording ideas.

Strategy 19-10: Assessing the Options

Purpose: To stimulate open-minded, critical thinking.
Description: Posing a problem and asking students to brainstorm possible solutions and then to assess the worth of each possibility.

Teachers ask many questions that have correct answers. But in real life, answers are not so easily judged correct or incorrect. People may disagree, for example, on the best way to speak to the boss, or drive to the airport, or handle unwanted pregnancies. Are different ideas, then, all a matter of opinion, or is there a way to determine if some ideas are more correct or more valuable than others?

Imagine a teacher helping students think about this. The teacher starts by posing a problem, such as

- How many different ways can we find the number of minutes in a year?
- How can we determine if global warming presents a serious problem?
- How can we know if Shakespeare really wrote that?
- How many ways can we find for estimating the space inside a circle?
- What would improve our playground?
- What are arguments for and against the death penalty?
- What might improve capitalism as an economic system?

Then, after students play with the question—perhaps first alone, then in pairs, and finally in the whole group—imagine that teacher saying, "We've listed a lot of ideas on the board. How can we tell which are the best ones or the most important ones? Let's discuss that a bit."

After students play with that question, imagine the teacher then saying this:

We've done good thinking today and generated a lot of ideas. Often there is not only one way to solve a problem. Sometimes when we face problems in life, it's useful to look at many ideas. And, of course, the more ideas we identify, the more likely we are to find good ones. Yet we must examine the ideas that come up and do some hard thinking to identify the best ones or the most important ones. Talking it over with others, like we did today, can help. How many changed their mind when they heard others tell why they thought an idea was good or important? Although we can hear others, we still must think for ourselves, however. Would you agree?

A lesson such as this is a worthy one, even though the teacher never said some answers were correct and others incorrect. Essentially, the process provides a strategy for helping students learn to think about thinking. It's a strategy commonly used by Asian teachers for mathematics lessons, which, Stevenson and Stigler (1992) suggest, may help explain the superior math scores of Asian students.

Strategy 19-11: Language to Advance Thinking

Purpose: To promote thinking in ordinary conversation.
Description: Using phrases that model mature thinking.

> Whatever your past has been, you have a spotless future.
>
> —*Anonymous*

If a child doesn't learn
the way you teach,
teach the way the
child learns.

—*Anonymous*

Costa and Marzano (1987) note that teachers can advance student thinking simply by modeling people who think carefully. For example, if a student says, "They wouldn't raise the budget," we might say, "Who are 'they'?" Instead of saying, "What did you think of the article?" we might say, "What conclusions can you draw from the article?" To model open-mindedness, we might say, "Here is what I have planned for today. We can always change if a better idea comes up." Other examples:

If a student says . . .	We might say . . .
• It never happened.	• Never, ever?
• I wouldn't have done what he did.	• Do you have reasons for your choice that you're willing to share?
• Plants need nitrogen.	• What went on in your head that led you to say that?
• The answer is 72.	• Tell us some of the steps that led to that answer.
• I don't know how to do that.	• What *do* you know about doing it?
• I don't know how to do that.	• How might you find out?
• I memorized it.	• What process did you use to memorize it?
• I hate to read that stuff.	• What makes you hate it?
• It's his fault.	• Did anything in your behavior contribute to the problem?
• I didn't finish the work.	• What do you need to think about to do better next time?
• I disagree.	• What, specifically, would you agree with?

Instead of saying . . .	We might say . . .
• Why did you do that?	• Do you know what led you to do that?
• I want you to do a good job.	• How can you motivate yourself to do a good job?

To model . . .	We might say . . .
• Thoughtfulness	• I'm confused about what to do about . . . [a classroom issue]. Let's brainstorm a list of possible options. Then help me see the pluses and minuses of each option.
• Avoiding emotional decisions	• My mind is not clear now. Let me come back to this another time when I feel more settled and can think more clearly.
• Empathy with others	• Considering their realities, they were probably having different feelings than we were.

Responding to Student Comments and Using Praise Appropriately

20

How should we respond after a student correctly answers a question? Should we dole out praise? And how about a student who gives an irrelevant answer? Can we, *should* we, hide our dismay? The basic question is this: What response from us will inspire students to develop their most healthy, constructive motives and bring those motives to their schoolwork? Or, to be more specific, what kinds of responses will inspire students to work with high personal dignity, steady energy, intelligent self-management, feelings of community, and keen awareness? That is the outcome we're aiming for. That is what will make teaching easiest for us and learning richest for students. This chapter has 12 strategies for this purpose. We recommend you give your first attention to the first eight, each marked with an arrow.

⏩ Strategy 20-1: Plain Corrects

Purpose: To confirm correctness without adding distracting emotions.
Description: Simply informing a student that an answer is correct.

The best response to a correct answer is often a plain, unemotional statement that, yes, that answer is correct. We might say

- Correct.
- Right.
- Yes, thank you.
- Yes, that is right.
- OK.
- Yes, that is just what I wanted.

Contrast these with such responses as, "Wonderful! Great answer! A brilliant response!" It's that kind of overblown praise that Plain Corrects are meant to replace. A Plain Correct treats students like intelligent, dignified people who prefer straight talk to overstatements. It provides a simple message: Your answer was correct; let's move on. A Plain Correct is a judgment, but unlike praise, which often feels like a judgment of the student, it is simply a judgment of the student's answer. It is an assessment by an expert, the teacher, of the accuracy of an answer and, as such, is quite helpful. Plain Corrects do not stir up emotions that might distract students from the intellectual work of learning.

Note that it's often useful to follow a Plain Correct with a restatement of the information (Saphier & Gower, 1997), as by saying, "That is right. Boyle's Law does deal with the expansion of gasses." This gives us a chance to reinforce the learning.

Strategy 20-2: Plain Incorrects

Purpose: To inform students that an answer is incorrect without adding distracting emotions.

Description: Simply informing a student that an answer is not correct.

Like our responses using Plain Corrects, our responses when students answer incorrectly might best be brief and unemotional:

- No, the correct answer is *Louisiana Purchase*.
- No, that is not what I wanted. Please use adjectives like those on the board.
- You had the first name right. The correct answer is Thomas *Jefferson*.
- That is an answer for kidney. *Bile* is the answer for stomach.
- No, but it's good you brought that up because others probably thought that, too. The correct answer is *metaphor*.

With the Plain Incorrect response, we simply give the correct answer and move on. There is no hint in this kind of response that students are so fragile they cannot make a mistake without being devastated.

Should we try to draw out an answer from a student who has answered incorrectly? It's tempting to do so, as in this example: "No, Keith, the capital of California is not Los Angeles. The correct answer starts with an *S*. Want to guess? Try again. Want another hint?" However, this procedure often puts the student on the spot and generates embarrassment, and is therefore not particularly useful for growing dignity. Furthermore, it slows down the quick pace that keeps all students actively involved. Usually, then, it is best to give the right answer and move ahead.

It is only with the heart that one can see rightly; what is essential is invisible to the eye.

—Antoine de Saint-Exupéry

Should we call on a second student? This, too, is often tempting, as in, "No, Keith, it's not Los Angeles. Can anyone else tell us the answer?" However, this procedure can make the first student feel inferior to the second student. We want to avoid pitting one student against another that way. Also, because we already have asked the question about California, all students have already had a chance to think about it. It's preferable to simply give the correct answer and offer another question for students to think about.

Strategy 20-3: Incorrects with Appreciation

Purpose: To acknowledge students' efforts.

Description: Informing a student that although the answer was not correct, the effort was commendable and we appreciate it.

Here are a few examples:

- The correct answer is *64,* but that was good risk taking on your part.
- The answer was *alternating current,* but that was good thinking.
- That is a good answer, but it doesn't really apply to this situation. In this situation, the best answer would be *hardly ever.*
- You have the first part right, and you sure are on the right track. The complete correct answer is . . .

This strategy shifts the focus from the answer itself to the process of thinking or to the willingness to risk speaking up, which is honestly commendable. We thereby balance any disappointment the student might feel with some positive feedback. That is often valuable for students with a shaky self-confidence.

Strategy 20-4: Praise and Rewards for All

Purpose: To encourage a group without slighting any student and to develop a close community in the classroom.

Description: Offering praise or a reward to the group as a whole.

Most students enjoy praise and rewards. Such attention makes them feel worthy and, presumably, motivates them to work harder and behave better. But a look under the surface might reveal undesirable side effects:

- *Addiction.* If students get too much praise and receive rewards too easily, the result can be like watching TV: easily attained satisfaction smothering the growth of independence, diligence, self-control, initiative. Or it can be like eating candy: a quick delight smothering interest in more nourishing choices. Praise and rewards can become addicting and, like other addictions, lead to endless desires for more of the same, making students further dependent on others for their feelings of worth.

• *Devaluation.* Many students notice that whereas some classmates receive a lot of rewards and praise, they rarely receive either. "We are not all appreciated in this class" is the message these students absorb, which too often leads to a sense of "I am not worth being appreciated."

• *Manipulation.* "Look how good the first row is," says the teacher, with the intention of getting students in all the other rows to straighten up. The subtler message that students receive is this: "The teacher is just saying that to get what she herself wants. She does not really care about us."

• *Puffery.* "Great answer!" gushes the teacher, followed by "Wonderful! Sensational! Super! Amazing! Let's give a round of applause to Kendra for that answer." Exaggerated praise can quickly devalue language and honest appreciation. Puffery can also lead students to say to themselves, "He must think I'm really dumb, expecting me to believe that nonsense," or "She must think I'm really weak, needing such hype."

The goal is to build personal dignity and motivate hard work and self-discipline without such harmful side effects (Brophy, 1981; Kohn, 1996; Marzano, Pickering, & Pollock, 2001). Does that mean never praising students? Not at all. One way to avoid these side effects is to offer praise to the group as a whole when we feel they genuinely deserve it. Some examples:

• This group is making good progress. I appreciate that. It's a pleasure for me to work with you.

• What a good group this is! Even though that material was hard, you folks stuck with it. I sure admire that perseverance.

• We did it right on time! Thanks for that.

• This sure is a powerful bunch, isn't it?

• Let's give ourselves a hand for the way we handled today's lesson.

• You all are working so well together! I told the principal today how special you are.

• This class is going so well I'm giving you all a treat today.

No one loses when praise and rewards are honest and are directed to the group as a whole. There is no envy. No one is left out. Besides, it encourages feelings of the class being one warm community.

Even when rewards cannot be distributed equally, we may want to communicate appreciation to everyone, as when we say something like, "I'm proud that one of our own classmates, Nicky, won first prize. And I'm proud of the way you people supported Nicky. So, in honor of the occasion, let's all give ourselves a hand."

But Praise and Rewards for All can be used manipulatively, as when a teacher offers a reward only when students do what the teacher wants. A class party on Friday because of diligent work all week often falls into this category. The motive of the teacher, then, is less to bring the class together for a delightful occasion, or to show appreciation, or to share good feelings with the class. The motive is more to shape the behavior of students. Not only is that less generous, it models manipulation and may well encourage students to try to manipulate others.

We recommend against making group praise or rewards contingent on student behavior. It is not advisable, then, to announce that if students do this or that they will get a reward. It is preferable to model someone who likes to bring joy into others' lives—and not only when it is earned. Indeed, we might better model someone who brings joy into the lives of people who are *not* earning it, for those are the people who most often need positive feedback. And if the intention is to bring out students' most positive, constructive traits, would we not want to model someone being positive and constructive?

◆ Strategy 20-5: Silent Response to Errors

Purpose: To avoid responding in unproductive ways to student mistakes.
Description: Noticing an error or problem and leaving until later a consideration of what, if anything, to do about it.

According to Pilon (1996), the best response to a mistake is often no response, other than a mental note to think about the issue later. Consider these examples:

• John is giving a report of his work to the class. Several times he says "ain't" and "ain't not." Often the best response to such errors is to say nothing and to make a mental note that he and perhaps others need more practice saying "isn't" and "is not."

• A student turns in a report that confuses *too* and *to*. Should we mark the error? If we do, two consequences are predictable. First, odd as it may seem, the student will continue making the error; that is, correcting such errors often fails to change a student's behavior. Second, the student will be less willing to write— sometimes less willing to write anything for anybody, even himself. Students rarely enjoy activities that lead to many corrections.

Instead of on-the-spot corrections, we might do nothing other than to remember the error and make a note to create an appropriate mini-lesson on another day for the whole class or for a small group. And at that time, we probably do not want to say, "We need to review *too* and *to;* we have not mastered that yet," or anything else that may communicate to students, "You should have already learned this." Such a message is unnecessary and may foster discouragement. We might instead simply teach the lesson as if it had never been taught before, perhaps as follows:

> Here on the board is an example of *too* used correctly in a sentence. And here is an example of *to* used correctly. It is, of course, easy to confuse them. I'd like each of you to please write a pair of sentences like these on scrap paper. In one, use *too* correctly. In the other, use *to* correctly.

When the students are finished writing, we might continue like this:

> Now please share your sentences with a partner. Check to see that the *to* and the *too* are correctly used in all sentences. If your partner wrote something interesting, you might also enjoy reading it.

In short, it's often wiser *not* to point out an error in order to get students to learn. Instead, simply teach a lesson about the topic again at another time. As long as the lesson has a quick pace, it will be an easy review for students who already understand and, for those who do not, a chance to learn it in a climate free of criticism or a sense of failure. Alternatively, we might teach the lesson only to the students who need it, allowing others to work at something else.

Keep in mind the message of one of the Truth Signs (Strategy 4-1): "We each learn in our own ways, by our own time clocks." Students sometimes encounter material they are simply not yet ready to master. We do well to accept such times as a natural part of the learning process and refrain from correcting all student misunderstandings on the spot.

Yet it is not always advisable to keep silent about errors. In solid, accepting relationships, people usually do not mind having someone point out a few of their mistakes. However, when unsure, choose the Silent Response to Errors. It is safer. Be like a physician who chooses the medicine most likely to avoid harmful side effects.

 ## Strategy 20-6: Can-You Questions

Purpose: To ask questions in a way that reduces the potential for damaging student dignity.

Description: Asking students if they *can* give an answer, rather than asking for the answer directly.

To understand the essence of this strategy, note that we recommend the first comment in each of these pairs:

"Can you say what you mean by . . . ?" in place of "What do you mean by . . . ?"
"Can you give an example?" in place of "What is an example?"
"Can you say what that might lead to?" in place of "What might that lead to?"
"Can you name the capital of Illinois?" in place of "What is the capital of Illinois?"

By using the phrase "Can you . . . ?" in this way, students are less likely to feel threats to their dignity. When they don't know the answer, they are less likely to manufacture an excuse or give a wild guess. They have a graceful way to respond. They can simply say, "No, I can't." When we use Can-You Questions, then, we can feel more comfortable asking questions of *all* students (as with Strategy 16-4, Whip Around, Pass Option), because the potential threat to student dignity is markedly diminished.

Strategy 20-7: Honest I Appreciates

Purpose: To remind students that at least one adult appreciates each of them.
Description: Telling a student we honestly appreciate something about him or her.

When a student answers a question correctly, we might say, if we intended to shower the student with praise, "Very good job, Shirley. The way you phrased your answer was top-notch." Notice that this is a "you" statement. It really says, "You did a good job." It carries the tone of one person judging the worth of another.

Or we could say, in the mode of giving rewards, "Extra credit for that, Shirley." Here the focus is not on the quality of the work but on a payment for the work.

Alternatively, we could make an "I" statement. We might say, "I appreciate the way you phrased your answer, Shirley." In this case the intention is not to praise—that is, not to give a boost to Shirley's self-esteem. The intent is merely to communicate honest, personal appreciation. It is an honest statement, not a mechanical platitude, certainly not an empty exaggeration.

Here are other ways to express Honest I Appreciates:

- Thank you. ("I give my thanks to you.")
- I appreciate that.
- I like the way you said that.
- I'm delighted that you spoke out like that.
- I'm happy that you took a chance with that tricky question.

Look well into thyself; there is a source of strength which will always spring up if thou wilt always look there.

—*Marcus Aurelius*

- That makes me smile.
- I sure like your taking that risk.
- Thanks for giving that a try.
- I liked the look in your eye when you did it.

Compared with praise and rewards, Honest I Appreciates are less likely to be seen as manipulative, judgmental, or mechanical. Also, as long as all students get their fair share, these comments rarely have negative side effects. Because we can almost always find something to appreciate about anyone—something said, a look in the eyes, a spring in the step, promptness, or neatness—we need not neglect any student.

This does not mean that we must distribute such responses absolutely equally. Sooner or later students must learn that some people elicit a more positive response than do others. That is a fact of life. Having a bit of imbalance in the distribution of Honest I Appreciates seems acceptable as long as every student experiences enough of them and no student gets too many. It is the extremes we need to guard against. To illustrate, consider the difference between a town of generally well-off people that has a few fairly rich folks, compared with a town that has some extremely wealthy people and others who do not have enough money for food and shelter. That resembles the extreme disparity that exists with positive feedback in many classrooms today.

 Strategy 20-8: I'm with You's

Purpose: To help students understand that they are not alone.
Description: Communicating an empathetic understanding and acceptance of a student's experience.

Consider these teacher comments to a student and the effect they might have:

- I might make that same mistake.
- Many of us feel that way.
- I can tell you're worried about that report.
- I can see how you would do that.
- I think I understand how you feel.
- I'd be proud to be in your shoes.
- I can share your sorrow.
- I understand why you would do that.
- It sounds like that was a great day for you.

The message of such comments is clear: "You are not alone. I am with you. It's OK for you to be the person you are." Often a student will say or do something that makes such a comment appropriate, as in this example, which also happens to include an Honest I Appreciate:

Teacher:	What is the formula for the area of a parallelogram?
Jane:	Uh, is it, uh . . . l times w?
Teacher:	I appreciate that effort, Jane. I could tell you weren't sure and yet you gave it a try. Good courage. But, no, the formula for the area of a parallelogram is b times h.

An I'm with You is another alternative to praise and rewards. Many students feel alone and essentially inadequate, unknown, isolated. It can be deeply empowering for them to hear that at least one teacher is with them, understands, and expresses that understanding empathetically.

Note that it is often appropriate to follow a Plain Incorrect statement with an Honest I Appreciate or an I'm With You, as in these examples:

• No, Bob, the answer is *9*. I can tell you're disappointed, but there is always next time.

• No, the answer is *southwest*. By the way, Tina, I like the power you used when you spoke.

Strategy 20-9: DESCA Inspirations

Purpose: To inspire new growth in dignity, energy, self-management, community, and awareness.

Description: Responding to students in a way that inspires them to develop the best they have in them.

You may recall from Chapter 1 the student motives represented by the acronym DESCA—students' natural desire to live with personal *dignity,* sustained *energy,* appropriate *self-management,* healthy *community,* and open-minded *awareness.* We believe it is especially important to acknowledge growth in these five areas. Not just excellent students, but *all* students can be successful with such growth. Furthermore, our everyday responses to students can inspire that growth.

The examples presented here illustrate how we can use Honest I Appreciates and I'm with You's for that purpose. You might want to imagine yourself using some of these responses. You will more likely, then, use them when appropriate situations arise. And you can then assess their effectiveness for yourself.

"Honest I Appreciate" Messages to Inspire DESCA Growth

Dignity:
- I really appreciate the way you just spoke up for yourself.
- I admire the confidence you are showing.
- I like the way you defended your friend.
- I like how you said it like you mean it.
- I sure appreciate the way you look straight into people's eyes.

Energy:
- I like it when you stick to it.
- I like it when you use your brain power.
- I like it when you pace yourself.
- I like it when you speak with energy.
- I like it when you go one more step even though you are ready to give up.

Self-Management:
- I like it when you organize your own papers neatly.
- I like it when you make a time plan.
- I like it when you pace yourself.
- I like it when you call on your ability to persist when you need it.
- I like it when you think it out for yourself.
- I like it when you ask for help when you need it.

Community:
- I like it when you respect the differences in others.
- I like it when you find something to appreciate in people so different from you.
- I like it when you lend a hand.
- I like it when you listen so well to others.
- I like it when you do more than your share of the work without being asked.

Awareness:
- Thank you very much for being so alert.
- Thank you very much for reading with an open mind.
- Thank you very much for bringing your attention back when it drifted.
- Thank you very much for ignoring the distractions outside.
- Thank you very much for noticing that someone needed help.

When someone loves you, the way they say your name is different. You know that your name is safe in their mouth.

—Billy, age 4

"I'm with You" Messages to Inspire DESCA Growth

Dignity:
- I can imagine how you felt after speaking up that way.
- I also feel proud of myself when I go that extra mile.
- I think I know how you felt when you insisted on your rights.
- It's sometimes hard, isn't it, to call on your willpower?
- There was a time when I, too, could not get all the courage I wanted.

Energy:
- I need rest, too.
- I enjoy moving about, too.
- I'm like you when it comes to taking the initiative.
- It's not easy to eat well all the time, is it?
- I, too, sometimes have trouble getting myself up when I feel depressed.

Self-Management:
- I, too, have trouble knowing when to speak up and when to say nothing.
- We can tell what is true for us, can't we?
- I understand how you know when you have had enough.
- Sometimes we must look twice to see what needs to be done, don't we?
- I, too, must sometimes remind myself not to be negative.

Community:
- I understand how you felt about cleaning up a mess you didn't make.
- It's fun to cheer people on, isn't it?
- I, too, like to show others my appreciation.
- You feel good when you reach out to newcomers, don't you?
- It feels good to me, too, when I can stand up for our class.

Awareness:
- I, too, sometimes do not manage myself as well as I want to.
- I, too, sometimes go too fast without noticing.
- I, too, sometimes think back over the day and wonder what I should do next time.
- I, too, sometimes need to pull myself out of daydreaming.
- I, too, sometimes wonder about my feelings.

A Few Words of Caution

It's not necessary to respond to everything students say or do, of course. If a student flaunts his good looks and clothing, for example, it might be advisable to avoid saying we appreciate today's new outfit. We might, indeed, generally avoid comments about clothing and looks. Such comments can encourage attention to superficial matters and, when overheard, can distress those unable to match someone else's appearance.

Similarly, we may choose not to respond to all superior work. You've probably heard stories of outstanding high school students who went to top colleges and attempted suicide after discovering they could no longer produce outstanding work. With that in mind, we may not want to overemphasize the importance of excellent work and underemphasize the importance of simply accepting people as they are. Furthermore, some students define their worth in terms of what they produce, just as some adults define their goodness in terms of status or possessions. When students with such self-definitions do excellent work and we say we are delighted, we risk reinforcing that definition. And we also risk hardening an assumption that if and when they cannot produce, they will be less worthy human beings.

Generally, we may want to avoid comments about excellent products when we sense that such comments will slight the dignity of those who aren't as capable. Besides, there is something more valuable to note and reinforce: not the products of work but the process of living—calling up courage, sticking to a tough task, lending a hand to a neighbor, thinking through an issue, expending honest effort, doing the very best one can with the task at hand.

▲ **TEACHER COMMENT**

I used to give rewards for everything. It got so the kids would do nothing unless they got a star or candy. No more. I use only I Appreciates and Spontaneous Delights. When a boy draws a picture now, I look him in the eye warmly and say, "I like it!" When a girl picks up the blocks, I smile and say, "Thank you!" It's all honest and polite and immediate. No big deal. The staff likes it too, and, somehow, the kids seem more self-composed.

—*Frances Fenton, Day Care Center Director*

Strategy 20-10: Spontaneous Delights

Purpose: To allow oneself to be spontaneously expressive and to demonstrate the reality that some people generate delight more readily than others.
Description: Expressing ourselves when students spontaneously delight us.

The preceding strategies suggest possible replacements for individual praise. They aim to give students supportive feedback and encouragement while avoiding problems of addiction, unfairness, manipulation, or puffery. Does that mean we should suppress the spontaneous delights we experience with certain students? No, not at all. It's easy to imagine, for example, statements such as these occurring naturally during the course of the day:

- I like the colors on that shirt, Tom.
- Good risk taking, Mike.
- What bright eyes today, Zack.
- Those were very neat papers you wrote yesterday, Linda.
- What good initiative you took, Paulo.
- I was delighted to see how you stuck with your friend, Terry.
- You were truthful, and that was not easy, Maru. I was very happy to see that.
- Great answer, Marissa. Very creative.

We call these Spontaneous Delights. The intent is simply to express spontaneous joy. Being willing to express such reactions is part of being genuine, and, we believe, teachers should be genuine.

A Spontaneous Delight is not meant to go on and on. We simply express it and move on: "Super design, Tony. I love it. Do you have any ideas for your next project?"

Spontaneous Delights are especially appropriate for young students, because young students have a special need to know they can bring delight to the world around them. Perhaps that is why adults naturally smile at young children. It is nature's way of eliciting the response those youngsters need.

> The truth is that I am enslaved . . . in one vast love affair with seventy children.
>
> —*Sylvia Ashton-Warner*

Strategy 20-11: Caring Attention Without Praise

Purpose: To support and encourage students without making them dependent on others' approval.

Description: Simply giving time and attention to a student, as by listening carefully.

Sometimes teachers fall into patterns of unnecessary praise. Imagine a young student coming to a teacher with a drawing just completed. A caring teacher might easily respond, "What a beautiful picture, Katie!" or "This is a lovely blue tree, Katie," or "You printed your name just perfectly." But such praise highlights the teacher's role as the authority and invites dependence, rather than encouraging the development of responsible self-management. Furthermore, many students would be quite satisfied with a response that showed true care and did not include praise. Honest I Appreciates or I'm with You's can do that.

Honest I Appreciates: "I really like this drawing, Katie. Thank you very much for showing it to me!" Or, assuming it's honest, "Oh, I really appreciate how carefully you did this drawing."

I'm with You's: "I can see you are happy with this. You have a big smile on your face, Katie. I would feel the same way if I did that drawing." Or "You look uncertain about your drawing, Katie. Am I right? When it comes to drawing, many of us are not very confident."

How else can we communicate that we really care for students, that we notice each of them, that each is important to us, without relying on "Good work!" and "Great job!"? Depending on the age and personality of the student and on our individual style, we might use these options:

- *Physical touch.* A pat on the arm, a hug around the shoulder, a shake of the hand.
- *Warm eye contact.* A look that communicates full personal attention.
- *Stimulating questions.* Perhaps, "What a bright blue tree, Katie. Did you enjoy doing this?" or "Looks like you used a lot of blue in this drawing. Do you like to draw with blue?" or "Thanks, Katie. This is just fine. What would you most like to do next?"
- *Time for the student.* Simply giving a bit of time to the student in whatever ways seem right at the moment, as in talking about a topic the student initiates, or allowing the student to remain nearby for a moment, even if we are talking with others.
- *Teaching.* Providing instruction or guidance in ways that show we care what the student might next be ready to learn: "I'd like you now to try drawing a face, Katie. Are you ready for that?"
- *Shows of concern.* Any response that comes to us that shows we are caring and that we wonder if we can help. For example: "You look tired, Katie. Is everything all right with you?"

In short, we will often want to show our care for students and to give them our attention. Many students, especially young ones, crave such care and attention. But we can provide it without inviting an addiction to praise. We can often give students healthy attention without any praise at all.

▲ TEACHER COMMENT

I was amazed at how empty my praise had become. So often I felt vaguely dishonest. Yet I, too, was addicted to praise. It wasn't easy to break the habit. I'm getting a non-praise habit, but slowly. I mainly ask opinion questions and respond with thank you's. I'm surprised how easy the shift was on students. I put the following list on my desk, and that is helping me:

- Honest I Appreciates: Thank you.
- I'm with You's: I understand. You are not alone.
- Plain Corrects: Yes. Right.
- Plain Incorrects: No, the answer is . . .
- Silent Responses: (Just note for possible future instruction.)
- Praise and Rewards for All: The group did well today.
- Spontaneous Delights: Truly felt compliments. (Am I neglecting anyone?)
- DESCA Inspirations: Who's showing dignity, working with energy, exercising self-management, cooperating, striking out in awareness?

—*Tom Clarence, High School History Teacher*

Strategy 20-12: Saying No Slowly

Purpose: To avoid having students feel that you do not listen to them.
Description: Being slow in saying no to student requests.

Be slow in saying no to a request. Many students believe teachers do not really listen to them, which is an affront to their sense of dignity. Failure to hear out a student request can hurt more than an unwillingness to go along with it. The antidote is to listen carefully and be sure we understand before responding. We might also ask for more time to think it over or talk to others about it. And if we can't accept the request, speak warmly and respectfully, not coldly and curtly, perhaps saying why we can't grant the request. The last thing we want is some students concluding "Teachers never listen to us."

What a wonderful life I've had! I only wished I'd realized it sooner.
—*Colette*

PART VI

Strategies for Ending Classes Efficiently

This part of the book contains chapters for handling tasks that typically show up at the end of a class—such as helping students to reflect, review, and summarize lessons; and providing effective homework assignments.

The language we choose as we handle these tasks makes a difference. What wording inspires forth the best motives students have within them? Consider these three comments and the messages they send:

Least inspiring: "You didn't do a good job in class today, so you'll have to do it again for homework."

In between: "The homework for tomorrow is on the board."

Most inspiring: "Have fun with this homework assignment. It has some real interesting challenges. Give it your best shot and don't worry about solving all the problems correctly. But do your very best."

Helping Students Review and Summarize a Class

21

A science lesson about heat might start with a demonstration showing how different materials react differently to heat, merge into a discussion of the implications of the demonstration, and end with the teacher announcing the evening's homework assignment. No summary of the heat lesson. No chance for students to reflect and to refine their understandings. Just a shift in attention to homework.

In another classroom students are busy completing worksheets with 15 minutes left before dismissal. Fifteen minutes later the teacher tells everyone to get ready to leave. No pulling together of the worksheet activity. No chance for students to reflect on their work and see if they can crystallize any learnings.

Such abrupt endings are high on our list of strategies to avoid. To work well, a classroom activity, like a good story, needs a proper ending. Without it, many potential learnings vanish, having had no time to take form.

Several strategies noted earlier help provide effective endings for lessons, including one of our favorites, the Review Test (Strategy 11-1). With the Review Test, the teacher poses a question based on the material covered and all students write an answer. The teacher gives the correct answer and students check their work. The teacher then promptly gives the next question. The process continues through 5 to 10 such questions, with a pace rapid enough to keep student awareness and energy high. Discussion is minimized. No grades are given. The activity provides a nonthreatening way to review material and correct misunderstandings. It also helps students appreciate the fact that they are making progress.

Another all-time favorite strategy, Outcome Sentences, leads off this chapter. Outcome Sentences and the three strategies that follow are each marked with an arrow, indicating they are recommended for your first attention.

Strategy 21-1: Outcome Sentences

Purpose: To inspire students to extract personal learnings from school experiences and to promote the habit of learning from all of life's experiences.

Description: Asking students to reflect back on an experience and write endings to such phrases as *I learned . . . , I was surprised . . . , I'm beginning to wonder . . .*

We want students to learn. Yet we want those learnings to be meaningful, to make sense to students, not merely to be strings of words they remember. Moreover, we want students to be lifelong learners, to learn how to learn on their own, so they can extract meanings from future experiences. For this purpose, Outcome Sentences is particularly effective.

A social studies teacher, for example, might tell about an event in history, show a map of the region involved, and explain what he thinks about the event. He might then say, "Please reflect back on the discussion and see what you can get out of it for yourself. Look at this chart I posted. Write some sentences starting with, for example, *I learned . . .* Or you might start by writing, *I was surprised . . .* or *I'm beginning to wonder . . .* Or any other such sentence. Think back over our discussion. Then see if you can find some learnings for yourself and write them down."

> • I learned . . .
> • I was surprised . . .
> • I'm beginning to wonder . . .
> • I rediscovered . . .
> • I feel . . .
> • I promise . . .

At this point, the teacher has various options. One that often works well is to ask if any students would like to volunteer to read one of their Outcome Sentences. Such sharing usually helps other students discover learnings they had not yet noticed. Another effective choice is to use the Whip Around, Pass Option (Strategy 16-4), giving each student a turn either to read aloud one Outcome Sentence they wrote or to say "I pass." Time permitting, either option could lead into a whole-class summary discussion, with the teacher adding points he would emphasize.

It's valuable to use this strategy often—for example, asking students to write Outcome Sentences on each chapter they read in the text, on each project they complete, on guest speakers' presentations, and on discussions about current events, films, units completed, holiday vacations, the first week of school, the stories they read, and the day in school.

Posting an Outcome Sentence chart like the one above provides students with handy sentence starters whenever we ask them to think about what they learned. Some teachers add other phrases to the chart, such as

- I now realize . . .
- I would someday like to . . .
- I would conclude . . .
- I cannot agree with . . .
- I would like to find out more about . . .

Note that this strategy does not carry an expectation that all students will get the same learning from a lesson. The aim rather is to inspire students to construct meaningful, personal learnings. Said another way, the goal is not for students merely to remember words or otherwise obtain only superficial knowledge. The aim is to stimulate students to think, digest information, and create meaning for themselves. It's the intent of what is often called constructivism, having students construct meanings for themselves.

It's often valuable for students to keep Learning Logs of Outcome Sentences, as suggested in Strategy 21-3. If they do, we can begin a class by asking for volunteers to read an item from their logs. This approach provides a convenient and useful review of prior learnings.

 ## Strategy 21-2: Like/Might Review

Purpose: To teach students to review their actions constructively and open-mindedly.
Description: Asking students to look back at their behavior and write what they *liked* about it and what they *might* do differently another time.

As John Dewey (1938) reminds us, we do not learn from our experience. We learn from processing our experience. In this strategy, students process experience by evaluating their own actions and, perhaps, learning something about what best serves them.

Two steps are involved. First, we ask students to think back over an experience, to consider what they did or did not do, and then to write a few sentences beginning with the phrase "*I liked the way I . . .*" Students might write, for example, *I liked the way I spoke up. I liked the way I took my time and changed my mind.* Whatever they write is, of course, acceptable.

When we notice that students are close to finishing their writing, we might say, "Just one more moment, please." We then announce the second step, which is to review their behavior again, but this time to write endings to the phrase "*Next time I might . . .*" To make that request clear, we could offer examples:

> You might write, for example, "Next time I might volunteer sooner," or "Next time I might pick a topic that is easier," or "Next time I might not rush so much." Write anything you might do differently the next time a similar situation arises. Not that you *promise* to do it, but that it is something you *might* do.

The "like" part of this strategy often moves students to notice their strengths and talents and to appreciate themselves. The "might" part reminds them that they don't need to repeat past behaviors; they can live and learn, adjust their behaviors, exert intelligent self-management.

There is no need for students to share their notes. It is the reflection itself that produces the most learning. But, if we like, we can invite sharing, perhaps by using the Whip Around, Pass Option (Strategy 16-4) or by asking students to sit in Sharing Pairs (Strategy 7-1) and discuss some of what they wrote, keeping private any parts they wish.

> The man who goes alone can start today; but he who travels with another must wait till that other is ready.
> —*Henry David Thoreau*

Strategy 21-3: Learning Log

Purpose: To help students monitor their own learnings.
Description: Regularly asking students to write about their learning experiences in a special notebook or folder that we can then review periodically.

Many teachers find it valuable to have students keep a record of what they are learning each day. Such Learning Logs help teachers take advantage of the reality that learnings are ultimately created by the learner, not given by the teacher.

We can have students create Learning Logs in several ways. One simple way is to ask students to keep the Outcome Sentences (Strategy 21-1) they write in one folder or to write them all in one notebook.

How might we use Learning Logs? Some possibilities:

• *To begin a lesson, as a review of prior work.* For example, ask students to read aloud something learned from yesterday's lesson.

• *To intensify and clarify learnings.* For example, ask students to look back over a week's learnings and write new Outcome Sentences showing what they learned from reviewing their prior learnings.

• *For giving grades.* For example, periodically collect Learning Logs to evaluate learnings and, perhaps more important, to assess student effort. You might even have students keep separate Learning Logs for different topics, to monitor progress in specific areas.

• *As a basis for discussions with parents.* This can be especially useful during report card conferences. Many parents appreciate seeing the samples of learnings written in Learning Logs, finding it more helpful than test scores or teacher anecdotes in understanding their child's progress.

Strategy 21-4: Concluding Whip Around

Purpose: To prompt all students to think back over the lesson and to get feedback on the students' experience of the lesson.

Description: Asking each student in turn to report something learned or enjoyed about the lesson just concluded.

This is a variation of the Whip Around, Pass Option (Strategy 16-4). At the end of a lesson we might conclude by saying something like, "Take a few seconds and make a note of one or two things you learned today." Then, after a brief pause, we introduce the strategy:

> Now, I'd like us to whip around the class, or as much of the class as we have time for, starting with Cleo. When it's your turn, tell us something you learned from the lesson, or tell us something you liked about the lesson. You can always say, "I pass." And remember, you can repeat something already said. You don't have to have an original idea.

Strategy 21-5: Mental Pictures

Purpose: To make learning more vivid for all students and to respect the needs of visual learners.

Description: Asking students to create a mental picture of concepts, processes, or learnings.

"Close your eyes for a moment," says the teacher after a lesson, "and think back to the work we just completed. What stands out for you?"

Mental Pictures can be useful for reviewing material or for introducing new material. We might also encourage students to create their own mental pictures whenever they want to, perhaps to summarize information for themselves. And we might remind students to call upon previous mental pictures to help them recall information during tests.

Mental Pictures can be useful in any subject area. In a history class, for example, the teacher might say, "Close your eyes for a moment and imagine you were there. Imagine seeing . . ." She continues to paint a word picture of an event she wants students to appreciate. A biology teacher might say, "Imagine seeing the spine of a normal person. Scan it top to bottom. Now notice the top vertebra . . ." In math class, the teacher might say, "In your mind, imagine seeing $4 \times 9 = 36$. Now turn that around so the picture shows $9 \times 4 = 36$. Can you make that picture into something that does not have numbers, maybe boxes or circles or apples, and that illustrates $4 \times 9 = 36$? I'd like several of you now to go to the board and draw something you visualized."

The secret of being a bore is to tell everything.
—Voltaire

Strategy 21-6: Learning Log Exchange

Purpose: To cross-fertilize student learnings.

Description: Asking students to exchange Learning Logs occasionally and give constructive feedback to one another.

Oddly, many students do more careful work with Learning Logs when they know peers will be reading those logs. In addition, student exposure to peer learnings often enhances their own understandings.

The procedure is based on the Paper Exchange and the Like/Might Review (Strategies 17-4 and 21-2). First, students exchange Learning Logs so they can read samples in three or four other logs. Students then have two jobs: (1) to write what, if anything, they liked about what they read; (2) to write what, if anything, they might do differently in the future when writing their own logs. Alternatively, students could write Outcome Sentences (Strategy 21-1) from the log review.

At another time, we might ask students to write feedback notes to one or more of their peers. This approach uses a modified Like/Might Review. We ask students to write notes telling the writer of the log (1) something they saw in the log that they liked, and (2) something they would recommend the writer consider doing differently in the future. It's wise to discuss beforehand the importance of being tactful when writing notes and to brainstorm some possible written comments, such as

I liked . . .
- Your honesty.
- The variety in your writing.
- That you added drawings.
- Your organization.
- How neat your work is.

You might . . .
- Include more details.
- Try to repeat yourself less.
- Include more examples.
- Try to be more organized.
- Try to write more neatly.

Strategy 21-7: Thought/Feel Cards

Purpose: To promote healthful self-awareness.

Description: Asking students to make notes, usually anonymously, of personal thoughts and feelings of which they are currently aware.

Imagine that after the viewing of an exciting video, a teacher distributes three-by-five-inch cards and says to his students,

> On one side of the card, write down some of the thoughts now in your mind. These could be thoughts about anything. You will not need to share what you write. This is just a chance to look inside yourself and notice what thoughts you find there. Then, on the other side, write some of the feelings you currently find inside yourself. How are you now feeling? Again, you will not need to show this to anyone.

Once the class climate is secure enough for students to handle this strategy honestly, it serves several valuable purposes. First, it sharpens the distinction between thoughts and feelings. Some students have trouble with that distinction and, as a result, have difficulty separating their emotional reactions from their reasoning powers, and that in turn can make it difficult for them to use their minds to manage their impulses.

This strategy also gives students a chance to vent their feelings, which, when used after an emotionally rich experience, prepares them to move ahead to whatever is next with a clearer mind. It also suggests that writing is always a safe way to vent one's feelings and, in that way, it teaches a useful life skill.

Finally, the Thought/Feel Cards strategy cultivates self-awareness and self-acceptance, and if the strategy is repeated from time to time, perhaps every three or four weeks, students tend to clarify their interests and concerns and become more intelligently self-managing.

What happens after students write their cards? Some possibilities:

- Invite volunteers to share either a thought or a feeling, which might lead into a Productive Discussion (Strategy 16-2).

It is while you are patiently toiling at the little tasks of life that the meaning and shape of the great whole of life shines down on you.

Phillips Brooks

- Start a Whip Around, Pass Option (Strategy 16-4), asking students to report a thought or a feeling or to say "I pass."
- Use Sharing Pairs (Strategy 7-1), asking students to take a moment or two to share with a partner something they are willing to reveal.
- Collect the cards after telling students they need not put their names on them. Perhaps then shuffle the cards and read one side aloud to the class, providing everyone with feedback about what is happening in the classroom. If you do this, take care not to reveal who wrote anything. Also, avoid reading a card that might embarrass someone. Some teachers who collect the cards wait until the next day to read a sampling to the group, allowing time to choose which cards are best not to read aloud. This feedback procedure helps some students feel they are not alone, not defective, not peculiar; they come to see that others in the class have the same unspoken thoughts or feelings as they do.

▲ TEACHER COMMENT

I was doing a tutorial when a thunderstorm occurred. The students lost all interest in what we were doing. I took advantage of the situation and had everyone complete a Thought/Feel Card. Then we did a Whip Around. Everyone felt so much better. Several students had been frightened, and the activity helped them see that others felt that way, too.

—*Hal Goldsmith, College Teacher*

Strategy 21-8: Mini-celebration

Purpose: To celebrate with energy and to strengthen feelings of community in the classroom.

Description: Pausing to recognize student effort with a moment of group applause or other celebratory action.

After finishing one segment of a lesson, we might say, "Let's give ourselves a hand for handling that lesson so well." Then we, preferably with shining eyes and true enthusiasm, start the applause.

If students are timid or if the applause lacks energy, we might call for a repeat. "Now let's do it as if we really *mean* it. Let's give ourselves a *big* hand for what we accomplished so far!"

At this point we recommend accepting what we get, not calling for another repeat. Student enthusiasm and participation tend to quickly increase when we keep using the procedure with strong, positive expectation.

Our colleague Neil Rothman offers these other options for Mini-celebrations:

- *Standing round of applause.*
- *Standing silent big* O *(for ovation).* Students stand, touch both hands above their heads to form a big *O*, and twist their big *O*s right and left, creating ripples of delight in the room.

- *Finger tapping.* Students tap their desktops with one finger.
- *Clamshell clapping.* As a silent celebration, students put one hand up, fingers bent forward, thumb snapping up and down against the four remaining fingers, like a clamshell opening and closing.
- *High-fives.* Students turn to nearby classmates and tap each other's palms.
- *Golf applause.* All applaud very quietly, as on a golf course.
- *Back pats.* All pat themselves on the back.

Strategy 21-9: Progress Proclamation

Purpose: To help students appreciate their progress.
Description: Occasionally reminding students how far they have progressed.

We can strengthen student dignity, community, and awareness by reminding students of their progress. We might fairly often tell the class, for example, that they have made great progress in

- Working independently.
- Making responsible decisions.
- Treating each another respectfully.
- Using self-control.
- Working cooperatively.
- Reading our difficult textbook.

We did not change as we grew older; we just became more clearly ourselves.

—Lynn Hall

22

Providing Effective Homework Assignments

Homework. The word brings as much joy to the average student as a toothache. Few homework assignments inspire students to do the very best work they can. Can homework be more inspiring? It sure can. The seven strategies of this chapter illustrate some possibilities. The first four are recommended for your first attention.

 ## Strategy 22-1: Assignments with Choice

Purpose: To grow self-responsible work habits.
Description: Providing homework assignments that give students some choice.

Many homework assignments are offered without choices: "Do the first 10 problems on page 36." Such no-choice assignments do not take advantage of the inherent opportunities in homework to individualize learning experiences, train students in responsible self-management, and, in the process, to communicate high respect for students. How can we take advantage of these opportunities? Some suggestions:

• *Give choice in **how much** to do.* "Do as many problems as you think you need to do to master this material." Or "Read the chapter and write as many Outcome Sentences as you can." Or "Do at least the first three problems, more if that would be good for you." Students then can do more or less, depending on personal judgments.

• *Give choice in **what** to do.* "Choose some spelling words that are difficult for you and practice writing each correctly at least four times." Or "Discuss any three of the problems on page 74." Such assignments allow students to individualize their focus.

• *Give choice in **how much time** to spend.* "Study the material for at least 20 minutes, more if that would be good for you." Or "Decide how long you want to work on the assignment. Set a timer and then stick to your commitment. Then write a statement about how well you did."

• *Ask students to **create their own** assignments.* "Design an assignment on this work that would be good for you." Or "Choose a partner and talk over what would be a valuable assignment for each of you. Be reasonable, honest, and helpful to each other. Then write down the assignment that you agree will be best for you and complete it for Monday."

Here are some other examples of homework with choice:

• For tomorrow, read any story from our class library.

• Create one or more real-life word problems based on this math work.

• From the list of words and phrases on the sheet distributed, be ready to read aloud as many as you can.

• For homework, please think back over today's activities and draw something or write a summary of what we discussed.

• Draw as many conclusions as you can from the information I presented and be ready to share it tomorrow with a partner.

Many students do more and better work with assignments that contain choices. Beyond that, Assignments with Choice, by regularly asking student to consider what is good for them and to make homework decisions on that basis, inspire healthy self-management. In time, then, we might expect students to make wiser decisions in other situations, perhaps even when their friends urge them to do something that, deep down, they know is not good for them.

Strategy 22-2: Homework Unlike Class Work

Purpose: To make homework more interesting.
Description: Designing homework assignments that are distinctly different from class work.

Many students find homework uninteresting simply because it too closely resembles what they did in class. One remedy is to assign homework that, although

I like nonsense—it wakes up the brain cells. Fantasy is a necessary ingredient in living. It's a way of looking at life through the wrong end of a telescope . . . and that enables you to laugh at all of life's realities.

—*Dr. Seuss*

related to class work, is distinctly different. If, for example, we *talked* about a science topic in class, we might ask students to *draw* something about it for homework. Some other examples:

• Find examples of today's grammar lesson in magazines or newspapers; cut them out and make a collage.
• Each day write at least one new entry in your Learning Log.
• Pick a topic from our past work that you would like to review and come prepared tomorrow to give a three-minute explanation of it to a fellow student.
• Write your best explanation of the reasoning behind the procedure we practiced today.
• Choose one or more new words mentioned today and look them up in a dictionary or an encyclopedia. Perhaps also ask someone in your neighborhood about them. Write what you discover.
• Practice reading aloud, anything you wish, to someone in your family. Come prepared to read it to a classmate tomorrow.
• Answer three questions from the end of Chapter 3, a chapter we finished weeks ago.

Strategy 22-3: Homework in Layers, Not Lumps

Purpose: To make homework more interesting and more efficient.
Description: Providing homework assignments that offer practice with current content, review old content, and preview new content.

Imagine a teacher explaining to his class that homework assignments will consist of many kinds of questions. Many of the questions will help students practice what they are currently learning in class. Others will help keep old learnings fresh, bringing up material from last week, last month, or even earlier. And sometimes homework assignments will contain especially challenging questions, perhaps about a topic the class has not yet studied. "When this happens," the teacher tells the students, "consider the possibilities for proceeding." He continues by offering some ideas:

> Is there something you already know that might help you with the new challenge? Is there someone you can ask for help? Is there an idea you might try, just to see what happens? Perhaps play with the questions, experimenting with different ways of approaching them. I do not want you to worry about getting everything right with such questions. I just want you to give it your best effort.

All virtue lies in individual action, in inward energy, in self-determination. There is no moral worth in being swept away by a crowd, even toward the best objective.
—*William Channing*

When we assign homework that layers back over old material, we provide students with a valuable review and with easy opportunities to experience success, something students appreciate. And by including questions that preview new content, we provide appropriate challenge for advanced students and motivate student interest in the new material. By the way, we need not worry about students answering preview questions incorrectly; see Strategy 10-4, Credit for Completing Homework, which discusses the advantages of giving full credit to students simply for completing homework, whether or not they answered questions correctly.

Strategy 22-4: Responsible Homework Discussions

Purpose: To improve students' homework self-management skills.

Description: Guiding students through discussions about how to make wise homework choices.

When it comes to students handling their homework intelligently and responsibly, it's fair to assume many students will be unskilled. It's valuable, then, to deal with this issue directly. Some examples of how various teachers discussed the issue during the first weeks of school:

Example 1. Because homework is important for learning and for reviewing learning, you will have an assignment every day, from the first day of school to the last. You will have to learn to manage your out-of-school time to do this. How can you manage that? Let's brainstorm some ideas.

Example 2. Even if you set aside time for homework, you may sometimes feel lazy or become distracted. That happens. But you can learn to say no to distractions. I encourage you to learn how to do that. One of the main jobs you have at this point in your life is your schoolwork. Yet we all have impulses and temptations that can distract us from our jobs. What are some distractions that might cause you or your friends to put off doing homework? What are some ideas for making it easier to say no to such impulses or temptations and to stick to our work?

Example 3. Doing homework is important. It is important for learning the subjects we're studying and also for developing self-discipline. I want you to do your homework, do it well, and do it every day. But I also want you to live intelligently, not to do everything everyone tells you to do just because they said so. As for making intelligent choices, sometimes you will not feel like even starting your work. And sometimes it will be very hard to stick with it and complete it. Is it intelligent to skip work in those situations? Why or why not?

Example 4. You will notice in this class that many homework assignments will include a choice. Sometimes the choice will be to do more or less of an assignment, such as how many vocabulary words to learn. Sometimes the choice will be whether to do this or that, such as whether you should study new words or review your old words. In addition, there is always the choice of how *well* to do what you do. I can emphasize the importance of doing the very best you can with homework, but it is up to you to learn what that means for you and to actually do it. No one else can live your life for you. I'd like to hear some of your thoughts about what doing your very best means to you.

Example 5. How carefully you do your homework is a choice you have to make. Have you noticed that you do some things more carefully than other things? I'm like that, too. Can you think of any advantages in learning how to do your homework very carefully every day? Do you know any hints for making it easier to work very carefully?

After such discussions, and especially if students still need help in self-managing homework, it's valuable to revisit the issue from time to time. Some questions we might ask—not all on the same day, of course:

How many are finding that you are doing more than the minimum homework some days? Do you ever not do that? How do you decide what is best for you to do?

What ideas have you come up with for managing your time so you don't have to struggle every day to make time for homework? How many need more ideas or, perhaps, a support buddy, to help you learn the art of time management?

How many have been aiming not only to do homework, but to do it very well—that is, seriously and carefully, so you can be proud of it? How many of you are perfectionists with homework, never fully satisfied, and might be better off relaxing a bit with homework? What can we learn about this issue of striving too hard versus not striving hard enough?

What temptations are getting in the way of homework for you? Do you have any tricks to share that help you say no to temptations that would not be good for you?

How many have had a day when it was intelligent not to do any homework at all, when something else really was more important to do? Is anyone willing to share an example?

Homework sometimes calls for persistence, "stick-to-itiveness." How many are good at sticking to tasks, even when those tasks are not easy or pleasant? How many are not so good at that? Perhaps we could list some things on the board that help people persist. Do you want to try some of these ideas? How about telling someone about your plan and, then, how things work out for you?

The general point is that it's advisable to actively help students learn to discipline themselves and complete homework conscientiously. It serves them—and us—better than complaining about their homework habits. It's especially valuable if we truly care about promoting lifelong learning.

Strategy 22-5: Homework Games

Purpose: To add a creative zest to homework.

Description: Inviting students to create a game for themselves that is connected to a homework assignment.

We might challenge students to create a personal game for themselves with some of their homework assignments. Some examples we might give students:

• One girl who had 25 problems to do set a timer and checked how long it took to do the first set of five. Her game was to see if she could do the next set of five faster and with the same degree of accuracy.

• In a science class, a popular game was to write fanciful stories with characters such as Mr. Osmosis, Ms. Fulcrum, Captain Spectrometer, Governor Pesticide—any word plucked from a recent unit. When the teacher wanted a fun change-of-pace activity, she invited a student to read aloud one of those stories.

• One student wrote his answers to homework questions and then had his grandmother write her answers. His game was to see who had more questions answered correctly each day.

Students can often come up with ingenious games. If we ask them to share their games with others, more students tend to play, a process that teachers report adds an entertaining new dimension to homework.

Strategy 22-6: Managing Long-Term Projects

Purpose: To improve self-management of long-term projects.

Description: Assisting students to plan well and stay on top of long-term projects.

We sometimes assign long-term projects and set due dates. But if we do nothing more to help students stay on top of such assignments, the result is often procrastination, sloppy work done at the last minute, and many late or incomplete projects.

The better approach is to help students learn the self-management skills that long-term projects require. How to do this? We might brainstorm ideas for avoiding procrastination with the class and then ask students to test those ideas, to see which might work best for them. We might then occasionally ask students to report to the class on which ideas they found to be working.

Success is not something that can be measured or worn on a watch or hung on the wall. It is not esteem of colleagues or the admiration of the community. . . . Success is a certain knowledge that you have become yourself, the person you were always meant to be.

—George Sheehan

We might also do the following:

• Ask students to turn in periodic progress reports. They might, for instance, submit three-by-five-inch "time cards" on which they have recorded time spent each day or week. Or students might keep a record of time spent in a log to be turned in with the completed project. This might be an optional activity; in the spirit of improving self-management, we might merely suggest it but not require it.

• Allow students to enlist the help of family members. For example, students could have a family member keep track of their time cards. We might also encourage students to discuss project work at home, or send a letter home informing parents of project requirements and due dates.

• Periodically use Sharing Pairs (Strategy 7-1) for the purpose of students telling each other what they've done so far.

• Occasionally call on students at random to report on progress.

Especially with students who are inexperienced in doing long-term projects, we might also break down the project into smaller pieces to be submitted over a period of time. Note, however, that it's often better to help students develop their own self-management skills than to make it unnecessary for them to learn such skills.

Strategy 22-7: Avoiding Homework Overload

Purpose: To minimize frustration caused by homework.
Description: Being open to student and parent feedback about homework and, when appropriate, individualizing the amount of homework given.

Homework should not be a burden. But it can, in fact, become one when it involves more work than students can reasonably handle, as sometimes happens when, for example, students do not have private space at home or must work after school. Simply stated, many students experience homework overload. How can we avoid this problem with our students? Some suggestions:

• Consider personalizing the amount of homework assigned. What is overload for some students may not be for others. Being open to individual adjustments can dramatically improve student responsiveness and parental support.

• Consider what is reasonable and healthy for the age and maturity level of the students. In one school, teachers gauge the amount of homework given by a system whereby 10 minutes of homework is given for each additional grade level—1st graders get 10 minutes; 2nd graders, 20 minutes; and so on.

• Be open to feedback from students and parents. You might, for example, discuss with parents, individual students, or the whole class what constitutes a "healthy" amount of homework for them—the amount that, given their realities, maximizes learning and minimizes frustration.

• Especially for young students, help family members find productive ways to support students in completing homework assignments. Sometimes it is enough to send home a letter with suggestions covering such topics as how to ask students about homework, when and how much to help, what materials and space to provide, what time of day is best for students to do homework, and what to do if students do not know what the homework is or do not understand how to do it.

Everybody gets so much information all day long that they lose their common sense.

—*Gertrude Stein*

PART VII

Strategies for Further Advancing Teacher Effectiveness

Our concern goes beyond helping students pass their final exams. We also want, for example, to help students become more skillful learners and more self-responsible, confident, mature citizens. And we know we will do our best with those goals if we also do well at taking care of ourselves. This part of the book deals with such topics.

The language we use as we attend to those tasks makes a difference. What wording, for example, would inspire students to become even better students? Consider these three comments and the messages they send:

Least inspiring: I was very disappointed to see so many careless errors in your work. From now on, I'm going to take points off for such carelessness.

In between: Some of you didn't check your work very carefully. Next time it might be a good idea for you to have someone look at your papers before you hand them in.

Most inspiring: Here is an interesting challenge: Take a look at this paper, in which I purposely included several careless errors. Work in pairs to see how many of the errors you can identify and fix, so the paper is more like the kind you would be proud to turn in.

Advancing Students' Learning Skills

23

Students, especially those who struggle, do better when teachers help them improve their learning skills (DeBacker & Nelson, 2000). Not incidentally, teaching such skills goes a long way toward helping students become lifelong learners. Many strategies already presented serve that purpose, including

- *Study Cards (Strategy 6-3),* which helps students learn to divide a mass of information into bite-sized pieces.
- *Know and Want to Know (Strategy 12-2),* which shows students how to build on what they already understand.
- *Think Aloud (Strategy 14-3),* which shows students how the teacher's mind works.
- *Plan, Do, Review (Strategy 17-10),* which gives students practice in planning, acting on plans, and then reviewing how well they did.
- *Outcome Sentences (Strategy 21-1),* which gives students a structure for constructing their own learnings.
- *Like/Might Review (Strategy 21-2),* which shows students a productive and satisfying way to learn from their own experiences.

This chapter presents five more such strategies. We recommend giving first attention to the first two, each of which is marked with an arrow.

Strategy 23-1: How-Read Discussion

Purpose: To help students read better.
Description: Teaching students several different ways of reading.

If we were to ask a group of adult excellent readers how they read a text, we would likely get a variety of answers. Some read carefully, word by word. Some outline readings. Some skim first, then choose how to proceed. Many say it depends on the reading and their purpose; for a well-written text, they may choose one approach, for a poorly written text, another. If their purpose is mastery of the reading, they may choose one approach, for general familiarity only, another.

But ask a group of typical *students* how they go about reading and chances are most will report reading word by word or, if candid, say they avoid reading altogether. One reason students avoid reading is that they assume word by word is the only way. A remedy, especially for students who are expected to do a lot of reading, is to teach them the variety of techniques used by good readers.

A high school teacher might simply ask students what different ways there are to read something and list the alternatives on the board. He might then explain more carefully a few of the options appropriate for that class. "Different people prefer different ways of reading," the teacher might conclude. "And smart readers choose different ways for different purposes."

One middle school teacher had students ask family members about different ways to read and then compiled a list, including these ideas:

- Ask questions first. Then read to find answers.
- Look at the pictures and headings. Read only those parts that look interesting.
- Set a time limit. Read only to that limit.
- Read little by little, so reading is not a heavy chore.
- Aim to write a summary of the entire reading or of sections of it.

Another teacher asked three different students to explain three different reading approaches to the class. All students then were asked to use all three approaches on two different passages and to log their experiences. Finally, the class discussed their logs and discovered, not surprisingly, that they preferred certain reading methods for certain tasks. The point was clear: It is intelligent to choose how to read in a way that suits you and the task at hand. Here are two other possibilities to consider:

- Include in reading assignments a request that students start by writing down the reading approach they choose to use. Afterward, ask students to reflect on the effectiveness of their choice.
- Discuss the helpful organizing systems found in many texts. Discuss uses of the table of contents and the index, and demonstrate how headings can assist

I lose all my good inspiration when my mom and dad fight.

—Sara, grade 3

in scanning and understanding. Perhaps note that some writers begin with summaries and some end with summaries, which can be helpful to understanding the reading.

Strategy 23-2: Note-Taking Options

Purpose: To help students master the art of note taking.
Description: Teaching students how to do more than make verbatim notes of what they hear and read.

Marzano, Pickering, and Pollock (2001) report that note taking is one of the most powerful tools available to students. But for many students note taking is nothing more than writing extracts from a book or a lecture, which according to Bretzing and Kulhary (1979) is among the least effective note-taking strategies. It is advisable to teach students more fruitful approaches, such as these two:

- *Notes in columns.* In this procedure, notes are written in columns. The first column might be for main ideas presented in the reading, the second for related details. Or the first might be for facts, the second for opinions of the author. Or the first might show evidence, the second conclusions of the author. Three columns can also be used—for example, for recording the author's evidence, conclusions, and remaining questions; or for listing past events, present situations, and future expectations/concerns (Santa, Havers, & Maycumber, 1996). This procedure automatically prompts students to think about what they are reading and to put notes in categories.

- *Notes with symbols.* Using this method, students code their notes as they proceed. They might identify important ideas with asterisks or underlining, for example. Student questions might be marked with a large capital *Q.* If two notes are related, they might both be coded with the same letter, a capital *A,* for example. Other related notes might be coded *B,* and so on.

Some other suggestions for helping students with note taking:

- Encourage students to experiment with different note-taking approaches, learning eventually how to choose an approach that works well for each situation they are in.

- Build in time for students to share notes, which can help them identify and correct misconceptions and identify the effective ways of note-taking used by classmates.

Anytime you see a turtle up on top of a fence post, you know he had some help.

—*Alex Haley*

- Instruct students to build on their initial notes, that is, to revise and expand them as they continue to think and learn (Anderson & Armbruster, 1986), so notes are active records rather than inert memories.
- Remind students to refer to notes when questions arise during class discussions or when they review for tests (Carrier & Titus, 1981).

You might also consider three other strategies that deal with note taking: Visual Aids and Graphic Organizers, Note-Taking Template, and Outcome Sentences (Strategies 13-4, 13-7, and 21-1).

Strategy 23-3: Detailed Oral Learning Statements

Purpose: To remember learnings longer and more clearly.
Description: Asking students to describe what they have learned in great detail, aloud, to themselves or a partner.

Want to remember well? Win Wenger (1989) suggests taking something just learned and describing it aloud in great detail. For example, if you're working on your golf swing, you might speak aloud to yourself, trying to describe exactly what you want to do:

> Keep my head in one spot, my nose pointing right at the ball. Put the center of my attention on my waist, aiming to take my power from my waist turn.

Or if you want to digest this strategy, so you understand it fully and recall it well, you might say aloud:

> To teach students how to digest a learning and remember it well, teach them to say aloud, in as much detail as they can, what they learned. The more detailed the description and the more vivid the speaking, the better.

This process works because it makes learnings more clear and specific and because it activates many learning modalities, including memory, visualization, vocalization, and hearing. Try it. Say aloud how you understand this strategy. See if that process clarifies and strengthens your understanding of it.

To apply this strategy to silent reading, instruct students to pause periodically during silent reading, then to close their eyes and momentarily visualize what they've read, and finally to whisper details about the reading to themselves. That is especially helpful when students must read material that is difficult for them to digest.

Strategy 23-4: Charts of Learning Tips

Purpose: To help students become more effective and more independent learners.
Description: Discussing and posting ideas that can help students take charge of their own learning.

To help students find their own way to learn, we might remind them that we all learn in our own ways, that there is no one best way to learn. Then ask the class for examples of how they personally were successful at learning certain material. Perhaps make a list of these options and suggest students try some of them, so all students have a toolkit of learning methods. Figures 16 and 17 show two lists that were posted in one classroom.

Figure 16
Poster for Learning from Others

To learn from a teacher or classmate . . .

- Don't feel bad if you are slow to understand, for we learn in our own ways, by our own time clocks.
- Communicate to those trying to help you learn. Tell them what is best for you.
- Give a time-out signal or say if you have had enough for now. (Sometimes we feel so confused that it is best to temporarily back off.)
- Say if you would like to have the material in writing.
- Say if you would like a classmate to explain it to you later, not now.
- Say if you would like more examples.
- Say if you would like a slower explanation.
- Say if it's the main point that you would like to hear again.
- Say what it is that you do not understand.
- Say if you think you need more practice or more examples.

Figure 17
Poster for Learning from Reading Materials

To learn from reading materials . . .

- Scan the material before reading carefully.
- Make an outline of the material as you read.
- Write notes about key points or questions you have as you read.
- Turn the reading into pictures or symbols that help you remember.
- Say aloud what you are getting from the reading.
- Turn your learnings into songs or poems.
- Tell someone what you are learning as you proceed.
- Give yourself a pat on the back for completing each part, perhaps even a stand-and-stretch moment.

Strategy 23-5: Teaching Specific Learning Skills

Purpose: To help students learn more easily and successfully.

Description: Teaching learning skills specific to the class grade level and subject matter.

Many students learn much better when they are taught specific skills for specific purposes. Some examples:

- *Prewriting.* To help students write better, recommend that before writing they brainstorm ideas, draw pictures, make lists of details, or draw a word map of their thoughts.
- *Visualized spelling.* To help students learn to spell, recommend that they visualize a word in their mind's eye after studying it, and when they want to recall the correct spelling, to visualize the word before trying to write it.
- *Scanning and questioning.* To help students read complex text material, teach them to first scan the material, to note questions that occur to them, and finally, to read with those questions in mind.
- *Reading and summarizing.* To help students remember more of what they read, suggest that they pause and summarize each part before going on, occasionally see if they can recall those summaries, and finally, summarize some or all of their summaries.
- *Math reasoning.* To help students handle word problems, teach them first to identify the question being asked, then to look for clue words indicating which operation or operations to use, then to eliminate unnecessary information, and finally, to create an equation and attempt to solve the problem.

When teaching students a new learning skill, it is useful, of course, to give them time for practice. Students might practice on their own and then compare experiences in Sharing Pairs (Strategy 7-1). Or they might practice together, using Learning Pairs or Practice Pairs (Strategies 7-2 and 7-4). You might also include skill practice as part of independent work time, as in a Do Now assignment (Strategy 6-1). In any case, it is wise not to assume that just because it is obvious to us how learning can best proceed, it will be obvious to the students.

Notice the difference between what happens when a man says to himself, "I have failed three times," and what happens when he says, "I'm a failure."

—*S. I. Hayakawa*

Making Learning More Real and Lasting for Students

24

The ideal is not for every runner to win the race. It's for all participants to run the very best they can. Similarly, the ideal school is not one in which all students write perfect exam papers. It's one that inspires all students to do the very best learning they possibly can. But there is a difference between students doing their best at reading popular magazines and reading good literature, at adding lists of numbers and thinking through real math problems. That is, the content of lessons makes a difference (Alexander, Kulikowich, & Schulze, 1994). The ideal school, we might say, has students doing their very best work on the most fruitful of content. Consider these four levels of content:

1. *Specific information.* Facts and details, names and dates, individual events, isolated skills. Learning at this level tends to have little use or lasting power.

2. *Concepts and generalizations.* The big ideas and the integrated skills. Learning at this level is far more valuable, especially for students able to understand and work with abstractions.

3. *Applications.* Practical applications of knowledge and skills. Learning at this level is the most real for the largest number of students.

4. *Personal values.* Issues that touch what students care about. Learning at this level is often most real, personal, and, perhaps most significant, lasting.

Figure 18 on p. 310 illustrates how the difference in these four levels might be evident in the kinds of questions asked in various subject areas.

With so much content to cover and so many constraints on our time, it is easy to neglect the richer levels of content. But we need not do that. Project work, especially Application Projects and Service Projects (Strategies 18-2 and 18-3), helps avoid that pitfall. Many textbook supplements also contain suggestions we can use. This chapter offers four additional strategies that teachers report help make subject matter both more real and lasting. The first one is marked with an arrow to indicate it deserves your first attention. But note: The most real and lasting learnings of all often emerge not from the content studied but from the process of studying, especially when that *process* stretches students' dignity, energy, self-management, community, and awareness.

Figure 18
Sample Questions for Four Levels of Content

Specific Information	• What is the date of the Declaration of Independence? • Where was the Declaration of Independence signed?	• What is the chemical symbol for water? For sodium chloride?	• Who wrote the story we read? • What reason did the husband give for his violence?	• What were the four main causes of World War II? • Who were the allies of the United States?	• What is 23 multiplied by 145?
Concepts and Generalizations	• What motivates people to declare their independence? • What is a declaration?	• How are elements joined into chemical wholes? • How are symbols derived?	• How are violent acts related to frustration? What else often leads to violence?	• What forces tend to contribute to warfare? To international co-operation?	• What is an efficient way to get a total from a group of identical amounts?
Applications	• What people nowadays want independence? What are they doing about it?	• What pollutes the water in our town? • How could you analyze a sample of the water in our town?	• What kinds of violence are increasing these days? What might be causing the increase?	• What kinds of conflicts are evident in our town? What might explain why these conflicts occur?	• What is the area of the floor of our room in square feet?
Personal Values	• How important is independence to you? • When is it hard for you to act independently?	• What elements in your life do you think are important? Can you draw symbols of those elements?	• How do you handle frustration? What would help you do better at dealing with frustration?	• Are there any conflicts now that concern you? Could you do more to deal with them?	• Can you recall occasions when you would have liked to do multiplication quickly and easily?

Strategy 24-1: Concept-Generalization Focus

Purpose: To bring learnings up to the level of concepts and generalizations.

Description: Selecting a concept or generalization and building lessons around that big idea.

We can organize a unit around a big idea, such as a concept or generalization. In science, for example, we can organize a unit on balance, evaporation, or plant growth. In art, the organizing concept could be color, movement, or sketching. In English, it could be poetry, metaphor, or comedy. This strategy calls for focusing our initial orientation and follow-up questions on the larger idea. Facts and details then serve mainly to illuminate the big ideas or general skills. Many students will remember the facts, of course, picking them up in passing, much as we learn the names of the streets in our neighborhood by passing them repeatedly. But more students will grasp something larger than these facts and details.

Some examples of teachers using this strategy:

In geography. Today we will start a unit on Europe. We will occasionally use flash cards to help you connect cities with their countries. We will see a film on rivers and mountains of Europe. We will read about people from different regions. And I will ask each of you to draw and label a map that shows the location of everything we study. This will bring up a lot of facts and details. Some of the facts will stick in your memory, of course, but you do not need to remember any particular fact. Aim to get the idea of Europe as a region, such as where it is, what it looks like, what its people are about. As we proceed, please make a list of interesting things you learned. At the end of the unit, I'll ask you to turn in your map and to summarize your list of learnings, so I know the main things you learned about Europe and, perhaps, what interested or surprised you most.

In math. Today we will start a unit on percentages. Your job is to prepare a scrapbook of several kinds of percentage problems, showing how you can correctly solve each one. This will require you to understand situations in which percentage problems occur in real life. You will have to figure out a way to solve such problems correctly. We'll explore all that and help each other. Many of you will master the process of doing percentage calculations during this unit. But that might still be tricky for some of you, so don't worry if your time for mastering the calculations has not yet arrived. Practice asking someone to help you solve your problems correctly. But be sure your scrapbook shows that you can identify several kinds of percentage problems and, by yourself or with help, can solve each one correctly.

In history. Today we will begin our unit on the Revolutionary War in America. Our approach will be to look closely at the daily lives of six different people who lived during that time, some famous and some not. As we do this, you will pick up

> Never tell people how to do things. Tell them what to do and they will surprise you with their ingenuity.
>
> —*George S. Patton*

many details and facts about that war and about life during that time. Some of you will remember the facts, but I would not like you to aim for that. Aim rather to get a general understanding of the war, and especially how people on different sides of the issue experienced it. At the end of the unit, I'll give you some time to work with one or two others, or alone if you like, to prepare a written or oral report, or perhaps a mural, dramatic skit, or model. Your task for this final work is to show some of the key things you learned about the American Revolution.

Concluding questions or summary evaluations would not, of course, focus on the facts of the lessons. Instead, they would focus on the big picture. Some examples:

- *What in general can you say about* . . . The three chemicals we've studied so far? The misspelled words on the board? The stories we read? How plants grow? The American history leaders we discussed?
- *Classify the specifics we studied into the concepts of* . . . Organic and inorganic chemicals. Spelling rules and exceptions to spelling rules. Subjective and objective writing. The plant-growth factors of soil, light, and temperature. Favoring democracy and opposing democracy.
- *Write some Outcome Sentences* about the lessons beginning with such phrases as *I learned . . . , I was surprised . . . , I'm beginning to wonder . . . , I promise . . . ,* or *I believe . . .*
- *Compare and contrast* . . . The three chemicals we studied in this chapter with chemicals we studied earlier. Subjective and objective writing. Early and late plant growth. The loyalists and the revolutionaries.

Many students realize that they forget facts soon after the final exam, and that even if they remember all the facts, those facts are often not very useful, other than for winning trivia games. Yet many students assume facts are what school is all about. For this reason, it's often prudent to explain when we want students to clarify a larger issue, or advance a general skill, or grasp a basic concept, not merely remember a batch of details. (See also Strategy 13-8, Signal for the Big Picture.)

Strategy 24-2: Using Subject Matter to Learn About Life

Purpose: To exercise mature thinking on real-life issues and to motivate academic study.

Description: Connecting a subject matter lesson to an issue students are likely to care about.

Often it is possible to begin a unit with a values-level discussion, that is, a discussion about an issue that students care about. Alternatively, we can end with such a discussion, as a demonstration of how academic study can connect to what matters in daily life. The following examples illustrate this strategy at work.

Example 1: Reading a Story

We might pick a concept from a story the class will study next and start the lesson with values-level questions likely to touch student concerns or interests, as in this example:

> Today we will begin a story by Clarkson. One person in the story is very sad, as you will see. Have you ever been sad? Make some notes to yourself about one or two times either you or someone you know was quite sad. What happened? How did the sadness go away? Later I'll invite you to share some of your thoughts with a partner, or to pass if you would prefer. We'll then talk a bit about sadness, seeing what we now know about it. Then we'll read the story and see what else we can learn.

A similar discussion after studying a piece of literature can turn the reading into a personally meaningful experience:

> One theme in the book we just finished was perseverance, not giving up even when the going got tough. Make some notes to yourself about times you or someone you know stuck to a task, even when that was very difficult. Then, thinking about your examples, note anything that made persevering easier. What ideas does our story suggest for handling times like that?

Example 2: A Person or Event in History

We might pick a concept related to a famous person or a historical event and similarly connect it to value issues that personally touch students, discussing it either before or after study. Here is an example of introducing a concept before study:

> Lincoln was sometimes unsure of what to do as president of the United States, as our next unit will make clear. How about you? Can you remember times when you were unsure of what to do? What is a good strategy for handling times like that? Let's think about this a bit now, and again after we study our unit, to see if we learn anything more about making choices when we are unsure. I will add my thoughts, too. People often must make a choice, even when they are not sure what the best choice is. In this unit, one of the things I want you to learn is something about how to make choices wisely.

An example of introducing a concept after study:

> As we learned, Alaska and Hawaii were the last states to be admitted to the United States, yet most of the people in Alaska and Hawaii were not unhappy about being last. How about you? Were you ever last or almost last at something?

How did you feel? What would make being last OK? What makes it harder when you are not among the first few to do something?

Example 3: Mathematics

Connecting mathematics to students' personal reality can effectively motivate new study and add a dimension of meaning to completed study. Here is an example of how we might do this before study:

> Before we move ahead with subtraction of large numbers, I want you each to come up with three examples of subtraction in real life. Use your imagination or ask family members, if you like. Then consider what would be very hard for you to subtract from your life. On the other hand, what would you love to get rid of?

An example of how we might do this after study:

> Before going on to our next unit in geometry, let's spend a few minutes talking about circles in the real world. We'll share ideas later, first in pairs and then as a whole class, but first make some notes about one or more of the questions I wrote on the board. What circles of things or people or ideas are important to you? What feelings, if any, do you have about circles? Do you have any broken circles in your life? Are there any circles you could complete for others? Can you draw a silly circle?

Three Steps for Adding a Values Discussion to a Subject Matter Lesson

Step 1: Seek a real-life issue that can be connected to the content. The connection can be very indirect. Figure 19 lists possible issues about which students might feel strongly.

Step 2: Ask questions in which the word "you" is central. Some examples:

- Have you ever experienced something like . . . ?
- Do you know someone who . . . ?
- Have you ever enjoyed . . . ?
- Have you ever had trouble with . . . ?
- What might you do if . . . ?
- What choice would make you feel best about yourself?
- What would you most want to avoid doing?

It is usually best to avoid hypothetical questions that are not likely to matter much to students. For example, a hypothetical question such as "How would life be different without cars?" is likely to elicit an indifferent reaction from students ("It won't happen, so why should I care?"). A better alternative would be "What would you like in your ideal car?"

> Great tranquility of heart is his who cares for neither praise nor blame.
>
> —*Thomas à Kempis*

Figure 19

Values Issues That Might Connect to Academic Lessons

- Money
- Luxuries
- Prejudice
- Honesty
- Special people
- Blind people
- Growing up poor
- Giving up
- Favorite games
- Things that are hard to wait for
- Stealing
- Winning a prize or an honor
- Love
- Strong personal beliefs
- Things I love to do
- Hugging
- Smiles
- Fear
- Hope

- Delight
- Generosity
- Courage
- Perseverance
- Fury
- Jealousy
- Deception
- Help in a strange place
- Crime in town
- Cars
- Telling the truth
- The way I look
- Surprise
- Grace and kindness
- Disappointment
- Sorrow
- Planning ahead
- Friends
- Giving compliments
- Death
- Loneliness

- Insecurity
- Keeping a secret
- Wanting something and not getting it
- Understanding others' points of view
- Teasing
- Bossiness
- Cruelty
- Pets
- Hobbies
- Being too short or too tall
- The future
- Tears and laughter
- A gift
- Strong positive or negative feelings
- A terrible mistake
- Hopes for the future
- Uncertainty
- Inability to act

Step 3: Structure a safe, thoughtful way to handle the questions. One option that works well is a Write-Share-Learn sequence (see Strategy 3-1, Action Flow Lessons). And it's advisable to offer students the option to pass on any question or any procedure. Doing so both protects student privacy and promotes student self-management.

On Values and Subject Matter

A common assumption is that lessons should begin at the fact-detail level— for instance, teaching relevant names and dates in history before studying what actually happened, or learning grammar and spelling before writing letters, or learning the parts of the microscope before beginning to use it. This approach has a certain logic, but it is a logic that often squeezes much of the life out of teaching. With some units and with some students, particularly students who have difficulty handling big ideas, it is advisable to start with facts and details, giving students success at that level. But, even then, whenever we can, it's wise to tag on at least a brief values discussion, to give students practice in serious think-ing about serious issues, as illustrated by the following examples.

In science. Now that we have looked at the earth's crust, I'd like to take a few min-utes to look at how people from different lands relate, or how people within one land relate when they are different from one another. Please make a note or two about how you feel when you meet someone from a foreign land or someone who is very different from you. You do not need to share this with anyone. Keep it private if you like . . . Sit with someone near you and share any thoughts you have about this that you care to talk about. We'll take just a moment or so for this . . . Let's all discuss how we want to behave with people who are different from us.

In math. Now that we have finished our unit on percentages, I'd like to take a few minutes to talk about percentages in your personal life. Please start by estimating the percentage of the time that you feel strong, capable, and confident. Then note what you might do to increase that percentage, if you have any ideas about that. I'll give you just a moment or two to make some notes. Then you'll have a chance to share thoughts with a partner, and, finally, we'll get together and I'll mention some suggestions I find useful for people who want to spend more time being their strong, capable, confident selves.

In history. Before we leave the Civil War unit, let's see if we can list on the board some ideas for talking over conflicts peaceably, resolving differences before they get into negative, hard feelings. Let's say two friends were in conflict. What kind of conflict might that be? What are some smart and not-so-smart ways to resolve such a conflict?

Value-level discussions, used either before or after study of facts, concepts, and applications, not only perk up students' interest but also can give students practice in thinking seriously about important life issues, practice that many stu-dents sorely need. Young people will face many complex choices in their lives. We find that they will face those choices with more balance and reason, and far less instability and impulse, when they have the opportunity to grapple with issues in the safety of the classroom.

Taking a unit up to the personal-values level of subject matter does not nec-essarily require a logical leap. For instance, on the concept of circles, we can leap from geometry circles to circles of friends or to circles of personal habits. On the concept of rocks, we can leap from categorizing hard rocks to wondering about hard people and how best to deal with them. On the concept of long division, we can leap to divisions in our personal lives or in the school or community.

Such leaps allow us to create powerful lessons, teach students about what is involved in good living, and keep schoolwork filled with rich variety. Students usually appreciate this and often grow a great deal as a result. Indeed, you may

It is the supreme art of the teacher to awaken joy in creative expression and knowledge.

—*Albert Einstein*

find that some students profit as much from such deliberations as from any academic studies.

Strategy 24-3: Application Brainstorm

Purpose: To broaden understanding and make learnings more relevant.
Description: Asking students to brainstorm ideas for applying a concept or learning to a new situation.

When we want to expand a subject matter lesson into the values arena, we can often make good use of the power of brainstorming to uncover nonobvious connections. For example, we might conclude a lesson on multiplication by asking students to brainstorm real-life situations in which using multiplication would be helpful. After teaching about the Bill of Rights, we might ask students to brainstorm situations in which the rights specified in the document are important. For hints on using brainstorming, see Strategies 16-8 and 19-9.

Strategy 24-4: Personalizing Learning

Purpose: To connect academic learning to real life.
Description: Asking students to expand on a topic by sharing examples from their own lives.

Nothing makes a lesson come alive for students more than having an opportunity to connect it directly to the people, events, or circumstances in their own lives. We might, for example, after reading a story, ask students to report incidents in their lives that were similar to those of the main character. In math class, we might conclude a lesson by having students report examples of how they might use the skill in their daily lives. In social studies, we might identify some controversial issues and ask if any students currently have positions on those issues.

When we personalize lessons in this way we must, of course, respect the boundaries of students and not ask them to speak about matters they would prefer not to. We therefore only invite personal comments, never require them.

25

Inspiring Students to Strive for Excellence

How can we inspire students to attack schoolwork with more of their best motivations, that is, with more of their natural motivations to live with full dignity, steady energy, intelligent self-management, feelings of community, and open awareness? In one way or another, that is the question addressed throughout this book, of course. Most of the chapters focus on a particular teaching task—from planning lessons to managing misbehavior—and suggest strategies for handling the task in ways that elicit such healthy motives. This chapter contains strategies that focus more directly on improving students' motivations. Our field tests suggest that the first four strategies deserve most teachers' first attention.

Strategy 25-1: High Expectations

Purpose: To take advantage of the power of expectations.
Description: Maintaining an expectation that students will do the best they can, even when there is no evidence they will do so.

As a teacher, we never want to give up on any students. When, for example, we plan a lesson, we are wise to fully expect that all students will get involved actively and responsibly. When some do not, we do well to assume they had good reason not to and, in the next lesson, they *will* become actively engaged. That is, we should never assume that any student lacks a willingness to be fully engaged. If we were to expect students *not* to become engaged unless, say, we gave them rewards and punishments, grades and tests, reminders and scoldings, they would likely oblige us. Expectations have power. We tend to get what we expect to get (Marzano, 2003).

It is valuable, then, to continually expect all students to be active learners. The message of this strategy is then simple: Find a way to hold that expectation. It is, we believe, one of our most influential, far-reaching strategies. If necessary, put a note on your desk or otherwise create a reminder that will help you keep that expectation alive.

If you're doubtful, remind yourself that your students probably tackle their hobbies with high spirit. Perhaps check it out. Ask them about their nonschool activities, their games, teams, social activities, the activities they really care about. The New or Goods strategy (Strategy 9-4) serves this purpose well. As students talk about the activities they enjoy, observe their spirit. Use that as a reminder that the capacity for active engagement exists in these young people. Is it not possible that we can bring that live energy into the classroom?

We suspect that few students want to be poor readers, clumsy calculators, ignorant of what goes on in the world. It is unlikely that they see any advantage in being unskilled and ignorant. Said another way, students' natural motives support active learning. If, then, we design Action Flow Lessons (Strategy 3-1) that keep students naturally, comfortably engaged, would it not be reasonable to *expect* that they will, in fact, do the best they can with those lessons?

This is not to say that it's not sometimes challenging to keep expectations high. Here is one teacher's observation:

> I had become disillusioned and frankly had low expectations for my students. I also had a lot of reason not to expect much. After all, none of the faculty was able to get much from them. At first I tried to imagine that my students would get actively involved in lessons, but it never lasted long and I had trouble believing it. Then my support buddy and I agreed to ask each other at lunch each day how we were doing at expecting active engagement, and that helped. In fact, we are now convinced that students do work harder when we expect them to. Yet, to be honest, we still need to remind each other at lunch. It's really hard, at least for us two, to hold high expectations in this depressed school.

It certainly can be hard. But it also can be easy! Try *expecting* it to be easy and see what happens. And consider getting a support buddy as this teacher did. Progress is almost always smoother when we proceed with a friend.

Strategy 25-2: Active Learning Thermometer

Purpose: To monitor active involvement and remind students of its importance.
Description: Regularly asking students to rate the level of their involvement in class work.

The quality of a person's life is in direct proportion to their commitment to excellence.

—*Vince Lombardi*

Can we expect equally high test scores from all students? That is unrealistic and ultimately discouraging, for there is no way all students will achieve equally high test scores. But we can expect all to do their personal best. And we can heighten that expectation by using the Active Learning Thermometer (Figure 20).

To introduce this strategy, we might tell students that we expect them all to stay fully involved in their work and to do the very best they can. "Because you all have different interests and backgrounds," we might say, "I do not expect all of you to accomplish an equal amount. But you can all be equal in working as hard as you can." Pointing to the Active Learning Thermometer, we might then explain the various numbers on the scale:

> Sometimes you might be very alert and actively involved in a lesson, doing the very best you can. You are then high up on this thermometer, up here, at *4*.
>
> Believe it or not, sometimes students are not at all active. Maybe they are feeling a little sick, or tired, or distracted, or upset. At such times they would be down here, at *1*.
>
> And sometimes students are in between. We might say they are *usually* alert and active, up about here, at 3. Or they might be *sometimes* active and alert, down about here, at 2.

After this explanation, we might ask students to think about how actively involved they were earlier in the day, when the class was involved in a particular activity. Then, demonstrating each movement, we might tell the students:

Figure 20
Active Learning Thermometer

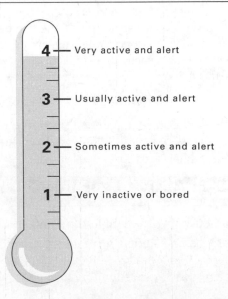

4 — Very active and alert

3 — Usually active and alert

2 — Sometimes active and alert

1 — Very inactive or bored

When I say "Go," leave both hands where they are if you would rate yourself *1*. Put a hand on your chest like this if you would rate yourself *2*. Put a hand on your neck like this if you would rate yourself *3*. Put a hand on your head like this if you would rate yourself *4*. Go!

When we see that everyone understands the procedure, we might tell students that we will repeat the activity from time to time to see how well everyone is doing at keeping actively engaged, and that our goal is to help all of them get to the top of the thermometer and stay there. "Your job will be to let me know what I can do to help you get up there. If we keep active involvement high, we can be sure that you will be taking as much learning as possible from this class."

After students are accustomed to the procedure, we need only point to the Active Learning Thermometer and direct students to use the hand movements to indicate how actively involved they were. Alternatively, we might ask students to write a number on a card or piece of scrap paper and hand it in. Either way, we'll be able to make a quick assessment of active learning. If we use the strategy regularly, we can chart progress, though doing so is not necessary. Used regularly, the hand-movement procedure itself is valuable. It reminds both us and our students that high, productive engagement is a prime goal. It's an easy way to keep alive the active learning goal.

If we do record scores, note that it's advisable to have several sample runs, so that students become accustomed to the procedure and settle in on some personal definition for each level on the "thermometer." We can then proceed in several ways:

- Have each student rate his or her level of engagement every day, recording the number on a slip that is then put in an envelope. Sort the slips and make a chart to show progress over time. Aim to gradually eliminate 1's and 2's and increase 3's and 4's.

- Do the above procedure on three consecutive days only once each month. Average the three daily scores to get one monthly score. Then chart the scores for September, October, and so on through the year, aiming, as before, to show progress toward eliminating 1's and 2's and increasing 3's and 4's.

- To simplify scoring, consider collapsing ratings 1 and 2 and chart them as "low involvement," and collapse ratings 3 and 4 and chart them as "high involvement." The aim then is to eliminate all low involvement.

- Consider having a responsible parent, other staff member, or even a student do the assessments. However, for consistency, if you want to track scores, use the same person and procedure each time.

Success is not a magic ingredient that can be supplied by teachers. Building on strengths allows students to create their own success.

—*Robert Martin*

◆◆◆ Strategy 25-3: Clarifying Excellence Discussion

Purpose: To help students appreciate the value of striving for excellence.
Description: Discussing what defines excellent work and encouraging students to strive for it.

> As essential as good technique is, I don't think education is basically a technological problem. It is a problem of drawing out of each youngster the best he has to give.
>
> —*Edgar Friedenberg*

Some students assume excellence is a high test score and each person must produce such a score or, unhappily, be a less than excellent person. However, what is excellent for one person may not be excellent for another. The best all students can do is strive *toward* excellence while taking care to avoid getting down on themselves when they have not yet reached it. It's when students get down on themselves and give up even trying that their motivation collapses and problems intensify. If there is one outcome we do not want, it is discouraged students. What is the best way to approach this issue? Teachers report that Truth Signs and Cushioning Questions (Strategies 4-1 and 4-2) are especially valuable. An open discussion of the issue can also be valuable. We can ask questions like these:

• *What are the advantages of striving for excellent results?* In the discussion we can acknowledge that it is usually more fun, of course, to play to win.

• *How are we to react when we have not yet produced excellent results?* The truth is that anything less than full self-acceptance makes further progress harder. It often makes it harder to get a good night's sleep, too.

• *How should we view people who do not care about reaching for excellence in some areas of their lives?* Discussing this question often leads to an understanding that minimum performance standards are necessary in some areas (such as driving a car, working in an office or factory, swimming in deep water), even when excellence is not required. The discussion also may lead students to see the unreasonableness of expecting a person to be excellent in all areas.

• *How do you know when you can be satisfied with your current work?* Here we might aim to help students appreciate the advantage of not relying entirely on others' assessments and to consider how they personally would judge their efforts: Did they do the best they could do at the time?

We might also consider continuing the discussion by

• Sharing with students our own positive and negative experiences in attempting to produce excellent results.

• Asking students to interview other adults using some of the same questions.

• Asking students to evaluate, then dramatize or illustrate, the strive-and-accept motto: "Strive to do your best. Accept whatever results."

 ## Strategy 25-4: Best-Work Lesson

Purpose: To clarify what it means to do one's best work.

Description: Asking students to review samples of their best work to clarify what is "best work" for them and then encouraging them to aim for that target in all future work.

Teachers often announce standards, but students do not always commit to them. One strategy to improve commitment to high standards is to help students develop their own definition of such standards. Here is a possible lesson sequence:

1. Ask students to identify samples of what they consider their "best" work. This may include work done at school or home, for themselves or others, including hobbies and jobs or chores around the house.

2. Ask students to list qualities that contributed to making the samples their "best" work, such as neatness, originality, effort.

3. Create a chart with a master list of the qualities students identify.

4. Conduct a discussion around questions like "Which qualities were mentioned most often?" "Do you think some of these qualities are more important than others?" "What qualities would you like to be represented in *your* future best work?"

5. Finally, ask students to make a personal list of qualities that would indicate to them that they did the best work they could do.

The next time we give an assignment, then, we can tell students to aim to have their completed work reflect their personal list of "best" qualities. (A somewhat open-ended and long-term assignment usually works best for this.) After this assignment is completed, student pairs might share work, noting for each other which "best" qualities they clearly see and perhaps which ones are lacking. Students might even give themselves a private "grade" for effort on the assignment and keep a record of such grades over time. Some teachers have used such private-effort grades to support notes to parents saying, for example, "Juan is more often doing the very best he can lately. I am proud of him."

Strategy 25-5: Inspiring Statements

Purpose: To inspire students to strive for excellence.
Description: Cheering students on to do their very best.

As all coaches know, the right comment at the right time can inspire people to reach down deep and exceed all expectations. If you are unpracticed in cheering students on, know that effective comments are rooted in genuine, respectful care. They say, in effect, "I'm with you." "I want this for you." "Working together, we can do the job." They do not say, "Do this for me." "I'm insisting on it." "It is required." They pull, rather than push. Consider the distinction:

Pushing: I want you all to master this material. It is extremely important. I will have no student of mine leaving here without knowing this backward and forward.

Pulling: You will really need this material. I'm committed to doing whatever I can to make sure you master it. Are you willing to work with me and go for it? It will be a challenge—let's do it!

It is often the care of one person for another that ignites an inner power that leads to inspired results. Words without genuine care are largely ineffective. And if the care is mutual, if the students, in fact, also care for the teacher, the inspiration flows along a highly charged path. It can be the path of inspired service, even love. We can then in full honesty communicate the message: "We are in this together, but I can't do the learning for you. You must do it. By now you know how much I care for you. I want to be proud for you, not for me. Show the world you can do it. Go to it!" The words, of course, are not the main thing. It's the intention behind the words that counts.

We once heard about an elementary school principal in Illinois, Frank Beczkala, who wanted to inspire students to do more reading. "If every student reads more," he announced, "I, who am deathly afraid of high places, will stand on the roof of this building and read aloud a story to those assembled below." The students met their challenge. And so did he.

Strategy 25-6: Going for the Gold

Purpose: To inspire students to strive for excellence.
Description: Challenging students to handle everyday tasks at a high level of excellence.

Consider asking students to do a simple task without trying very hard, say, drawing 3 circles or writing the first 10 letters of the alphabet. Then tell them to repeat the task, this time doing their best. This means, you might explain,

• *Striving:* Doing the very best you can, not doing just an ordinary job. Reaching far beyond the level of work you might do without this special challenge. Perhaps reaching for a level of excellence you never attained before. In essence, going for the gold.

• *Risking:* Trying new behaviors. Not staying with what you know you can readily handle. Perhaps reaching out for unfamiliar skills, speed, accuracy. Stretching yourself.

• *Persisting:* Not giving up. Sticking to it. Overcoming any urge to handle the task at a level below your very, very best. Absolutely refusing to accept less from yourself.

You might conclude by discussing which experience felt more satisfying and which produced better results. Some follow-up questions:

• How did you do? What was hard? What was fun? Did anything surprise you?

• Why do you think it's important to accept yourself if, this time, you didn't do your very best? What might happen if you didn't accept yourself in this situation?

• What if someone's best is not as good as another person's best?

• What would you say about this quote: "It's not whether you win or lose. It's how you play the game."

• How many of you would sometimes like to challenge yourself to go for the gold? When might you do that?

• How can we celebrate our efforts? What would encourage us again to go for the gold? Why would we want to do that?

Evidence suggests that such lessons increase student achievement more than do lessons on ways to improve comprehension or manage study time (Craske, 1985; Van Overwalle & De Metsenaere, 1990; Wilson & Linville, 1982).

As teachers, we give students many tasks: academic tasks, such as completing a project or a homework assignment; and administrative tasks, like cleaning up after art or running errands. We would want students to know that striving for excellence is a choice always available when handling any of these tasks.

Strategy 25-7: E-for-Effort Certificates

Purpose: To reinforce the value of doing one's very best.
Description: Regularly acknowledging student effort and occasionally offering certificates to formalize such acknowledgment.

Students are often inspired when they know teachers appreciate a big effort. Offering E-for-Effort Certificates occasionally is one way to keep communicating

The good school sees the student, not as a vessel to be filled, nor a lamp to be lighted. Both metaphors suggest that the student is something to be done to, when in reality he or she is something that does, a body that moves, a mind that purposes, a spirit that soars, a life that lives. The good school sees the student as a life to be lived.

—Royce S. Pitkin

such appreciation. Such certificates are especially valuable as a follow-up to the preceding strategy, Going for the Gold. Consider the following excerpt from Marzano, Pickering, and Pollock (2001):

> Ian MacIntosh was a new student at Prairie Elementary School. It did not take him long to discover that even though the teachers and students seemed nice enough, the school was considered to be what they called a "low-performing school." They had low scores on the state tests, and everyone knew it because the results were published in the local newspaper. The test was given soon after Ian arrived and, like other students, he just wanted to get through it.
>
> The next year, the school got a new principal, Ms. Heichman. Things began to change. Ian's teachers started telling stories of famous people who achieved their goals because they believed that if they tried hard enough, they could do anything. Even students were asked to give examples, and Ian told the story of his grandfather's belief that he could make his farm successful. Ian's teachers started giving students "E for Effort" certificates. Ian earned two in one week. It made him feel more confident and made him want to do better. His classmates all seemed a bit more confident, too, especially when the whole class received the principal's "E for Effort" award because the class beat their own previous class average on math quizzes, twice in one month. He was proud when the banner went up over the door—and he enjoyed the ice cream the room mothers had promised them if they hit their goal.
>
> The best news came when the state test scores returned. The school was in the headlines as the school that had improved the most. Ian knew he and his schoolmates still had a long way to go, but he believed they could do it. (p. 49)

In addition to giving E-for-Effort Certificates, we can also consider these actions:

- Remind students often that they will learn much more when they try much harder. Other strategies in this chapter can provide such reminders.
- Include grades for effort on report cards, and emphasize their importance, as suggested by Strategy 32-2, Dual Grades.
- Make calls or send notes to parents of students who markedly increase their effort, as suggested by Positive Parent Schedule and Surprise Personal Notes (Strategies 27-9 and 32-4).

Strategy 25-8: Personal Model

Purpose: To communicate high expectations through teacher modeling.
Description: Exemplifying a person who works with high DESCA—dignity, energy, self-management, community, and awareness.

Historian and author Will Durant reminds us that "we teach more by what we are than by what we teach." What we are speaks loudly—perhaps more loudly than

> People travel to wonder at the height of the mountains, at the huge waves of the seas, at the long course of the rivers, at the vast compass of the ocean, at the circular motion of the stars, and yet they pass by themselves without wondering.
>
> —St. Augustine

anything we can say. It is best, then, to practice what we preach. If we want to see our students working with high DESCA—dignity, energy, self-management, community, and awareness—we would do well to strive to do the same. More specifically, we should strive to act

- With dignity, ready to assert our own needs.
- With energy, not drained by too many commitments.
- With self-management, not afraid to take initiative.
- With a sense of community, not trying to go it alone.
- With awareness, alert to the needs of our students and ourselves.

When we shine our own light, we are more likely to see our students shining theirs.

Strategy 25-9: Inspiring Stories

Purpose: To strengthen student idealism and encourage students to act on their ideals.
Description: Calling attention to people with inspiring life stories.

Many teachers report it worthwhile to call attention to people who exemplify high levels of idealism or who successfully overcame serious obstacles, such as Helen Keller, Jackie Robinson, Nelson Mandela, and Thomas Edison. We might ask students to reflect on the stories of such people, to write about or illustrate their lives, or to role-play how they themselves might handle similar situations. For one rich source of inspiring stories, see the *Chicken Soup* series by Jack Canfield and Mark Victor Hansen. We might also take time to share inspiring stories from our own life and encourage students to do the same. And we might create an area for posting inspiring stories, quotes, pictures, or anything else that we or our students find inspiring. Inspired students, after all, are most likely to produce inspired schoolwork and to grow up to become positive, inspired citizens.

Strategy 25-10: DESCA Challenges

Purpose: To advance students' capacity to do excellent schoolwork.
Description: Challenging students to stretch their ability to live and work with dignity, energy, self-management, community, and awareness (DESCA).

Teachers can empower students profoundly by occasionally offering nondemanding but stimulating challenges aligned with the five themes of DESCA. Some examples for each quality follow.

Challenges to increase dignity:

- Stand tall.
- Move ahead with confidence.
- When someone is being teased, step up and defend the person.
- Walk away when people are gossiping.
- Even if it feels risky, call up your courage and do what you think is best.
- Speak up for yourself.
- Respect your own ways, your own time clock.
- Show your willpower.
- Look people in the eye.
- Refuse to be put down.
- Show you can take it.
- Say it as if you mean it.
- Show your inner strength.
- Stand up for what you believe in.
- Sit tall in your chair.
- Reach deep inside for your courage.
- Act with authority.

Challenges to increase energy:

- When you are ready to give up, take one more step.
- Stick to it.
- Use all your brain power.
- Go for it—put your all into it.
- Walk briskly.
- Take initiative.
- Use your whole self.
- Practice stepping with a joyful aliveness.
- Speak with full energy.
- Make your eyes bright.
- Relax now to be strong later.
- Get yourself ready.
- Make sure you get enough exercise.

- Move right along.
- Reach down for more ability to persist.
- Make sure you get plenty of sleep.

Challenges to increase self-management:

- Control your impulses.
- Take care of unfinished tasks.
- Think things through for yourself.
- Go past the first idea.
- Ask for help when you need it.
- Look ahead and plan.
- Trust that you will know what to do.
- Proceed by your own time clock.
- Notice when something needs to be done.
- When feeling stuck in inactivity, get up and do something.
- Tell yourself you do not have to be negative.
- When you are angry, slowly count to 10.
- Practice starting immediately.
- Practice stopping immediately.
- Manage your own time.
- Take control of your behavior.
- Organize your papers.

Challenges to increase community:

- Respect the differences in others.
- Practice going out of your way for others.
- Be all for one, one for all in this class.
- Listen to others.
- Help clean up.
- Do more than your share.
- Accept compliments.
- Care for those who need it.
- Cheer people on.
- Show your appreciation.
- Reach out to newcomers.
- Be honest.

> The good teacher . . . discovers the natural gifts of his pupils and liberates them. . . . The true leader makes his followers twice the men they were before.
>
> —*Stephen Neill*

- Accept all people for who they are.
- Tell people when you do not understand.
- Stand up for our group.
- Look for the good in everyone.
- Let us know when we make mistakes.
- Do something good for the community.
- Do something extra at home.
- Ask family members how you can help them.
- Pick up trash when you see it.
- Connect to someone new.

Challenges to increase awareness:

- Keep alert.
- Read with an open mind.
- Call up your intelligence.
- When your attention drifts, bring it back, stay awake.
- Enjoy hearing, seeing, feeling, smelling, tasting.
- Practice ignoring distractions.
- Recall past ideas.
- Notice when someone needs help.
- Notice nonverbal messages.
- Focus your attention.
- Look closely at details.
- Look below the surface.
- Wonder "what else?"
- Open yourself up to big ideas.
- Keep a log of your thoughts, dreams, feelings.
- Notice what is being left undone.
- Notice what is going on.
- Keep alert to the state of your body.
- Pay attention to colors and sounds.
- When you are going too fast, back off.
- Notice your feelings. Where do feelings show up in your body?
- End each day by asking what you liked and what you might do differently next time.

Strategy 25-11: DESCA Proclamation

Purpose: To create a classroom climate that empowers student growth.

Description: Proclaiming "This is a high DESCA classroom" to assert an intention that we and our students are expected to highly value the use of dignity, energy, self-management, community, and awareness.

Announce to the class, "This is a high DESCA classroom," and explain how, as humans, everyone is naturally motivated to live and work with dignity, energy, self-management, community, and awareness—what we call DESCA—and that you want students to learn to live and work that way in your classroom. Some teachers post a sign with this proclamation. Some also have students do a choral reading of the DESCA Proclamation from time to time, typically before a test or other activity in which students might stretch those DESCA abilities.

Every individual has a place to fill in the world and is important in some respect, whether he chooses to be so or not.

—*Nathaniel Hawthorne*

Advancing Students' Self-Responsibility

26

Students behave better and present fewer discipline problems when teachers inspire self-management rather than try to enforce rules, and when they use the first few days to create a positive class climate (Eisenhart, 1977; Emmer, Evertson, & Worsham, 2002; Moskowitz & Hayman, 1976). Part of this effort involves taking the time to have students understand and master basic classroom procedure, as with Student Procedure Mastery (Strategy 5-1) and Setting Procedures and Expectations (Strategy 8-1). Another part involves giving students many choices to make, as with Assignments with Choice (Strategy 22-1). This chapter presents four strategies specifically designed to nurture more healthy self-responsibility. Our field tests suggest that the first two strategies deserve first attention, which is why each is marked with an arrow.

 ## Strategy 26-1: Common Sense Comments

Purpose: To encourage students to make full use of their common sense.
Description: Saying to students at appropriate times, "Does that make sense?" "Do what makes sense," and "It's up to you. You decide."

Consider these scenarios:

• A student is making noise in the hall. A teacher asks mildly, "Does that make sense?"

• A student gives a thoughtless answer to a question. The teacher smiles and responds, "Does that answer make sense?"

• A student says, "I'm finished. What should I do now?" The teacher responds, "Do what makes sense."

- A student asks, "Does this have to be typed?" The teacher responds, "Do what makes sense."

- A student asks, "What should I do first?" The teacher responds, "It's up to you. You decide."

In ways such as these we can remind students that they are intelligent, aware beings, capable of managing their lives responsibly. They do not have to bring every little question or issue to us. They can be more successfully self-reliant than they may have assumed.

Some teachers like to announce early on that it is a class requirement that each person make good use of his or her own common sense and not, for example, ask unnecessary questions or act in ways that cause unnecessary problems for others. However, it is probably more effective to respond consistently with phrases like those in the examples above. By doing so, students keep hearing a valuable message: "I believe you are intelligent and can think for yourself."

Strategy 26-2: Shared Responsibilities, Personal Responsibilities

Purpose: To cultivate a cooperative classroom community.
Description: Discussing the difference between shared and personal responsibilities and brainstorming ways to keep the classroom running smoothly.

Several elementary school teachers have reported that it is valuable to have a discussion that begins somewhat like this:

> In our classroom I'd like us to live as a cooperative community. That means we have shared responsibilities and personal responsibilities. For example, we are all responsible for taking care of our personal belongings—coats, books, lunchboxes, and the like. That is a personal responsibility. But we also have many books and other materials in our classroom that do not belong to one person, and they too must be taken care of. Because that job is too big for any one person, I call it a shared responsibility. Let's brainstorm now some other personal responsibilities. Then afterward, let's identify some shared responsibilities that will help us to keep our classroom community running smoothly.

We cultivate community whenever we encourage students to work together for the good of all. However, we do well also to encourage self-management, for when students act as responsible community members *and* responsible individuals, classrooms function most smoothly and efficiently and we teach a basic lesson about life itself.

A new position of responsibility will usually show a man to be a far stronger creature than was supposed.

—*William James*

Strategy 26-3: Self-Management Goals

Purpose: To provide opportunities for personal growth in self-management.
Description: Inviting students to set and track a personal goal for the day.

To help students become more intelligently self-managing, we recommend occasionally beginning class by inviting students to set a personal goal for themselves for the day. We might say, for example

> Let's all think about the kind of person we would like to be for today. You may want to be more relaxed or more confident, or less chatty or more thoughtful. Or you may want to *do* something special today, perhaps take more risks or be more outgoing. Take a moment now to see if you can find one goal you would like to choose for today. If you have chosen one, please record it in your logbook. You might want to begin with the phrase "My goal for today is . . ." At the end of the day, check back to see how well you succeeded. We may have time later to share some goals and share reports on how well you did. But for now, let's keep our goals private.

By asking students to make such a note in a logbook from time to time, we stimulate them to become more self-aware and self-managing. Time permitting, at the end of the day we might give students time to reread their goals and record a few comments about how successful they were. We might also invite some students to share their experiences, in pairs perhaps or with the class as a whole. We might also conduct a discussion on how best to choose such a daily goal and successfully reach it.

But most of the power of this strategy, we suspect, comes from the simple request at the outset to consider choosing a goal for the day and then to aim to reach it.

Strategy 26-4: Rights, Responsibilities, Rewards

Purpose: To help students learn to live responsibly.
Description: Discussing the natural connection between rights, responsibilities, and rewards and how to make use of that connection in the classroom.

Imagine a teacher posting a chart with three large Rs on it and telling students that this is to be a "Class of 3 *R*s." The first *R* is for *Rights*. The teacher then lists a few key rights she wants the class to enjoy—for example, *to feel safe, to get help when we need it, to walk about the room when we need to.*

The teacher then reminds students that with rights comes a second *R, Responsibilities.* For the rights mentioned earlier, for example, certain responsibilities reasonably flow: *to refrain from making others feeling unsafe; to do our best before asking for help; to move about the room without disturbing others.* The teacher discusses each responsibility listed, giving enough examples of responsible and irresponsible behavior to make each point clear to students.

The third *R* is for *Rewards,* the ways students will be happier and learn better if they exercise each right and fulfill the accompanying responsibilities.

Throughout the year, then, the teacher can refer back to the list of key Rights, Responsibilities, and Rewards from time to time, to reinforce responsible acts and to remind students why some actions are not responsible. The teacher might say something like this:

> There are rewards when we all fulfill our responsibilities and problems when we do not. And that is why I want us to be clear about our responsibilities—when we know what they are and we fulfill them, we avoid unnecessary problems. I think I know what my responsibilities are. They include helping each of you to learn each day and doing so in ways that are good, dignifying for you. Let's review and make a list of your responsibilities. I'd like to start with, Thinking before asking questions. What others might we list?

Thus students move toward a more mature understanding of what it means to live a rewarding, responsible life (Barr & Parrett, 1995) and to work as a cooperative, effective group (McEwan, Gathercoal, & Nimmo, 1997).

What happens when a student fails to fill reasonable responsibilities? We recommend treating the incident as a normal discipline problem, which means doing what is appropriate to help that particular student learn better self-control. As discussed in other chapters on discipline, we might, depending on the student and the circumstances, start with a Calm Reminder (Strategy 33-2), move to an assertive Authority Statement (Strategy 8-3), and, if necessary, then design a Self-Management Contract (Strategy 34-2) that includes whatever we judge will best help that student do better. Such a contract may include punishments for continued misbehavior, or rewards for improving behavior, or nothing more than a self-reminder checklist the student maintains. Just as each teacher is unique, each student is unique. As a result, we risk denting students' dignity if, for instance, a violation of a rule leads to the same consequences for all. In contrast, students' dignity is nourished when we do our best to give each of them what will best help them learn intelligent self-responsibility.

27 Advancing Students' Self-Confidence

Some students come to class with healthy self-esteem and appropriate self-confidence, but many do not. They may be anxious in class, have trouble concentrating, or avoid asking questions that might make them look foolish. These students tend to do far less than their best work. We can, however, reduce their anxieties and build their confidence. Several strategies already introduced do that effectively, especially the strategies in Chapter 4, which include Truth Signs, Cushioning Questions, and the Intelligence Call-up. We build confidence, too, when we

• Teach in Layers, Not Lumps, spiraling back over content until mastery is achieved (Strategy 3-2).

• Use strategies that allow for full participation even when understanding is low, such as Learning Pairs, Review Test, Choral Work, and I Say Review (Strategies 7-2, 11-1, 11-2, and 11-3).

• Allow time for every student to speak but permit every student to pass, as with the Whip Around, Pass Option (Strategy 16-4).

• Express appreciation for excellent effort even when it hasn't produced excellent results, as by using Credit for Completing Homework, Incorrects with Appreciation, Praise and Rewards for All, and E-for-Effort Certificates (Strategies 10-4, 20-3, 20-4, and 25-7).

We can also nourish student self-confidence more pointedly. This chapter has nine strategies for doing so. The first four are marked with arrows to indicate they are recommended for your first attention.

Strategy 27-1: Validations

Purpose: To help students appreciate themselves.

Description: Showing all students, including those who upset us, that we see them as worthy human beings.

Someone may smile warmly at us in passing, for no special reason, just because he or she is happy. It can be heartwarming. We can get the same experience from an unanticipated little gift, or someone taking the time to listen to our everyday ramblings. Such events can strengthen the feeling that we are valid human beings, that our existence is worthwhile, that we matter even when we do nothing special. Such messages might be called "validations." They validate our very existence.

Compare such messages with praise. "Good job!" someone may say. That might strengthen the certainty that we are successful, competent, or respected. But it often is a *conditional* worth, conditional on our doing a good job. It does not necessarily strengthen our certainty that we are worthwhile even when we do not do a good job. Too many students believe they are worthwhile only if they succeed or please others. They are not so sure they have inherent worth, unconditional value, essential dignity, just because they exist. And that self-doubt can make it difficult for them to relax with themselves, to handle the risks of living and learning with a comfortable self-confidence. How can we validate students simply for being the way they now are? Several of the strategies in Chapter 4 will help us. In addition, we might

> Your children need your presence more than your presents.
>
> —*Jean Kerr*

• Remember that we can't give self-confidence; it's the *self* that must provide self-confidence. We can, however, stimulate the self to provide that sustenance by smiling warmly at students and responding to them with, for example, Honest I Appreciates, I'm with You's, and Spontaneous Delights (Strategies 20-7, 20-8, and 20-10). Doing so enlivens students' positive inner selves.

• Provide all students with unanticipated little treats or special events, communicating the message "It's for no special reason. It's not because you worked hard or behaved well, but just because I enjoy having you in class, just because I like you. Thank you for being yourselves."

• Give students validating messages even when we do not give treats. If we use the power of language, the words themselves then become the treat. To one student, we might say something like, "I sure like seeing you," or "Your eyes are sparkling today, John." To the whole class we might say something like, "This is a fun group," or "It's so good to see you all again after the weekend."

• Simply but sincerely, be polite to all students. We do well to frequently say "thanks" and "please" and "I appreciate." The value of politeness is probably rooted in the satisfactions that come from being treated as an inherently worthwhile person. Similarly, we do well to apologize when, for example, we can't listen patiently, we inadvertently slight one or more students, or accumulated pressures prevent us from being our own best selves.

• Give all students warm eye contact and let it linger a bit, perhaps when they turn in papers or walk through the door.

• Find ways to show interest in students' ideas, feelings, and concerns. One way to do this is through New or Goods (Strategy 9-4), as when we start a class by asking, "Anything new or good in your lives?"

⟫ Strategy 27-2: Recognition for Everyone

Purpose: To help students lacking academic talent to shine in the class.
Description: Searching for ways all students can play an active, constructive role in the class community.

It's relatively easy for students who have scholarly strengths to stay active and feel successful. How can you help your other students avoid feeling completely unrecognized or unappreciated? One way is by ensuring that nonacademic strengths can be expressed and appreciated. Some possibilities:

• *For students with artistic abilities.* Invite all students to illustrate any work they turn in. Instead of decorating the room or bulletin boards yourself, have a committee of artistic students do it. Set up a classroom art gallery and invite all students to post work.

• *For students with athletic abilities.* In preparation for times when you want the class re-energized, ask some of those students to be ready to lead a brief exercise session. Identify strength or endurance challenges that would fit into the classroom, such as push-ups, and invite volunteers to set goals for themselves, to practice in and out of the classroom, and to post their progress. Look for chances to call on students to help with tasks—for example, to reposition your desk or lug books—and announce you need some strong volunteers for that. Perhaps invite someone to teach a few yoga postures to these students, maybe during lunch or other free time.

- *For students with musical abilities.* Appoint a committee to select and play recorded music while the class enters or leaves the room, or appropriate background music during quiet study time. The committee could also play upbeat music if, at times, you want students to stand and re-energize. Some might even be able to play live music. To provide opportunities to shine for those with both musical and physical talents, perhaps use dancing as a brief class energizer.

- *For students who excel at handiwork.* Invent tasks for such students—making charts, folding papers, making stands to hold classroom items, constructing place mats, tending class plants—and publicly recognize their work.

- *For students with creative or inventive abilities.* Ask students to invent, say, a better way to take attendance, store books, identify owners of found objects, prevent lost objects, handle class paperwork, or send messages to and from the office.

- *For all students.* Announce that you want to hear about individuals' special interests and talents. Invite students to share them with you and look for ways to share the information with the whole class. Perhaps include a show-and-tell time in class. Consider Supportive Report Card Comments (Strategy 32-3) to acknowledge nonacademic successes to students and parents. Consider writing Surprise Personal Notes (Strategy 32-4) any time you sense students might need extra support and encouragement.

Strategy 27-3: Promoting Kindness

Purpose: To promote positive peer relationships.
Description: Encouraging students to speak and act in ways that communicate civility, kindness, and respect.

In terms of bolstering self-confidence, the way students are treated by their peers can be most significant. Accordingly, we might pose these two questions and brainstorm answers with the class:

- What words would we like to hear from one another?
- What actions would we like to observe?

We might then create a poster showing questions and the answers the students came up with, like the example shown in Figure 21 on p. 340, and hang it in the classroom. Such a poster can serve as a useful reminder to students. We can even extend this to what Dick Mulbauer, a middle school teacher, calls Kindness Cards. He reports good results from giving students the option of occasionally presenting another student with such a card. It's simply a three-by-five-inch card students write

The true teacher defends his pupils against his own personal influence. He inspires self-distrust. He guides their eyes from himself to the spirit that quickens him. He will have no disciple.

—*Amos Bronson Alcott*

Figure 21
Poster for Promoting Kindness

What words would we like to hear from one another?

- Thank you.
- You're welcome.
- Excuse me.
- I like the way you did that.
- You showed great dignity.
- That was a good thing to do.
- Do you need help?
- Stop acting like a bully.

What actions would we like to observe?

- Holding the door for someone.
- Picking something up when a person has dropped it.
- People holding back and giving others a chance to talk.
- Reporting a potential danger to a teacher.
- Reminding someone who's lost control to pause and count to 10.

to recognize an act like the ones listed in Figure 21. Reports Mulbauer: "Students usually give me the card to present to the student, which I usually do privately. Receiving such peer appreciation has a dramatic impact on some students."

Strategy 27-4: Distress-Easing Comments

Purpose: To provide support for students in distress.
Description: Reaching out to ease the distress of a student.

While teaching we may notice certain students appearing to be unusually distressed. How might we react? Some suggestions for things we might say, usually best in private:

- *"I'm with you."* Sometimes we can say something that communicates to students that they are not alone, that we are with them.
  - "I think I understand how you feel, Michael."
  - "Shantal, the same kind of thing happened to me once. I can appreciate what you're going through."
  - "I see the hurt in your eyes, Jorge. And I hurt with you."
- *"Take the time you need."* It might be appropriate to reassure students that they need not hide their real feelings and can take the time they need to work through a difficult time.
  - "Take your time with it. There is no need to rush back into your class work. We'll somehow help you catch up."

○ "There is no need to pretend you don't feel what you feel. Is there any way I can make it easier for you here in school?"

• *"You are absolutely worthy."* We might reassure students that their experience does not diminish them in our eyes. Perhaps we tell students that what they experience has nothing to do with their essential dignity and worth.

○ "You may have failed at that. But I still care for you, and I always will. Your essential goodness is not touched."

○ "It's OK to feel what you are feeling. You are no less strong or worthy for it. Many of us have had to suffer the same thing."

• *"Want to talk about it?"* Perhaps we gently invite students to share their experience. Some might be willing to share with the whole class, and it might be good for everyone if they did.

○ "Would you like to tell the class, or some of them, about what is going on? Or would you like to have me tell them? It might be good for them to know."

○ "Many of us have experienced the death of a loved one. I wonder if you would mind my talking about this issue with the class, not mentioning you or your situation. Then, if you choose, you could tell them about what happened to you. But perhaps such a discussion is best put off for a while. Do you have any thoughts about this?"

Some students get sufficient emotional support from family members, so such comments are not so important. But that is not the case for all students. For some, words such as these can prevent a serious crack in confidence or faith. Indeed, some teachers have told us that they themselves were deeply affected in a positive way by a teacher who once reached out to them in ways like that.

Strategy 27-5: What-I-Like-About-You Reports

Purpose: To give students a boost to self-confidence.
Description: Occasionally providing time for students to write one thing they like about each class member.

It can be difficult for students to feel confident when they don't feel they are liked by their peers. For some students, it is impossible. It's useful, then, to have students occasionally prepare What-I-Like-About-You Reports for one another.

One way to proceed is to have each student write his or her name on a blank sheet of paper. All students then pass their sheets to the next person. Students

> The only thing necessary for the triumph of evil is for good men to do nothing.
>
> —*Edmund Burke*

think of something they can honestly say they like about the person whose sheet they have—perhaps something they did or a personal quality they sometimes exhibit; or perhaps something they do not do, like interrupt their friends. If students have such a comment, they write it, with or without including their own names, as they choose. Students also have the option to pass, that is, to write nothing. When all the students have had a chance to write something on all the sheets, we can return the sheets to the students, perhaps at the end of the day or week, and allow each student to enjoy reading a list of things that "my classmates say they like about me."

Strategy 27-6: Sensible Risk Taking

Purpose: To help students learn how and when to take risks.
Description: Seeking opportunities to help students clarify for themselves what is and is not a risk worth taking.

"We can learn more and do more when we're willing to take a risk." So says one of the signs included in Truth Signs (Strategy 4-1). But taking a risk is risky. For students with low self-confidence, learning how and when to take a risk is not easy. Here are some ideas for ways to support such students.

• *Occasionally make time for discussions about risk taking.* Some ways to begin such a discussion:

Example 1. Some risks would be foolish to undertake. But some risks, like making a speech in class or jumping off a low diving board, can *feel* dangerous but not *be* dangerous at all. Can you think of other examples? It has been said that a wise risk is one that offers benefits but not serious dangers. Do you agree? How can you tell if a situation that feels risky is really not at all dangerous? How can you tell when it *is* dangerous and you would be smart *not* to act?

Example 2. When we face something that makes us anxious, we can call up our courage and act. We can define *courage* as the quality we have that allows us to act even when the action feels risky. Can you give examples of when you believe you acted with courage? Do you have any ideas about how you could more often access your courage?

Example 3. Timid people are reluctant to take risks that many others readily take. But many of us are timid in some situations but not in others. Are there situations in which you tend to be timid? Are there situations in which you tend to act recklessly?

The worst sin towards our fellow creatures is not to hate them, but to be indifferent to them; that's the essence of inhumanity.

—*George Bernard Shaw*

Example 4. An impulsive act is different from a courageous act. When an act feels dangerous and we choose to act anyhow, we use our courage. An impulsive act does not require courage. Are there situations in which you typically act impulsively? Courageously? Do you think animals can act courageously?

• *Use Risk Language (Strategy 4-3) when inviting students to speak in class.* Rather than saying, "How many are willing to share a thought?" we say "How many are willing *to risk* sharing a thought?" In that way, we acknowledge risks might be involved and invite a more thoughtful choice. Perhaps we add Cushioning Questions (Strategy 4-2): "Would it be OK if some choose not to risk sharing right now?" "Sure," students might say. "How come?" we might ask. Someone might answer, "We each have our own ways and time clocks." And in that way any anxiety raised by the invitation to share is cushioned, and students can then think more clearly about whether to share and what to share.

• *Use ordinary topics to raise the issue of risk taking.* If, for example, a person in a story, a history lesson, or a current events discussion took a risk or backed away from a risk, we might take a moment to ask:

Did the person take a wise risk or a foolish risk? What makes a risk wise? What makes a risk foolish? What could that person have done to make a wiser choice?

What would you likely have done if you were in that person's situation? What would you have been most proud of doing?

Have you ever actually been in a situation like that? How did you handle it? How would you like to be able to handle it if it ever happens again?

Strategy 27-7: Prize Sprinkle

Purpose: To honor students for simply being who they are.
Description: Randomly choosing students to receive a prize.

When students have risen to a challenge or come to the end of a long project or managed a difficult learning, it's often valuable to acknowledge them in some way. We can use the Mini-celebration (Strategy 21-8) for this purpose. We might also consider randomly sprinkling prizes throughout the year, even when students have done nothing in particular to earn it. By doing so, students receive a message more valuable than any reward for excellent work or good behavior—a message that says they are valued not for what they do, but for simply being who they are.

We might, for instance, write each student's name on a slip of paper and have one student draw one name each week to receive a token prize. To ensure that no

344: Strategies for Further Advancing Teacher Effectiveness

one is left out, drawn slips can be put aside until all students have been selected. Says one teacher, "Not only do students enjoy the fun element this adds to the class, but I enjoy it, too. For an extra kick, I include two slips in the jar that say *ALL*, and when one of those slips gets chosen, we *all* get a special snack. Loads of fun for all."

Some ideas for possible prizes:

- The privilege of sitting anywhere for a day, being the line leader for the day, or drawing the slip for the next week's prize.
- If music is included in the classroom routine, the privilege of choosing the music for the day.
- The honor of sitting with the teacher while she calls home with a special message for the parents.
- A special button, hat, or T-shirt to wear.
- Any small treat, such as pencils, candy, erasers, notepads.

Whatever the prize may be, it probably won't matter nearly as much to students as the feeling of being the day's winner.

Strategy 27-8: Star of the Day

Purpose: To give every student a regular validating reminder.
Description: Giving each student a turn to be the Star of the Day.

Many elementary school students are deeply nourished by being the Star of the Day. The Star of the Day might also be given token privileges: first in line, first to run errands, and the like. A simple rotation plan works well. Perhaps end each day by announcing the next day's star, or have the Star of the Day make the announcement. The next day could even begin with yesterday's star introducing the new star, who might then stand, take a bow, and receive the applause of the class. Later on, at a designated time before lunch or dismissal, that day's star might also be given a moment in the spotlight, perhaps to

- Read a poem or short passage from a favorite book.
- Share a favorite item from home.
- Tell the class a riddle.
- Show something he or she created.
- Sing, dance, or play an instrument.
- Say what he or she liked best about the day.
- And, finally, announce the name of the next day's star.

Also consider the related strategy, Class Leaders (Strategy 5-6).

Strategy 27-9: Positive Parent Schedule

Purpose: To improve family support for students.
Description: Creating a procedure that makes it easy to send positive messages home to parents.

Sarah Schmidt, a 4th grade teacher, typically sets aside an hour on some weekends to phone every student's family with a quick message, something like this:

> Mrs. Jones, this is Sarah Schmidt, Tom's teacher. I want to take a second to let you know that I am delighted with how Tom has been participating in our class. I don't have time now to get into details, but you can certainly be very proud of your son. Please say hello to him for me. Goodbye.

"I've learned to expect," says Sarah, "that the parent will soon ask Tom what on earth he did that was so good, and that Tom will himself wonder. Often students ask me on Monday. I just say I want parents to appreciate their children, and, in fact, I am delighted with how well things have progressed so far. I don't make more of it than that, and it works just fine."

We might make general statements to parents, such as saying we are delighted with the way the student is participating, learning, cooperating, or progressing. Or we could write ourselves a note when something in particular shows up and then report that the student, say, reached out to help someone as a partner; arrives on time every day, ready to work; shows real responsibility; is willing to risk sharing his answer even when he might be wrong; had a beautiful, happy smile when he walked in one day; often volunteers to clean up.

To facilitate this process of sending home positive messages, some teachers address a postcard to each family or have the students themselves address the cards. The teachers then write notes on each card and send them out, aiming to get all the cards sent before starting a new set. Teachers might also use e-mail in some cases. In this way we may improve family support for students, which may well beef up student dignity and grow confidence in the classroom.

We make a living by what we get; we make a life by what we give.

—*Winston Churchill*

28 | Advancing Students' Maturity

The strategies of this book are designed to help us handle our ordinary teaching tasks in a way that keeps nourishing healthy, mature behavior. This chapter has six strategies that nourish healthy, mature student behavior more directly. As such, they contribute directly to DESCA engagement, that is, to a classroom in which students work with high personal *dignity*, with sustained *energy*, with intelligent *self-management*, with a sense of supportive *community*, and with high *awareness*. Of the six strategies in this chapter, we recommend giving first attention to the first two.

 ## Strategy 28-1: Strength-Building Challenges

Purpose: To inspire students to further develop their personal strengths.
Description: Challenging students to increase their inherent strengths.

"Say it as if you mean it," says a teacher to a student mumbling along with low energy, hoping to trigger more of the student's positive powers. All humans, of course, carry such potential powers—to speak up, to stand tall, to remain committed, to think before acting. Yet students are not often challenged to develop these powers. Here are other examples of how we might challenge students:

- In your Sharing Pairs, practice looking your partner straight in the eye.
- Read aloud to your partner with quiet power and strong intention.
- Practice speaking up for yourself this weekend. Practice living with all the integrity you can muster.
- If you talk about it, talk about it truthfully.
- When you do it, put yourself fully into it. Don't do it halfheartedly.

Some teachers post a chart listing examples of such challenges and refer to it from time to time. Figure 22 is an example of such a chart. And some teachers like to discuss the positive powers inherent in human beings as a prelude to offering such challenges.

A caution is in order here. Some students may not be ready for one or more such challenges. So issue the challenges in a way that allows students to skip them if they prefer. We don't want to pressure students to try to be something beyond their current capabilities.

Self-confidence is the first requisite to great undertakings.

—*Samuel Johnson*

Figure 22
Strength-Building Challenges

As a human being you have the power to . . .

- Speak up for yourself.
- Tell the truth.
- Stand by a friend.
- Apologize after causing hurt.
- Do a good deed.
- Say it as if you mean it.
- Stop what you are doing.
- Change your mind.
- Do what you need to do.
- Pull yourself together.
- Open your mind.

- Stick to your principles.
- Defend other people.
- Call on your courage.
- Think for yourself.
- Take your own time.
- Say "no" when you must.
- Say "yes" and mean it.
- Go for the gold.
- Accept whatever you get.
- Make choices.
- Be yourself.

Strategy 28-2: Personalized Challenges

Purpose: To inspire students to further develop their personal strengths.
Description: Challenging students to choose their own way to strengthen themselves and to practice doing so.

Students can design their own personal-growth challenges. Here is an example of a teacher introducing the idea:

> Here is an optional project. I'd like each of you to consider a personal strength you would like to develop, and I'd like you to dare yourself to work on it this weekend. Possibilities: Controlling your impulses to watch TV. Apologizing to someone. Eating better. Risking starting a conversation that you really want to

have, perhaps to talk something over with a friend. What other challenges might be worth taking? Let's share some ideas.

On Monday I'll ask how many accepted this challenge and how things worked out. Take a few minutes now in your groups to talk over what you might do. You might even be cheerleaders for someone in your group who would appreciate such support. You might phone them with encouragement, for example. Do whatever you think makes sense. As our sign says: "It's intelligent to ask for help. No one need do it all alone." Winning is much easier when we have cheerleaders cheering us on!

Challenges can spur the development of important life skills, including perseverance, wise self-management, impulse control, collaboration, and communication. Some of the most valuable challenges revolve around the issue of self-acceptance. To get a feel for such a challenge, consider something about yourself that you still do not fully accept—your looks, your age, your personality, anything. Pledge to take a week to practice being more accepting. See what happens. You might also risk sharing the experience with your students.

Some students might want to undertake a long-term personal challenge, perhaps to break a bad habit or start a new one, such as exercising more, holding one's temper, or overcoming procrastination. Students usually need support and planning if they are to succeed at such challenges. The Self-Management Contract (Strategy 34-2) can serve that purpose.

Strategy 28-3: Gratitude Journal

Purpose: To expand students' appreciation of what is good and positive in their lives.

Description: Asking students to keep a record of what in their lives they can be grateful for.

"How many of you," we might ask a class, "are grateful for the way someone takes care of you? How many can feel grateful for your ability to run? How many can feel grateful for a toothache, which could be a signal that you need to see a dentist before matters get worse? What other things in your life might you be grateful for if you stopped and thought more about it?" After a discussion, we might then ask students to start a list of things for which they can be grateful. Afterward, at least once a week, we can ask them to add to the list or to check items already listed. In this way, we can remind students what they can be grateful for.

Why do this? Many students are primarily aware of what is lacking in their lives, their frustrations, their unmet needs. And many grow up to be adults who

We strain hardest for things which are almost but not quite within our reach.

—*Frederick Faber*

feel more sorry for themselves than grateful for, say, the sun in the sky, those who force them to stop and examine what they're doing, their innate ability to forgive and forget. The Gratitude Log, then, provides a means of expanding student awareness so it includes more of what is right about life, including life itself. Incidentally, the Gratitude Log is also a fine source of ideas for writing assignments.

Strategy 28-4: Whole-Self Lesson

Purpose: To teach students how to live more often as their preferred selves.
Description: Guiding students through a lesson on self-acceptance and appreciation of personal possibilities.

The Whole-Self Lesson helps students, as well as teachers, be accepting of themselves. Here is an example of such a lesson. It's in a form that one of us, Merrill, used recently when working with a group of teachers. You might reflect on each lesson segment as if you were in that teacher group. Doing so will probably best prepare you to craft your own version of the lesson.

A Whole-Self Lesson with Adults

1. *The open self.* Merrill begins by talking a bit about himself, describing himself as a person who, as he sees it, includes several selves. "For example, I am sometimes my easy-going, open-minded, flexible self. That is a self I have inside me these days," he notes, "for these are fairly good days in my house, and if the winds are just right, I can be this good self. I call this my *open* self. Your *open* self will likely be different from mine, because, of course, we are all different." He asks the participants to write on a piece of paper one or two qualities that they exhibit when they are their easy, open selves. After a pause he asks if anyone is willing to share something noted.

2. *The narrow self.* Merrill notes that at other times he is much more "self-centered, narrow-minded, irritable, and tight. I do not feel at all easy and flexible." He tells the participants that he calls this his "*narrow* self" and that it is also part of his current personality. "How about you?" he asks. "Make a private note about what comes up for you when you feel tight, small, narrowed down. Anyone willing to share something you wrote?"

3. *Four selves.* "Look at this chart," Merrill then says, pointing to a chart like that in Figure 23 (on p. 350). "It has headings for four of my selves and a few qualities that describe each." He notes the first heading, referring to a *former* self. "That is a self that showed up when I was much younger and rarely

shows up nowadays. I suspect it lies dormant inside me. I hope it stays dormant," he says.

He goes on to explain the other headings on the chart: "Then I included notes on my current narrow and open selves," he says. "Finally, I added what feels like a *possible* self, a self that is not now available to me but that I sense exists deep inside me someplace. A self that might, and then again might not, emerge as an available self. I call that my *possible* self."

Merrill invites the participants to go through a similar exercise. "Try drawing a chart like this for yourself—or, I should say, for your *selves*," he says. "You can skip your former and possible selves if you like. It is most important that you write notes describing your current narrow and open selves. See what turns up for you."

4. *The inevitability of narrow selfhood.* Merrill notes that most people feel more comfortable when they are their "open" selves than when they are their "narrow" selves. "Should we regret it when our narrow selves show up?" he asks. "Is that unfortunate? Wouldn't it be far better for us to learn how to live always as our open selves?"

Responding to his own questions, he tells the participants that they can try it if they like, but they may find it impossible. "Toothaches occur. A disappointment shows up. We look in a mirror and don't like what we see. Stuff happens that gets us feeling off balance, tight, uncomfortable, not at all our open, balanced selves." He shares his contention that humans naturally experience both narrowed and open selves. "It's part of the human condition," he notes.

5. *Accepting the inevitable.* "I do not believe humans are meant to live only in their open selves," he says. Instead, he continues, humans have both narrow and open selves, and they naturally spend time in each. "It makes no sense, then, for me to try to live only as my open self," he notes. "I have to remind myself of that

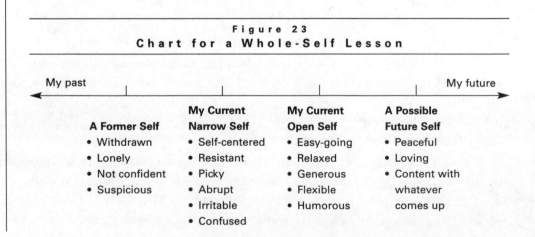

Figure 23
Chart for a Whole-Self Lesson

My past			My future
A Former Self	**My Current Narrow Self**	**My Current Open Self**	**A Possible Future Self**
• Withdrawn	• Self-centered	• Easy-going	• Peaceful
• Lonely	• Resistant	• Relaxed	• Loving
• Not confident	• Picky	• Generous	• Content with
• Suspicious	• Abrupt	• Flexible	whatever
	• Irritable	• Humorous	comes up
	• Confused		

from time to time because I have a tendency to get down on myself when I am my narrow, tight self and not my good open self. How about you?"

He continues by stating that he also does not believe that humans outgrow their current selfhood and move to a new one before the time is right for such growth. "A child cannot be an adult before the time is right," he says. "It makes no sense, then, for me to regret that I have not yet become my possible self, the self I sense I might someday be." He tells the participants that he has to remind himself of this idea because he has a tendency to be self-critical when he is not as good as the person he senses he might someday become. "I sometimes say to myself, 'The sun does not rise before sunrise. Things are what they are. Me too. I am not yet better than I now am. Furthermore, I am not always as good as I sometimes can be. Sometimes I get into my tight, narrow self. No sense getting down on myself for that.'" He then asks the participants to consider how good they are at accepting themselves as they are.

6. *Practicing acceptance.* He says he would like classroom teachers to make it as easy as possible for students to accept themselves, even when they are not being their best selves. His reason is simple: "When people are not accepting of themselves, they have two problems rather than only one." He explains by sharing an example. "Let's say I am angry, so angry I cannot think too clearly. If that is my only problem, I can say, this too will pass, ups and downs happen, and I might even be able to do something to get myself beyond it—say something positive to myself, walk among the trees, think of my wife's lovely smile, whatever." But, he continues, if he does not *accept* his anger, if he not only feels angry, but also feels guilty about his anger, or childish for being angry or resentful of what sparked his anger, then he has a second set of problems. "It will certainly be harder to think clearly about what is going on and what I might do next," he points out. "Indeed, it is being down on ourselves for being down that is often the larger problem. Said another way, when we do not accept ourselves when a narrow-self quality shows up, as sooner or later it will, we are rejecting a part of ourselves." If such behavior becomes habitual, it leads to all kinds of ills, both mental and physical, he says. "It is hardly empowering to reject a part of oneself."

Merrill then offers a recommendation: "I recommend we practice accepting ourselves as fallible human beings," he says. "When I have slipped, and when I notice it, I like to say, 'Well, there I go again. I'm being my narrow self. But no sense getting down on myself for that. Time to move on!'" He tells participants that sometimes he finds it useful to say such self-encouraging words aloud, sometimes to the people around him. "Such an admission makes it easier for me to avoid getting stuck in a deeper slump," he says, and then asks, "How about you? What works to

Ever tried. Ever failed. No matter. Try again. Fail again. Fail better.

—Samuel Beckett

Stumbling is not
falling.

—Portuguese proverb

help you accept yourself when you notice you are your narrow self?" He suggests that if participants have a difficult time accepting their narrow selves, they might remember Mark Twain's explanation of why people are less than perfect: "Man," Twain said, "was made at the end of the week's work, when God was tired."

7. *The whole self.* Shifting the topic to what he calls the "whole self," Merrill says the concept is no mystery. "It is all of me." Referring to the chart of "selves" featured earlier (Figure 23 on p. 350), he says that if he were to draw a circle around what are now his narrow and open selves, the circle would represent his current whole self. "For good or ill, that's me," he says. "Want to know yourself more clearly?" he asks. "Simply return to your own assortment of selves and put a circle around all of them. When sages tell us, 'Know yourself,' I believe they want us to know the parts in our circle. When sages tell us, 'Accept yourself,' I think they want us to accept our whole self." Recalling a more personal example, Merrill says, "And when my own father told me, as he often did, 'Be yourself; don't put on airs,' I think he was giving me the same message. What do you think?"

8. *Calling up the open self.* Next Merrill suggests that the participants test those ideas for themselves to see if they serve a useful purpose. He recommends two experiments:

> First, try calling up your open self at a time when you believe it might be especially useful to you. You might wait for an important appointment. Or you might wait for the next time a tricky choice comes up. Or perhaps some pattern or habit of yours that you dislike will show up and you will wonder how to handle it. When such an occasion shows up, pause and say to yourself, "How would my open self handle this situation?" or "What would my open self want me to do?"
>
> Or try calling up your whole self the next time you feel off, tight, or anxious. Perhaps say to yourself, "Now wait a minute. I am now being my narrow self. I can see that. But that is not *all* of me. I am sometimes other than the way I am now. Let me not forget that." See what happens.

A Whole-Self Lesson with Students

Here is how a 3rd grade teacher adapted the Whole-Self Lesson to her class.

1. *Whole class, 5 minutes; followed by individual writing, 2 minutes.*

I told the class about my own open and narrow selves. (I didn't talk about my former self or my possible self. I was not sure their concept of time could handle that.) I made two circles on the board, filled in several qualities of my open and narrow selves in each, and then asked students to fill in two circles for themselves.

2. *Whole class, 2 minutes; followed by Sharing Pairs (Strategy 7-1), 5 minutes.*

I asked for three volunteers to read any one of their open and narrow self quali-ties. Almost all volunteered, so I called on five students. Then I asked all to sit in pairs and either to share some of their notes or talk about what I said about myself. I didn't want to force talk if some wanted to keep things private. All seemed to go at this with good energy.

3. *Whole class, 5 minutes.*

I then talked about how it's OK when we are our narrow selves, how narrowness happens to me (they laughed), and how it happens to everyone. I asked if some would tell when *they* became their narrow selves. Tests and scolding were the win-ners. This produced many comments all could identify with and many good-natured smiles all around. They all seemed to recognize their common humanity.

4. *Whole class, list creation, 4 minutes.*

Next I asked them what helped them become their open selves when they felt "off," and we made a list on the board: playing with friends, hugs from Mom, and the like. These students seem to have a much clearer perspective on life than many adults. I believe this step opened up new ideas to some students.

5. *Whole class, speak-write, 5 minutes.*

I told them I wanted to explain more about this. I said I would talk and, when I paused, I wanted them to think and make notes. I gave three mini-lectures on the whole self. I started by drawing one large circle around my two circles and labeled that my "whole self." Then I talked about how I and people we studied in history had whole selves, and how each student has a whole self. I ended by recommending that they appreciate their whole selves, especially when they feel like a failure or when someone treats them badly. "We all have narrow-self times." But as humans, I said, we also have open-self times. We are whole human beings.

6. *Individual writing, 2 minutes; Whip Around, Pass Option (Strategy 16-4), 10–11 minutes.*

After they made their last notes, I had them think back on all we had talked about so far. I pointed to the Outcome Sentence beginnings I have posted and asked each to write one or two Outcome Sentences (Strategy 21-1). After a minute or two, I asked if anyone would share something they had written, and almost all hands went up, so I used the Whip Around, Pass Option and had all either read one or say "I pass." No one passed!

Here is how the teacher summarized her experience with this lesson:

The lesson led to many new ideas for them. Several said they better understood their parents and why parents sometimes seemed upset. Two said they wanted to take the lesson home, to see what others in the family thought were their narrow and open selves. Several students referred to their "bad selves." I just suggested they call it their "narrow" selves, and they seemed to do that afterward. Later that day, I heard one boy ask another, "I was my open self on the playground, wasn't I?" They seemed to get it. I'll follow up in some way, although I haven't decided how yet. As I think about it now, I will invite all students to ask their open selves for advice next time they have a choice to make.

Some follow-up possibilities. After the class has absorbed the concepts contained in the Whole-Self Lesson, it is natural for students to talk about their "open," "narrow," and "whole" selves. These words become valuable tools in developing an appreciation for oneself and others; an appreciation, too, of the magnificence of life in general. One teacher put up a new sign to keep the Whole-Self Lesson alive:

> We can accept our narrow selves,
> become our open selves, and in
> that way be our whole selves.

▲ TEACHER COMMENTS

It's a running, lighthearted gag now. Since I taught that lesson, when I am "off" or a student is "off," someone is likely to suggest the person is stuck in narrowed selfhood. Almost always when that suggestion is voiced, everyone, including me, the person who most often is "off," relaxes, even smiles. Not bad at all.

—*Don Keefe, College Teacher*

I know they learned it because I hear things like this: "I'm my open self today, so I should do well," and "Be your whole self, man; don't get down on yourself."

—*Tom Hughes, High School Physical Education Teacher*

Students now use being in narrow selfhood as an excuse, as "I can't do good work today because I'm my narrow self." . . . It's not that they didn't give excuses before. But although they talk more about narrow selves, they *act* more like open selves, so I am happy to say something is working.

—*G. S. Tarentello, 6th Grade Teacher*

Strategy 28-5: Choose, Be, Review

Purpose: To help students expand their powers of choice.
Description: Teaching students a procedure for more often being the way they want to be.

Be choices are different from *do* choices. Very often we consider what we should do. Should I phone Pat? Should I go shopping? Should I do this now or later or not at all? Some days we make a detailed to-do list. Those are what can be called *do* choices. We choose what we will do.

Less often do we make *be* choices. Yet we can make *be* choices as often as do choices. If we go shopping, for example, there are several ways we can *be* while we are shopping. We can be efficient, aiming to get in and out of the store quickly. We can be friendly, taking time to smile at open faces. We can be adventurous, on the lookout for new foods to try, new corners to explore, new people to meet. When we go shopping, there are many ways we can be, and we can *choose* which of those ways to be: efficient, friendly, adventurous, thrifty, or whatever. We can even choose to be without a *be* choice. That is, we can choose to be spontaneous, open to whatever shows up. All of these options can be called making a *be* choice.

The Importance of the *Be* Choice

Be choices sometimes make all the difference in the world. Let's say, for example, that you choose to phone Ashley. That is what you will *do*. And let's say Ashley is a tricky person for you to talk to. It might be well for you to pause and consider how you want to be during the call. Do you want to be your accepting, listening self? Your assertive, straight-talking self? Your open-minded, flexible self? There are several ways you can be when speaking to Ashley. And if you deliberately choose a way to be, it is much more likely that you will, in fact, be that way—which might make a difference in the outcome of the conversation.

Using the *be* choice, then, requires pausing and choosing how we want to be in the time ahead. One occasion when we might want to use the *be* choice is when we prepare lesson plans. On the top-right corner, for example, we might write how we want to be as we teach that lesson. We might write "Be flexible, tuned in to students." Another possibility might be "Be clear and brief" or "Be energetic and upbeat." The choice will depend on what we sense the students most need for that lesson. We might also want to teach the *be* choice to students.

> The great danger for most of us is not that our aim is too high and we miss it, but that it is too low and we reach it.
>
> —*Michelangelo*

Teaching the *Be* Choice

When we teach this lesson to students we might start by distinguishing between do and be choices, much as in the earlier discussion. We can make the distinction by offering examples of our own do and be choices. Then we might say

> Let's try making a *be* choice here. In a moment, I will ask you to look around the room for, perhaps, 10 seconds. As you look around, please be your ordinary self, just as you might look around the room if I were busy and you had nothing else to do. No talking, just looking around. Start now.
>
> Thank you. Now let's do that again, but this time I want you to write a *be* choice before you look. Let me give two suggestions. Perhaps choose to be your curious self. Be on the lookout for something new or interesting. Most of us have curiosity inside us; so, if you like, you can look around as your curious self. Or perhaps choose to be your careful self, looking closely at details, not letting your eyes slide past something too quickly, really looking into whatever your eyes see.
>
> So choose now which way you would like to be—curious or careful, or some other way, if you like—and write your personal *be* choice on a piece of scrap paper. Writing down a *be* choice makes the choice more certain inside ourselves. OK, please look around now, being the way you wrote you wanted to be.

After asking students to share any differences between the two look-arounds, we might then say

> Please write on your scrap paper how you want to be for the rest of the lesson today. You cannot always choose what you can *do* here. But you can always choose how you want to *be*. In class now, for example, you might choose to be relaxed or intelligent or careful or happy. What are other ways a person could be in a class like this? Choose any way you want to be and write it down now. Writing it usually plants it more solidly and certainly in our awareness. If we have time, I'll ask you later if that *be* choice made any difference for you today.

We might follow this experiment by saying something like this:

> In general, I would recommend you experiment with *be* choices. After school, for example, you might pause and ask yourself how you want to be when you walk in the door at home. Or, whenever you see some friends ahead, you might pause and choose how you want to be as you meet your friends. Do you want to be your cooperative self? Your leadership self? Your energetic self? Experiment with *be* choices in whatever seems interesting to you. Perhaps next time I'll ask if someone would be willing to share an experience.

We might also talk about using *be* choices when a conflict arises and cite an example from a lesson recently studied:

> The labor union conflict we studied ended with no real winners. How could it have been handled differently? Notice how both parties took a win-lose position. Both were full of conflict, were oppositional, were antagonistic. What do you

think would have happened if one or both sides had paused and made a different choice? If, instead of being full of conflict, they had chosen to be open, that is, to come at the problem seeking a resolution both might agree on?

We might also apply this to a disciplinary situation, as in this example:

About the argument you two had yesterday, as I understand it, each of you thought you were right, the other was wrong. And both of you were stubborn, insistent. Let's imagine that one or both of you paused before things got too bad and made a different *be* choice. Let's say you chose not to be stubborn but, say, to be open about the argument; that is, you chose to be open-minded and to try to see the whole picture. And let's say you asked someone to sit with the two of you to help you talk about the argument and better understand the whole picture. Can you see how that might have prevented some of the worst of what happened yesterday? Can you see how someone in a conflict could, in fact, pause and choose not to be argumentative, but to be open-minded? Tomorrow I'd like to role-play such a situation with the whole class. You two can play yourselves in the skit, or we can get others to play the parts and you can watch. We'll talk more about this kind of *be* choice tomorrow. I'm telling you now to give you time to think about this beforehand.

If we have already taught the Whole-Self Lesson (Strategy 28-4), so our students understand the terminology, we might include references to it in one of our discussions:

You can choose to be your open self if you like. Of course, you may not remain your open self even if you choose it. For you also have a narrow self. That is also part of you. But if you *choose* to be your open self, chances are you will more often or more fully *be* that way than if you made no choice at all. Experiment and see.

It is particularly effective for teachers to model someone who makes *be* choices as well as *do* choices. As mentioned, writing personal *be* choices on daily lesson plans is one way to do this. Not coincidentally, doing so can also help us maintain good balance in the classroom.

Strategy 28-6: Goodness Log

Purpose: To inspire students to exercise their good-heartedness.
Description: Asking students to keep a log of times they did something unusually good for others or themselves.

We might assign students the task of keeping a special log, perhaps called "My Goodness." In it they are to note times they did or said something that they would

Confidence is
contagious. So is
lack of confidence.
—*Vince Lombardi*

judge to be, for them, unusually good, positive, constructive. It could be good for themselves or for others. And it could be an incident in or out of school. We might explain that we all do good deeds as a normal part of our days, and what you're looking for in this log are actions that are not common for them, times they stepped beyond their normal good-heartedness.

Occasionally, then, perhaps as a break from studies, we could ask volunteers to read from their logs. We might also periodically ask students to review their entries and write Outcome Sentences (Strategy 21-1). Reports one teacher: "I called for reports whenever the class needed a pick-up of good feelings. I especially liked the way the strategy gave slow students an equal chance to stand out. And when I wanted students to practice a writing skill, I would often invite them to write about one of the notes in their Goodness Log."

Advancing Our Own Personal Balance

29

It's easy for teachers to feel overstressed. Given enough pressure, we can all get thrown off balance. What helps us regain it? We each have our own methods. We go for a long walk. We talk to a close friend. We buy a new pair of shoes. And then there are the strategies of this chapter, which teachers report are almost always less expensive than shopping. Better yet, these strategies can help us strengthen ourselves so we lose our balance less often. All five strategies are equally worth your attention.

Strategy 29-1: Self-Acceptance Monologue

Purpose: To maintain peace of mind.

Description: Reminding ourselves that we cannot expect to behave perfectly at all times.

Let's say, for example, that you are not in the habit of making "I Statements." You may prefer to do so, but often you fail, and you berate yourself for these failures:

> I still complain and blame. "Why did you do that?" "*You* should know better than that." "*You* have to stop that." *You, you, you.* Ugh! Why don't I say, "*I* can't understand why that behavior continues." "*I* thought we had handled that." "*I* need that to stop." I have wanted to make that change for so long now!

When you fail at this or any other preferred behavior, we recommend a firm self-accepting monologue, which might go like this:

> OK, I'm still not perfect. It would have been better if I had acted the way I wanted to act, but I didn't. Should I focus on such failures, inadequacies? No. That won't help. I am not yet perfect. I might as well accept that. And I don't want to keep focusing on the past. That is not helpful. The question is, what, if anything, do I want to do *next* time? So, let's see, what *do* I want to do next time?

Most likely you want the students in your classrooms to look at their inappropriate acts without guilt, without resignation, without dismay. You want them to think about what happened and learn from it. You do not want them stuck in discouraging memories or obsessed by personal imperfections. You want them confident about doing better. Ditto for yourself.

Incidentally, we advise sharing this strategy with students. You might tell students how you used a Self-Accepting Monologue in your life, reporting what you might say to yourself and why. This models a valuable life skill. You might then ask students if any of them sometimes talk that way to themselves and how it works out. Finally, you might invite students to experiment with a Self-Accepting Monologue and, if appropriate, to let you know if it helped them in some way.

◄► Strategy 29-2: Reality-Acceptance Monologue

Purpose: To maintain peace of mind.
Description: Taking a moment to remind ourselves that not all bothersome behavior can be eliminated.

Teacher Judy Kupsky tells of a 3rd grade boy who was keeping her awake nights:

> He was wired with high energy and no self-control. Nothing that anyone could think to do had any effect. He kept calling out, moving about, bothering people around him, messing up the class. It was driving me crazy. The harder I tried to stop his disruptions, the worse it got. Finally I gave up trying to change him. Like living with my stringy hair, I realized there was nothing to do but live with it as best I could. He just was not going to change. After I gave up, I realized the other students were not nearly as bothered as I was. Now, somehow, I don't expect him to change, and I don't fight it, and things are not nearly so bad. Fighting with it was the worst part. Now I have more energy to live with it.

Somehow people assume bothersome behavior should always be eliminated. When they have a student whom they are unable to change, they can easily become stuck in a double problem. Instead of just suffering the student's antics, they must also suffer the frustration of being unable to win the "change him" game. If you suffer this kind of experience, it often helps to remind yourself that, like all humans, you have limited powers. You cannot always get things to turn out the way you want. You might as well accept realities you cannot change and move on from there, perhaps saying to yourself:

> I realize I was assuming I could get him [or her, or them] to change. It looks like that won't happen, at least not now. There is no sense in continuing to fight that

reality. I might as well accept it. After all, there are aspects of myself that cannot be changed. I might as well assume that the same applies to my students.

Most students probably have less difficulty adjusting to bothersome students than do teachers, perhaps because students do not assume they can change others. For them, it's more a matter of how to best minimize the difficulties. To them, it is not an overblown issue.

Strategy 29-3: Healthy Response to Misbehavior

Purpose: To maintain personal balance when facing misbehaving students.
Description: Checking to ensure we react to problem students in a healthy way.

What is your experience when a student misbehaves? Do you get terribly upset, as if no student should ever disrupt your classroom? Or do you react as if handling misbehavior is simply another part of your job? Compare these teacher responses:

Upsetting	Part of the Job
• The guys in the back are driving me crazy.	• Teaching is sure not easy, but I'll handle those guys one way or another.
• She just wants to make trouble for me.	• She obviously still can't or won't control her anger.
• I'm furious at the way he keeps messing up.	• I haven't yet figured out what to do with him.
• She should stop making noise.	• Even though she knows it bothers me, something keeps motivating her to make noise.

If student disruptions elicit a response from us that resembles those in the second column, chances are we will preserve our personal balance very well. On the other hand, if our response resembles those in the first column, we will likely suffer more upsets than is necessary, which is neither good for our mental health nor our ability to make sound decisions.

Enough practical and effective strategies for handling discipline exist so that, once mastered, we can handle misbehavior much like we handle nuisance phone calls and dead car batteries—as stuff that happens, not as distressing personal affronts. Remember, too, that the strategies of this book were selected for their ability to bring out the best from students, and, therefore, they will help us minimize student disruptions. If minimizing student disruptions is one of your prime concerns, you might give special attention to these strategies, which are among those teachers report as being most helpful for that purpose:

- Truth Signs (Strategy 4-1)
- Cushioning Questions (Strategy 4-2)
- Let Them Be (Strategy 4-9)
- Authority Statement (Strategy 8-3)
- Whole-Class Problem Solving (Strategy 8-9)
- DESCA Challenges (Strategy 25-10)
- Whole-Self Lesson (Strategy 28-4)
- Choose, Be, Review (Strategy 28-5)
- Asserting Our Priorities (Strategy 29-4)
- Calm Reminder (Strategy 33-2)
- Honest I Statements (Strategy 33-4)
- Silent Response to Misbehavior (Strategy 33-12)
- Apologizing (Strategy 33-13)
- Person-to-Person Dialogue (Strategy 34-1)

The key is to notice if we are letting misbehavior problems upset us and, if so, to remember that such a reaction is not only uncomfortable but also unnecessary and unwise. Handling misbehaving students need not cause distress. We can view it as just part of the job. And if we do experience distress, we do well to let it go as soon as we can. Curwin and Mendler (1988) speak to this point:

> It is critical for you not to carry anger, resentment, and other hostile feelings once a discipline situation is over. If you are angry with a student from an incident that happened the day before, you might enter a power struggle just to flex your muscles and show who is boss. Don't. Start fresh each day. (p. 105)

⟫ Strategy 29-4: Asserting Our Priorities

Purpose: To escape feelings of being overburdened.
Description: Noticing when we feel overburdened, backing off to see the whole picture, using our priorities to regain personal balance, and being willing to say no.

It's not unusual to feel overburdened. "It's crazy in my school," writes one teacher. "We have so many difficult students and not nearly enough staff or support. The parents don't even support us. In fact, they make matters worse. And now they want me to attend all these extra meetings about preparing students for those unnecessary state tests!" What is a teacher to do? We recommend two things: (1) clarifying priorities and (2) maintaining the courage to say no.

Clarifying Priorities

When we can't do everything asked of us at a high professional level, we can sort the demands in terms of our priorities. We can then go about at least handling the high-priority tasks. That is a better option than pretending that we can, in fact, do it all. In terms of teaching priorities, of course, high on our list would be promoting active learning, particularly DESCA learning, for when we inspire students to apply their best motives to daily schoolwork in that way, all our other professional goals are well served.

Finding the Courage to Say No

Many of us need to practice saying no more often. Too often we want to do everything for everyone and sink under that impossible burden, burning out in the process, which serves no one. How can we learn to say no to requests we find burdensome? There is no easy method. However, teachers who have worked at it and succeeded offer the following suggestions:

- *Imagine yourself gracefully declining.* Write a statement that you would like to be able to make and practice saying it aloud. You might write, for example,

> I would like to be able to do what you ask, but it would be better for me not even to try. I must learn to get better balance in my life. I'm already at the limits of what I can do well. Please forgive me for saying, sorry, but no. It's hard for me to say that, but I now feel the need to risk saying it. Can you see my point of view?

- *Ask someone to support you.* Tell someone that you need to make more space in your life and want to back off from too many commitments. Suggest that the person ask you from time to time how you are doing, as a reminder, and as an encouragement to take better control of your life.
- *Post a note on your refrigerator.* Such a note might say something like this: "I can't take care of others very well if I do not also take care of myself. And it starts by no longer overcommitting."
- *Be patient with yourself.* Start promptly. Don't delay and forget. Say "Sorry, but I'm already too busy" even when you are unsure; you can always change your mind. But if you make no immediate progress, accept that fact and say no next time. After all, we each learn in our own ways and by our own time clocks. Insuring yourself against burnout is worth patient and persistent effort.

Have patience with all things, but chiefly have patience with yourself.

—*Saint Francis de Sales*

Strategy 29-5: Respecting Our Own Stage

Purpose: To avoid frustrations and disillusionment that may come from unrealistic expectations.

Description: Reminding ourselves that teachers go through stages of development and it is unwise to expect more of ourselves than is now appropriate.

Are you an experienced teacher? If so, this book will probably help you improve quickly. Are you a beginning teacher? If so, this book should help you move through the three stages most teachers experience:

Stage 1: Pleasing others. Beginners often start with a mind that is set on mastering job requirements, getting accepted, and, especially, pleasing those in authority. They want students to like them. They want parents to like them. And they want whoever is in authority to like them, at least enough to offer them a permanent job. Some teachers call this the "survival" stage.

Stage 2: Teaching the subject matter. After some experience, particularly after receiving tenure, teachers typically enter a stage when what is most important to them is getting students to learn the subject matter they were hired to teach. Such teachers are willing to confront students, to push them to work hard, even to confront parents: "I believe your son would do better if he did not watch so much TV." Teachers at this stage often feel it is important to cover the subject matter. Pleasing others has reduced priority.

Stage 3: Teaching beyond subject matter. After some time at Stage 2, many teachers notice that no matter what they do, some students never learn much subject matter and many of those who do promptly forget it, often within days of exams. Furthermore, the teachers may come to see that students who do not forget what they learned hardly ever use it. How often, after all, are adults asked to find the area of a parallelogram or name the battles of the Civil War? This realization leads teachers to reevaluate the importance of subject matter. Typically, then, they become less obsessive about covering subject matter, more willing to allot class time to other matters, for example, to events that excite or worry students. Such teachers typically open their concerns beyond subject matter to show respect for good living as well as good learning.

If you are a beginner, you will almost certainly start at Stage 1. Guard against expecting so much from yourself that you invite disillusionment. Similarly, if you have recently moved into Stage 2, you may find it wise to allow yourself to remain where you are as long as you need to be there. In short, respect your own time clock. Know that this book will help you move through your teaching stages smoothly. And if you are one of the few beginners willing to risk starting with a Stage 3 focus, know that the book will make success easier. You might even discover, as others have, that you will not displease others by being a Stage 3 teacher. You might find many people absolutely delighted that you can teach in

> Something awful happens to a person who grows up as a creative kid and suddenly finds no creative outlet as an adult.
>
> —*Judy Blume*

inspiring ways. You will also discover that you will not slight subject matter mastery by becoming a Stage 3 teacher. In fact, we know of no better way to advance learning than by teaching in a way that inspires students to apply the very best they have to daily schoolwork.

PART VIII

Strategies for Evaluating
Student Learning

The chapters in this part of the book focus on strategies for evaluating student work, testing and grading, and reporting on student progress. In these tasks, which might evoke student apprehension, inspiring language is especially important. Consider the following three comments and compare the messages they send to students:

Least inspiring: "I've posted the test scores by the door. Some of you clearly need to give more time to your studies."

In between: "Here are the graded tests. Come up when I call your name and I'll give you your test paper."

Most inspiring: "You tried hard, class. I can tell that you did your best. Many of you showed especially great progress. I'll walk around now and give each of you your paper."

Handling Students' Written Work

30

How can we best handle students' written work so it is not excessively time-consuming for us but still is maximally beneficial to students? Several strategies covered earlier are helpful, especially Paper Exchange, Student Self-Evaluation, and Learning Log Exchange (Strategies 17-4, 17-11, and 21-6). In addition, the strategies of Chapter 10, Handling Completed Homework, can easily apply to all written work. Here are four more strategies. Teachers report that the first two are especially worthy of first attention.

Strategy 30-1: Response to Undone Work

Purpose: To respond wisely to students who fail to do their work.
Description: Avoiding blaming students who fail to do required work and rather responding in a way likely to inspire students to do better.

Students occasionally will fail to turn in written work. Some students will fail on many occasions. We can count on it. We do well to treat such events as uneventful. We do not want to get overly upset. We do not want to react as if our integrity is being violated, as if students are being defiant. Students are simply doing what students always do. It will not help to get overly emotional and blame the students. Instead, we want to remain cool-headed and treat the task of choosing our reaction as just another part of the job. Just as we must plan lessons and give grades, we must also respond to students who fail to turn in written work.

We also do well to avoid reacting in a way that is likely to do more harm than good. Accordingly, scolding, sarcasm, punishment, and nagging are not recommended. These approaches seldom work for long, and even when they do, they are more likely to produce unhealthy resentment or new guilt than to lead to the kind of self-responsible work we want from students. Here is a better set of options to consider when we're deciding how to react:

- *Respectful reminder.* "Sean, please complete the work later."

- *Next-time message.* "Next time we have this work, please turn it in by the requested time."

- *Inspirational prod.* "Rosa, this is not the first time. There is no reason for you to fall into the habit of missing assignments. I'll bet you're smart enough to find a way to avoid such a habit. How about challenging yourself to get all future papers in right on time? I know you can do it. Are you willing to go for it?"

- *Honest offer to help.* "Was the assignment too difficult for you?" "Are there any ways I can help you or get help for you?" "How about doing just the parts you can do?"

- *Honest I Statement (Strategy 33-4), with a discussion of natural consequences.* "You agreed to stay after school to finish that work, right? Because you didn't do it, there are consequences we both have to live with. For example, I now have more difficulty trusting your promises. More serious yet, you may have difficulty trusting your own word. Not keeping your agreement may have weakened your faith in yourself. Besides, you continue to fall behind in your work. We need to deal with this situation. Let's see if we can agree on where we go from here." Such a statement requires a follow-up discussion, which might well take the form of a Person-to-Person Dialogue (Strategy 34-1).

- *Respectful insistence.* "Sit there and finish that page now." Note that we believe it's sometimes perfectly acceptable to insist that work be done and, for students who might need that kick, be done right now. But we best insist only in cases in which we sense the student is ready to profit from it. We want such insistence to bring out the best within students, not to be merely an assertion of our authority. Can you recall a time when someone insisted you do something, and deep down, even if you resisted doing it, you knew it was good for you? You knew the person was not diminishing you in any way, not needing to control you, not disrespecting you; you knew rather that the person was challenging you to dig out more of your positive abilities. Similarly, when we insist something must be done, we want to be sure students know we are insisting because we care for them, for their welfare, not our own sense of righteousness.

- *Acceptance of reality.* We might, of course, do nothing. Sometimes it is best to accept the reality that nothing we know to do will produce a positive result. There is no advantage to getting upset in such a circumstance. Nor do we want to get the student more upset. When we see no constructive option, we may well

> If we treat students as they can be rather than as they now are, we are most likely to see them become that kind of person.
>
> —Haim Ginott

choose to do nothing. Sometimes this gives us time to find a constructive way to handle the situation. Sometimes it gives the student time to grow into more healthy self-responsibility. And sometimes, alas, neither occurs. But each seed has its time to germinate. It doesn't make sense to get upset if that time has yet to arrive.

The issue here is perspective. Let's keep in mind that the goal is not only to teach subject matter but also to do that in ways that are beneficial to students. When we keep that goal in mind, we are less likely to handle undone work in ways that are harmful to the students or frustrating to ourselves. As teachers, we have much power. We do well to avoid becoming corrupted by that power and placing our own ego needs ahead of the needs of our students. That would not be good for the students and would not be good for us either.

 ## Strategy 30-2: Next-Time Feedback

Purpose: To shift the focus from evaluating student work to providing constructive feedback.

Description: Writing comments on written work that give students specific guidance on what to do next time to improve their work.

What should we do with written work that falls short of high standards? Imagine a student receiving a paper with the comment, "Javier, you should have known this by now. We've gone over it many times." That sting may not inspire Javier to work more carefully in the future. And how about the student whose returned paper is covered with red marks and a low grade? That student, too, will likely feel more disheartened than encouraged. How many of us, after all, feel encouraged after negative feedback?

Aware of the consequences of negative feedback, some say, "Ignore student errors. Focus on the positive. When responding to written work, note only the good parts." That advice can get teachers to dole out endless stickers and smiley faces or to rely heavily on praise and rewards. But extrinsic motivators like that also have costs. It certainly does little to activate students' *intrinsic* learning motives. It's often wise to include praise in comments on poor work, but it's even more valuable to offer advice on how, practically speaking, students can do better next time.

One way to do this is to write comments that tell students what, specifically, they might do to produce better work. Some examples:

• Excellent thinking here. However, there are many silly grammatical errors. Perhaps next time have several people read your work before you turn it in.

- You're on the right track, but next time make sure to include only information relevant to your topic. I've marked the places where I think you drifted off the topic.
- You seem to understand the process of long division but have errors in your multiplication. I recommend you spend more time with multiplication flash cards.
- After writing your first draft, perhaps take some time away from the work, then come back to it later. Doing so often gives us a fresh perspective.

Marzano, Pickering, and Pollock (2001) remind us that the sooner students get such constructive feedback, the better. The usefulness of such feedback can be further enhanced when it indicates where students are in relation to specific learning targets (Crooks, 1988; Wilburn & Felps, 1983).

Strategy 30-3: Avoiding Paperwork Overload

Purpose: To make paperwork more manageable.
Description: Reducing the number of papers we check and grade.

Not all learning can be measured by grades.
—*Beth, age 16*

A seemingly endless stream of papers to be read and evaluated can make a teacher feel overwhelmed. That is not a feeling that is likely to increase our effectiveness. How might we avoid it? Some suggestions:

- We might consider what Pilon (1996) calls "respectful disposal." In her Task Workshop, students spend a large part of each day engaging in a series of brief independent learning tasks, tasks that produce many student papers every day. Pilon recommends that those papers be neither graded nor returned to students. Teachers might scan the papers at the end of the day, to get a sense of students' progress, but the papers are then to be respectfully discarded. The assignments did their job. They helped students stay productively engaged. The papers they generated have no further significant value. Might as well discard them, says Pilon. Similarly, when we conclude that there is little to be gained by checking and returning students' papers, we might consider appreciatively, respectfully, and discreetly discarding them.
- We might not collect homework frequently—perhaps only rarely. We might, however, provide frequent opportunities for peer evaluation and self-evaluation, perhaps by distributing rubrics that outline standards of excellence, perhaps by displaying correct answers against which students can compare their answers. We might also use Homework Sharing Pairs, Homework Self-Correcting, or Homework Hearing Time (Strategies 10-1, 10-2, and 10-3).
- When we do collect homework or class work, we consider Strategy 10-4, Credit for Completing Homework, which allows us to monitor who completes

assignments and approximately how well they did without the burden of correcting and grading the papers.

• Limit the number of tests we grade. In some cases, students might exchange papers and grade each others'. We might even reduce the number of tests given. Experience shows that frequent testing rarely produces higher grades or more learning. And because it consumes time that otherwise could be used for more productive learning experiences, frequent testing can be counterproductive. Limiting the number of tests also tends to reduce student anxiety and increase student confidence. Indeed, when we regularly assess student learning in a variety of ways, we need not rely on tests as our primary assessment tool. For more on this, see Chapter 31, Handling Testing and Grading.

Strategy 30-4: Positive Feedback Notes

Purpose: To encourage weak students to keep striving.
Description: Highlighting what is right and good about poor work.

At times we may have no clear sense of what some students can do to improve their work. Perhaps we just don't know how they can get from where they are to a higher level of competence. We therefore cannot offer specific, constructive feedback. But we can encourage the students to keep trying. We can do it by looking for something positive to say and expressing it honestly, sympathetically, warmly. We might say, for example, "You still have a way to go before reaching mastery, yet . . ." Or "I know you are not satisfied with this level of work, and yet . . ." Or "I can tell you are still struggling to master this and . . ." And then add something like this:

- Great effort.
- I admire your persistence.
- I wish all papers were as neat as this.
- You can be proud of the progress you continue to make.
- This is a novel approach, and I appreciate that.

It might take some searching to find positive statements we can offer honestly, and it's important to truly believe what we say. We might be encouraged to take the time to do so if we remember that writing such encouraging comments will help inspire students to remain actively engaged. And then, even if students never reach mastery, we are at least doing our best to help them learn to handle life's issues actively and constructively—which, of course, is one of education's primary goals.

I'm not a teacher; only a fellow-traveler of whom you asked the way. I pointed ahead—ahead of myself as well as you.

—*George Bernard Shaw*

31 # Handling Testing and Grading

As is probably clear by now, all the teaching strategies of this book are meant to

• Stimulate students to make more use of their constructive motives—especially their natural desire to work with dignity, flow with energy, be appropriately self-managing, be part of a community, and use their rich human awareness. Students then naturally become engaged in learning and that reduces any need we have to rely on tests and grades as motivators.

• Provide many ways to assess student progress while students are in the process of learning, so we need not spend so much time on testing and grading.

• Give priority to striving to do one's best, rather than reaching certain predetermined objectives by certain deadlines. Every individual, then, can reasonably experience success—that is, the satisfaction of having done one's best at that time.

• Generally take the emphasis off grades, which, of course, reduces discouragement among those students who are slow to learn—a discouragement that often leads such students to cease even trying to learn.

Yet most of us will still want to give some tests and grades. This chapter has 11 strategies for handling that. We recommend giving first attention to the first five.

Strategy 31-1: Dignifying Grading Practices

Purpose: To develop a balanced, comprehensive, dignifying grading plan.
Description: Creating a plan for grading that considers both professional requirements and the best interests of students.

What might be the best way to handle testing when we want to *inspire* students to work hard, not rely on grades to *pressure* them to do so? Here are some options and observations:

- *Minimum testing.* After students have been in class for a few weeks, we can usually tell quite accurately who is learning a lot and who is learning little. We may need to look at students' learning logs, homework papers, portfolio items, or other such material. But we rarely need many tests to identify the successful and less successful learners. If we give occasional tests, then, not to scare students into studying but to give them chances to summarize and "show their stuff," we will almost certainly have enough data to scale learners into grading categories.

This is the minimum-testing approach, and it often works very well. Grades are not based on tests alone but on all the data available, objective and subjective. And because the approach minimizes the time consumed by preparing, giving, and grading tests, it maximizes the time available for teaching and learning.

- *Professional statement.* What if a student or parent complains, "You cannot rely on subjective judgment. I want to see hard evidence that supports your grades." How might we respond? We favor telling the truth, by making a statement such as this:

> I certainly understand your concern that Ben be graded fairly. But, as a dedicated professional, I need to be trusted with my judgments. Students would have less time for learning if I had to take the time to collect and document all the data everyone would like to see. Please visit my class if you think that might reassure you that learning is taking place or that I am aware of what students are doing.

Being criticized is, of course, uncomfortable. It is uncomfortable even to worry about being criticized. It is tempting, therefore, to avoid the problem, even if that means using more time and energy for testing than you may believe is wise. Professionally and personally, it's better to do the best job we can in the classroom and to be prepared to call up our courage when necessary to respond to criticism. We also recommend thinking ahead about what we might say about our grading and perhaps writing for ourselves a statement like the one above.

- *The upgrade option.* We can reduce many students' preoccupation with grading and get them to pay more attention to learning simply by making any one grade earned less significant. Some teachers do this by collecting large numbers of grades. They might grade daily work, weekly tests, monthly reviews, and so on, so no single grade is critical. But this procedure is more likely to increase the

The statistics on sanity are that one out of every four Americans is suffering from some form of mental illness. Think of your three best friends. If they're okay, then it's you.

—*Rita Mae Brown*

attention and anxiety associated with grading than to decrease it. And collecting more grades adds to our noninstructional chores.

An alternative is to collect fewer grades and to make any one less significant by allowing students to do extra work whenever they are not happy with the grade earned. "If you would like to improve your grade," we might say, "let's sit and write a contract saying what you will do to earn extra credit. If you then do what I judge to be quality work on your upgrade project, you will get a better grade." This is a win-win approach. Students end up learning as much as they need to learn to get a good grade—and learn self-responsibility as well—and we do not need to consume a lot of teaching time with excessive testing.

• *The certain makeup.* Similarly, we favor telling students they can always make up missed work. We might insist that the students find their own helpers or tutors, which they usually can do from within the class. Compared with penalizing students for work avoided or missed, this approach is less punitive, more respectful, and more in tune with concern for developing self-management. Is it coddling? No. Making up work missed, like doing extra work to raise a grade, is not easy in a student's busy life. This is especially so when new work keeps pressing in on students' time.

• *Goal agreement.* Many students are accustomed to hearing a teacher announce course expectations, content to be covered, requirements, and the like. It is possible to make such an announcement, invite students to agree with our expectations, and then ask students if they want to create some of their *own* expectations for the course, as in this example:

> That is my proposed outline. Are you willing to go along with it? How about starting this way and later taking another look to see how we all feel about our progress? Also, I wonder if you can find any goals of your own related to the focus of this class. If you have personal goals, perhaps we can find ways to help you reach them. You might, for example, write a personal learning contract. Or we might set up groups to help you reach your goals. Do you want to search for some personal goals?

If we give grades, then, and they relate to how well students have fulfilled course expectations, it is more likely that grading will proceed amicably. If our goals have become the personal goals of our students, students are more likely to see us as being on their side, rather than as someone apart, simply making judgments about them. Most significant perhaps, we will be teaching and advancing personally responsible learning.

• *Procedure agreement.* Sometimes we can seek agreements on procedures that relate to grading. For example, we might say, "Here are several samples of what

The smart man solves a problem. The wise man prevents it.
—*Albert Einstein*

I consider excellent work. Let's study these together so my definition of excellence is clear." Or we might say something like this: "As for rating your work, here is what I propose . . . Any suggestions for improving that process? Are you willing to go along with it, at least for now, until we find something better we can agree on?"

• *Success for all.* Because it is difficult for individuals to persist when they rarely succeed, providing many success experiences is critical to maintaining motivation, especially for students likely to struggle academically. This is another argument for dignifying and personalizing the grading process, as suggested by other strategies described in this chapter. We might consider Strategy 6-4, Independent Learning Assignments, which recommends that students choose and execute personal learning goals with the teacher acting as an academic coach. We might also consider using Portfolios (Strategy 31-3) as part of an assessment program; for they offer many opportunities to find something to appreciate about students' work and, therefore, make it easier for us to provide success experiences to all.

• *Grades for participation.* We do not recommend giving credit for participation in class discussions. Some students naturally speak up in class, and others learn better when they can relax and just observe. It seems unfair, an indignity really, to tell the quiet people they must speak up or suffer a penalty. After all, we each have our own ways.

 ## Strategy 31-2: Tests with Choice

Purpose: To improve students' likelihood of succeeding on tests.
Description: Including various types of questions on tests and allowing students some choice in which questions to answer.

To help students experience success, we might design our tests in ways that maximize chances that students will have a success experience. We might, for example, instruct students to choose three out of five essay questions, or skip up to 10 short-answer questions. Or we might append something like this to our test questions: "Now write two questions you wish had been on this test and write answers to both." Giving students such choices individualizes testing. It makes it easier for students to feel smart and earn good grades. It also protects student dignity and decreases the negativity that often surrounds testing. In addition, as students make decisions about what questions best serve them, they develop skills of self-management and awareness. All this can be accomplished without significantly reducing our opportunity to evaluate how much and what students have learned.

Strategy 31-3: Portfolios

Purpose: To give students responsibility for organizing and evaluating their work.
Description: Asking students to keep a collection of their work, both for their own review and for our review.

Portfolios are simply collections of student work that the students themselves manage and present. In an elementary class, each student might have a folder that contains collected writings, worksheets, and drawings. At the end of a week, each student might be asked to sort through the folder, write some Outcome Sentences (Strategy 21-1) based on the week's papers, star the items they feel best about, and perhaps select items they want to take home to show their families.

Portfolios develop self-management abilities and are broadly adaptable for many grade levels. They reduce the need to test students; they can be used as a supplement to testing or as a replacement for it. The following is a handout that one of us, Merrill, has distributed to students in a college class to provide them with information about how to develop an effective portfolio.

Self-Managed Evaluation Process

Many college students are accustomed to asking about requirements and then fulfilling them. However, that approach does not empower learners or learning. Indeed, it rather serves passivity and uncritical obedience. This is not the approach our faculty intends. Our commitment is to instruct in ways that strengthen people, that expand their ability to learn intelligently and self-responsibly. We are also committed to reducing disconnection between courses and between what is learned and what happens in real life. A key element in our approach is the student portfolio. This is a request for you to take responsibility for building one for yourself. We recommend you build it with three purposes in mind:

- To organize and integrate the whole of your work, so you can clearly track your progress and interests.
- To reflect on your current experiences and the choices ahead, so you can maximize the amount and the relevance of your learnings.
- To keep your work in a coherent and tangible form, so your progress can be communicated to the faculty.

Portfolios are meant to be self-managed and designed. As you begin building yours, you might consider including some of the elements below.

Personal Goals. You could have one section of your portfolio include notes about your long-term and short-term targets. You might begin by listing some. You might state goals broadly or with a focus only on teaching. For teaching, you might list

---

When a teacher is in a bad mood, there's no way I'm going to ask to go to the bathroom.

—Angela, age 11

- *Knowledge Goals,* what you want to understand: Why some people don't learn, what B. F. Skinner proposed, how values are developed.
- *Skill Goals,* what you want to be able to do: Get a job, handle misbehavior, avoid overwork, get appreciated, keep all students involved all the time.
- *Being Goals,* how you want to be as you do what you do: Be flexible, be confident, be empathic, be caring, be optimistic, be assertive.

Experience Log. You might include in your portfolio a log of significant experiences related to your professional growth. Perhaps list courses you took, books and other materials you read, conversations that were meaningful, experiments you tried, family events that made a difference.

Learning Log. You might include a method of tracking your professional development. You could base this on your learning goals. Perhaps indicate somehow which goals have been met and which new ones are emerging. You might also include a section that logs what you were able to extract from your experiences. You might simply include an ongoing, dated list of sentences with such beginnings as

- I learned . . .
- I am beginning to wonder . . .
- I was surprised . . .
- I rediscovered . . .
- I now better appreciate . . .
- I now promise to . . .

- I have become more skilled at . . .
- I'm getting clearer about . . .
- I uncovered a new question about . . .
- I was proud of the way I . . .
- I reevaluated the assumption I once had about . . .

These could be categorized in some way, such as learnings about teaching methods, psychological principles, useful references, ideas for different units of study, and so on.

Supporting Items. Your portfolio might also include a table of contents and examples of work you produced. Perhaps include papers you wrote, summaries of different theories that interested you, tapes of yourself teaching at different points in your program, or feedback forms from students. In many cases, you will want to have a home reservoir of materials and assemble your portable version, your portfolio, to share with others in whatever way is appropriate at the time. In all sections, unless the faculty directs otherwise, say as little or as much about any element as serves your best interests.

Note this special request: Please treat your portfolio as a learning tool. Do not highlight its use as an assessment tool. Do not build a portfolio to impress the faculty. That may erase much of its power to serve you. It may even erase some of your own respect for learning and growing. You will occasionally be invited to show parts of your portfolio to the faculty. That can help them assess your work accurately. And you may occasionally be asked to create and include special items, such as a summary of your learnings to date or a list of current interests and needs. But you will never be asked to reveal parts of your portfolio you choose to keep private. If you want to impress the faculty, use your portfolio to demonstrate your sincere, steady, intelligent strivings to get the most from your learning experiences.

Strategy 31-4: Focus-on-Learning Statement

Purpose: To emphasize learning rather than grading.

Description: Informing students of our intention to focus on learning, not grading, and inviting students' suggestions and cooperation.

Some teachers find it valuable to state openly to students that they intend to place the class focus more on learning, less on grading. They might take time to discuss this carefully enough so students are not thrown by such a shift and willingly cooperate with it. To do this, a teacher might simply ask students, "How can we take some of the heat out of testing and grading and give more of our attention to serious learning?" Often a more detailed approach works better, as in the lesson outlined below.

One Teacher's Approach

The lesson presented here is from a junior high school math teacher. She introduces the topic by saying, "Many students are preoccupied with grades. For some it's more important to get a good grade than to learn something. How many here feel a bit like that? Who would be willing to risk sharing their thoughts?" As the teacher listens, she often offers a supportive comment, saying something like, "Yes, I can understand that." Then she continues:

> I'd like us to take a different approach in this class. I'd like us to focus on studying and learning and to keep testing and grading in the background. This might be a difficult switch for some. But there is a downside to focusing on testing and grading. See if each of you can think of one or more downsides to testing and grading. Make notes for yourself and then let's see if we can make a group list on the board.

Students then offer various ideas, which the teacher writes on the board:

- Grading makes us anxious.
- Some are not good at taking tests.
- Makes some of us sick.
- Wastes a lot of class time.
- Makes some want to cheat.
- It makes us feel bad if we fail.
- It makes some of us not want to come to class.
- When we learn for the test, we forget right away.
- Makes some uncomfortable when they get better grades than their friends.
- Keeps our parents on our backs.

A master can tell you what he expects of you. A teacher, though, awakens your own expectations.

—Patricia Neal

- No one learns much by taking tests.
- Many of us don't get good grades.

The teacher tells the students that she has to give grades, but she wants to take the emphasis off grading. She explains:

> Actually, I do not need many tests to know how much each of you is learning. After a while, as I keep working with you, I can tell. That is how I know what I need to reteach and when we can go to a new topic. I watch and listen, and you, too, probably can tell how much you are learning. We don't need a lot of tests to tell us that.
>
> We may want to have a test from time to time, not because I need to be sure how much you learned, but because a test can be a good way to pull a unit together.
>
> That won't hurt us—as long as we know tests are not the main thing. It may even help some of you keep your attention on this class work. There are many out-of-school pressures and temptations, after all, and pressures from other classes, too. If we had no pressure here, some of you might not be able to resist putting all your energy elsewhere. Do any of you fall into that category? Is it OK to have some but not a lot of tests here?

After the students have an opportunity to respond, the teacher continues the discussion by telling the students that she doesn't want some of them to feel they are better than others. She lets them know that she likes and respects all of them, that she believes that each of them has a lot of goodness inside, and that she doesn't want grades to come across as "labels of more goodness and less goodness." She also brings up the matter of time clocks, reminding the students of the sign posted on the classroom wall (from Strategy 4-1, Truth Signs):

> Remember that we all learn some things now and some things later anyhow, so why get too anxious about it? You may zip ahead in your math learning later in the year, or next year. That sometimes happens. It is more likely to happen if you do not get discouraged when your time clock for learning indicates you're not ready to learn right now, but you keep at it anyhow, doing the best you can.

The teacher then says that, nevertheless, she must give grades. Before she presents her proposal for grading, she invites the students to think about her suggestion and to give her feedback, "Think about this, and if it does not feel right to you, sometime let me know privately," she says. "Then we'll talk and see if we can come up with a different plan the two of us can live with." Then she outlines her proposal:

> First, I will give a passing grade, at least a *C,* to all who show up in class regularly and who keep doing the best they can. My job is to help you get into learning. If I cannot do my job well, or if your time clock for learning is different, or if other things are more important in your life at the time, well, that is no one's fault. That is just the way things were at the time. We all might be able to do better in the future. No sense giving someone a grade lower than *C* and risk making anyone

feel bad because of it. That will do more harm than good, I'd say, especially because the grade you get in this course will not qualify you or disqualify you for anything very important. I could not say this if this was a course in piloting airplanes!

I will give an extra good grade, which I call a *B*, for work that I feel is extra good. Does that mean that *B* grades are better than *C* grades? Not necessarily. It may just mean that those getting *B* grades had time clocks that allowed them to get extra good learnings. Or maybe our class methods just suited them fine. No big deal.

I will give a top grade, an *A*, to work that is a clear step ahead of extra good work, for work that seems to me outstanding, exceptional. Are people who get *A*s better than people who get *B*s and *C*s? Who can guess why I would not say so?

As she presents her proposal, the teacher occasionally points to the Truth Signs and the messages they convey. She notes that some students may have difficulty with her proposal to de-emphasize grading and tests. They may still view grading and tests as being very important. "I can accept that," she says. "I merely want to reduce the time and energy we take away from learning in our class." She then brings up another point:

This may help you to go for a top grade without worrying that you will not succeed. And if you worry less, chances are you will learn more and enjoy math more.

Here is the plan. Get into your class work. Give it your all. Forget about grading. And then let's see after a while what grade I think best fits your learning. If you are not satisfied with that grade, I'll mark down an *I*, for "in progress," or leave the grade blank and explain that your work is still in progress, and I can't quite be sure yet. Then you and I can plan what extra work would be good for you to do, so you can, in fact, end up earning a grade more satisfying to you. But be careful, because this will mean extra work while you have your regular work to do. But if the trouble is worth it to you, I'm willing to offer that upgrade option.

The "upgrade option" that the teacher mentions is included in Strategy 31-1, Dignifying Grading Practices.

Wrapping up the discussion, the teacher suggests that the class try her proposed system for a while. She concludes by saying

If problems come up, speak to me privately, or, if you prefer, let's talk about it as a whole class. I'll bet we can brainstorm and come up with a creative remedy to a problem that comes up. But for now, let's put the issue aside. I will point up errors in your work, but I won't grade papers. I won't grade homework. I won't grade class participation. I'll just react in ways that I think might help you learn better.

Things to Consider When De-emphasizing Grading

Unlike the teacher in the paraphrased lesson, some teachers are not willing to give a passing grade to students just because they come to class every day and work diligently at learning. We recommend that such teachers simply adjust their comments to say what is required for a *C* grade. One can de-emphasize grading and testing while also insisting on minimum competence for a passing grade.

We also recommend that teachers who wish to conduct a discussion like the one above share their proposed approach beforehand with other teachers and, if appropriate, with administrators, asking for feedback and suggestions. It is not easy to move far from the current assumptions about the importance of tests and grades. The more ideas we gather about making such a move the better. And, as with any change from old habits, the more support we have the better.

Do not underemphasize the time it may take for students and parents—and us, too—to become comfortable with a focus that shifts away from grading and toward learning. For many, good grades have become an addiction. We may need to occasionally restate our concerns and support those who are having trouble breaking old habits. Fortunately, because the core purpose of schooling centers more on learning than grading, truth is on our side. We are not likely to proceed for long without finding others supporting us.

Also keep in mind that, as with many issues, no grading plan is likely to satisfy everyone. Some people, of course, will believe that a heavy emphasis on grading is ill-advised. Unfortunately, those individuals are less likely to complain loudly than are those who become dissatisfied when we de-emphasize grades. It is advisable, then, to be clear about our intentions, not naive about expecting to please everyone, and strong in our professional commitment. We will likely need to call up courage.

The issue of emphasizing or de-emphasizing grading is similar to the question "Should we promote or retain failing students?" In the long run, we believe retention does not help students learn more. Moreover, retention does tend to diminish self-esteem. Our desire to serve both learning and living, then, leads us to favor promotion for all students. We would, however, make exceptions. Sometimes a particular student is clearly better served by retention.

Once we have initiated a policy that de-emphasizes grading, it's best to give the issue minimum class time. The more attention we give to grades and tests, the more important and convoluted the issues become. We recommend making our best judgments and setting the topic aside. The less we talk about grading in the classroom the better. There are, after all, more worthy things to attend to—learning, for example.

> To me inspiration is the planting of a seed that flowers into action.
>
> *—Greg Matthews*

Strategy 31-5: Retest Offer

Purpose: To help students suffering from test anxiety to show their true learning.
Description: Allowing students to retake any test or to demonstrate accomplishment in another way.

Even good test-takers can have a bad day. But tests can make some students so anxious that every test day is a bad day, no matter how well they have learned the material. One way to support students through the occasional bad test day and to reduce test anxiety for all students is to make a standing Retest Offer. "Students not satisfied with their grade always have the option to retake any test," we might announce. In certain cases, when retesting does not seem viable, we can allow students to demonstrate learning in any other way that is mutually agreeable. Oddly, offering a retest option reduces the likelihood we will need to use it. The offer itself reduces test anxiety.

Strategy 31-6: Pre-final Exam

Purpose: To help students successfully prepare for final exams.
Description: Giving students a pre-final exam that includes questions resembling all those that will be on the final exam.

As with any test, we want to help students succeed on final exams. To do so, consider the Pre-final Exam strategy. Here is one possible sequence:

1. Prepare and distribute to students a pre-final exam that contains the kinds of questions you plan to use on the final, plus several others.
2. Give students time to complete the pre-final, which they might do in or out of class, working alone or in small teams.
3. Review with students the correct answers to all questions.

As long as students find this strategy motivating, it can be repeated until students are properly prepared for the exam ahead.

Strategy 31-7: Rubrics

Purpose: To clarify for students what good work is and is not.
Description: Presenting, discussing, and using rubrics as criteria for evaluating student work.

A rubric makes clear what distinguishes good and poor results, usually by providing samples of results at different levels of excellence (see Figure 9 on page 165 for an example). Rubrics thereby clarify for students what is required to succeed. Students' goals then tend to be more precise and their work more focused. In general, research has shown that when feedback on student work is based on a

Sometimes you need a little push to go down the big slide.
—*Cynthia Copeland Lewis*

rubric, students learn more from their mistakes than when work is merely graded *A, B, C* (Crooks, 1988; Wilburn & Felps, 1983).

Rubrics are most helpful when discussed before work is begun, as suggested in Strategy 12-7, Specific Levels of Excellence. Here are some other suggestions:

• Students can grade their own work by using a rubric that assigns a grade to each level of excellence. Students might then compare that grade with the grade given by another student who examines their work, or with the teacher's grade. Discussing discrepancies can help students understand what they are missing and how they might improve.

• After students have completed an assignment, we can ask them to grade one another using a rubric. Applying rubrics to one another's work helps students better understand how rubrics can be used to guide their own work.

• When assigning a long-term project, the class as a whole might design a rubric for assessing the results. Or we might simply present a rubric we've created. Rubrics are especially valuable for such projects. They give students a clear target and give students and parents a clear picture of what was done well and what needs to be improved. They can also make grading such projects easier for us, eliminating the need to write many comments about each student's work.

▲ TEACHER COMMENT

Students used to always complain about my grades and argue with me. But then I started giving them copies of learning goals with rubrics that showed various levels of excellence. I ask them to demonstrate the level they achieved in a unit. Grades flow naturally from that. And that somehow eliminated those arguments about how many points I get for this or that and what grade is fair or unfair. The question is always, What level did you reach? And students can see that for themselves.

—Polly Pennington
Middle School Social Studies Teacher

Strategy 31-8: Failure Insulators

Purpose: To help students with test anxiety.
Description: Providing many successful test-taking experiences at the start of the school year.

Students who have failed in the past often begin a school year expecting to fail again, and, says Ciaccio (2004), to help them change their self-defeating ways, they must be convinced that they have a real chance of success with a new teacher. Accordingly, we might consider these options:

• *Give easy early tests.* Adjust the difficulty of tests early in the year so all students experience high achievement, build confidence, and reduce their test-taking anxiety.

- *Don't grade every test.* Especially in elementary school, do not grade many early tests. Instead, simply respond with a general comment such as "You seem to understand" or "You may need to study more."
- *Use* A, B, *"Needs improvement."* If you must give grades, restrict grades to *A, B,* or "Needs improvement." When you give a "Needs improvement" grade, it's especially useful to offer specific suggestions for how to do better or, if possible, to make available peer tutoring or adult volunteer tutors.
- *Offer extra credit.* Give extra-credit opportunities to students who did not do well. Or offer them an oral make-up test, which can be evaluated more subjectively than a written test and, therefore, can provide more ways for students to experience success.
- *Don't count the test.* If the failure seems particularly damaging to a student—if, for example, there was unusual anxiety or an extenuating circumstance—simply find a plausible reason for not counting the test.

Strategy 31-9: High-Achievement Comments

Purpose: To make grades more meaningful to high achievers.
Description: Writing comments that recognize exceptional student achievement.

For students who easily get *A*s, another *A* on a test or a report card provides little satisfaction and may not inspire them to do their very best work. Accordingly, find a way to give "super-excellent" grades. We might, for example, write on test papers and add to report cards comments such as "Better than *A* work. Shows unusual insight and understanding." Or "Better than *A* work. Shows exceptional creativity and persistence." This strategy is especially useful in times of grade inflation, to both encourage and reward exceptional achievement.

Strategy 31-10: Self-Selected Learning Reports

Purpose: To individualize learning reports.
Description: Allowing students to choose their own way to show what they have learned.

In place of an examination at the end of a unit of study, some teachers like to let students choose their own way to show evidence of learnings. An artistically inclined student, for example, might choose to create a poster, a collage, or a model of key learnings. A student with musical ability might write and perform a song about the topic. A practical-minded student might create a new application of a concept. A social student with good communication skills might conduct an appropriate interview and report on that. Self-Selected Learning Reports also provide a helpful alternative for students who do not perform well on tests. Perhaps brainstorm possibilities for such reports with the whole class. Some ideas to start the process:

- Creating a concept map
- Writing and performing a skit
- Preparing a test with answers
- Assembling a portfolio
- Teaching someone else until that person achieves mastery
- Submitting a Learning Log (Strategy 21-3) with critical items highlighted
- Reviewing Learning Log entries and submitting a new set of Outcome Sentences (Strategy 21-1) that shows what was learned by the review.

Strategy 31-11: Quick Feedback

Purpose: To help students learn more from tests.
Description: Providing test feedback as quickly as possible, including explanations and opportunities for student self-evaluation.

Students typically take tests and wait to see their grades. Teachers often return graded tests with feedback indicating little more than what is correct and incorrect. Too rarely do students or teachers approach tests, or the ensuing feedback, as learning experiences. But after analyzing almost 8,000 studies, Hattie (1992) concluded that feedback is "the most powerful single modification that enhances achievement" (p. 9). Feedback need not be given solely by the teacher—students can effectively contribute through self-evaluation (Wiggins, 1993), peer evaluation, and by monitoring their own progress (Trammel, Schloss, & Alper, 1994). This strategy supports the use of three other methods— Homework Self-Correcting, Review Test, and Student Self-Evaluation (Strategies 10-2, 11-1, and 17-11). Some additional ways to give students quick feedback:

- When possible, give shorter tests that can be taken and reviewed during one class period. Shorter math tests, for example, can be self-checked or checked by another student while we explain or demonstrate the solution for each problem.
- For spelling tests or other tests with simple right/wrong answers, ask students to write their answers in ink and after each question provide the correct

An error means a child needs help, not a reprimand or ridicule for doing something wrong.

—*Marva Collins*

If you do badly on a report card or test that you take home on a Friday, you should wait until Sunday night to ask your parents to sign it.

—Hannah, age 14

answer. Have students then write your correct answer in pencil or in another color ink—even if their original answer was correct, as a reinforcement of the correct answers. Answers written correctly twice then count toward the grade.

• When tests consist of questions that require more involved responses, the test might contain only three or four questions. Then, after students write responses to each question, you might discuss possible answers, perhaps including an explanation of what makes answers correct or incorrect. Students might grade each of their responses themselves (*excellent, fair, inadequate*), or they might exchange papers and grade each other's.

Reporting Students' Progress

32

Ideally, we would want grades to empower students, not to diminish them. Yet, as noted by Tomlinson (2001), many current grading practices generate more discouragement than diligence. Can our grading and reporting practices better serve us and our students? Tomlinson's research points out the importance of having grades support, not criticize, students' efforts. The strategies of this chapter suggest ways we can do this. Our field tests suggest that the first strategy be given your first attention.

Strategy 32-1: Report Card Plan

Purpose: To increase consistency between report card procedures and key school purposes.

Description: Creating a plan for report cards that is considerate of both professional requirements and the best interests of students.

Although report cards are often the central symbol of an evaluation system, they often oversimplify and complicate our mission. Sometimes they make it difficult to avoid sending an undesirable message: *You are a failure.* Or to avoid sounding arbitrary: *What matters is what I say, not what you say or think.* Or to avoid fostering envy: *You are below average.* Or to avoid narrow judgments: *Only what is listed here is worth attention.* Or to avoid oversimplification: *Your work was worth a* B. What might be an improvement over a reliance on standard report cards? Here are some possibilities:

• *Revised report cards.* It may be wise to campaign for an improved report card. In general, the best cards allow for multiple grades and subjective comments.

Dual grades—for example, one grade for achievement and another grade for effort—is much more effective than is a single grade.

* *Student-teacher dialogues.* The importance of report cards is diminished, along with their potential for negative side effects, when they are augmented with other reporting procedures. Individual student-teacher dialogues are especially useful. Some teachers regularly set aside a few days each reporting period for such dialogues, keeping students busy on other tasks while they meet one-on-one. (See Strategy 17-9, Consult Time.) A teacher might ask students to bring to the meeting notes about recent progress. From the teacher's perspective, a dialogue sequence might follow four steps: *How do you see your progress? Here is how I see it. Any ideas about what you or I might do in the future? All things considered, what grade should we list for this work?*

* *Open visitor policy.* We recommend actively encouraging parents and other community members to visit classes at any time, even without notice. When visitors see students busy at work, most conclude that, yes, learning is taking place and that is what is most important. Parents, then, tend to become less concerned about report cards and more supportive of what goes on in their schools. Consider preparing a standard sheet of "Do's and Don'ts for Visitors." A student committee member, or the student of the day, might give a copy to each visitor. The sheet might also include options for doing more than observing. Observers might be invited, for example, to offer tutoring to students who seem stuck or to participate directly in learning activities, something many visitors enjoy doing.

* *Parent-teacher conferences.* Parent-teacher conferences are particularly worthwhile for neutralizing the problems of report cards. Phone conferences, with the teacher initiating calls to each student's family, can play a valuable role in communities where parents do not usually visit the school.

Strategy 32-2: Dual Grades

Purpose: To use grades to give more than ordinary information to students and parents.
Description: Giving separate grades for effort and accomplishment.

Tomlinson (2001) speaks of the advantages of giving dual grades, one for effort and one for accomplishment. A high grade for effort will be especially important for struggling students or late-starters. It also reflects the reality that the best all students can do is the best they can do; the effort grade, then, might well be seen as the prime grade. Dual grading also gives valuable information to bright students

> Others will treat you with the amount of respect you feel you deserve.
> —Marie Hackett

who repeatedly excel at tests without much effort. When a student, for example, gets a report card with an *A* for accomplishment and a *D* for effort, it informs him and his parents that there is room for improvement. Many bright students need such information if they ever are to make the most of their gifts. Tomlinson suggests two ways to handle dual grading:

• *Give separate grades for effort and mastery.* Or, similarly, give one grade for progress toward personal goals, perhaps as written in a personal learning contract, and one grade for achievement. This could be communicated in one box by using a letter and number, such as *A3*. The *A* could mean the student's effort was top-notch, the best that could be expected for this particular student. The *3* could mean that the student was average in mastering the material thus far.

• *Give separate grades for personal growth and relative standing.* In this model, letter grades might be used to indicate student growth. For example, an *A* means excellent growth, *B* means very good growth, *C* means some growth, *D* means little growth, and *F* means no observable growth. A numerical notation might then be used to indicate the student's standing relative to peers or to curriculum benchmarks. For example, a *1* means the student is working above grade level, a *2* means the student is working at grade level, and a *3* means the student is working below grade level. Also see E-for-Effort Certificates (Strategy 25-7).

Strategy 32-3: Supportive Report Card Comments

Purpose: To make report cards more personal and positive.
Description: Adding personal comments to report cards acknowledging something positive about each student.

Adding written notes to report cards makes them more personal and, not incidentally, shows that we care, something students and parents much appreciate. It also gives us an opportunity to highlight the positive, which is especially valuable for struggling students. We can even do this with cards not designed for such comments by attaching a note to the card. Some teachers find it useful to prepare a list of possible comments, such as these:

• Not the best grade in class, but _____ is doing the very best he can.
• Showing much progress.
• Attitude is coming around beautifully.
• She'll do even better next time.

- I couldn't ask for more cooperation and diligence.
- He needs work on _____, but on _____ and _____ he is doing just fine, and I am proud of him.
- I'm delighted to have _____ in our class.
- He started slow but has begun to show improvement.
- _____ continues to be a pleasure to teach.

Strategy 32-4: Surprise Personal Notes

Purpose: To give students support and encouragement between report cards.
Description: Occasionally sending surprise notes home with some good news.

Report card time is often a particularly busy time for teachers. Fortunately, it does not take much effort to devise a convenient system to send home a positive message between report cards. One teacher, for example, takes a few minutes each week to write notes to two students. She calls these Surprise Personal Notes. She announces at the beginning of the year that sometimes she will give a student a note to take home saying something positive. Some examples of her notes:

- Tamara was wonderful today with . . .
- On time every day this week.
- Always helpful to others.
- Reached out to a new student.
- Appreciate the way he tries so hard.
- Walks with dignity.
- Works with energy.
- Growing beautifully in self-management.
- A respected and well-liked member of our class community.

Strategy 32-5: Reverse Report Card

Purpose: To obtain input from families about how we might help students do better.
Description: Defining student behaviors we would like to promote and asking families to observe and periodically report on changes in these behaviors.

Pilon (1996) once suggested initiating what might be called Reverse Report Cards. These are cards not from the teacher to the parents, but from the parents to the teacher. To use this strategy, we start by defining student behavior we would like to see developed, such as

- Engages in self-initiated reading.
- Uses new vocabulary words when speaking.
- Handles everyday calculations willingly and accurately.
- Listens respectfully to what others say.
- Expresses ideas in artistic ways.
- Walks and speaks like someone with full dignity.
- Maintains comfortable energy flow throughout the whole day.
- Manages own time and materials appropriately.
- Is willing to share and participate with others.
- Lives with awareness of the things and people nearby.

We then ask each student's family to be on the lookout for changes in these behaviors, and to send us a card each marking period noting which behaviors have progressed and, perhaps, any other noteworthy changes observed in the student. We would then have valuable data for class planning; we would know what students are learning in ways that actually show up in real life—at least as the parents report it—and perhaps what more is needed for certain students or the whole class.

We might also ask parents to note their concerns—for example, how their child is progressing socially, improving impulse control, developing independence—and make it a point to include their observations on the Reverse Report Cards. This strategy has the additional benefit of helping parents feel that they and the teacher are working as partners in the education process.

We could set up a similar system that would ask not parents but rather each student to report on progress. "In which categories have you noticed progress?" Again, this could provide valuable data for future planning. It could also invite more student self-responsibility for progress and be useful in private teacher-student conferences about progress.

Educate your children to self-control and you have done much to abolish both misery from their future lives and crimes from the society.

—Daniel Webster

PART IX

Strategies for Maintaining Discipline

The two chapters in this part of the book focus on strategies for maintaining all aspects of discipline, from handling routine misbehavior to dealing with more serious and chronic misbehavior.

Inspiring language is particularly important when students might feel they are being criticized. Consider the following three comments and the messages they send to students:

Least inspiring: Teacher says from the front of the room, "Bill, you know better than to make noises like that. Stop it. And I mean *now*."

In between: After walking near Bill, the teacher says, "Bill, do we need to talk again about how to behave in class?"

Most inspiring: After walking near Bill, the teacher says, "It's too hard for me to teach with that noise, Bill. Please stop it."

Handling Routine Misbehavior

33

Like a stitch in time, preventing discipline problems is the way to go. The best way to do this is by (1) keeping students productively, comfortably involved in learning, and (2) being a teacher who is clearly confident and caring. Yet students will be students; problems will arise. We will, for example, likely encounter students who are uncontrollably angry, or who get immense pleasure from resisting authority, or who act the clown at just the wrong time. It's not that they are "bad" people. Nor is it that they chose to have those personalities. It's just the way some humans are, and we must be prepared to teach while they are in our classrooms.

How might we prepare ourselves? Chapters 4 and 8 identify strategies that help to prevent problems; review especially Strategies 8-1, 8-2, 8-3, and 8-11. This chapter and the next should help with the problems that are not prevented. The basic principle throughout is simple: When confronted by a discipline problem, avoid acting in a way that will elicit the worst in students, such as their ability to be hostile. Rather act in a way that will bring out the best in students, such as their willingness to cooperate. The strategies below illustrate ways of doing just that. Of the strategies in this chapter, teachers report that the first seven are deserving of first attention, which is why each is marked with an arrow.

⟩ Strategy 33-1: Broken Record

Purpose: To persist in asserting authority without arguing.
Description: Repeating a statement that a student seems not to be respecting.

Canter and Canter (1976) suggest what they call the broken record technique. Here is an example:

Teacher:	Jimmy, we do not fight in this room. I want you never to fight here again. I never want anyone hurt.
Jimmy:	Bryan started it. He hit me first.
Teacher:	That might well be. But we do not fight in this room. Please remember that.
Jimmy:	What am I supposed to do when someone pokes at me then?
Teacher:	Good question. Let's talk about that another time. For now I just want to make clear that I do not want you or anyone else ever to fight here again.

This broken record strategy is especially effective, say Canter and Canter, when students do not seem to acknowledge our original statement. It clearly communicates to students that we will not engage in an argument with them. Charles (1996), however, reports three cautions:

• When you repeat your original statement, preface it with a comment showing that you heard what the student said—for example, "That might well be. Yet I'd like everyone to hold comments until I'm through talking." Or "I understand your feeling. However, I need you to stay in your seat."

• Don't ask questions. Just make statements.

• Repeat your statement a maximum of three times. Do not slip into a verbal power struggle with an obstinate student. If a student is not agreeable after three restatements, it's best to simply put the issue aside, go on to something else, and consider later what, if anything, would be a wise next step.

Strategy 33-2: Calm Reminder

Purpose: To keep class proceedings running smoothly without generating negativity.

Description: Calmly reminding students what we want.

Even well-intentioned students forget. It is a truth *we* sometimes forget. And when we do forget it, we may resent having to restate a requirement. Yet sometimes a calm restatement is the best choice. To preserve student dignity, it is certainly better than a response that might bite or diminish, such as "Weren't you paying attention the first time I said it?" or "Didn't I explain that already?" Far better are these alternatives: "Nick, I'd like you to notice if the hall pass is on the hook before asking about it," or "Tom, when our hands go up, it's the signal to end small-group talk."

Rather than complain or fuss, it is sometimes better to just explain the procedure again, as if we had never said it before. No blame. Just a simple restatement.

The unspoken message is this: "I guess this did not register in your memory. No big deal." This is not to say, however, that we should always remind students of procedures. It takes a judgment about what is best in a particular situation. See the Once Principle (Strategy 5-4) for a strategy that aims to eliminate unnecessary reminders.

And this caution about reminders has special applicability to behavior problems. Compare these two examples:

Example 1. "Don't talk to your neighbors, Bill."
Later, said more sternly: "Bill, I said don't talk to your neighbors."
Still later, said with clear irritation: "Bill, I do *not* want you talking to your neighbors. Face the front and pay attention."

Example 2. "Please don't talk to your neighbors, Bill. It's distracting to me."
Later, said with a smile and a wink: "Bill, you are talking again."
Still later, said with no hint of irritation: "Bill, we need to talk later about your side conversations. Let's talk at noon."

The first sequence is to be avoided. The tone is bossy; Bill is likely to want to resist us. Also, by allowing irritation to take root in us, we fall into conflict with the student when we would do well to be above that. See Strategies 29-3 and 33-5.

Why is the second sequence better? The tone is less bossy, more simply informative; we are informing Bill that his talking is disturbing us. As a result, Bill is less likely to resist and more likely to cooperate.

What can we learn from this comparison?

• We best limit our reminders to deliberately misbehaving students. We want students to know we mean what we say. Repeating our reminders suggests that we expect our messages to be disregarded.

• There are reminders that inspire cooperation and those that inspire resistance. Said another way, we can remind students in ways that respect their dignity or in ways that do not, that rather insist on our own needs. The respectful path is almost always more effective.

• It is entirely possible to be strict *and* respectful. We can insist that students behave respectfully in class in a way that is respectful of them. We do well to master ways of doing that.

• One thing that helps us make reminders respectful is to give reasons for our requests (such as, "It's distracting"), so they don't feel arbitrary and students are more likely to cooperate.

• It's difficult to make our reminders respectful when we have lost our emotional balance and begun to feel angry. We then project not care for the well-

Everyone who remembers his own educational experience remembers teachers, not methods and techniques. The teacher is the kingpin of the educational system. He makes and breaks programs.

—Sidney Hook

being of the class as much as we project rejection of the misbehaving student. In the second example above, the teacher's ability to speak with a wink and a smile suggests she maintained her balance. In general, we think better and act more wisely when we deepen and strengthen our personal balance.

 ## Strategy 33-3: Next-Time Message

Purpose: To correct students' behavior without discouraging them.

Description: Saying what behavior we want next time as a way of reminding students what was wrong this time.

Teachers often invite guilt into the room by focusing on what went wrong. Instead, Moorman and Moorman (1989) note that teachers can correct students gracefully by focusing on next time, not this time. For example, "Seth, next time remember to put your paper in the box," or "Kim, next time please ask before you use my pencil."

Next-Time Messages are best delivered matter-of-factly. When we use them, we do not want our tone to communicate "You should know better." We do not want to focus on what is already done. We simply intend to remind students of what would be the ideal behavior for next time. Note, however, that it is wise to avoid using Next-Time Messages when students might interpret their use as a hesitancy to make Authority Statements (Strategy 8-3).

 ## Strategy 33-4: Honest I Statements

Purpose: To communicate honestly without blaming and without generating defensiveness or guilt and to model a valuable interpersonal skill.

Description: Honestly expressing personal needs and feelings, avoiding comments about what "you" did or "you" failed to do.

Communication theory teaches us that "I" statements have a very different effect than "you" statements. Compare the following pairs of statements:

"I" Statement: It upsets me to be interrupted. It makes me feel like what I say is unimportant.

"You" Statement: You keep interrupting me! You have no respect for what I say.

"I" Statement: I feel frustrated when I must say the same thing three times!

"You" Statement: I wish you would listen to me! You did not hear me the first two times I explained it.

"I" statements often lead to mutual understanding. "You" statements more likely communicate blame and lead to arguments, resistance, withdrawal, resentment, and retaliation.

"I" statements help students to understand the effect their behaviors are having on others. They help students see the consequences of their acts in very personal terms, terms they can understand clearly.

"I" statements, therefore, are effective in showing students natural consequences of misbehavior. They maximize the likelihood that students will want to cooperate and be supportive. It's smart, then, to become practiced in making such "I" statements when misbehavior shows up.

Here is an example of one of us, Merrill, sharing an Honest I Statement with a group of teachers:

> I used an Honest I Statement with my neighbors the other day. They play music too loudly and too late into the night, and we can hear it. It sometimes makes it hard to sleep. I mentioned it to them last week, just telling them that we were having trouble with the loud music. I asked them if they would mind turning it down. But nothing changed, and I was getting upset.
>
> So I called them and said, "Mr. Smith (not his real name), I am getting very upset over here. When I hear music from your house, my blood pressure zooms up. My family is getting upset with me because I am getting too nervous, and I just wanted you to know how serious a problem that is for me."
>
> That is all I said. It was an Honest I Statement. The neighbor said he'd try to keep the sound lower, but it's too soon to tell. An Honest I Statement does not always solve a conflict between people. But it's a lot easier and safer than fighting or suffering endlessly.

A Lesson for Students

In addition to using "I" statements ourselves, we can teach students to make such statements. Here is how one teacher introduced the idea to her class:

> If a classmate does something that is disturbing to you, you might want to tell the person exactly what it is that is disturbing. Maybe the classmate was not aware of the effect of the behavior. You might say something like, "The tapping on your desk is really annoying to me right now. Maybe you didn't know that."
>
> If you absolutely need them to stop, tell the truth; tell them you need it. Learn to make what I call "Honest I Statements." Say something like, "I really need more quiet to concentrate and do my work."

The teacher explains that an Honest I Statement says how someone really feels or what someone really wants. The focus is on *I*—what *I* feel, what *I* want—not on the other person, not on what *you* are doing or what *you* need to stop doing. She tells the students that "you" statements make people feel criticized and put down. "We don't want that in our classroom," she says.

What is learned in high school, or for that matter anywhere at all, depends far less on what is taught than on what one actually experiences in the place.

—*Edgar Friedenberg*

She expresses her hope that the students will be honest about their needs and will do their best to help people get what they need.

In the long run, we will all get along better and appreciate one another's real needs if we learn to make Honest I Statements. We may not always be able to do what others want, but we can always respect what they say.

The teacher then uses a role-play to illustrate how someone might use an Honest I Statement. Portraying a student, she says, "I might say to a classmate, 'What you are doing is bothering me. It's hard for me to do what I'm trying to do.' That would be an Honest I Statement if it were true—that is, if it was really hard for me to do what I wanted to do." She then continues:

Notice that I put the emphasis on what *I* want or need, not on what the *other* person was doing. I don't want to risk putting others down or to treat them with less than full dignity. Blame often does that. Honest I Statements make it easier for other people to understand our situation without feeling blamed.

The teacher then asks the students to pretend for a minute, to imagine someone is messing up their work. She asks them to write a sentence or two that, first, would be honest and, second, would not so much blame or complain but that would be an "I" statement—that would express the individual's own feelings or wants or needs. "Try it," she says. "Then we'll see if someone will risk reading what he or she wrote. We can then work together, aiming to get all the potential blame out of each statement. Let's practice this a few times."

Expanding Language Awareness

Ginott (1972) talks about a special advantage of using eloquence and variety when making "I" statements. Students' vocabulary is enriched and their emotional awareness is refined when they hear such language as "I am feeling indignant," or "I am chagrined," or "I feel bewildered and confused about what is best to do next." Consider making a list of words that convey emotion, words whose meanings and nuances students would benefit from understanding more fully.

▲ TEACHER COMMENT

I was not sure what to expect, but I thought I'd try teaching my 2nd graders the Honest I Statement way to resolve conflicts. We talked about conflicts in life, and about fighting and war, and laws against hurting others, and even the United Nations. Then I said they themselves have conflicts, and we role-played a situation in which a brother kept changing the TV channel and the sister was getting angry. Instead of hitting or complaining to a parent, the sister, quite coolly, I thought, told the brother how she felt. I asked the students to guess how the brother felt when he heard that. The class concluded that the brother would have felt a lot worse if he had gotten into trouble with his parents. The next day one boy said he used an Honest I Statement when an uncle changed the TV channel while he was watching a program he was allowed to watch. He said it worked! And I think a girl on the playground used it the other day. . . . I'll bet there will be fewer arguments and fights in this group.

—*2nd Grade Teacher*

Then review the list from time to time, so the words are readily available when an opportunity to use one comes up. Possibilities include *guilty, sorrowful, panicky, anguished, remorseful, suspicious, infuriated, depressed, awkward, fearful, anxious, glum, gloomy, ecstatic, irritated, manipulated, conflicted, regretful.*

Strategy 33-5: Conciliation Statement

Purpose: To turn a conflict with another into a win-win discussion.

Description: When in conflict with a student, communicating a desire for mutual understanding and conciliation.

Chick Moorman (2005) suggests that before trying to make a problem with a student smaller, we might try to make ourselves larger. How? In general, by awakening our full respect for the student's dignity and communicating a desire for a mutually respectful outcome. We might say, for example:

- Let's both take a 10-minute time-out.
- How can we both get what we want?
- Let's search for a solution together on this one.
- I'm willing to compromise. Are you?
- Let's negotiate.
- What's your opinion?
- Help me understand your point of view.
- How can we see this in a different way?
- It feels like we're working against each other on this. Let's both remember we're on the same team here.
- I'd like your input on this.

If the situation is not urgent, we might even use two or three such conciliatory statements before calling on another discipline strategy.

Strategy 33-6: Conflict-Resolution Lesson

Purpose: To teach students how to solve problems in a nondestructive, mutually respectful way.

Description: Teaching students how to talk honestly about a conflict and, if the problem remains, how to brainstorm a list of possible solutions.

First say to yourself what you would be; and then do what you have to do.

—*Epictetus*

Conflicts, even if they are quite intense, can often be resolved by a straightforward two-step process. The first step is for the parties to the conflict to make Honest I Statements to one another (Strategy 33-4). Sometimes an impartial person is needed to allow such an exchange to flow smoothly. The second step, to be used if the first step has not dissolved the conflict, is for the parties to the conflict to brainstorm a list of possible resolutions, writing their list, and then going back over it, seeking agreement on which option to choose.

Imagine the following lesson, outlined by an elementary teacher, whose intention was to teach the first step to her class:

> Let's say someone kept messing up your games, or kept teasing you, or otherwise made you angry. What could you do? You could scream or hit or cry. But there is a more intelligent way to react.
>
> Let's say a girl, we'll call her Jaime, keeps pushing to get to the front of the line. And let's say you get very angry at that. You might go up to her and say, "Jaime, I don't like it when you don't wait your turn. It makes me mad." You might say this after Jaime pushed into line. Or if it was not a good time to talk, you could wait until later and then tell her how you feel.
>
> You do not have to do more than that. Just tell Jaime the truth about how you feel. Maybe Jaime did not know she was causing such bad feelings. Maybe she would be willing to cooperate better if she knew that people were getting upset.
>
> That is a healthy way to settle conflicts. What you do is make what we call Honest I Statements. We simply tell the person honestly how we feel, such as "I feel furious." The idea is not to hurt the other person or make him or her angry, but just to get the feelings out, so the other person knows, and so we do not have to keep bad feelings locked inside us.
>
> Let's try a little role-playing. Let's say someone took your pen and did not give it back, and that made you angry. Who would be willing to play a person like that? Thank you, Nikki. Who would be willing to act out the person who took the pen? OK, Paula, you stand there. Now imagine she has your pen, Nikki. Go over to her and simply tell her the truth about how you are feeling.

A role-play like this might require several trials. A follow-up role-play another day might also be wise. Especially valuable are follow-up questions: "Who can remember what I said last week about a healthy way to handle conflicts when they come up?" or "Who can tell me what I mean by an Honest I Statement?" or "Has anyone used an Honest I Statement in the last few days? Are you willing to tell us about it?"

The second part of this strategy focuses on answering this question: What if you make an Honest I Statement and it doesn't work? Then it's time to call on the second step. Here is a middle school teacher explaining this second step to his class:

> Sometimes you will find that making an Honest I Statement does not solve the problem. Perhaps, for example, you told two neighbors that their loud bickering

The greatest evil that can befall man is that he should come to think evil of himself.

—Goethe

makes it difficult for you to concentrate, but they continued. What might you do next? It is usually best for all involved to work together to brainstorm a list of possible solutions. You might begin by making another Honest I Statement, such as, "Your talking is still bothering me," followed by something like, "I'd really like to find a solution that will make us all happy. What options might exist for this situation?" Then take turns hearing each other's suggestions, writing them down so you can go back to them later. When you've got a list of ideas, talk honestly about which one or ones you'd be willing to try. See if you can agree on a solution and give it a shot. You may want to have one of our Peer Mediators [Strategy 33-8] help you with that process.

It's not always easy for students to follow that sequence, and, therefore, we recommend having students role-play one or two examples of it.

Note that we can use this two-step process with students who continue to cause us problems. The process would have us starting by making Honest I Statements, such as, "Sam, your sarcasm is very distressing to me. I can't take it any longer and I want you to be aware of that." If the problem persisted, the second step would have us sitting with the student and brainstorming together a list of as many ideas as we can come up with for dealing with the situation. After the brainstorm, we might say something like, "Well, of all the items we listed, I can go along with numbers 2 and 5. How about you?" If this process was carried out without rancor or blame, but rather in the spirit of two dignified human beings seeking a way out of a conflict, there is, in our experience, a good chance for the problem to ease.

Unfortunately, some students, especially those who seem to deliberately and willfully create conflicts, may soon create a new problem for us. And for that we may need to go beyond this two-step conflict resolution process. The next chapter, Handling Serious and Chronic Misbehavior, suggests some possibilities for doing so.

▲ TEACHER COMMENT

We began using our detention room for lessons on good living. Last week I had the best lesson in a long time. I taught students how to make Honest I Statements when they were in conflict with each other and how to negotiate differences when honest talk alone doesn't solve the problem. I used a three-step model: (1) Person-to-Person Dialogue on the conflict. (2) If the conflict remains, write a brainstormed list of possible resolutions. (3) Go back over the list and try to agree on resolutions to try. As we talked about this and role-played this model, it was clear to me that no one in the room (there were about 15) had any idea conflicts among themselves could be resolved in nondestructive ways.

—*Lauren O'Leary, High School Counselor*

⚙▶ Strategy 33-7: Behavior Checklist

Purpose: To correct misbehavior in a way that inspires growth in self-management.

Description: Working with a problem student to create a behavior checklist the student can then use to monitor behavior and take responsibility for improving.

Some students have difficulty maintaining focus, following classroom procedures, or controlling an impulse to call out or talk to neighbors. Sixth grade teacher Julia Symer crafted a strategy that focuses on building self-responsibility in such students. The first step is to sit with the student and brainstorm:

> I'm going to show you how to make it much easier for you to succeed in this classroom. To start, let's ask, "What could you say to yourself that would show you succeeded?" For example, you might say
>
> - I put away my coat and book bag.
> - I placed my homework in the homework bin.
> - I put my lunch clip on the appropriate side of the lunch tally.
> - I sat down and began the Immediate Work Assignment.
> - When I noticed I was talking too much, I stopped myself.
>
> What are some others? Let's brainstorm and make a list of lots of behaviors that would show you were doing a good job.

The second step is to narrow down the list so we and the student agree it shows a reasonable target. We might then say, "I'd like you to keep a copy of the list and tomorrow check off every item you can. If you slipped up on an item, just don't check it. At the end of the day, I'll ask you to show me your list so I can see how many checks you made. That will show how well you succeeded. OK?"

Then, when the student shows us a list, Symer suggests we offer honest, positive feedback, such as the following:

> You were able to make only one check today but you remembered the checklist and I very much appreciate that. A good start, Shawn. Please keep the list tomorrow and we'll see if you can give yourself even more checks.

> I'm impressed how well you did on the first day, Angie. Please do this again tomorrow. I'd like to see if you can do as well or, maybe, even better!

Symer writes:

> I find this strategy works best when I give lots of positive feedback during the first few times the student shows me a checklist. I do this by making many Honest I Appreciates. I then gradually reduce the amount of such praise, to help the student become self-responsible. Soon enough, sometimes in days, sometimes in weeks, students indicate they no longer need a checklist, so we drop it. Yet I still take the time to occasionally voice Honest I Appreciates for mature behavior. But then, for many students, even that becomes unnecessary. Good self-management becomes a habit, and, as efficient life habits serve us adults, I let efficiency be its own reward. In general, I find the strategy solves many of my behavior problems. Furthermore, it does so in a way that both respects the dignity of students and grows healthy intrinsic motivations.

Discipline is not a simple device for securing superficial peace in the classroom; it is the morality of the classroom as a small society.

—Emile Durkheim

Strategy 33-8: Peer Mediators

Purpose: To give students a role in managing conflicts.

Description: Training small groups of students in the conflict-resolution model and then asking them to help handle problem situations.

The Conflict-Resolution Lesson (Strategy 33-6) teaches all students two skills for resolving their conflicts: making Honest I Statements and brainstorming possible solutions. Yet when actual conflicts arise and emotions run high, students often revert to bickering, name calling, tattling, sometimes even physical aggression. Whole-Class Problem Solving (Strategy 8-9) is one option in such situations. Even more helpful is turning to trained peer mediators. Here is how to implement this strategy.

- *Choose mediators.* We can use any of a number of options for choosing mediators. We can give all students a turn at being a mediator. We can ask for volunteers and have the rest of the class elect the current mediators from the volunteer pool. Or we could appoint mediators ourselves, trying to include students who are struggling academically or socially, for they are often the ones most in need of positive experiences in the class community.

- *Train mediators.* Using the Conflict-Resolution Lesson as a guide and using a lot of role-playing, we train the mediators to hear all sides to a conflict, to elicit Honest I Statements, and, when necessary, to lead a brainstorming session to find possible solutions, seeking agreement from all involved. We or another faculty member or an adult volunteer might provide that training, or expert students could do it.

- *Activate peer mediation.* We might then say to students something like this:

My aim is for you to learn to solve your own problems. But while you are learning, you might need help. That is what our peer mediators are for. Try your best to handle whatever comes up. But if you feel yourself getting too emotional or losing control, know that our mediators are here for us. If, for example, you are arguing with a classmate, you might say, "Fighting is not helping us solve this. Let's get a mediator." Then calmly ask one of our mediators for help. You might even ask a mediator for help in solving a conflict with me or another teacher.

For more information on peer mediation, see Lam (1989) and Smith and Daunic (2002).

I now perceive one immense omission in my psychology—the deepest principle of human nature is the craving to be appreciated.

—*William James*

Strategy 33-9: Visitor's Chair

Purpose: To keep disruptive students near the teacher until they can manage their own behavior.

Description: Without communicating any displeasure, asking a student to sit in a chair near us as "time out."

When young students are working individually, one will sometimes talk too loudly or tease others or otherwise be disruptive. Often this problem will soon enough disappear. However, if the incident is seriously disruptive or if it continues, the use of the Visitor's Chair might be in order (Pilon, 1996). The following example illustrates how this strategy can be implemented.

The teacher introduces the procedure to her students by acknowledging the possibility that sometimes people lose their composure and somehow disturb others. She asks the students to practice "intelligent self-management" when they notice themselves doing something like that by stopping their own disruptive behavior. "No one is perfect," she says. "We all have impulses that can prompt us to disturb others. Be aware when that happens to you and stop it."

She continues: "If someone near you is disturbing others, and you see that the person is not aware enough, or not self-managing enough to stop it, hold out a hand like this to send them a signal that it's time to settle down." She demonstrates holding her hand flat, parallel to the floor. "That might help them become aware and settle down," she says. "Let's help each other that way."

The teacher then explains how the Visitor's Chair can be used:

> If I notice you are not settling down right away, I may go over to you, or ask one of our other class members to go to you, and say quietly, "Visitor's Chair." Your job then is to come sit in a chair close to me, wherever I happen to be in the room, until you settle down, at which time you may go back to your place.

She suggests that a student in the Visitor's Chair may want to do a Clock Focus (Strategy 8-5), or, if she's working with a group, she may invite the student to work along with the group. "In any case," she says, "you may go back to your own place whenever you decide you can be properly self-managing again. You do not need to ask my permission. All of you are intelligent enough to know when you can do that."

She concludes by reminding the students that everyone sometimes behaves in ways that disrupt others:

It may well be that the greatest tragedy of this period of social transition is not the glaring noisiness of the so-called bad people, but the appalling silence of the so-called good people.

—*Martin Luther King Jr.*

We can all lose self-control at times. Me too. Does that mean I'm a bad person? No, just that I'm a human being. We can all lose self-control and make mistakes. That is what humans do.

Note that when we want someone to sit in a Visitor's Chair, we should not call out the student's name, as in "Charles! Visitor's Chair, please." Such a public announcement often grates on pride, denting dignity and inviting resentment. We should either go over and speak to the student quietly or send a messenger over with instructions such as "Speak very quietly to Charles and ask him to sit in this Visitor's Chair."

If Charles is not being dangerous to himself or others and is not being seriously disruptive to other students, we may prefer to use a Silent Response to Misbehavior (Strategy 33-12). Perhaps we are more annoyed by Charles than are other students. And perhaps we and the students both would do well to learn to keep working when the surroundings are not perfectly calm and peaceful.

Strategy 33-10: Waiting Place

Purpose: To provide a place for a student to be alone briefly while waiting for a private conversation with the teacher.

Description: Sending a student to a place where he or she can conveniently wait until we have time to talk with the student.

Some classrooms of younger students benefit from having a special spot designated as a Waiting Place. Consider the following:

> Girls and boys, sometimes I find it useful to speak to a student privately, to tell about a prize earned or to give some personal advice. And sometimes I'll be too busy to do it right away. I'll want you to wait for me, so we can talk privately when I have a moment. For our waiting place, I'd like to use that area, right near the door. Let's call that our Waiting Place. To demonstrate, Victor, will you please go to the Waiting Place? A little farther back, Victor. Yes, that is the spot. From now on, whenever I ask you to go to the Waiting Place, please stand over there and wait for me. You might do a Clock Focus [Strategy 8-5] while waiting. I'll try not to be too long. Then we can talk privately before you go back to your work.

Soon after introducing this strategy, it might be advisable to ask a student to wait in the designated Waiting Place. It's also advisable to have such initial uses not involve disciplinary events. We might use the Waiting Place, for example, when we want to send a message home with one child or to give a private compliment to someone.

Subsequently we can use the procedure whenever we want a student to disengage briefly from his activities while we are busy elsewhere. Or we might use it to give a student time to settle restless energies. Or we can use it as a place for a student to wait until we can conveniently offer an Authority Statement, a Calm Reminder, a Next-Time Message, or an Apology (Strategies 8-3, 33-2, 33-3, and 33-13). It can also serve as a place for a student to wait safely when we have made a Silent Response to Misbehavior (Strategy 33-12) and feel the need to do more but, at the moment, are unsure what is best. For older students, teachers report similar success in sending a student to a colleague's room, where they are to sit in the back and, perhaps, write about the incident.

Strategy 33-11: Redirecting Student Energy

Purpose: To dissolve misbehavior without generating negativity.
Description: Turning the attention of a misbehaving student to something not disturbing.

Jack keeps tapping his pencil, making loud noises. To use a nonverbal Authority Statement (Strategy 8-3) as a signal, we might walk over to Jack while continuing the lesson and gently touch the arm holding the pencil. If that does not stop the noise, we might take the pencil from him, perhaps smiling warmly because we know he can be hyperactive and must struggle to control himself, and say, "Take your pencil from my desk later, when you feel more settled."

Or we might try to get Jack more involved in the lesson, perhaps by asking him a question. Or perhaps we could ask Jack to help emphasize a key point: "Jack, say to the whole class clearly—1 percent is always equal to one-hundredth." In other words, we do not focus on what is wrong. We avoid calling attention to misbehavior. Rather, we use creativity to redirect the student's energy to something less disturbing, letting the misbehavior evaporate. Consider the following examples:

• *John keeps giving his opinions to a neighbor during class discussion.* "John, please write a note of any comments you have about this issue. Later I'd like you to share them with me."

• *A student is strolling about, distracting other students during quiet reading time.* "Bob, please fetch me that dictionary from the back before you sit down to read."

• *Two students are arguing too heatedly.* "You two seem excited. Let's try some mental arithmetic. Val, guess which is larger, a third of a hundred or two dozen. Tess, do you agree? Here's one for you: What is 5 times 13? Take a moment and work it out on paper, both of you, and see if you are correct."

The intent here is to keep behavior in reasonable bounds without generating negativity. Indeed, redirecting student attention in this way often communicates our respect for them. We appreciate that although they might not yet be able to manage themselves well enough, they need not lose dignity because of it. Strategy 33-2, Calm Reminder, has a similar effect.

Strategy 33-12: Silent Response to Misbehavior

Purpose: To give students room to solve their own problem and to avoid a hasty, inappropriate response.

Description: Mentally noting misbehavior and leaving until later the consideration of what, if anything, to do about it.

A student fails to bring in the required notebook, chats with a neighbor while we are talking, neglects to do work assigned, or makes a smart-aleck remark. Sometimes the best response is a Silent Response, a response to oneself that says, "There is a problem here. Let me note it now and see, later, if I want to do something about it and, if so, what." Sometimes such later attention is, in fact, needed. But sometimes it is not. The problem may disappear on its own. That outcome is especially likely if the class climate is lively, kind, and supportive and students have a growing respect for the teacher, who, by responding silently to misbehavior, demonstrates a self-confidence that itself inspires a positive response. In such cases it makes no sense to use our limited energies to respond immediately to every incident, especially when the problem is in no way dangerous and might well solve itself or soon be solved by student-initiated self-responsibility.

▲ **TEACHER COMMENT**

I like the Silent Response to Misbehavior. I use it all the time. If I had to react to each and every little disturbance, both the students and I would go crazy. My first reaction is to ignore a problem. If I reacted every time someone disturbed the class, I bet some students would only mess up more frequently and get pleasure out of that.

—*Stuart Rabinowitz, Junior High School Teacher*

Other Reasons to Use a Silent Response

In addition to the possibility that a problem will disappear on its own, why else should we respond only by making a mental note to ourselves? Some reasons to consider:

• The Silent Response models an adult with personal security, someone who is not worried that one incident will destroy the group climate. It can be reassuring and educational for students to witness such a leader.

• The Silent Response communicates a confidence and trust in students. It demonstrates our confidence that they can and will learn to self-manage their behavior, that they do not need to be babied, told what is right and what is wrong at every turn. The Silent Response strengthens the power of positive expectations.

• The Silent Response seems to strengthen our own personal security and sense of community, perhaps partly because as we practice going with the flow, not trying to control every event around us, we learn how to live more peacefully ourselves.

• The Silent Response gives us the space to choose a response that will produce the best long-term effect. It helps us avoid a more impulsive response, one more likely to aggravate our problems. It is the wisdom of counting to 10 before acting.

• An immediate response to a student who has just misbehaved calls attention to the misbehavior. Often it's preferable to call attention to the behavior we *want* in the classroom, to accent the *positive,* rather than add attention to those acts we'd prefer to disappear. This is especially important in terms of our concern for student dignity and growth in self-management. When we call attention to an act of misbehavior by responding to it, a student with questionable self-worth often experiences a further weakening of self-worth, concluding that "I was bad," not "The act was bad."

Further Considerations

• *Demonstrating security, not timidity.* Teachers who respond to misbehavior by only making a mental note, not doing anything overtly, are not timid. They are secure—or at least strong and wise enough to act as if they feel secure until that security does emerge.

• *When silence is inappropriate.* A Silent Response is not appropriate when danger is involved—for example, a book is tossed across the room; a fight breaks out between students; a student waves a knife. Physical danger calls for direct, forceful action.

• *Silence now, action later.* Withholding an immediate overt response does not equal no response at any time. We might note a behavior problem and then,

▲ TEACHER COMMENT

Ginger was repeatedly late to my class, but only a few seconds late. At first it bothered me. Then I sensed Ginger was playing an independence game, that her style was not to go along with authority figures. She was bright enough so her lateness was not serious, and it was not prompting others to be late, so I decided to ignore the issue and let her live her life in her way. Interestingly, when her lateness stopped bothering me, Ginger stopped being late. Odd, eh?

—Benj Ho, High School Teacher

the next day, teach or reteach a lesson to some or all of the class. For example, if we notice too much aimless walking about, we can role-play walking in class with efficient purpose and dignity, without criticizing any students for prior behaviors.

- *Reflection and learning.* In some cases we may conclude that there is nothing we can do to prevent the misbehavior. We thereby accept reality. And we might do well to reflect on what we can learn from it, asking questions like, Could that misbehaving student be providing me with an opportunity to learn more about treating people who displease me with dignity? About remaining calm in the midst of chaos? About finding new ways to run my classroom? Great lessons, after all, often come from experiences initially judged unfortunate.

- *Avoiding excessive intervention.* In general, minimal interventions are preferable. It's important to give students enough space to practice and eventually master the art of self-discipline. A Silent Response, indeed, can actually make things a lot easier for us. No action is often the best action.

Strategy 33-13: Apologizing

Purpose: To model behavior that is healthy for mature relationships.
Description: Honestly apologizing to a student, modeling respectful social behavior.

It's strange how often apologies are misused. Some people feel they should never admit being wrong. Others feel they are always admitting they are wrong. Yet an apology can be healthful for all concerned if it is clean, caring, and honest—especially if it comes from a teacher. "I'm sorry," we might say, "that I nagged so much yesterday about your lab reports. I wish I hadn't done that. Now for today's lesson . . ." Just a simple statement, without elaboration or discussion, can work wonders.

We might also encourage students to learn the art of apologizing, perhaps saying something like this:

> Class, I'd like to see us apologize when we make a mistake and hurt someone. As you will probably notice, I will apologize from time to time. Sometimes I get too impatient, or too irritable, or too tired, or too something. I might snap at someone or, sometimes, snap at the whole class. I may not realize that until later. In those cases, I like to come back and say I'm sorry once I get better perspective.
>
> I might say to someone, for example, "I'm sorry I got so angry and talked so irritably yesterday. No one deserves such treatment. I hope I didn't hurt your feelings. I don't want to hurt you or anybody else. It's just that sometimes I am unable to do better. I'm sorry if I hurt you." You, too, might apologize in class sometimes.

I don't know who my grandfather was; I am much more concerned to know what his grandson will be.

—Abraham Lincoln

▲ TEACHER COMMENT

Nowadays I go out of my way to apologize to my little tikes. Some of them only know scolding and, too often, beatings. I doubt if some of them ever in their whole lives heard an apology from an adult. It seems to be catching. Little Timmy the other day got angry and blasted some blocks that messed up others. Another boy was ready to hit back, but Timmy said, "I'm sorry I did that," and immediately all seemed to have been forgotten.

—Tanya Torrez, Preschool Teacher

It clears the air. It often dissolves guilt. It helps keep a group running smoothly. Usually it makes us all feel a bit closer.

To give us a bit of practice now, imagine you have made a mistake and acted in a way that was not your best self. Maybe start by imagining what you could say or do that might be hurtful to someone. Then write possible words you might say, maybe the next day, to that person. After a few moments, I'll ask you to share your ideas with a partner. Maybe someone would be willing to role-play such talk for us all. Let's see what we can learn about phrasing apologies.

Such a lesson may be unnecessary. Simply modeling the behavior—that is, simply apologizing in the classroom when you do something you regret—often leads students to pick up on the strategy and begin to apologize to each other more often. Such behavior can contribute substantially to a healthy class community.

Strategy 33-14: Mindset Switch

Purpose: To interact with students constructively, positively.
Description: Noticing when we have slipped into a negative mindset and switching out of it.

Leon avoids speaking up in Ms. B's classroom. He is certain he can never answer questions as well as other students. Early on Ms. B noticed him averting his eyes whenever she looked his way. He seemed to hunch over as if trying to disappear. Not wanting to embarrass Leon, she now hardly ever calls on him.

Things are different in Ms. C's classroom. From the outset Ms. C expected Leon and everyone else to participate fully, and Leon knew it, so he was ready to do the best he could when called on. After all, he didn't want to be surprised when his name was called—and he knew it would be. Now he doesn't even try to disappear in that room. He stays ready to speak if necessary, which is turning out to be not nearly as painful as he thought it would be.

Polly is not at all like Leon. She loves to speak up. In fact, she seems to demand attention, often blurting out questions and complaints and even more often chatting with her neighbors. Ms. B expects Polly to be disruptive and is wary of her. Polly has noticed this wariness, and not wanting to be surprised by a reprimand when she least expects it, she seems to purposely provoke one by continuing to talk until the teacher reacts. Then Polly, looking hurt, sulks and pays no attention to lessons for some time.

Things are different in Ms. C's classroom. Like Ms. B, Ms. C also has noticed Polly's habits of talking, but somehow she trusts that Polly will not persist, that she will control herself for the good of the class. Also, Ms. C does not often reprimand Polly for being disruptive, and when she does caution her to hold down her talking, she speaks to Polly rather mildly, more as a reminder than a scolding. As a result, Polly is not worried about being surprised by a reprimand and so feels no need to provoke one, as she does in Ms. B's room. Moreover, Polly senses Ms. C's trust in her ability to learn self-control and, not wanting to let her down, does much better at controlling her talking.

The point is simple: We get what we expect. Ms. B expects Leon to be a nonparticipant and he is, even though he speaks up quite readily in Ms. C's class. Ms. B expects Polly to keep disrupting the class and she does, even as she is controlling herself in Ms. C's classroom. As noted elsewhere, expectations make a difference. If, then, we are facing too many discipline problems, we might check our mindset. Have we learned to expect these problems? If so, we would be wise to practice switching our mindset. Once we develop the knack, it's not difficult. As Michelangelo reminds us, "The great danger for most of us is not that our aim is too high and we miss it, but that it is too low and we reach it." Consider the following pairs of expectations:

Unproductive: The student is bad. I expect bad behavior.
Productive: The student is troubled and would like to do better. With proper support, he will learn to do so.

Unproductive: The student is hopeless. There is nothing constructive I can do.
Productive: Right now I don't know what to do. But I can keep modeling someone who cares, which might reassure him that he is not rejected by everyone. Maybe later I'll discover something more I can do.

Unproductive: She's driving me crazy. I feel as if she's attacking me personally.
Productive: She is just being the way she is. Why, I wonder, can I not deal with it without being so upset?

Unproductive: He shouldn't be that way and behave that way.
Productive: No use my resenting him for being who he is, living his own life. Until he changes, I will simply deal with it and keep expecting him to do better.

I'm glad I've got delusions of grandeur. It makes me feel a lot better about myself.

—*Jane Wagner*

Unproductive: I'm worried she will keep causing me problems.
Productive: I don't want to exude worry. I want to exude trust and confidence in her ability to be happy, so I'll imagine her being happy.

Unproductive: He deserves a stiff punishment. He can't keep getting away with it.
Productive: He needs a striking wake-up call, so he knows how serious this is. What will best serve that purpose?

Unproductive: She's purposefully disruptive.
Productive: Her disruptive impulses are strong. How can I better bring out and strengthen her constructive impulses?

Unproductive: I expect to have trouble with him again.
Productive: I expect him to behave very well today.

Finally, consider this vignette from Marzano (2003), illustrating one teacher's technique for changing her mindset:

> Ms. Young's mantra is "Don't hold a grudge." She desperately needs this mantra when she finds herself spending an entire evening obsessing about the behavior of a student that day. Before she goes to bed, she also makes a commitment to herself that she will say three positive things to the student during the following two days. "Even if all I can find to compliment is the color of the student's clothes, I always find three things. The act of saying the positive things aloud changes my perceptions of that student, even if my positive statements are met with a scowl. By the time I have said the third positive thing, I almost always feel the tensions in my shoulders ease, and I feel ready to develop a different relationship with the student. To paraphrase C. S. Lewis, I say the positive things not because it changes the students, but because it changes me." (pp. 73–74)

Strategy 33-15: Ask for Help

Purpose: To broaden the base of a teacher's options and supports.
Description: Sharing problems with other professionals, requesting suggestions and assistance.

Trained psychologists have difficulty knowing what to do with some of the students in schools today. It is unfair to ask teachers with all their other responsibilities to be more self-sufficient. To fulfill their management responsibilities most wisely, we recommend that teachers not hesitate to ask for help. More specifically, consider picking two or three other people you could approach with a tricky problem, and then, when such a problem arises, ask for their ideas or their

Until you can have a heart for your own failings and suffering, you won't do very well having a heart for other people's. Yet it requires courage to hear yourself in pain, and to observe your pain with respect, understanding, caring, and fairness.

—*Tom Rusk*

reactions to your ideas. Teacher support teams provide one way to continually advance our professional development. The more consultation we seek and the sooner it is initiated, the better the situation is likely to be for us and our students. Know, too, that some students will best be handled by someone other than ourselves. Let's be willing to acknowledge that truth.

34 Handling Serious and Chronic Misbehavior

When the discipline strategies of Chapter 33 are combined with satisfying instruction and used by a confident, caring professional, most students manage to control themselves. But not all. Additional strategies may well be necessary. This chapter contains several effective strategies, all of which are consistent with our inspiring approach to motivation. That is, all help us manage problem students in a way likely to elicit their positive, constructive motivations, not fuel their negative impulses, their angers or resentments.

Some of this chapter's strategies have us forcefully confronting students. For some students, such confrontation may be necessary. Some students seem to require the shock of a confrontation to break free of unproductive habits. A serious or chronic misbehavior problem, then, may be a blessing in disguise for us. It may offer us the opportunity to help a youngster turn a life around. In any case, it is advisable to be prepared to handle serious problems. It's part of the job. The strategies of this chapter help prepare us for that task. Consider at least the first four, each of which is marked with an arrow; our field tests indicate they deserve first attention.

Strategy 34-1: Person-to-Person Dialogue

Purpose: To advance mutual understanding between the teacher and student.
Description: Talking with a student privately, relying mostly on "I" statements.

Carla has been disrupting the class by persistently talking to her neighbors. Yesterday the teacher tried making an Authority Statement (Strategy 8-3): "I need you to be quiet during lessons. I find your talk to nearby students quite distracting."

No luck. Today Carla is continuing her distractions—if anything, more defiantly. The teacher asks Carla to talk with her in the hall while the rest of the students are busy with independent work.

The teacher begins by saying, "Carla, I must admit your talking is getting to me. I find it very hard to take." She pauses, and Carla, remaining silent, looks down. "I'm not sure what to do, Carla," the teacher continues. "The situation is beginning to feel serious to me." Carla then speaks up: "Well, stop picking on me." Speaking gently, the teacher acknowledges Carla's comment. "It seems like I'm picking on you." "Sure," Carla replies. "You never look at other people in the class who are also talking. Others talk just as much as I do." Wanting to communicate that she fully understood what Carla said, the teacher repeats Carla's comment: "The other students seem to talk as much as you." Carla nods. "Yeah. Right." She seems to have nothing more to say.

"I don't want to pick on you, or anyone else. I want to be fair to all my students," the teacher says. "Then stop picking on me!" Carla blurts out. "I'll try to watch that, Carla," the teacher says. "I'm sorry if I did that. I wonder, though, if that will solve my problem. I mean, I'm still worried that you will talk to your neighbors during the lessons, distracting me and other students." The teacher pauses, not wanting to make this a lecture, and Carla fills in the gap with a repetition of her point: "Well, then, stop picking on me." "Yes," the teacher says, "I'll make sure I don't do that." Carla is clearly ready for the conversation to end. "Can I go now?" she asks. With some uncertainty, the teacher replies, "Maybe we've talked enough for now. I guess you understand that it bothers me a lot when you talk to neighbors during lessons. And I understand that you don't want to be picked on. So let's leave it at that."

This conversation may not have accomplished much. But it probably did nothing to make the situation worse, as it might have if Carla had sensed dislike or rejection from the teacher. And it's possible that the respect the teacher demonstrated for Carla will impress Carla enough to make her feel more cooperative, more willing to curb her distracting talk in the future. In fact, such dialogues often do have such an effect. Experience shows that they sometimes resolve quite serious problems.

It is not always easy to engage a disruptive student in such conversations, however. The chief danger is that the student will feel blamed and, as a result, will become defensive and resistant to future efforts. To avoid that problem, it's wise not to assume the conversation will solve the problem. Instead, we recommend choosing a more modest target: an increase in mutual understanding. Aim to talk

> Men are men before they are lawyers or physicians or manufacturers. And if you make them capable and sensible men, they will make themselves capable and sensible lawyers and physicians.
>
> —*John Stuart Mill*

in a way that communicates that you are not blaming. You are merely talking about a conflict. In the example, the conflict is between Carla's desire to act as she does and the teacher's need for those actions to stop. A Person-to-Person Dialogue can bring such conflicts more clearly to the surface in a way that encourages students to change.

We do not recommend persisting if a conversation gets bogged down or keeps getting off track. In such cases you might simply disengage with a comment such as "I don't know where to go from here. I'd like to put this conversation on the shelf for now and think about it. Maybe we should talk together later." If the situation poses a danger, of course, "later" might occur very soon, or something other than talking might be called for.

Guidelines for a Person-to-Person Dialogue

A Person-to-Person Dialogue is a private talk between teacher and student. It is meant to be free of blame, rancor, or argumentation. Its aim is mutual understanding between two dignified human beings, for the moment leaving in the background the fact that one is a student and one a teacher. In the dialogue, the teacher is more an ordinary person than an authority figure. Here are four guidelines for the dialogue:

- *Make Honest I Statements (Strategy 33-4) about your thoughts and feelings.* Avoid focusing on what the student does or does not do. Aim to be truthful. Risk communicating your ideals, anxieties, frustrations, needs, fears. Help the student see that you, too, are a feeling human being.
- *Defer to the student.* Pause often. When the student wants to speak, stop and allow it. Don't make mini-lectures. Help the student see that you want to understand.
- *Every time the student speaks, show that you heard.* Perhaps pause and take time to digest the student's words. Summarize what the student said. Repeat a few of the words the student used. Or just show attentiveness by nodding.
- *Avoid asking questions.* Questions such as "Why did you do that?" or "Did you think I changed the class rules?" often make students feel controlled, manipulated, defensive. Questions in disciplinary situations tend to make students feel inferior and accused. You might avoid such a reaction by turning questions into statements: "I'd like to know if you had a reason for what you did." "I wonder if you thought I don't care about the class rules."

Sometimes your best move is blocked by your own checkers.

—Cynthia Copeland Lewis

Strategy 34-2: Self-Management Contract

Purpose: To solve a discipline problem in a way that develops individual self-responsibility.

Description: Engaging a misbehaving student in a Person-to-Person Dialogue, then brainstorming a written list of possible next steps, ending with a written agreement on exactly what is to be done next.

The Self-Management Contract is similar to what some people call "contingency management" or "contingency contracting." There are three steps to the process, which begins with a step similar to the Person-to-Person Dialogue (Strategy 34-1).

Three Steps in the Self-Management Contract Process

Step 1: The teacher makes an Honest I Statement of feelings, thoughts, or needs.

- Risk being as truthful as possible.
- Every time the student speaks, listen and show that you heard.
- Avoid asking questions. If necessary, say what you need.

Step 2: The teacher writes down a brainstorm list of possible next-step actions to help the student improve self-control.

- Use paper or the board to list the first option mentioned and every one thereafter.
- Avoid judging any idea, yours or the student's.
- Seek more than three options, even if some are unrealistic.

Step 3: The teacher and student seek agreement on a specific action plan.

- Start by saying which ideas you might accept. Mark them on the list.
- Ask the student which ideas he or she might accept. Mark them on the list.
- Seek the best option on which you both can agree.

A Classroom Example

In this example, the teacher is implementing Step 1 in the Self-Management Contract strategy: *The teacher makes an Honest I Statement of feelings, thoughts, or needs.*

Marco, I asked you to talk with me because your negativity in class is really getting to me. I see you continually making noise and moving around and generally bothering the people around you. It is certainly distracting to me. I get the feeling you don't care to listen to my lessons. Today I even sensed—and I may be wrong—that you enjoy disturbing my lessons, that you get pleasure out of it. Sometimes I even feel as if I'm being teased. That makes me very uncomfortable. And I'm frustrated about what to do. I wonder if you can tell me anything about this.

Sometimes Step 1 is all that is necessary to resolve the problem. The key is to be honest and to show the student that we, too, are persons with feelings and needs. Often a student will respond to such an honest statement more or less apologetically and, thereafter, behave more or less satisfactorily.

But not always. Here is how the discussion with Marco might proceed if Step 1 was not sufficient.

Marco: It's not always my fault. Jan does the same thing and you don't notice him!

Teacher: I see. I understand, Marco. It seems like I'm ignoring Jan. But I want to talk about my concerns with your self-management now. I wonder if you would be willing to practice better self-control.

Marco: I'm not that bad. What do you want me to do, anyway?

Teacher: Well, I guess the main thing that bothers me is the way you move about and distract me and, I suspect, others during a lesson. I really need you to practice controlling that better.

Marco: I'm just kinda restless. I like to move. Jan does the same thing and others, too, and you never pick on them.

Teacher: Perhaps. But I wonder if you would be willing to consider making a plan to control yourself better.

Marco: What do you mean?

Teacher: Well, let's brainstorm a minute. Let's list some things you might do that could help you better handle your restlessness during lessons. Let's just imagine wildly and list some ideas for now. Later we can go back and see if any of the ideas are worth a try. For example, you might put a reminder sign on your desk, maybe one that says "Relax." I'll write that on this paper as Number 1. [Teacher writes "*1. Reminder sign on desk.*"] Or maybe you could ask a neighbor to signal you every time you get restless and don't notice it yourself, so you could pull yourself together and settle down. I'll list that as Number 2. [Teacher writes "*2. Ask neighbor to remind me.*"] Any ideas you can think of?

Marco: Nah. Jan needs to be here too, you know.

Teacher: I might have to talk to Jan sometime; but now, let me think. For three, you could talk this issue over with a friend, tell a friend how I said that behavior was bothering me. See if that turns up any good ideas. I'll write here, "*3. Talk it over with friend.*" Any other possibilities come to mind?

Marco: Nah. I guess I could walk around some. That might help.

Teacher: That's an idea. [Teacher writes "*4. Walk around.*" Long pause.] How about asking one of your parents to help us with this problem?

Marco:	No way. I'd probably get killed if you called my mother.
Teacher:	OK, that doesn't sound like it would help us, but because we want to list all our ideas I'll write it down. [Teacher writes "*5. Talk with parents.*" Pause.] I could perhaps make up a special signal for you when I need you to settle down, like touch my left ear.
Marco:	Nah. I don't want any special signals. Jan and some others need that too, you know.
Teacher:	OK. But now we're just brainstorming, and we want to write down all the ideas we can think up. Later we can see if we both agree that some are worth trying. Let me write that so I don't forget it: *6. Special signal to settle down.*
Marco:	I could quit this class.
Teacher:	That's another idea. [Teacher writes "*7. Quit this class.*"] Any other ideas?
Marco:	Nah.
Teacher:	I have one more. You could use a Self-Report Card. That helped other students control themselves and it could help you. What you do is, every 10 minutes or so, you take out the card and rate how you did for the last 10 minutes. Give yourself an *A+* if you controlled every impulse to act out, an *F* if you failed completely, and a grade in between if your self-control was in between. You could even do it more often if you think that would be better for you. Then you show me the card before you leave. I may even give you a high-five! The Self-Report Card is a good way to stay aware when you're trying to change a habit. So let me add that to our list of possibilities as Number 8. Do you have any more ideas?
Marco:	Nah.

This dialogue illustrates Step 2 of the strategy: *The teacher writes down a brainstormed list of possible next-step actions to help the student improve self-control*. All ideas are to be accepted. And—this is critical—all ideas must be written on a piece of paper, the board, any convenient place. Brainstorming does not work well if all options are not recorded.

In the process, it is important to acknowledge all student comments. We might paraphrase student comments or say that we understand, much like the teacher did when the student mentioned Jan. The students must know that we are listening to them, just as we want to be listened to. We need to give students plenty of time to talk. Not deliver mini-lectures.

Also, we best avoid asking questions. Instead, we do well to make statements. We do not ask "What can you do about your restlessness?" and we certainly do not ask such a question as "Don't you know better than to keep behaving that way?" Instead, we want to state what is on our mind: "I wonder if you have any ideas about what you can do to better control yourself." Or "If you have any ideas, please let me know." When we turn our questions into statements, and then

Above all things we must take care that the child who is not yet old enough to love his studies does not come to hate them and dread the bitterness which he has once tasted, even when the years of infancy are left behind.

—*Marcus Fabius Quintilianus*

pause so students have room to respond or not, as they choose, we reduce student defensiveness and, more important, we keep demonstrating that we respect students' power to manage their lives.

After brainstorming the list of options, Step 3 follows: *The teacher and student seek agreement on a specific action plan.* Here is how this step plays out in the interaction between the teacher and Marco:

Teacher: Maybe we will think of more ideas to write down later, but for now let's see if we both agree that any ideas on this list are worth trying. Let's look at this sheet together. I'd be willing to go along with Numbers 1 and 3 and 8. And I guess I'd go along with Number 2. Would you agree to any of those?

Marco: [Student pauses, squints, hesitates.] I guess I'd agree to try Number 1, maybe. And 4.

Teacher: Well, we both agree on Number 1, "*Reminder sign on desk.*" Let's try that for a few days. Maybe we can think of some other ideas to try later. But, for Number 1, let's be real specific now and work out the details. Where shall we start . . . ?

Follow-up Discussions

The Self-Management Contract process sometimes requires several follow-up discussions. These might reinforce or adjust the action plan. Follow-ups are especially appropriate for students who have unusual difficulty in managing emotions or impulses, or who have learned not to expect respectful treatment from teachers, or who are accustomed only to rewards and punishments and do not respect their own potential for learning to self-manage their lives intelligently. In this sample follow-up, note that the teacher is not complaining, but is holding the student to his agreement:

Teacher: I did not see a sign on your desk today.

Marco: I can't find it. Maybe the cleaning people threw it away.

Teacher: Marco, we agreed you would keep a reminder sign on your desk.

Marco: I know, but it got lost.

Teacher: What was our agreement?

Marco: OK, OK, I'll make a new one. You sure are pushy!

Teacher: [Teacher ignores the implied insult.] OK, Marco. See you later.

Questions and Answers

• *Is it worth the time to go through this process?* From a narrow, selfish viewpoint, it certainly is. A Self-Management Contract often prevents much stress for us later on. From a larger, more fundamental perspective, it can be the best means to teach a difficult student an especially meaningful lesson: At least one adult knows the student can learn to live as an intelligent, self-managing citizen, and, furthermore, one adult cares enough to take the time to help the student do that. It is, for some students, a sobering, heartening lesson.

• *Is it guaranteed?* Does agreement on a plan always emerge? Do students always follow through? No and no. But many teachers find that the process itself lowers the heat from problems. Many problems cease being serious. Why? Two reasons come to mind: (1) the process helps teachers to better understand the student and, therefore, to be better able either to accept the behavior or find new ways of handling it; (2) the student now better understands or appreciates the teacher's concern, senses the teacher's respect, and has a new willingness to go along.

• *Should we insist misbehavior stop?* How strongly should we press a student to end misbehavior? Strongly enough to communicate that we trust the student can do it, that we have faith in him, that he is not hopeless or a bad person, that he can change if and when he chooses to do so. But not so strongly that we communicate that he must do so and do it now, whether his time clock for better self-management is ready or not, whether he chooses to or not. We do not want to communicate that his dignity and readiness for self-management are not important. We want to take care not to get into a power struggle with a student. The goal is not to break a student's will. In some cases it might be better to wait for another time, another opportunity. After all, there were probably times in our own lives when we couldn't control our behavior. Let's be real here.

Strategy 34-3: Parent Notification

Purpose: To use the power of parents to help resolve discipline problems.
Description: Using the possibility that parents will be notified to emphasize the seriousness of the problem to students and, if parents are likely to be helpful, inviting them to assist in the solution.

"If this keeps up, I'll have to talk to your parents." It's a statement that can work wonders with some students. On the other hand, when a student's caregivers are themselves irresponsible, which is not uncommon, a message home may do nothing more than remind students that their caregivers don't really care; and in extreme cases, messages to parents have been known to result in severe beatings. Neither of these results is likely to help solve our problems, especially in a way that advances student self-responsibility.

But there are two ways to use parent notification that are effective.

1. *Use parent notification as a question* ("Would it be useful to involve your parents in this?") *or as a tentative comment* ("I wonder if I should talk with your

parents."). *Do not use parent notification as a threat* ("Next time it's a note home to your parents.").

The question or comment approach provides the same kind of wake-up call to students as does the threat approach—students are now alerted that parents might get involved—but it leaves open the possibility that we may, in fact, choose not to involve parents. And, depending on the student response, that may be the choice we end up making. If, for example, the student responds with honest alarm ("My father would break my arm again!"), we may choose not to notify parents. Or if the student responds, "No one at home cares about what I do," we may similarly choose not to involve parents. The point is, when we embed parental notification into a question or into a tentative comment, we may get the positive results we want—students sense that the stakes are dramatically raised and they may put new effort into self-management—without locking ourselves into a threat that we may well decide is not in our best interests. (For an example of the use of parent notification as a question, see the dialogue related to Step 2 in the Self-Management Contract strategy above.)

2. *Use parental notification to seek a conference with parents to discuss the best way to handle the situation. Do not use parent notification simply to get parents to lean on students on your behalf.*

Many parents would be happy to sit with teachers, hear about their child's behavior in class, share their perceptions and ideas, and generally engage in an open discussion about what might be best next steps. In some cases, and depending on the age of the student, we may want to include the student in such a conference. The discussion may conclude that the parents should reinforce our demand for a change of behavior with, say, a loss of TV or music privileges the next time we report a problem. Or the discussion may conclude that we should try a new approach to the issue—if, for example, we learn that the student fears failure more than we suspected and might do better with more instructional support. Or, even if the student does not attend, the discussion may bring the student to realize that the situation is serious enough to warrant trying harder. There is no way to predict the outcome of such a discussion. The key is not to assume that more parental pressure is our best next step, but rather to explore the issue openly with parents. We will likely then have more information and often more allies, which will put us in a better position to help the student improve self-management.

▲ TEACHER COMMENT

The parents and I came up with the idea that next time Lexie was a problem, I would have Lexie call her mother at work and tell her briefly about the current incident. Then that night Lexie would write about what happened and what she planned to do next time to manage herself better, and her mother would sign the paper. I would then return that paper to her mother, via Lexie, with my comments and a note about how Lexie did that day. After we made that agreement, I had to have Lexie call only twice all the rest of the year! Up to then, Lexie was a daily pain.

—*Barbara Ehrenreit, Middle School Teacher*

Strategy 34-4: Cool-Quick-Certain Control

Purpose: To protect the safety of all.
Description: Assertively taking control and managing a problem situation.

We may occasionally face a student behaving like a wild animal. In a preschool class, Stephen runs about screaming shrilly, heeding for only a split second the teacher's insistence that he sit down. In junior high, Mary is antagonistic. Ask her to lower her voice and she sneers bitterly. Ask her to stop poking Tanya and she gives a harder poke and then sneers. What to do? Here are three examples that illustrate the components of the Cool-Quick-Certain Control strategy.

- *Be cool—do not show hostility.* Act as unemotionally as possible. Certainly do not show anger or fear. Treat out-of-control students as they are—out of control—not as persons deliberately planning to do damage. Just as we would not blame a colicky infant for crying, we should not blame students for thrashing out of control. Besides, blame invites resentment, making future interactions harder. Blame also invites self-condemnation, which is even harder to counter. Simply take action, as coolly as possible, as if a car were rolling with the brake off.

- *Be quick—act immediately.* Do not hesitate. If the student has exceeded safe limits, act promptly, even if we are unsure that our actions are the best. If appropriate, we can always apologize later or change our plans. Do not show ambivalence. Do not communicate that what is clearly unacceptable might be allowed.

- *Be certain—act with confidence.* Communicate without doubt that we mean what we say. Be specific and clear. Request specific actions, as by saying, "Sit down now," "Put both hands in your lap now," "Sit in this chair by me," "Stand up and come with me." Or use a Dramatic Distraction (Strategy 34-5), as by saying, "Count backward by threes from 57." "Do you remember the name of the capital of New York State?"

Do not say things such as "Control your temper" or "You'll hurt someone." Such messages are difficult for students to respond to. Do not nag, whine, or scold. Do not punish or otherwise add to the student's pain. Be the controlling force the student now lacks. At this point, aim solely to stop the behavior.

There is an art to this, of course, an art that we can best perform when we stay in touch with our best selves. There is art, too, in deciding what is dangerous and needs to be stopped, and what, no matter how uncomfortable it makes us feel, is really not dangerous. There is no simple guideline for this. Note, however, if an act is not particularly dangerous and may merely violate our personal boundaries, it might best be handled not immediately but in cooler moments.

> Where I was born and where and how I have lived is unimportant. It is what I have done with where I have been that should be of interest.
>
> —Georgia O'Keeffe

Strategy 34-5: Dramatic Distraction

Purpose: To prevent problems from getting worse and give time for positive student motives to emerge.

Description: Dramatically turning student attention away from problem behavior, as by getting students to talk or by posing a surprising question.

This strategy resembles Strategy 33-11, Redirecting Student Energy, but is much more forceful. The following scenarios show how it might be implemented.

Example 1

A teacher is confronting two high school boys fighting. The teacher does not touch either young man but speaks loudly, authoritatively, insistently to both:

> Kevin, put that hand down. Move over there. Right there! Eric, sit down right where you are. Sit right down! NOW! Kevin, in a minute I will ask you what is behind this. But first, Eric, I want you to tell me what you think caused this!

Blame, threat, whine, complaint, groan, or words to that effect, is Eric's response. Then Kevin does the same. But no matter. Teachers who intervene with a force of personality often get fighters to pause long enough to allow a verbal venting to begin. This is a Dramatic Distraction, for it begins by distracting students from the battle at hand. It usually would not matter at all what the students said about the fight. What is important here is shifting hostile energies from punches to words.

After the teacher senses enough energy has gone out of the fight, she might announce:

> OK, both of you. Get back to your work. We do not want people here acting out such angry feelings. We all get upset. But intelligent human beings learn to manage upsets so they do not do serious damage. Both of you, pull yourselves together. We want to live together here as one community. Now move on.

Example 2

Here is an example from a teacher familiar with Workshop Way (Pilon, 1996). She came across two students fighting in the hall, neither of whom she knew by name. "You," said the teacher, facing one boy, "count backward from 100 by twos. Go!" After mumbled responses from the boy, she turned to face the other boy: "You, count upward by threes, starting with 10. Go!" These odd commands, probably coupled with something inside the students that preferred to end the fight, if they could only do so without losing face, did the job. The fight stopped and the teacher sent the students on their way.

To remain whole,
be twisted!
To become straight,
let yourself be bent.
To become full,
be hollow.
Be tattered, that you
may be renewed.

—*Lao-tzu*

Example 3

A group of 6-year-olds bring Sarah to the principal's office. "She was stamping on our feet, hard," several students complain. "I see," says the principal. "Well, Sarah, would you like to apologize to these boys and girls?" "No," insists Sarah, head down, eyes stony. "Well, boys and girls, Sarah is not ready to apologize now. Maybe another day. Before you all go back, who can count from 2 to 12 by twos? Anyone?"

The principal can be said to have ended that conflict by distracting the students. Perhaps he assumed the time was not right for a more healthful healing or a long-term remedy. In any case, it is noteworthy that the principal did not agree that Sarah did wrong or say something like, "We do not want people to be hurt like that, Sarah. Please do not do that again." Such a statement likely would have not registered meaningfully.

That incident occurred in one of Grace Pilon's Workshop Way schools, and, in talking about it, Pilon (1996) says

> Students do have common sense. They do know what is right. And they know they know what is right. Scolding, even frowning, sends a very different message. It tells them I do not believe they know what is right. I never want to get students to doubt themselves that way. (p. 166)

In the incident with Sarah, the principal probably avoided adding to Sarah's negative self-concept. Sarah may even have learned that a responsible adult trusts her to know right from wrong and appreciates that, for one reason or another, she is just unable now to manage herself better. If so, Sarah might have learned a valuable lesson. Later on, of course, the principal might think about what else could be done to help Sarah improve her self-discipline. But all problems do not need to be solved in one visit to the principal's office.

Strategy 34-6: Calamity Procedure

Purpose: To regain control of a classroom that has slipped into bedlam.
Description: Rapidly, forcefully calling out questions and directing students to write answers to them.

Sometimes a whole class can use a Dramatic Distraction (Strategy 34-5). For such times, Pilon (1996) recommends keeping on hand several sets of questions that can be used to capture students' attention. As an example, imagine a teacher has just walked into a chaotic classroom. She speaks forcefully, with certainty:

Everyone! Take out a piece of scrap paper and write the number *1*. Look in your English text, on page 45. Write the last three words you see on that page.

The teacher writes on the board: *1. Under the stars.* No discussion follows. The teacher shows no concern that most students have not yet even moved to find their texts. The teacher assumes students will follow and moves right along:

Write the number *2*. Look on page 26. Write the three-word subheading in the middle of the page.

The teacher pauses very briefly and writes on the board: *2. Nouns and Pronouns.* Again, no discussion follows and the teacher quickly moves forward:

Write the number *3*. Look on page 104. Write the first three words of the first full paragraph.

And so it goes. Rapid-fire directions to students to write the next question number, find the page called out, hunt for and then write the material indicated.

Write the number *4*. Page 34. Write the caption under the picture.

Write the number *5*. Page 190. Write the names of two people mentioned in the second full paragraph.

Write the number *6*. Page 12. Write the first word on that page that rhymes with river.

Write the number *7*. The title page. Write the full name of the author.

Write the number *8*. Page 87. Write the place where whales were hunted in 1911.

Write the number *9*. Back pages of the book. Write *true* or *false:* There is no index in the book.

Write the number *10*. Page 122. Write the full name of the man pictured on the opposite page.

After calling out each question, the teacher pauses a beat, then writes the correct answer on the board. The tone is firm enough to get the attention of some students at the outset, and as the procedure goes on, increasing numbers of students follow the teacher's lead. Students see that simply by paying attention and working promptly they can write correct answers and experience success. By the time 10 questions are finished, the teacher can expect the class to be at least somewhat settled, ready to move on. "Fine," the teacher might say at the end. "Please put that away and let's begin our review of yesterday's work." Or the teacher might choose to address the disruption directly: "We need to talk about what was happening when I entered the room."

No criticism. No complaints. Just a quick-paced request for specific acts, aiming to round up the energies of students and direct them to something they can successfully handle. And because the teacher had prepared a list of questions and answers for just such an emergency, she had no need to check the book herself to find the answers.

Pilon (1996) suggests that 10 questions be used, for it sometimes takes that many to secure the involvement of the bulk of the class. If, however, the questions are interesting enough and the pace is fast enough, fewer than 10 might do the trick. Consider these possibilities:

- Write your name in fancy letters on the top of a piece of paper.
- On the left side of the page, list one person and three things that whistle.
- On the right side, list four things you would never find on the moon.
- In the center draw a picture of yourself jumping about on the moon.
- When finished, fold your paper five times and write your name on an outside fold.

A single question might even be sufficient, if it captures and holds the class's attention. And note: It's wise to practice this Calamity Procedure once when the class is not disorderly, so that you and your students become familiar with it and can implement it more smoothly if the need ever arises.

Strategy 34-7: Bully Lesson

Purpose: To reduce the likelihood that bullying will occur and to prepare students to handle incidents that do occur.
Description: Discussing and role-playing with students ways to handle bullying.

Bullying is more common among students than many people suspect. One easy step to take: Instruct students to promptly report all incidents. The offender and the victim might then be carefully counseled. As for victims, it is important that they not be left to feel alone, without support, or to feel that they are to blame for being picked on. It is also valuable to help them think through what they might

▲ **TEACHER COMMENT**

The room was in an uproar when I came in, and I did not even know why. But I knew I had to do something, so I yelled, "Everyone sit down and start writing pairs of rhyming words. Go!" I called that out a few times because this class liked inventing simple rhymes; and as some students actually began doing it, which surprised me, actually, I went over to students I thought might begin writing if I looked them straight in the eye. Finally I was able to get all but one girl sitting and at least thinking about writing. She was furious with another girl for flirting with her boyfriend.

—*Bruce Maskow*
Special Education Elementary School Teacher

do if they are again victimized, such as the advantages and disadvantages of taking it passively, speaking out assertively, striking out aggressively, trying to escape, yelling for help, reporting incidents promptly, avoiding certain places or people, or avoiding being drawn into a verbal exchange.

For offenders, it's important they not feel disrespected. Bullying is often their way of compensating for a weak self-concept, and we don't want to exacerbate that problem. It is also important, of course, that offenders be helped to find a way to control any bullying impulses that may again arise. We might discuss, for example, what they might do or say if they are in a group that starts picking on someone.

In any case, a healthy community cannot tolerate bullying. Moreover, when it's allowed to persist, it often escalates. It's noteworthy, too, that those who persist in being either a bully or a victim are more likely eventually to carry weapons and use them.

One way to reduce the severity of bullying is by having students role-play appropriate responses. For observers, an appropriate response might be an Honest I Statement (Strategy 33-4) such as "I don't like to see kids picked on like that!" A person who is being victimized and who is willing to be assertive might make a similar statement—for example, "I don't like it when people say or do things like that." Perhaps consider brainstorming with your class other possible responses both by observers and victims, discussing the relative merits of each. Humor is often useful for defusing an incident, and students can often come up with examples of that.

Also consider a more detailed lesson about bullying, perhaps with the following steps:

1. *Discuss bullying in general.* Tell your class that some young people have strong impulses to tease others, push others, put others down, bully them. They usually need extra help in controlling these bullying impulses. At the same time, some young people are often the victims of bullies. They usually need extra help in standing up to bullies. These things are just a fact of life, not a judgment. Many of us need extra help, and bullies and victims of bullies often are in that category.

2. *Initiate role-playing.* One student portrays a bully, the other portrays a victim. Tell the bully to act however a bully might act. Instruct the victim to try to ignore the bully for a second or two, but if the bully persists for more than that, to turn and face the bully and say loudly something like, "I don't like your teasing. Please stop it." Repeat the role-playing several times, as necessary. Then ask

all students to pair up and role-play such a scene; after that, have pairs switch roles and do it again.

3. *Initiate another role-play.* Again have a bully and a victim. But this time include a third student who is to act as a bystander. In this role-play, the victim is to hesitate more than two seconds, and the bystander is to step in and speak out, saying something like, "I don't like your bullying. Please stop it." "We want to help one another," you might say to the class, "and sometimes we all need the help of others."

4. *Initiate a third role-play.* Sometimes a single bystander will not feel strong enough to face very aggressive bullies. For that situation, role-play a scene with two bullies picking on one victim, with several other students strolling nearby. Instruct the victim to not defend himself or herself. After the bullying persists for a few seconds, you might say, "I want one of you bystanders to gather a few others, so you are not alone, and then to face the bullies as a group. One of you, whoever is up to it, should start by saying something like, 'We don't like that kind of behavior here. Please stop it.' The others can then join in and say something similar."

It's also valuable to have bullies shake hands with victims afterward and apologize by saying perhaps, "I'm sorry I didn't control myself better. Please accept my apology." In addition, it is valuable to instruct students who experience actual bullying that it's usually unwise to fight with bullies, for that often escalates the problem. "It's often best to face the bully," you might say, "responding in one of the ways we role-played. However, it's sometimes best to ignore the bully and just walk away." In some cases, you may want to ask parents to reinforce this lesson.

Strategy 34-8: Temporary Removal

Purpose: To give a teacher temporary relief from a problem situation.
Description: Instructing a student to leave the group temporarily.

It is sometimes appropriate to ask a student to leave the room, perhaps to go to a colleague's classroom or sit in the back, though we recommend this as a last-resort measure. We also recommend it as only a temporary measure. Experience shows that neither the student expelled from the group nor the class as a whole is likely to profit from this procedure over the long haul. Sometimes, however, there seems to be no other option. Sometimes a student can be too upsetting to be in the group. See also Strategy 33-10, Waiting Place.

> A little knowledge that acts is worth infinitely more than much knowledge that is idle.
>
> —*Kahlil Gibran*

The aim, when separating a student from peers, is to find a way to get the student back as soon as possible. "I wish I knew what to do," you might explain to a student, followed by something like this:

> I want you to be with all of us in the class. But I cannot accept these disturbances. When you are certain you can rejoin us with better self-control, let me know. I once had a student who came in and then, before he knew he would lose his self-control, left the group again. It was a self-managed system. Let me know if you want to try that. I'll talk to you later and see where we go from here.

This is the kind of statement a student would probably like to hear. It might even inspire the student to turn over a new leaf. Important here is what part of us, as teachers, is being expressed. Are we expressing an angry, punitive part of ourselves? If so, positive results are unlikely. If, however, we are expressing the part of us that honestly regrets sending the student away from the class, the positive instincts of the student may be touched, which will make it much more likely the student will be inspired to work at improving.

When we send a student away, we do well to instruct the student to fill out a Think Time Sheet (Strategy 8-7). Research shows that when we send students away from the group, discipline problems are reduced afterward only when students are inspired to use the time away to do constructive, reflective thinking (Sugai & Colvin, 1996). More specifically, the research suggests we ask students to write answers to three questions: (1) What is the behavior that was considered inappropriate? (2) What do you need to do differently in the future? (3) How able are you to perform those replacement behaviors? The paper the student writes, then, can be used as a ticket of admission back to the class and as the basis of a discussion with the teacher as well as, perhaps, a Self-Management Contract (Strategy 34-2).

▲ TEACHER COMMENT

We have a signal. When I point to a student and say "Out please," he knows it's time to stand outside the door. He also knows I am not intending to punish him. It's not a punishment for misbehavior. I often tell the class that we have no punishments here, that I do not believe that punishment helps people in the long run. I therefore say "Out" calmly, without any scold in my voice. The student then stands outside and knows that he can come back in the room anytime he thinks he has himself under control. I told the class, "You are all intelligent persons and able to know when it will be all right for you to return to your work." Students seem to appreciate my respect of their intelligence. That is the only way I use "time out," and it works very well for me.

—*Barbara Teitz, Special Education Teacher*

Strategy 34-9: Discipline Squad

Purpose: To help teachers who are vulnerable to feel more secure and to have a system in place for handling extreme classroom problems.

Description: Arranging an emergency system that will quickly bring several nearby adults to the classroom.

In some schools a teacher can feel so threatened that calm, confident teaching is hardly possible. Canter and Canter (1976) suggest that such teachers consider asking three or four other teachers or administrators to be ready, when called, to come immediately to help handle extreme situations, as when one or more students are dangerously violent.

Here is one way this might work: A problem arises that is beyond the teacher's ability to safely manage. The teacher calls loudly to the class, "Summon the discipline squad!" Students have been told in advance what to do. Following these directions, some might immediately, say, phone the office, notify all nearby teachers, or run to the counselor's office.

Sometimes the teacher's announcement alone settles the problem enough so the teacher can handle it. However, the discipline squad soon arrives. As members arrive, they stand and wait for commands from the classroom teacher. They do not initiate any actions without directions. The classroom teacher is still to be clearly in charge. If the problem has by then eased enough so the teacher can handle it, the other adults can be thanked and dismissed. If not, the classroom teacher directs members of the squad, by saying, for example, "Separate those two young men. Remind all others to take their seats. Take the one with the red shirt to the hall. Help me check the room for weapons. I'll start here. Mr. Jenkins, please begin there."

Arranging for such a procedure often helps teachers feels secure enough to handle problems on their own. They therefore rarely, if ever, need to summon the Discipline Squad. The risk of the strategy is in its potential to weaken feelings of teacher authority and student respect for the teacher. When the strategy is restricted to problems so extreme that students can clearly see why one adult alone could not handle it, that risk is minimal. It is further minimized when the classroom teacher remains in control of the actions of the Discipline Squad.

Strategy 34-10: Safety Drill

Purpose: To generate orderliness in disorderly classes and to build a healthy class community.
Description: Helping students master a process of structured group walking.

Are there many impulsive, angry, disrespectful, disorderly students in your class? Sixth grade teacher Amanda Treben recommends setting up a Safety Drill procedure. Then, at the first hint that disorder is growing, announce a Safety Drill:

> It's time we line up to practice a Safety Drill. Remember, I want you to be safe here in school and outside of school. For that, we need to master self-control. We

I am an idealist.
I don't know where
I'm going, but I'm
on my way.

—*Carl Sandburg*

also need it in case of a fire or other emergency. So now, everyone line up and do so absolutely silently. Not a peep. Go!

Students are then to line up in a prescribed order and in a prescribed place, a process we will have to teach students beforehand. Students have no choice in this lining-up process. If we see a student disrupting the process, we get that student's attention, even if we must move directly to the student. We then make eye contact that communicates firm disapproval but no hostility. Hostility violates our concern that students learn for their sake as well as ours. Hostility does not serve student welfare. As writer J. S. Knox once put it, "You can't antagonize and influence at the same time."

Students are then to walk, silent and mindful, in an orderly way around the room or, better yet, outside the room—perhaps in the halls or up and down the stairs; maybe around the gym or through the aisles of the auditorium. All the while we repeatedly give them self-control messages in a quiet, clear, supportive voice:

> We all need to learn to manage ourselves and to get along with others. No one can make it in life without self-control. We can't run a classroom without self-control. There is no reason we can't all master self-control. It may not be easy, but it's never too late to learn. We all can do it. And we will learn to do it in this class. You are doing a good job right now. Look at how well you are walking. We need to remember how well we can control ourselves, work together, cooperate, not mess up our class. We all need to learn to manage ourselves.

We will need to be patient in teaching students how to walk this way. If we venture outside the room, we might appoint a monitor at the head of the line who is to stop after every dozen or so steps, allowing the line to condense and at the same time teaching students to adjust to change without disruption. We could even teach simple marching moves, such as "about face," at which time students turn to their right and walk in the opposite direction. And we might consider pairing up some students with other, more reliable students, to help keep them in line and on task.

The idea is to get students moving silently as an orderly group. We want the experience to be educational and satisfying, to build security and to reinforce students' natural thirst for rhythm and order.

How often might we use Safety Drills? For very troublesome classes Treben recommends using it very often the first week or two, even once an hour, until habits of self-control begin to take hold. After that, she recommends using it as needed, even if only a few students in the class need it. If the Safety Drill is brief, say three to six minutes, it can be a welcome break from seatwork and invigorate subsequent learning time.

The real menace in dealing with a 5-year-old is that in no time at all you begin to sound like a 5-year-old yourself.

—*John Lubbock*

Says a middle school teacher in a difficult, urban school: "I tried it last month and found that students actually enjoy Safety Drills and end up not only growing in self-control and as a class community, but do more intense academic work afterwards because of it."

Strategy 34-11: Diagnosing Student Motivations

Purpose: To handle underlying reasons for misbehavior.
Description: Considering what might be motivating a misbehaving student and, when appropriate, making a plan to ease the student's problem.

Occasionally we can discover what is fueling the behavior of persistently troublesome students. Sometimes that discovery is helpful. For this, Dreikurs (1968) highlights three student motives: attention, power, and revenge.

Attention

Some students thirst for attention from others. They want to be heard, noticed, recognized. They sometimes talk a lot and loudly, or ask bothersome questions, or move about intrusively. They may prefer negative attention to no attention at all and will cause trouble until they get sufficient notice. Annoyance is a characteristic reaction to such students; when we feel annoyed by a student, it is often because that student is driven to get attention.

How can we ease a drive for attention? Not by forcing the student to be quiet; that rarely helps. In the short run, try these strategies: Clock Focus, Visitor's Chair, Waiting Place, or Redirecting Student Energy (Strategies 8-5, 33-9, 33-10, and 33-11).

In the long run, aim to help the student have more experiences of being noticed in a healthful way, perhaps through Support Groups (Strategy 7-8), frequent work in Sharing Pairs and Learning Pairs (Strategies 7-1 and 7-2), and cooperative learning activities. Also look for opportunities to help these students grow in preventive self-control, as by using Intelligence Call-ups (Strategy 4-4) and, especially, Self-Management Contracts (Strategy 34-2). And seek ways to provide such students with more healthful attention, as by tutoring younger students or joining out-of-school group activities.

Power

Some troublesome students are driven by a need to exert control. They may be motivated by a need for personal freedom, perhaps to be free of close supervision. Sometimes the motive will flow from an irrational fear that harm might result if they do not control matters, as if an inner voice were saying, "If I'm not in charge, I don't know what will happen." Students who carry a strong power force often resist teachers. They are sometimes furiously defiant. Threat is a characteristic reaction to such students; when we feel threatened by a student, it is often because the student has a drive for power.

How can we ease a drive for power inside students? Not by engaging in a power struggle; that rarely helps. When incidents occur, aim to defuse passions by using cooling-off periods, Clock Focus, Visitor's Chair, Dramatic Distractions, or Temporary Removal (Strategies 8-5, 33-9, 34-5, and 34-8). In the long run, aim to help students feel safe, perhaps by referring frequently to classroom Truth Signs (Strategy 4-1), especially the sign about time clocks, and using lessons on community living, Intelligence Call-ups, Honest I Statements, and Self-Management Contracts (Strategies 4-4, 33-4, and 34-2).

Also consider healthful ways for the student to exercise power constructively, perhaps by participating in recreation activities, tutoring slower students, and engaging in appropriate sports or hobbies.

Revenge

Some students seem intent on doing harm. They may damage property or tease others. Sometimes it seems as if they are paying the world back for pains they once experienced, and sometimes those pains can be identified. But sometimes no cause for destructive impulses can be found. Feelings of hurt are a characteristic reaction to such students; when we feel hurt by a student's behavior, it is often because that student is motivated by revenge.

How can we help students with vengeful impulses? Not by overlooking actions or delaying responses; that rarely helps the student and often leads to further harmful actions. Punishment is also rarely helpful; punishments typically further fuel impulses to do harm. Prompt, assertive, nonpunitive reactions are more appropriate, as by using respectful disapprovals, Honest I Statements, Visitor's Chair, and Temporary Removal (Strategies 33-4, 33-9, and 34-8).

Over the long run, we recommend aiming to eliminate painful experiences from the classroom and to increase students' self-acceptance and acceptance by others. For this, we can use Truth Signs (Strategy 4-1), cooperative learning, all activities that increase group togetherness, and consistent demonstrations that we remain fully accepting of all persons, even while not accepting certain behaviors. It can also be helpful to encourage humor as a safe vent for hostile emotions, and vigorous exercise or high-energy sports as a safe vent for physical energies.

You can work miracles by having faith in others. To get the best out of people, choose to think and believe the best about them.

—*Bob Moawad*

Glossary

Ability Salute Telling groups we appreciate how much effort they are putting into learning. Strategy 4-10, page 69

Action Flow Lessons Planning lessons around active-learning strategies that flow together smoothly, coherently, interestingly. Strategy 3-1, page 29

Active Learning Thermometer Regularly asking students to rate the level of their involvement in class work. Strategy 25-2, page 319

Apologizing Honestly apologizing to a student, modeling respectful social behavior. Strategy 33-13, page 413

Application Brainstorm Asking students to brainstorm ideas for applying a concept or learning to a new situation. Strategy 24-3, page 317

Application Projects Encouraging students to apply learnings to real-life situations. Strategy 18-2, page 254

Ask a Friend Encouraging students who need help to ask a friend. Strategy 5-3, page 74

Ask for Help Sharing problems with other professionals, requesting suggestions and assistance. Strategy 33-15, page 416

Asserting Our Priorities Noticing when we feel overburdened, backing off to see the whole picture, using our priorities to regain personal balance, and being willing to say no. Strategy 29-4, page 362

Assessing the Options Posing a problem and asking students to brainstorm possible solutions and then to assess the worth of each possibility. Strategy 19-10, page 262

Assignments with Choice Providing homework assignments that give students some choice. Strategy 22-1, page 292

Attentive Lecture Watching students while lecturing and changing either content or procedure before attention slips. Strategy 13-1, page 166

Authority Statement Making a simple, direct statement of our authority as teachers. Strategy 8-3, page 112

Avoiding Homework Overload Being open to student and parent feedback about homework and, when appropriate, individualizing the amount of homework given. Strategy 22-7, page 298

Avoiding Paperwork Overload Reducing the number of papers we check and grade. Strategy 30-3, page 372

Avoiding Re-explanation Limiting the number of times we re-explain and, instead, reassuring students that no one needs to understand everything right now. Strategy 16-11, page 217

Background Music Playing music that is soothing or refreshing to students as they enter the room or work independently. Strategy 6-6, page 92

Behavior Checklist Working with a problem student to create a behavior checklist the student can then use to monitor behavior and take responsibility for improving. Strategy 33-7, page 405

Best Choice Debate Instructing students to pair up, consider one side of a controversial issue, and then share their thoughts with a pair that has considered the other side of that issue. Strategy 17-14, page 240

Best-Work Lesson Asking students to review samples of their best work to clarify what is "best work" for them and then encouraging them to aim for that in all future work. Strategy 25-4, page 323

Boss/Secretary Asking student pairs to take turns dictating answers to a list of questions. Strategy 17-8, page 232

Brain Drain Giving students a few minutes to vent their thoughts in writing. Strategy 9-7, page 136

Brainstorm/Sort Asking students to brainstorm options for handling an issue and then to sort the options, seeking the best. Strategy 16-8, page 213

Brainstorming Asking students to think open-mindedly about a topic and to generate a list of ideas without worrying if any idea is reasonable or not. Strategy 19-9, page 262

Broken Record Repeating a statement that a student seems not to be respecting. Strategy 33-1, page 397

Bully Lesson Discussing and role-playing with students ways to handle bullying. Strategy 34-7, page 431

Calamity Procedure Rapidly, forcefully calling out questions and directing students to write answers to them. Strategy 34-6, page 429

Calm Reminder Calmly reminding students what we want. Strategy 33-2, page 398

Can-You Questions Asking students if they *can* give an answer, rather than asking for the answer directly. Strategy 20-6, page 270

Caring Attention Without Praise Simply giving time and attention to a student, as by listening carefully. Strategy 20-11, page 277

Challenge Opener Posing a problem that generates many student questions, confusions, or frustrations and only then presenting the information we want students to learn. Strategy 12-4, page 161

Charts of Learning Tips Discussing and posting ideas that can help students take charge of their own learning. Strategy 23-4, page 307

Checklist for Effective Lectures When planning lectures, keeping in mind the importance of (1) generating initial interest, (2) maintaining student engagement, and (3) helping students construct learnings. Strategy 13-11, page 178

Check-Yourself Message Directing students to check what they have done, with the expectation that they will then notice corrections needed. Strategy 4-5, page 64

Choose, Be, Review Teaching students a procedure for more often being the way they want to be. Strategy 28-5, page 355

Choral Work Flashing a series of cards to which a class responds in unison. Strategy 11-2, page 148

Clarifying Excellence Discussion Discussing what defines excellent work and encouraging students to strive for it. Strategy 25-3, page 322

Clarifying Questions Asking questions that get students to think about material presented. Strategy 16-1, page 205

Class Agreement Announcing a topic or problem and asking for students' input and agreement on the best way to deal with it. Strategy 5-2, page 73

Class Leaders Choosing daily class leaders for special responsibilities. Strategy 5-6, page 77

Class Meeting Teaching students when and how class issues can be regularly and thoughtfully considered in a class meeting. Strategy 5-5, page 75

Class Tutors Establishing a procedure whereby students can readily be tutored by other students. Strategy 17-12, page 236

Clear Learning Target Providing a clear learning target for students. Strategy 12-6, page 163

Clear-to-Muddy Groups Asking students to put themselves in one of three groups—clear, buggy, or muddy—depending on how clear their present understanding is. Strategy 17-1, page 221

Clock Focus Having students stand and watch the second hand of a clock circle one, two, or three times, as they choose, then sit to resume work. Strategy 8-5, page 117

Common Sense Comments Saying to students at appropriate times, "Does that make sense?" "Do what makes sense," and "It's up to you. You decide." Strategy 26-1, page 332

Communicating Confident Authority Exuding a confidence that we can handle whatever discipline problems arise. Strategy 8-2, page 109

Community Living Lessons Occasionally presenting lessons and activities that help students appreciate what is involved in living as a cooperative classroom community. Strategy 5-8, page 81

Comparing Asking students to compare two items and note both similarities and differences. Strategy 19-3, page 258

Computers and the Internet Tapping into appropriate programs available on the Internet. Strategy 17-16, page 245

Concept Charts Creating and maintaining a classroom chart of important concepts studied. Strategy 13-6, page 173

Concept-Generalization Focus Selecting a concept or generalization and building lessons around that big idea. Strategy 24-1, page 311

Conciliation Statement When in conflict with a student, communicating a desire for mutual understanding and conciliation. Strategy 33-5, page 403

Concluding Whip Around Asking each student in turn to report something learned or enjoyed about the lesson just concluded. Strategy 21-4, page 287

Confidence Builders Before asking students to engage in lessons, making a reassuring statement, such as "We'll go over this again, so don't worry if you don't grasp it right now." Strategy 4-6, page 65

Conflict-Resolution Lesson Teaching students how to talk honestly about a conflict and, if the problem remains, how to brainstorm a list of possible solutions. Strategy 33-6, page 403

Consult Time Organizing activities so there's time for each student to visit briefly with the teacher. Strategy 17-9, page 232

Cool-Quick-Certain Control Assertively taking control and managing a problem situation. Strategy 34-4, page 427

Cooperative Reading Groups Teaching students a structure for discussing a reading in small groups, with each student taking turns playing a different role in the group's discussion. Strategy 15-4, page 193

Creating Groupings Asking students to sort items into categories they themselves create. Strategy 19-7, page 261

Credit for Completing Homework Checking homework assignments but not grading homework or penalizing students for not completing it. Strategy 10-4, page 143

Cushioning Questions Before asking students to demonstrate how much they learned, reinforcing basic truths about learning by asking such questions as "Is it OK if someone gives us a wrong answer today? Why?" Strategy 4-2, page 56

DESCA Challenges Challenging students to stretch their ability to live and work with dignity, energy, self-management, community, and awareness (DESCA). Strategy 25-10, page 327

DESCA Inspirations Responding to students in a way that inspires them to develop the best they have in them. Strategy 20-9, page 273

DESCA Proclamation Proclaiming "This is a high DESCA classroom" to assert an intention that we and our students are expected to highly value the use of dignity, energy, self-management, community, and awareness. Strategy 25-11, page 331

Detailed Oral Learning Statements Asking students to describe what they have learned in great detail, aloud, to themselves or a partner. Strategy 23-3, page 306

Diagnosing Student Motivations Considering what might be motivating a misbehaving student and, when appropriate, making a plan to ease the student's problem. Strategy 34-11, page 437

Dignifying Acts Doing little things that show we value students as persons, not only as learners. Strategy 5-9, page 84

Dignifying Grading Practices Creating a plan for grading that considers both professional requirements and the best interests of students. Strategy 31-1, page 374

Directed Reading Actively guiding students through a reading, frequently requesting student responses, offering comments when appropriate. Strategy 15-6, page 195

Discipline Plan Taking the time to make a plan for handling the situations we are likely to face. Strategy 8-11, page 124

Discipline Squad Arranging an emergency system that will quickly bring several nearby adults to the classroom. Strategy 34-9, page 434

Discovery Lesson Posing a problem and allowing students to puzzle on it before providing an answer. Strategy 14-1, page 180

Distress-Easing Comments Reaching out to ease the distress of a student. Strategy 27-4, page 340

Do Now Providing independent work for students to handle as soon as they arrive. Strategy 6-1, page 86

Dramatic Distraction Dramatically turning student attention away from problem behavior, as by getting students to talk or posing a surprising question. Strategy 34-5, page 428

Dramatic Reading Modeling dramatic reading and then asking students to read important passages aloud with as much dramatic flair as they can manage. Strategy 15-9, page 200

Dual Grades Giving separate grades for effort and accomplishment. Strategy 32-2, page 390

Efficient Classroom Structures Settling on a few classroom routines that maximize learning and ease teaching. Strategy 3-4, page 38

E-for-Effort Certificates Regularly acknowledging student effort and occasionally offering certificates to formalize such acknowledgment. Strategy 25-7, page 325

Encouragement Offering verbal encouragement to students who struggle academically or personally or both. Strategy 4-7, page 66

Experience Before Concept Giving students a meaningful experience of a concept before discussing it abstractly. Strategy 12-5, page 162

Explanation Back-off When continuing an explanation would turn off more students than it would help, backing off and doing something else. Strategy 13-3, page 169

Face-off Game Asking questions to students sitting in pairs, with each person in the pair representing a different team. Strategy 16-10, page 215

Failure Insulators Providing many successful test-taking experiences at the start of the school year. Strategy 31-8, page 385

Family Introductory Letter Sending an upbeat message to students' families early in the year. Strategy 5-10, page 85

Finger Feedback Preparing lectures that include questions to which students respond by holding up fingers. Strategy 13-9, page 176

Focus-on-Learning Statement Informing students of our intention to focus on learning, not grading, and inviting students' suggestions and cooperation. Strategy 31-4, page 380

Getting-to-Know-You Activities Providing time for activities that involve personal sharing. Strategy 5-7, page 78

Going for the Gold Challenging students to handle everyday tasks at a high level of excellence. Strategy 25-6, page 324

Goodness Log Asking students to keep a log of times they did something unusually good for others or themselves. Strategy 28-6, page 357

Gratitude Journal Asking students to keep a record of what in their lives they can be grateful for. Strategy 28-3, page 348

Group Challenge Challenging small groups to find ways to help one another learn something. Strategy 7-9, page 104

Group Role Sheet Before starting group work, familiarizing students with the roles and responsibilities they can expect. Strategy 7-10, page 105

Grouping Students for Instruction Considering the options for grouping students and choosing those that best suit us and our classes. Strategy 7-7, page 102

Guided Discovery Leading students through a set of practices that help them circle in on mastery. Strategy 14-4, page 185

Hand-Raising Signal Silently raising a hand as a signal that it's time to discontinue individual work or small-group discussions. Strategy 9-1, page 131

Healthy Response to Misbehavior Checking to ensure we react to problem students in a healthy way. Strategy 29-3, page 361

High Expectations Maintaining an expectation that students will do the best they can, even when there is no evidence they will do so. Strategy 25-1, page 318

High-Achievement Comments Writing comments that recognize exceptional student achievement. Strategy 31-9, page 386

Homework Games Inviting students to create a game for themselves that is connected to a homework assignment. Strategy 22-5, page 297

Homework Hearing Time Meeting briefly with individual students to hear about their completed homework. Strategy 10-3, page 140

Homework in Layers, Not Lumps Providing homework assignments that offer practice with current content, review old content, and preview new content. Strategy 22-3, page 294

Homework Self-Correcting Asking students to check homework against an answer key with little or no teacher involvement. Strategy 10-2, page 139

Homework Sharing Pairs Asking students to pair up and share completed homework. Strategy 10-1, page 137

Homework Unlike Class Work Designing homework assignments that are distinctly different from class work. Strategy 22-2, page 293

Honest I Appreciates Telling a student we honestly appreciate something about him or her. Strategy 20-7, page 271

Honest I Statements Honestly expressing personal needs and feelings, avoiding comments about what "you" did or "you" failed to do. Strategy 33-4, page 400

How-Read Discussion Teaching students several different ways of reading. Strategy 23-1, page 303

I Say Review Asking pairs of students to share what they would say about certain subject matter. Strategy 11-3, page 149

I Start, You Finish Reading the first part of a sentence aloud, then pausing to let the whole class read the remainder of the sentence in unison. Strategy 15-5, page 195

I'm with You's Communicating an empathetic understanding and acceptance of a student's experience. Strategy 20-8, page 272

Incorrects with Appreciation Informing a student that although the answer was not correct, the effort was commendable and we appreciate it. Strategy 20-3, page 267

Independent Learning Assignments Guiding students through steps that help them successfully design and complete independent learning projects on topics of their choice. Strategy 6-4, page 89

Inspiring Statements Cheering students on to do their very best. Strategy 25-5, page 324

Inspiring Stories Calling attention to people with inspiring life stories. Strategy 25-9, page 327

Intelligence Call-up Reminding students frequently that they are intelligent beings, each with the capacity to stop and think and to make responsible choices. Strategy 4-4, page 62

Jigsaw Asking quartets of students to each read or study part of a topic and then meet to share what they learned. Strategy 15-10, page 200

Know and Want to Know Starting a lesson by asking students to note what they already know or might want to know about the topic. Strategy 12-2, page 158

Language to Advance Thinking Using phrases that model mature thinking. Strategy 19-11, page 263

Learning Centers Setting up activity or task centers in the classroom in which students can work on their own. Strategy 6-2, page 87

Learning Challenges Posing an assignment not as a responsibility or a chore, but as a challenging opportunity. Strategy 4-8, page 66

Learning Log Regularly asking students to write about their learning experiences in a special notebook or folder that we can then review periodically. Strategy 21-3, page 286

Learning Log Exchange Asking students to exchange Learning Logs occasionally and give constructive feedback to one another. Strategy 21-6, page 288

Learning Map Helping students develop a method of taking notes that integrates words, symbols, pictures, and other images connected to a central topic. Strategy 17-3, page 225

Learning Pairs Asking students in pairs to help each other learn something new or to drill each other on past learnings. Strategy 7-2, page 96

Learning Sheets Helping students to engage a reading by providing a question sheet that guides and stimulates their learning. Strategy 15-8, page 197

Lesson Agreement Announcing our general plans for the lesson ahead and inviting student agreement. Strategy 9-5, page 134

Let Them Be When we suspect students have not learned because they are not yet ready to learn, letting them be, not attempting to force something before its time. Strategy 4-9, page 69

Like/Might Review Asking students to look back at their behavior and write what they *liked* about it and what they *might* do differently another time. Strategy 21-2, page 285

Lingering Board Notes Not erasing important board notes. Strategy 13-5, page 172

Make a Prediction Asking students to make predictions. Strategy 12-3, page 160

Managing Long-Term Projects Assisting students to plan well and stay on top of long-term projects. Strategy 22-6, page 297

Mastery Learning Game Asking review questions in a gamelike setting without keeping score. Strategy 16-9, page 214

Mental Pictures Asking students to create a mental picture of concepts, processes, or learnings. Strategy 21-5, page 287

Mindset Switch Noticing when we have slipped into a negative mindset and switching out of it. Strategy 33-14, page 414

Mini-celebration Pausing to recognize student effort with a moment of group applause or other celebratory action. Strategy 21-8, page 290

Mini-task Assigning a task that students can complete within one session that is likely to give them a feeling of satisfying accomplishment. Strategy 17-2, page 223

Models and Manipulatives Enhancing learning by using models and manipulatives. Strategy 16-13, page 218

Motivational Question Asking a question, both to focus attention on a topic and to start the process of student thinking. Strategy 12-1, page 158

New or Goods Asking students if anything is new or good in their lives. Strategy 9-4, page 133

Next-Time Feedback Writing comments on written work that give students specific guidance on what to do next time to improve their work. Strategy 30-2, page 371

Next-Time Message Saying what behavior we want next time as a way of reminding students what was wrong this time. Strategy 33-3, page 400

Nod of Recognition Nodding to a student who has just volunteered to speak so as to communicate that we noticed the offer, yet looking about so as to give more time for others to consider volunteering. Strategy 16-7, page 212

Note-Taking Options Teaching students how to do more than make verbatim notes of what they hear and read. Strategy 23-2, page 305

Note-Taking Template Using a sheet of paper to help focus, organize, and engage awareness during a lesson. Strategy 13-7, page 174

Once Principle Announcing that from now on directions will be given only once and that students not hearing directions are to use a dignified, intelligent way to catch up. Strategy 5-4, page 74

One Say, All Say Having one volunteer read something aloud and then having the whole class repeat what was read. Strategy 11-4, page 150

One-Minute Warning Allowing students to continue working only as long as they are actively engaged. Strategy 9-2, page 132

Option Display Instructing groups to construct a display showing several options for solving a problem, the likely consequences of each option, and the group's preferred solution. Strategy 17-18, page 247

Outcome Sentences Asking students to reflect back on an experience and write endings to such phrases as *I learned . . . , I was surprised . . . , I'm beginning to wonder . . .* Strategy 21-1, page 284

Paired Reading Asking pairs of students to take turns reading to each other. Strategy 15-1, page 189

Paper Exchange Asking students to read one another's papers and to write feedback notes. Strategy 17-4, page 226

Parent Aides Inviting parents and other adults to visit often and, perhaps, to serve as teacher aides. Strategy 8-10, page 124

Parent Notification Using the possibility that parents will be notified to emphasize the seriousness of the problem to students and, if parents are likely to be helpful, inviting them to assist in the solution. Strategy 34-3, page 425

Parking Lot Writing on the board student questions that are best deferred, as a reminder to us to return to them later. Strategy 16-14, page 219

Partner Restatement Pausing during a presentation and asking students to pair up and restate points that were made. Strategy 13-10, page 178

Pass the Q&A After announcing a question and an answer, having students pass them along down the rows or around their tables. Strategy 11-6, page 152

Peer Mediators Training small groups of students in the conflict-resolution model and then asking them to help handle problem situations. Strategy 33-8, page 407

Personal Inspiring Power Learning to bring out our own best selves in the classroom. Strategy 3-5, page 46

Personal Model Exemplifying a person who works with high DESCA—dignity, energy, self-management, community, and awareness. Strategy 25-8, page 326

Personalized Challenges Challenging students to choose their own way to strengthen themselves and to practice doing so. Strategy 28-2, page 347

Personalizing Learning Asking students to expand on a topic by sharing examples from their own lives. Strategy 24-4, page 317

Person-to-Person Dialogue Talking with a student privately, relying mostly on "I" statements. Strategy 34-1, page 418

Physical Movement Enhancing learning by providing opportunities for students to move their bodies. Strategy 16-15, page 219

Plain Corrects Simply informing a student that an answer is correct. Strategy 20-1, page 265

Plain Incorrects Simply informing a student that an answer is not correct. Strategy 20-2, page 266

Plan, Do, Review Having students plan how they will handle an assignment and then, afterward, reviewing how well they did. Strategy 17-10, page 233

Portfolios Asking students to keep a collection of their work, both for their own review and for our review. Strategy 31-3, page 378

Positive Feedback Notes Highlighting what is right and good about poor work. Strategy 30-4, page 373

Positive Parent Schedule Creating a procedure that makes it easy to send positive messages home to parents. Strategy 27-9, page 345

Practice Pairs Giving practice problems to students sitting in pairs, so they can help each other master the material. Strategy 7-4, page 97

Praise and Rewards for All Offering praise or a reward to the group as a whole. Strategy 20-4, page 267

Pre-final Exam Giving students a pre-final exam that includes questions resembling all those that will be on the final exam. Strategy 31-6, page 384

Presentation for Task Assigning a task and then presenting the information needed to complete it. Strategy 13-2, page 168

Prize Sprinkle Randomly choosing students to receive a prize. Strategy 27-7, page 343

Procedures That Energize Using classroom procedures that help keep minds and bodies active. Strategy 8-4, page 116

Productive Discussion Continuing a class discussion only as long as all students are productively engaged. Strategy 16-2, page 206

Progress Proclamation Occasionally reminding students how far they have progressed. Strategy 21-9, page 291

Project Work Helping students design independent learning projects, complete them successfully, and report their learnings appropriately. Strategy 18-1, page 249

Promoting Kindness Encouraging students to speak and act in ways that communicate civility, kindness, and respect. Strategy 27-3, page 339

Question Exchange Asking students to write questions about material that was studied and then to discuss each question with others. Strategy 17-5, page 228

Question, All Write Asking all students to write an answer to a question before calling on someone to reply. Strategy 16-3, page 209

Quick Feedback Providing test feedback as quickly as possible, including explanations and opportunities for student self-evaluation. Strategy 31-11, page 387

Quick Pace Noticing when students are losing interest and promptly making a change. Strategy 3-3, page 37

Reading for Task Giving students a task that requires them to read thoughtfully. Strategy 15-2, page 190

Reality-Acceptance Monologue Taking a moment to remind ourselves that not all bothersome behavior can be eliminated. Strategy 29-2, page 360

Reciprocal Teaching Asking students to take turns reading aloud in a small group and then to take turns leading a group discussion of the reading. Strategy 15-3, page 191

Recognition for Everyone Searching for ways that all students can play an active, constructive role in the class community. Strategy 27-2, page 338

Redirecting Student Energy Turning the attention of a misbehaving student to something not disturbing. Strategy 33-11, page 410

Relaxation Exercise Providing a mini-exercise that prepares students to do their best work. Strategy 9-6, page 135

Report Card Plan Creating a plan for report cards that is considerate of both professional requirements and the best interests of students. Strategy 32-1, page 389

Respecting Our Own Stage Reminding ourselves that teachers go through stages of development and it is unwise to expect more of ourselves than is now appropriate. Strategy 29-5, page 363

Response to Undone Work Avoiding blaming students who fail to do required work and rather responding in a way likely to inspire students to do better. Strategy 30-1, page 369

Responsible Homework Discussions Guiding students through discussions about how to make wise homework choices. Strategy 22-4, page 295

Reteach Review Overlapping lessons by briefly reteaching prior material before introducing new material. Strategy 11-7, page 153

Retest Offer Allowing students to retake any test or to demonstrate accomplishment in another way. Strategy 31-5, page 383

Reverse Report Card Defining student behaviors we would like to promote and asking families to observe and periodically report on changes in these behaviors. Strategy 32-5, page 392

Review Test Posing a set of review questions and having students (1) write answers and (2) immediately check their work against the provided correct answer. Strategy 11-1, page 145

Rights, Responsibilities, Rewards Discussing the natural connection between rights, responsibilities, and rewards, and how to make use of that connection in the classroom. Strategy 26-4, page 334

Risk Language When soliciting responses from students, using wording that encourages participation, as by asking, "Who is willing to risk an answer?" Strategy 4-3, page 61

Rotating Pairs Asking student pairs to share ideas or to work together briefly, and then to rotate partners, so each student can compare thoughts with yet other students. Strategy 7-3, page 96

Rubrics Presenting, discussing, and using rubrics as criteria for evaluating student work. Strategy 31-7, page 384

Safety Drill Helping students master a process of structured group walking. Strategy 34-10, page 435

Saying No Slowly Being slow in saying no to student requests. Strategy 20-12, page 279

Selecting Group Size Selecting the smallest group size feasible for learning, preferably pairs. Strategy 7-5, page 98

Selecting Members for Groups Asking students to select their own group members and assisting them in doing so only as necessary. Strategy 7-6, page 98

Self-Acceptance Monologue Reminding ourselves that we cannot expect to behave perfectly at all times. Strategy 29-1, page 359

Self-Discipline Lesson Teaching a lesson about making wise choices in stressful situations, how important it is to do so, and how we can help one another do it. Strategy 8-8, page 121

Self-Management Contract Engaging a misbehaving student in a Person-to-Person Dialogue, then brainstorming a written list of possible next steps, ending with a written agreement on exactly what is to be done next. Strategy 34-2, page 421

Self-Management Goals Inviting students to set and track a personal goal for the day. Strategy 26-3, page 334

Self-Selected Learning Reports Allowing students to choose their own way to show what they have learned. Strategy 31-10, page 386

Sensible Risk Taking Seeking opportunities to help students clarify for themselves what is and is not a risk worth taking. Strategy 27-6, page 342

Service Projects Encouraging students to engage in projects that provide service to others. Strategy 18-3, page 255

Set of Speakers Requesting volunteers to speak and, then, from all volunteers, choosing a set that will take turns speaking. Strategy 16-5, page 211

Setting Procedures and Expectations Establishing very clear classroom expectations without mentioning consequences for misbehavior. Strategy 8-1, page 107

Shared Responsibilities, Personal Responsibilities Discussing the difference between shared and personal responsibilities and brainstorming ways to keep the classroom running smoothly. Strategy 26-2, page 333

Sharing Pairs Asking students to pair up and briefly share thoughts on a question or topic. Strategy 7-1, page 94

Signal for the Big Picture Doing something special to call students' attention to a big idea or a general principle. Strategy 13-8, page 175

Silent Response to Errors Noticing an error or problem and leaving until later a consideration of what, if anything, to do about it. Strategy 20-5, page 269

Silent Response to Misbehavior Mentally noting misbehavior and leaving until later the consideration of what, if anything, to do about it. Strategy 33-12, page 411

Sketching to Review Before reviewing a topic, asking students to draw part of what they remember. Strategy 11-5, page 151

Solving a Problem Asking students to solve a problem that lacks an obvious solution. Strategy 19-8, page 261

Sorting the Items Asking students to sort through items and place them in certain groups. Strategy 19-4, page 258

Special Energizing Activities Inserting energizing activities into the classroom when a slump or restlessness emerges. Strategy 8-6, page 118

Specific Levels of Excellence Before giving an assignment, reviewing with students a written rubric with characteristics of good and poor work. Strategy 12-7, page 165

Spontaneous Delights Expressing ourselves when students spontaneously delight us. Strategy 20-10, page 276

Star of the Day Giving each student a turn to be the Star of the Day. Strategy 27-8, page 344

Strength-Building Challenges Challenging students to increase their inherent strengths. Strategy 28-1, page 346

Student Procedure Mastery Spending enough time teaching classroom procedures early on so they become comfortable, automatic routines for students. Strategy 5-1, page 71

Student Question Writing Defining three levels of questions—recall, thinking, and personal—and then asking students to create questions on as many levels as they can. Strategy 17-6, page 229

Student Self-Evaluation Providing students with opportunities to evaluate their own work. Strategy 17-11, page 235

Study Cards Asking students to create and study a set of cards containing material to be memorized. Strategy 6-3, page 88

Summarizing Asking students to summarize information on a topic. Strategy 19-6, page 260

Support Groups Forming stable student groups, usually groups of fours, and giving them the assignment to support one another. Strategy 7-8, page 103

Supportive Report Card Comments Adding personal comments to report cards acknowledging something positive about each student. Strategy 32-3, page 391

Surprise Personal Notes Occasionally sending surprise notes home with some good news. Strategy 32-4, page 392

Task Group with Communication Practice Instructing small groups to work at a task and, while working, practice an interpersonal skill. Strategy 17-15, page 242

Task Group, Share Group Instructing students to work together to complete a brief task and then to pair up and report results to each other. Strategy 17-17, page 245

Task Workshop Providing a standing set of sequential learning tasks and asking students to work independently at those tasks during class time. Strategy 6-5, page 91

Teacher Role-Play Asking students to work individually to learn something and then to role-play being a teacher who teaches that material to others. Strategy 17-7, page 230

Teaching in Layers, Not Lumps Planning not for mastery at any one time, but rather planning to return to topics as often as necessary until mastery is reached. Strategy 3-2, page 36

Teaching Specific Learning Skills Teaching learning skills specific to the class grade level and subject matter. Strategy 23-5, page 308

Temporary Removal Instructing a student to leave the group temporarily. Strategy 34-8, page 433

Tests with Choice Including various types of questions on tests and allowing students some choice in which questions to answer. Strategy 31-2, page 377

Think Aloud Talking aloud while working out a problem so students hear how we think. Strategy 14-3, page 184

Think Time After posing a question, allowing time for all students to formulate an answer for themselves before inviting students to share ideas. Strategy 16-12, page 217

Think Time Sheet Asking students to think about how a behavior problem might best be handled. Strategy 8-7, page 120

Thought/Feel Cards Asking students to make notes, usually anonymously, of personal thoughts and feelings of which they are currently aware. Strategy 21-7, page 289

Timed Reading Giving students two to three minutes to read, scan, or simply turn pages of some text. Strategy 15-7, page 196

Truth Signs Posting and discussing signs that remind students of core truths about learning. Strategy 4-1, page 50

Tutor Training Teaching students skills for effectively giving and receiving help. Strategy 17-13, page 236

Underexplain and Learning Pairs Explaining material briefly, so only some students understand it, then asking pairs to work together to help each other more fully understand. Strategy 14-2, page 182

Using Subject Matter to Learn About Life Connecting a subject matter lesson to an issue students are likely to care about. Strategy 24-2, page 312

VAK Attack Providing visual, auditory, and kinesthetic learning experiences. Strategy 14-5, page 187

Validations Showing all students, including those who upset us, that we see them as worthy human beings. Strategy 27-1, page 337

Visitor's Chair Without communicating any displeasure, asking a student to sit in a chair near us as "time out." Strategy 33-9, page 408

Visual Aids and Graphic Organizers Using visual aids and graphic organizers to enhance presentations. Strategy 13-4, page 170

Voting Questions Asking general-interest questions to which students can respond by raising hands. Strategy 9-3, page 132

Voting Questions to Assess Understanding Rather than asking "Any questions?" asking "How many of you have questions?" or "How many would like to move on and come back to this topic another time?" Strategy 16-6, page 211

Waiting Place Sending a student to a place where he or she can conveniently wait until we have time to talk with the student. Strategy 33-10, page 409

What Might Explain? Asking students to think back and consider what might explain an event. Strategy 19-5, page 259

What's the Difference? Asking students in what ways two items are different. Strategy 19-1, page 257

What's the Same? Asking students what is similar about two items. Strategy 19-2, page 258

What-I-Like-About-You Reports Occasionally providing time for students to write one thing they like about each class member. Strategy 27-5, page 341

Whip Around, Pass Option Asking students to speak one at a time, in turn, on an issue or, if they prefer, to pass. Strategy 16-4, page 210

Whole-Class Problem Solving Asking students to brainstorm a list of possible solutions to a class problem and then seeking agreement on what options are best for all concerned. Strategy 8-9, page 122

Whole-Self Lesson Guiding students through a lesson on self-acceptance and appreciation of personal possibilities. Strategy 28-4, page 349

Bibliography

Abbott, J., & Ryan, T. (2001). *The unfinished revolution: Learning, human behavior, community, and political paradox*. Alexandria, VA: Association for Supervision and Curriculum Development.

Abrutyn, L., & Danielson, C. (1997). *An introduction to using portfolios in the classroom*. Alexandria, VA: Association for Supervision and Curriculum Development.

Adams, A., & Bebensee, E. L. (1983). *Success in reading and writing*. Glenview, IL: Good Year.

Adkins, G. (1990). Educating the handicapped in the regular classroom. *Educational Digest, 56*, 24–27.

Akin, T. (1992). *The best self-esteem activities for the elementary grades*. Spring Valley, CA: Innerchoice.

Alexander, P. A., Kulikowich, J. M., & Schulze, S. K. (1994). How subject-matter knowledge affects recall and interest. *American Educational Research Journal, 31*(2), 313–337.

Allan, S. D., & Tomlinson, C. A. (2000). *Leadership for differentiating schools and classrooms*. Alexandria, VA: Association for Supervision and Curriculum Development.

Allen, D. (1995). *The tuning protocol: A process for reflection*. (Studies in Exhibitions, No. 15). Providence, RI: Coalition of Essential Schools, Brown University.

Allport, G. (1955). *Becoming: Basic considerations for a psychology of personality*. New Haven, CT: Yale University Press.

Alson, A. (2002, December–2003, January). The minority student achievement network. *Educational Leadership, 60*(4), 76–78.

Ames, C., & Ames, R. (Eds.). (1985). *Research on motivation in education: Vol. 1. Student motivation*. Orlando, FL: Academic Press.

Ames, C., & Archer, J. (1982). Achievement goals in the classroom: Students' learning strategies and motivation processes. *Journal of Educational Psychology, 80*, 260–267.

Anderson, J. R. (1983). *The architecture of cognition*. Cambridge, MA: Harvard University Press.

Anderson, L. M. (1989). Implementing instructional programs to promote meaningful, self-regulated learning. In J. Brophy (Ed.), *Advances in research on teaching: Teaching for meaningful understanding and self-regulated learning* (Vol. 1, pp. 311–343). Greenwich, CT: JAI.

Anderson, L. M. (1989). Classroom instruction. In M. C. Reynolds (Ed.), *Knowledge base for the beginning teacher* (pp. 101–115). Oxford, England; New York: Pergamon Press.

Anderson, L. W., & Anderson, J. C. (1982, April). Affective assessment is necessary and possible. *Educational Leadership, 39*(7), 524–525.

Anderson, R., Hiebert, E., Scott, J., & Wilkinson, I. (1985). *Becoming a nation of readers: A report of the Commission on Reading*. Washington, DC: National Institute of Education.

Anderson, T. H., & Armbruster, B. B. (1986). The value of taking notes during lectures. (Tech. Rep. No. 374). Cambridge, MA: Bolt, Beranek & Newman; and Urbana, IL: Center for the Study of Reading.

Anderson, V., & Hidi, S. (1988, December–1989, January). Teaching students to summarize. *Educational Leadership, 46*(4), 26–28.

Andrade, H. G. (2000, February). Using rubrics to promote thinking and learning. *Educational Leadership, 57*(5), 13–18.

Annis, L. (1979). The processes and effects of peer tutoring. *Human Learning, 2,* 39–47.

Applebee, A. (1986). Problems in process approaches: Toward a reconceptualization of process instruction. In A. Petrosky & D. Bartholomae (Eds.), *The teaching of writing: 85th yearbook of the National Society for the Study of Education* (pp. 95–113). Chicago: University of Chicago Press.

Armstrong, T. (1998). *Awakening genius in the classroom.* Alexandria, VA: Association for Supervision and Curriculum Development.

Armstrong, T. (2000). *Multiple intelligences in the classroom* (2nd ed.). Alexandria, VA: Association for Supervision and Curriculum Development.

Aronson, E., & Patnoe, S. (1997). *The jigsaw classroom: Building cooperation in the classroom* (2nd ed.). New York: Longman.

Ashton, P. T., & Webb, R. B. (1986). *Making a difference: Teachers' sense of efficacy and student achievement.* New York: Longman.

Augustine, D. K., Gruber, K. D., & Hanson, L. R. (1989, December–1990, January). Cooperation works! *Educational Leadership, 47*(4), 4–7.

Bailis, P., & Hunter, M. (1985, August). Do your words get them to think? *Learning, 14*(1), 43.

Bandura, A. (1965). Behavior modification through modeling procedures. In L. Krasner and L. P. Ullman (Eds.), *Research in behavior modification: New developments and implications* (pp. 310–340). New York: Holt, Rinehart & Winston.

Bandura, A. (1986). *Social foundations of thought and action: A social cognitive theory.* Englewood Cliffs, NJ: Prentice-Hall.

Bandura, A. (1997). *Self-efficacy: The exercise of control.* New York: W. H. Freeman.

Bangert-Downs, R. L., Kulik, C. C., Kulik, J. A., & Morgan, M. (1991). The instructional effects of feedback in test-like events. *Review of Educational Research, 61*(2), 213–238.

Banks, J. A., & McGee Banks, C. A. (1995). *Handbook on research on multicultural education.* New York: Macmillan.

Barclay, J. R., Bradford, J. D., Franks, J. J., McCarrell, N. S., & Nitsch, K. (1974). Comprehension and semantic flexibility. *Journal of Verbal Learning and Verbal Behavior, 13,* 471–481.

Barr, R. D., & Parrett, W. H. (1995). *Hope at last for at-risk youth.* Boston: Allyn & Bacon.

Bateson, G. (1972). *Steps to an ecology of mind.* New York: Ballantine.

Baum, H. (1982). *The biochemist's songbook.* Oxford, England; New York: Pergamon Press.

Baumann, J. F. (1992). Effect of think-aloud instruction on elementary students' comprehension monitoring abilities. *Journal of Reading Behavior, 24*(2), 143–172.

Bear, G. F. (1998). School discipline in the United States: Prevention, correction, and long-term social development. *School Psychology Review, 27*(1), 14–32.

Bellanca, J., & Fogarty, R. (1990). *Blueprints for cooperative learning in the thinking classroom.* Palatine, IL: Skylight.

Bennett, W. J. (Ed.). (1997). *The book of virtues for young people.* New York: Simon & Schuster Books for Young Readers.

Benninga, J. S. (Ed.). (1991). *Moral, character, and civic education in the elementary school.* New York: Teachers College Press.

Benson, H., & Proctor, W. (2003). *The breakout principle: How to activate the natural trigger that maximizes creativity, athletic performance, productivity and personal well-being.* New York: Scribner.

Berliner, D. C. (1979). Tempus educare. In P. L. Peterson & H. J. Walberg (Eds.), *Research in teaching* (pp. 120–135). Berkeley, CA: McCutchan.

Berliner, D. C. (1984). The half-full glass: A review of research in teaching. In P. I. Hosford (Ed.), *Using what we know about teaching* (pp. 511–577). Alexandria, VA: Association for Supervision and Curriculum Development.

Biddle, B., & Anderson, D. S. (1986). Theory, methods, knowledge, and research on teaching. In M. C. Wittrock (Ed.), *Handbook of research on teaching* (3rd ed., pp. 230–252). New York: Macmillan.

Biehler, R. F., & Snowman, J. (1991). *Psychology applied to teaching* (7th ed.). Boston: Houghton Mifflin.

Bohlin, K., & Ryan, K. (1999). *Building character in schools: Practical ways to bring moral instruction to life.* San Francisco: Jossey-Bass.

Borg, W. R., & Ascione, F. A. (1982). Classroom management in elementary mainstreaming classrooms. *Journal of Educational Psychology, 74*(1), 85–95.

Borko, H., & Niles, J. A. (1987). Descriptions of teacher planning: Ideas for teachers and researchers. In V. Richardson-Koehler (Ed.), *Educators' handbook: A research perspective* (pp. 167–187). New York: Longman.

Bower, B., Rolheiser, C., & Stevahn, L. (2000). *The portfolio organizer: Succeeding with portfolios in your classroom.* Alexandria, VA: Association for Supervision and Curriculum Development.

Bower, G. H. (1981). Mood and memory. *American Psychologist, 36,* 129–148.

Boynton, M., & Boynton, C. (2005). *Educator's guide to preventing and solving discipline problems.* Alexandria, VA: Association for Supervision and Curriculum Development.

Brandt, R. (1984, September). Teaching of thinking, for thinking, about thinking. *Educational Leadership, 42*(1), 3.

Brandt, R. (1989, May). A changed professional culture. *Educational Leadership, 46*(8), 2.

Brandt, R. (Ed.). (1989). *Readings from* Educational Leadership *on teaching thinking.* Alexandria, VA: Association for Supervision and Curriculum Development.

Brandt, R. (1992, December–1993, January). On outcome-based education: A conversation with Bill Spady. *Educational Leadership, 50*(4), 66–71.

Brandt, R. S. (2000). *Education in a new era (2000 ASCD yearbook).* Alexandria, VA: Association for Supervision and Curriculum Development.

Bransford, J. D., Barclay, J. R., & Franks, J. J. (1972). Sentence memory: A constructive versus interpretive approach. *Cognitive Psychology, 3,* 193–202.

Bretzing, B. H., & Kulhary, R. W. (1979, April). Notetaking and depth of processing. *Contemporary Educational Psychology, 4*(2), 145–153.

Bridges, W. (1980). *Transitions: Making sense of life's changes.* Reading, MA: Addison-Wesley.

Brimijoin, K., Marquisse, E., & Tomlinson, C. A. (2003, February). Using data to differentiate instruction. *Educational Leadership, 60*(5), 70–72.

Brody, N. (1983). *Human motivation: Commentary on goal-directed action.* New York: Academic Press.

Brooks, J. G., & Brooks, M. G. (1999). *In search of understanding: The case for constructivist classrooms.* Alexandria, VA: Association for Supervision and Curriculum Development.

Brophy, J. E. (1979, April). *Advances in teacher effectiveness research.* East Lansing, MI: Institute for Research on Teaching, Michigan State University.

Brophy, J. E. (1981). *Teacher praise: A functional analysis.* (Occasional Paper No. 28). East Lansing, MI: Institute for Research on Teaching, Michigan State University.

Brophy, J. E. (1982). Supplemental group management techniques. In D. Duke (Ed.), *Helping teachers manage classrooms* (pp. 32–51). Alexandria, VA: Association for Supervision and Curriculum Development.

Brophy, J. E. (1983). Conceptualizing student motivation. *Educational Psychologist, 18*(3), 200–215.

Brophy J. E. (1989). *Advances in research on teaching: Vol. 1. Teaching for meaningful understanding and self-regulated learning.* Greenwich, CT: JAI.

Brophy, J. E. (1996). *Teaching problem students.* New York: Guilford.

Brophy, J. E. (1998). *Motivating students to learn.* Boston: McGraw-Hill.

Brophy, J. E., & Good, T. L. (1986). Teacher behavior and student achievement. In M. C. Wittrock (Ed.), *Handbook of research on teaching* (3rd ed., pp. 328–375). New York: Macmillan.

Brophy, J. E., & Kher, N. (1986). Teacher socialization as a mechanism for developing student motivation to learn. In R. Feldman (Ed.), *The social psychology of education: Current research and theory* (pp. 257-288). New York: Cambridge University Press.

Brown, D. (1971). *Changing student behavior: A new approach to discipline.* Dubuque, IA: W. C. Brown.

Brown, J., & Moffett, C. (1999). *The hero's journey: How educators can transform schools and improve learning.* Alexandria, VA: Association for Supervision and Curriculum Development.

Bruner, J. S., Goodnow, J. J., & Austin, G. A. (1956). *A study of thinking.* New York: John Wiley and Sons.

Bruner, J. S., & Kenny, M. J. (1966). *Studies in cognitive growth.* New York: John Wiley and Sons.

Bugental, J. (1967). *Challenges of humanistic psychology*. New York: McGraw-Hill.

Bugental, J. (1989). *The search for authenticity: An existential-analytic approach to psychotherapy*. New York: Irvington.

Bugental, J. (1990). *Intimate journeys: Stories from life-changing therapy*. San Francisco: Jossey-Bass.

Cain, D. J., & Seeman, J. (Eds.). (2002). *Humanistic psychotherapies: Handbook for research and practice*. Washington, DC: American Psychological Association.

Caine, R., & Caine, G. (1991). *Making connections: Teaching and the human brain*. Alexandria, VA: Association for Supervision and Curriculum Development.

Calkins, L. (1986). *The art of teaching writing*. Portsmouth, NH: Heinemann.

Camp, R. (1990, Spring). Thinking together about portfolios. *National Writing Project and the Center for the Study of Writing and Literacy, 12*(2), 8–14, 27.

Campbell, B., & Campbell, L. (1999). *Multiple intelligences and student achievement: Success stories from six schools*. Alexandria, VA: Association for Supervision and Curriculum Development.

Canfield, J. (1990, September). Improving students' self-esteem. *Educational Leadership, 48*(1), 48–50.

Cangelosi, J. S. (1990). *Designing tests for evaluating student achievement*. New York: Longman.

Canter, L., & Canter, M. (1976). *Assertive discipline: A take-charge approach for today's educator*. Seal Beach, CA: Canter & Associates.

Canter, L., & Canter, M. (1989). *Assertive discipline for secondary school educators* [Videotape].

Carr, E., & Ogle, D. (1987, April). K-W-L plus: A strategy for comprehension and summarization. *Journal of Reading, 30*(7), 626–631.

Carr, J. F., & Harris, D. (2001). *Succeeding with standards: Linking curriculum, assessment, and action planning*. Alexandria, VA: Association for Supervision and Curriculum Development.

Carrier, C. A., & Titus, A. (1981, Winter). Effects of note taking, pre-training and test mode expectations on learning from lectures. *American Educational Research Journal, 18*(4), 385–397.

Carter, C. J. (1997, March). Why reciprocal teaching? *Educational Leadership, 54*(6), 64–68.

Carter, K. (1990). Teacher's knowledge and learning to teach. In W. R. Houston (Ed.), *Handbook of research on teacher education* (pp. 291–310). New York: Macmillan.

Cavalli, T. F. (2002). *Alchemical psychology: Old recipes for living in a new world*. New York: Tarcher/Putnam.

Cazden, C., & Mehan, H. (1989). Principles from sociology and anthropology: Context, code, classroom and culture. In M. C. Reynolds (Ed.), *Knowledge base for the beginning teacher* (pp. 47–57). Oxford, England; New York: Pergamon Press.

Channon, G. (1970). *Homework*. New York: Outerbridge.

Charles, C. M. (1996). *Building classroom discipline* (5th ed.). White Plains, NY: Longman.

Chen, Z. (1999). Schema induction in children's analogical problem solving. *Journal of Educational Psychology, 91*(4), 703–715.

Childre, D., & Paddison, S. (1998). *HeartMath discovery program: Daily readings and self-discovery exercises for creating a more rewarding life*. Boulder Creek, CA: Planetary.

Ciaccio, J. (2004). *Totally positive teaching: A five-stage approach to energizing students and teachers*. Alexandria, VA: Association for Supervision and Curriculum Development.

Clarke, J. H., Sanborn, S. D., Aiken, J. A., Cornell, N. A., Goodman, J. B., & Hess, K. K. (1998). *Real questions, real answers: Focusing teacher leadership on school improvement*. Alexandria, VA: Association for Supervision and Curriculum Development.

Cohen, J. (1999). *Educating minds and hearts: Social emotional learning and the passage into adolescence*. New York: Teachers College Press.

Cole, J. C., & McLeod, J. S. (1999). Children's writing ability and the impact of pictorial stimulus. *Psychology in the Schools, 36*(4), 359–370.

Coles, R. (1997). *The moral intelligences of children: How to raise a moral child*. New York: Random House.

Collins, M. (1992). *Ordinary children, extraordinary teachers*. Norfolk, VA: Hampton Roads.

Combs, A. W. (1982). *A personal approach to teaching: Beliefs that make a difference*. Boston: Allyn & Bacon.

Cooper, H. M. (1989). *Homework*. New York: Longman.

Cooper, H. M. (1989). *Integrating research: A guide for literature reviews* (2nd ed.). Newbury Park, CA: Sage.

Cooper, H. M., & Good, T. L. (1983). *Pygmalion grows up: Studies in the expectation communication process.* New York: Macmillan.

Cooper, H. M., & Tom, D. (1984, September). Teacher expectation research: A review with implications for classroom instruction. *Elementary School Journal, 85*(1), 77–89.

Corno, L. (1979). Classroom instruction and the matter of time. In D. Duke (Ed.), *Classroom management: 78th yearbook of the national society for the study of education* (Ch. 8). Chicago: University of Chicago Press.

Costa, A. L. (1984, November). Mediating the metacognitive. *Educational Leadership, 42*(3), 57–62.

Costa, A. L. (Ed.). (1991). *Developing minds: A resource book for teaching thinking and programs for teaching thinking* (Rev. ed., Vols. 1 and 2). Alexandria, VA: Association for Supervision and Curriculum Development.

Costa, A. L., & Lowrey, L. F. (1989). *Techniques for teaching thinking.* Pacific Grove, CA: Midwest Publications.

Costa, A. L., & Marzano, R. J. (1987, October). Teaching the language of thinking. *Educational Leadership, 45*(2), 29–33.

Cotton, K. (1999). *Research you can use to improve results.* Alexandria, VA: Association for Supervision and Curriculum Development.

Cotton, K. (1999). *The schooling practices that matter most.* Alexandria, VA: Association for Supervision and Curriculum Development.

Covington, M. V. (1992). *Making the grade: A self-worth perspective on motivation and school reform.* New York: Cambridge University Press.

Crary, J. (2001). *Suspensions of perception: Attention, spectacle, and modern culture.* Cambridge, MA: MIT Press.

Craske, M. L. (1985). Improving persistence through observational learning and attribution retraining. *British Journal of Educational Psychology, 55*, 138–147.

Crocker, J., Fiske, S. T., & Taylor, S. E. (1984). Schematic bases of belief change. In J. R. Eiser (Ed.), *Attitudinal judgment* (pp. 197–226). New York: Springer.

Crooks, T. J. (1988). The impact of classroom evaluation practices on students. *Review of Educational Research, 58*(4), 438–481.

Crump, C. (1970, April). Teachers, questions, and cognition. *Educational Leadership, 27*(7), 657–660.

Csikszentmihalyi, M. (1990). *Flow: The psychology of optimal experience.* New York: Harper Perennial.

Cummings, C. (1980). *Teaching makes a difference.* Edmonds, WA: Teaching, Inc.

Cummings, C. (1983). *Managing to teach.* Edmonds, WA: Teaching, Inc.

Cummings, C. (2000). *Winning strategies for classroom management.* Alexandria, VA: Association for Supervision and Curriculum Development.

Curwin, R. L., & Mendler, A. N. (1988). *Discipline with dignity.* Alexandria, VA: Association for Supervision and Curriculum Development.

Curwin, R. L., & Mendler, A. N. (1997). *As tough as necessary: Countering violence, aggression, and hostility in our schools.* Alexandria, VA: Association for Supervision and Curriculum Development.

Cushman, K. (Ed.). (1996, November). Looking collaboratively at student work: An essential toolkit. *Horace, 13*(2), 1–12.

Daniels, H. (1994). *Literature circles: Voice and choice in the student-centered classroom.* York, ME: Stenhouse.

Danielson, C. (2002). *Enhancing student achievement: A framework for school improvement.* Alexandria, VA: Association for Supervision and Curriculum Development.

D'Arcangelo, M. (2000, November). How does the brain develop? A conversation with Steven Petersen. *Educational Leadership, 58*(3), 68–71.

DeBacker, T., & Nelson, R. (2000, March/April). Motivation to learn science: Difference related to gender, class type, and ability. *Journal of Educational Research, 93*(4), 245–254.

deCharms, R. (1976). *Enhancing motivation: Change in the classroom.* New York: Irvington.

Deci, E. L. (1978). Application of research on the effect of rewards. In M. Lepper & D. Greene (Eds.), *The hidden costs of reward: New perspectives on the psychology of human motivation* (pp. 193–203). Hillsdale, NJ: Lawrence Erlbaum.

Deci, E., & Ryan, R. (1985). *Intrinsic motivation and self determination in human behavior.* New York: Plenum.

Delisle, R. (1997). *How to use problem-based learning in the classroom*. Alexandria, VA: Association for Supervision and Curriculum Development.

Derrida, J. (1995). *Points . . . : Interviews, 1974–1994*. Stanford, CA: Stanford University Press.

Dewey, J. (1933). *How we think*. Boston: D. C. Heath.

Dewey, J. (1938). *Experience and education*. New York: Macmillan.

DiCaprio, N. S. (1983). *Personality theories: A guide to human nature*. New York: Holt.

Dillingham, B. (2005). Performance literacy. *The Reading Teacher, 59*(1), 72–75.

Dillon, J. T. (1984, November). Research on questioning and discussion. *Educational Leadership, 42*(3), 50–56.

Dillon, J. T. (1988). *Questioning and teaching*. New York: Teachers College Press.

Dillon-Peterson, B. (1986). Trusting teachers to know what is good for them. In K. Zumwalt (Ed.), *Improving teaching (1986 ASCD yearbook)* (pp. 29–35). Alexandria, VA: Association for Supervision and Curriculum Development.

Directors of the Child Development Project. (1994). *At home in our schools: A guide to school wide activities that build community*. Oakland, CA: Developmental Studies Center.

Dishon, D., & O'Leary, P. W. (1998). *A guidebook for cooperative learning: Techniques for creating more effective schools* (3rd ed.). Holmes Beach, FL: Learning Publications.

Donald, M. (1991). Origins of the modern mind: Three stages in the evolution of culture and cognition. Cambridge, MA: Harvard University Press.

Doyle, W. (1986). Classroom organization and management. In M. C. Wittrock (Ed.), *Handbook of research on teaching* (3rd. ed., pp. 392–431). New York: Macmillan.

Drabman, R., Spitalnik, R., & O'Leary, K. (1973). Teaching self control to disruptive children. *Journal of Abnormal Psychology, 82*, 10–16.

Drake, S. M. (1998). *Creating integrated curriculum: Proven ways to increase student learning*. Thousand Oaks, CA: Corwin Press.

Dreikurs, R. (1968). *Psychology in the classroom* (2nd ed.). New York: Harper & Row.

Dreikurs, R., Grunwald, B., & Pepper, F. (1982). *Maintaining sanity in the classroom* (2nd ed.). New York: Harper & Row.

DuFour, R., & Eaker, R. (1998). *Professional learning communities at work: Best practices for enhancing student achievement*. Alexandria, VA: Association for Supervision and Curriculum Development.

Dunson, M. (2000). *From research to practice and back again: TIMSS as a tool for educational improvement*. (CPRE Policy Brief No. RB-30). Philadelphia: Consortium for Policy Research in Education, University of Pennsylvania.

Durlak, J. A., & Weissberg, R. P. (2005, August). *A major meta-analysis of positive youth development programs*. Invited presentation at the annual meeting of the American Psychological Association, Washington, DC.

Eisenhart, M. (1977, May). *Maintaining control: Teacher competence in the classroom*. Paper presented at the American Anthropological Association, Houston, TX.

Elkman, P., & Friesen, W. (1975). *Unmasking the face*. Palo Alto, CA: Consulting Psychologists Press.

Emmer, E. T. (1988). Praise and the instructional process. *Journal of Classroom Interaction, 23*(2), 32–39.

Emmer, E. T., & Evertson, C. M. (1981, January). Synthesis of research on classroom management. *Educational Leadership, 38*(4), 342–347.

Emmer, E. T., Evertson, C. M., & Worsham, M. A. (2002). *Classroom management for secondary teachers* (6th ed.). Boston: Allyn & Bacon.

English, L. D. (1997). Children's reasoning in classifying and solving computational word problems. In L. D. English (Ed.), *Mathematical reasoning: Analogies, metaphors, and images* (pp. 191–220). Mahwah, NJ: Lawrence Erlbaum.

Erwin, J. C. (2003, September). Giving students what they need. *Educational Leadership, 61*(1), 19–23.

Esme, R. C. (1999). *Educating Esme*. Chapel Hill, NC: Algonquin Books.

Evertson, C. M. (1989). Classroom organization and management. In M. C. Reynolds (Ed.), *Knowledge base for the beginning teacher* (pp. 59–70). Oxford, England; New York: Pergamon Press.

Fantuzzo, J. W. (1990, Winter). An evaluation of reciprocal peer tutoring across elementary school settings. *Journal of School Psychology, 28*(4), 309–323.

Farnan, N., & Kelly, R. (1991, July–September). Keeping track: Creating assessment portfolios in reading and writing. *Quarterly of the National Writing Project and the Center for the Study of Writing and Literacy, 14*(1), 14–17.

Feshbach, N. D. (1975). Empathy in children: Some theoretical and empirical considerations. *The Counseling Psychologist, 5*, 25–29.

Feshbach, N. D. (1984). Empathy, empathy training, and the regulation of aggression in elementary school children. In R. W. Kaplan, V. J. Konecni, & R. W. Novaco (Eds.), *Aggression in children and youth.* The Hague; Boston: Martinus Nijhoff Publications.

Feuerstein, R. (1980). *Instrumental enrichment: An intervention program for cognitive modifiability.* Baltimore: University Park Press.

Firth, G. (1985). *Behavior management in the schools: A primer for parents.* New York: Thomas.

Fisher, D., & Roach, V. (1999). *Opening doors: Connecting students to curriculum, classmates, and learning.* Colorado Springs, CO: PEAK Parent Center.

Flanders, N. (1969). Teacher effectiveness. In R. L. Ebel (Ed.), *Encyclopedia of educational research* (4th ed., pp. 1423–1437). New York: Macmillan.

Flavell, J. H. (1976). Metacognitive aspects of problem solving. In L. B. Resnick (Ed.), *The nature of intelligence* (pp. 231–235). Hillsdale, NJ: Lawrence Erlbaum.

Flick, L. (1992). Where concepts meet precepts: Stimulating analogical thought in children. *Science Education, 75*(2), 215–230.

Fox, L., & Weaver, F. L. (1990). *Unlocking doors to self-esteem.* Torrance, CA: B. L. Winch.

Fraser, B. J., Walberg, H. J., Welch, W. W., & Hattie, J. A. (1987). Synthesis of educational productivity research. *Journal of Educational Research, 11*(2), 145–252.

Frazer, R., & Fadiman, J. (1984). *Personality theories and personal growth.* New York: Harper.

Freiberg, H. J. (Ed.). (1999). *Perceiving, behaving, becoming: Lessons learned.* Alexandria, VA: Association for Supervision and Curriculum Development.

Freiberg, H. J., & Driscoll, A. (2000). *Universal teaching strategies* (3rd ed.). Boston: Allyn & Bacon.

Frick, W. R. (1981). *Humanistic psychology: Conversations with Abraham Maslow, Gardner Murphy, & Carl Rogers.* Bristol, IN: Wyndham Hall Press.

Gabbert, B., Johnson, D. W., & Johnson, R. (1986). Cooperative learning, group-to-individual transfer, process gain, and the acquisition of cognitive reasoning strategies. *Journal of Psychology, 120*, 265–278.

Gall, M. (1970, December). The use of questions in teaching. *Review of Educational Research, 40*(5), 207–220.

Gardner, H. (1993). *Creating minds.* New York: Basic Books.

Gendlin, E. (1980). *Focusing.* New York: Bantam.

Gibbs, J. (1987). *Tribes: A process for social development and cooperative learning.* Santa Rosa, CA: Center Source Publications.

Ginott, H. G. (1972). *Teacher and child.* New York: Avon.

Ginsberg, M. B., Johnson Jr., J. F., & Moffett, C. A. (1997). *Educators supporting educators: A guide to organizing school support teams.* Alexandria, VA: Association for Supervision and Curriculum Development.

Glasser, W. (1985). *Control theory in the classroom.* New York: Perennial Press.

Glasser, W. (1990). *The quality school: Managing students without coercion.* New York: Harper & Row.

Glasser, W. (1998). *Choice theory: A new psychology of personal freedom.* New York: Harper Collins.

Goldenburg, C. (1985). *The paradox of expectations: Two case studies.* Paper presented at the annual meeting of the American Educational Research Association, Chicago.

Goleman, D. (1995). *Emotional intelligence: Why it can matter more than IQ.* New York: Bantam.

Good, T. L. (1987, July–August). Two decades of research on teacher expectations: Findings and future directions. *Journal of Teacher Education, 38*(4), 32–47.

Good, T. L., & Brophy, J. E. (1990). *Educational psychology: A realistic approach.* New York: Longman.

Goodlad, J. (1984). *A place called school.* New York: McGraw-Hill.

Gordon, S. P., & Maxey, S. (2000). *How to help beginning teachers succeed* (2nd ed.). Alexandria, VA: Association for Supervision and Curriculum Development.

Gordon, T. (1989). *Teaching children self-discipline at home and at school.* New York: Times Books.

Grof, S. (1988). *The adventure of self discovery*. Albany, NY: SUNY.

Gross, S. J. (1998). *Staying centered: Curriculum leadership in a turbulent era*. Alexandria, VA: Association for Supervision and Curriculum Development.

Grossman, P., Wilson, S. M., & Shulman, L. S. (1989). Teachers of substance: Subject matter knowledge for teaching. In M. C. Reynolds (Ed.), *Knowledge base for the beginning teacher* (pp. 23–36). Oxford, England; New York: Pergamon Press.

Guskey, T. R. (1996). *Communicating student learning (1996 ASCD yearbook)*. Alexandria, VA: Association for Supervision and Curriculum Development.

Guzzetti, B. J., Snyder, T. E., & Glass, G. V. (1993). Promoting conceptual change in science: A comparative meta-analysis of instructional interventions from reading and science education. *Reading Research Quarterly, 28*(2), 117–155.

Hanson, J., Silver, H., & Strong, R. (1991). *Thoughtful education*. Princeton, NJ: Hanson Silver Strong & Associates.

Hargreaves, A. (Ed.). (1997). *Rethinking educational change with heart and mind (1997 ASCD yearbook)*. Alexandria, VA: Association for Supervision and Curriculum Development.

Harmin, M. (1990). *How to plan a program for moral education*. Alexandria, VA: Association for Supervision and Curriculum Development.

Harmin, M. (1990, September). The workshop way to student success. *Educational Leadership, 48*(1), 43–47.

Harmin, M. (2002). *Strategies to inspire active learning*. White Plains, NY: Inspiring Strategy Institute.

Harris, T. A. (1969). *I'm OK–you're OK: A practical guide to transactional analysis*. New York: Harper & Row.

Hart, L. (1975). *How the brain works*. New York: Basic Books.

Hart, L. (1983). *Human brain, human learning*. New York: Longman.

Hart, T., Nelson, P. L., & Puhakka, K. (2000). *Transpersonal knowing: Exploring the horizon of consciousness*. New York: SUNY Press.

Harter, S. (1999). *The construction of self: A developmental perspective*. New York: Harper & Row.

Hattie, J. (1992). Measuring the effects of schooling. *Australian Journal of Education, 36*(1), 5–13.

Hattie, J., Biggs, J., & Purdie, N. (1996). Effects of learning skills and intervention on student learning: A meta-analysis. *Review of Educational Research, 66*(2), 99–136.

Havighurst, F. (1952). *Developmental tasks and education*. New York: Longman.

Heiman, M., & Slomianko, J. (Eds.). (1987). *Thinking skills instruction: Concepts and techniques*. (Building students' thinking skills series). Washington, DC: National Education Association.

Henson, K. (1988). *Methods and strategies for teaching in secondary and middle schools*. New York: Longman.

Herman, J., Aschbacher, P., & Winters, L. (1992). *A practical guide to alternative assessment*. Alexandria, VA: Association for Supervision and Curriculum Development.

Hidi, S., & Anderson, V. (1987). Providing written summaries: Task demands, cognitive operations, and implications for instruction. *Reviewing Educational Research, 56*, 473–493.

Hirsch, E. D. (1987). *Cultural literacy: What every American needs to know*. Boston: Houghton Mifflin.

Hirsch, E. D., Kett, J. F., & Trefil, J. (2002). *The new dictionary of cultural literacy*. Boston: Houghton Mifflin.

Hoerr, T. R. (2000). *Becoming a multiple intelligences school*. Alexandria, VA: Association for Supervision and Curriculum Development.

Holubec, E. J., Johnson, D. W., & Johnson, R. T. (1994). *Cooperative learning in the classroom*. Alexandria, VA: Association for Supervision and Curriculum Development.

Hoyle, J. R., English, F. W., & Steffy, B. E. (1990). *Skills for successful school leaders* (2nd ed.). Arlington, VA: American Association of School Administrators.

Hunkins, F. P. (1989). *Teaching thinking through effective questioning*. Boston: Christopher-Gordon.

Hunter, M. C. (1969). *Teach more—faster!* El Segundo, CA: TIP Publications.

Hunter, M. C. (1976). *Rx: Improved instruction*. El Segundo, CA: TIP Publications.

Hunter, M. C. (1984). Knowing, teaching, and supervising. In P. Hosford (Ed.), *Using what we know about teaching* (pp. 169–192). Alexandria, VA: Association for Supervision and Curriculum Development.

Hunter, M. C., & Carlson, P. V. (1971). *Improving your child's behavior*. Glendale, CA: Bowmar.

Hyde, A. A., & Bizar, M. (1989). *Thinking in context: Teaching cognitive processes across the elementary school curriculum*. New York: Longman.

Hyerle, D. (1996). *Visual tools for constructing knowledge*. Alexandria, VA: Association for Supervision and Curriculum Development.

Ilfeld, E. (1996). *Learning comes to life*. Ypsilanti, MI: High Scope Education Research.

Jackins, H. (1974). *Human side of human beings*. Seattle, WA: Rational Island.

James, W. (1980). *Principles of psychology*. Mineola, NY: Dover.

Jensen, E. (1998). *Teaching with the brain in mind*. Alexandria, VA: Association for Supervision and Curriculum Development.

Jensen, E. (2001). *Arts with the brain in mind*. Alexandria, VA: Association for Supervision and Curriculum Development.

Johnson, D. P. (2005). *Sustaining change in schools: How to overcome differences and focus on quality*. Alexandria, VA: Association for Supervision and Curriculum Development.

Johnson D. W., & Johnson, R. (1975). *Learning together and alone*. Englewood Cliffs, NJ: Prentice-Hall.

Johnson, D. W., & Johnson, R. (1987). *Creative conflict*. Edina, MN: Interaction Book Company.

Johnson, D. W., & Johnson, R. (1988, May). Critical thinking through structured controversy. *Educational Leadership, 45*(8), 58–64.

Johnson, D. W., & Johnson, R. (1989). *Cooperation and competition: Theory and research*. Edina, MN: Interaction Book Company.

Johnson, D. W., & Johnson, R. T. (1995). *Reducing school violence through conflict resolution*. Alexandria, VA: Association for Supervision and Curriculum Development.

Johnson, D. W., Johnson, R. T., & Holubec, E. J. (1994). *The new circles of learning: Cooperation in the classroom and school*. Alexandria, VA: Association for Supervision and Curriculum Development.

Johnson, D. W., Johnson, R. T., Holubec, E. J., & Roy, P. (1984). *Circles of learning: Cooperation in the classroom*. Alexandria, VA: Association for Supervision and Curriculum Development.

Jones, B. F., Amiran, M. R., & Katims, M. (1985). Teaching cognitive strategies and text structure within language arts programs. In J. W. Segal, S. F. Chipman, & R. Glaser (Eds.), *Thinking and learning skills: Relating instruction to research* (Vol. 1, pp. 259–297). Hillsdale, NJ: Lawrence Erlbaum.

Jones, B. F., Palincsar, A. S., Ogle, D. S., & Carr, E. F. (Eds.). (1987). *Strategic teaching and learning: Cognitive instruction in the content areas*. Alexandria, VA: Association for Supervision and Curriculum Development.

Jones, F. (1987a). *Positive classroom discipline*. New York: McGraw-Hill.

Jones, F. (1987b). *Positive classroom instruction*. New York: McGraw-Hill.

Jones, V. F., & Jones, L. S. (1990). *Comprehensive classroom management: Motivating and managing students* (3rd ed.). Boston: Allyn & Bacon.

Jordan, B. (2000). *Social work and the third way: Tough love*. Thousand Oaks, CA: Sage Publications.

Jourard, S. (1963). *Personal adjustment: An approach through the study of healthy personality*. New York: Macmillan.

Jourard, S. (1980). *Healthy personality: An approach from the point of view of humanistic psychology*. New York: Macmillan.

Joyce, B., & Weil, M. (1991). *Models of teaching*. Englewood Cliffs, NJ: Prentice-Hall.

Kagan, S. (1980). Cooperation-competition, culture, and structural bias in classrooms. In S. Sharan, P. Hare, C. Webb, & R. Hertz-Lazarowitz (Eds.), *Cooperation in education* (pp. 197–211). Provo, UT: Brigham Young University Press.

Kagan, S. (1989, December–1990, January). The structural approach to cooperative learning. *Educational Leadership, 47*(4), 12–15.

Karlin, M. S., & Berger, R. (1972). *Discipline and the disruptive child: A practical guide for elementary teachers*. West Nyack, NY: Parker.

Katzenmeyer, M., & Moller, G. (2001). *Awakening the sleeping giant: Helping teachers develop as leaders*. Thousand Oaks, CA: Corwin Press.

Kaufman, B. (1964). *Up the down staircase*. New York: Harper.

Kearns, J. F., Kleinert, H. L., & Kennedy, S. (1999, March). We need not exclude anyone. *Educational Leadership, 56*(6), 33–38.

Kendall, J. S., & Marzano, R. J. (1996). *A comprehensive guide to designing standards-based districts, schools, and classrooms.* Alexandria, VA: Association for Supervision and Curriculum Development.

Kerman, S., & Martin, M. (1980). *Teacher expectations and student achievement.* Bloomington, IN: Phi Delta Kappa.

Kerr, M. M., & Nelson, C. M. (1983). *Strategies for managing behavior problems in the classroom.* Columbus, OH: Merrill.

Kessler, R. (2000). *The soul of education: Helping students find connection, compassion, and character at school.* Alexandria, VA: Association for Supervision and Curriculum Development.

Kilpatrick W., Kilpatrick, G., & Wolfe, S. M. (1994). *Books that build character: A guide to teaching your child moral values through stories.* New York: Touchstone.

Kindsvetter, R., & Wilen, W. (1989). *Dynamics of effective teaching.* New York: Longman.

Kintsch, W. (1979). On modeling comprehension. *Educational Psychologist, 1,* 3–14.

Knight, P. (1992, May). How I use portfolios in mathematics. *Educational Leadership, 49*(8), 71–72.

Kobrin, D. (1992). *In there with the kids: Teaching in today's classrooms.* Boston: Houghton Mifflin.

Kohn, A. (1993). *Punished by rewards: The trouble with gold stars, incentive plans, A's, praise, and other bribes.* Boston: Houghton Mifflin.

Kohn, A. (1996). *Beyond discipline: From compliance to community.* Alexandria, VA: Association for Supervision and Curriculum Development.

Kohut, S., & Range, D. G. (1979). *Classroom discipline: Case studies and viewpoints.* Washington, DC: National Education Association.

Kounin, J. S. (1977). *Discipline and group management in classrooms.* Huntington, NY: R. E. Krieger.

Kozminsky, E., & Kozminsky, L. (2003, September). Improving motivation through dialogue. *Educational Leadership, 61*(1), 50–53.

Krumboltz, J. D., & Krumboltz, H. B. (1972). *Changing children's behavior.* Englewood Cliffs, NJ: Prentice-Hall.

LaBerge, D., & Samuels, S. J. (1974). Toward a theory of automatic information processing in reading. In H. Singer and R. B. Riddell (Eds.), *Theoretical models and processes of reading* (pp. 548–579). Newark, DE: International Reading Association.

Lam, J. (1989). *The impact of conflict resolution programs on schools: A review and synthesis of the evidence* (2nd ed.). Amherst, MA: National Association for Mediation in Education.

Lasley, T. J. (1985). Fostering nonaggression in the classroom: An anthropological perspective. *Theory into Practice, 24,* 247–255.

Lasley, T. J., & Wayson, W. W. (1982, December). Characteristics of schools with good discipline. *Educational Leadership, 40*(3), 28–31.

Lee, A. (1989, Fall). "I'll tell you right from the beginning, Mrs. Lee, I hate reading." *American Educator,* 19–20.

Lemlich, J. (1988). *Classroom management: Methods and techniques for elementary and secondary teachers* (2nd ed.). New York: Longman.

Lepper, M., & Greene, D. (Eds.). (1978). *The hidden costs of rewards: New perspectives on the psychology of human motivation.* Hillsdale, NJ: Lawrence Erlbaum.

Levin, B. (2001). *Energizing teacher education and professional development with problem-based learning.* Alexandria, VA: Association for Supervision and Curriculum Development.

Levine, S. L. (1999). *A passion for teaching.* Alexandria, VA: Association for Supervision and Curriculum Development.

Lewin, L., & Shoemaker, B. J. (1998). *Great performances: Creating classroom-based assessments tasks.* Alexandria, VA: Association for Supervision and Curriculum Development.

Lickona, T. (1983). *Raising good children.* New York: Bantam Books.

Lickona, T. (1991). *Educating for character.* New York: Bantam Books.

Lopez-Reyna, B. A., & Bay, M. (1997). Enriching assessment: Using varied assessments for diverse learners. *Teaching Exceptional Children, 29*(4), 33–37.

Maeroff, G. (1988). *The empowerment of teachers.* New York: Teachers College.

Marsh, D. D. (1999). *Preparing our schools for the 21st century (1999 ASCD yearbook).* Alexandria, VA: Association for Supervision and Curriculum Development.

Martin, G., & Pear, J. (1983). *Behavior modification: What it is and how to do it* (2nd ed.). Englewood Cliffs, NJ: Prentice-Hall.

Martin-Kniep, G. O. (2000). *Becoming a better teacher: Eight innovations that work*. Alexandria, VA: Association for Supervision and Curriculum Development.

Marzano, R. J. (1992). *A different kind of classroom: Teaching with Dimensions of Learning*. Alexandria, VA: Association for Supervision and Curriculum Development.

Marzano, R. J. (2000). *Transforming classroom grading*. Alexandria, VA: Association for Supervision and Curriculum Development.

Marzano, R. J. (2003). *What works in school: Translating research into action*. Alexandria, VA: Association for Supervision and Curriculum Development.

Marzano, R. J., Brandt, R. S., Hughes, C. S., Jones, B. F., Presseisen, B. Z., Rankin, S. C., Suhor, C. (1988). *Dimensions of thinking: A framework for curriculum and instruction*. Alexandria, VA: Association for Supervision and Curriculum Development.

Marzano, R. J., Marzano, J. S., & Pickering, D. J. (2003). *Classroom management that works: Research-based strategies for every teacher*. Alexandria, VA: Association for Supervision and Curriculum Development.

Marzano, R. J., Pickering, D. J., & Pollock, J. E. (2001). *Classroom instruction that works: Research-based strategies for increasing student achievement*. Alexandria, VA: Association for Supervision and Curriculum Development.

Maslow, A. (1999). *Toward a psychology of being* (3rd ed.). New York: John Wiley & Sons.

Mathematical Science Education Board. (1990). *Reshaping school mathematics*. Washington, DC: National Academy Press.

Maurer, R. (1988). *Special educator's discipline handbook*. West Nyack, NY: Center for Applied Research in Education.

May, R. (1984). *The courage to create*. New York: Bantam.

McCarty, H., & Siccone, F. (2001). *Motivating your students: Before you can teach them, you have to reach them*. Boston, MA: Allyn & Bacon.

McCombs, B. L., & Whisler, J. S. (1997). *The learner-centered classroom and school*. San Francisco, CA: Jossey-Bass.

McCourt, F. (2005). *Teacher man: A memoir*. New York: Scribner.

McEwan, B., Gathercoal, P., & Nimmo, V. (1997, March). *An examination of the application of constitutional concepts as an approach to classroom management: Four studies of judicious discipline in varied classroom settings*. Paper presented at the annual meeting of the American Education Research Association, Chicago. (ERIC Document Reproduction Service No. ED418031)

McIntyre, T. (1989). *The behavior management handbook: Setting up effective behavior management systems*. Boston: Allyn & Bacon.

McLeish, J. (1976). Lecture method. In N. L. Gage (Ed.), *The psychology of teaching methods: Part I. 75th yearbook of the National Society for the Study of Education*. Chicago, IL: University of Chicago.

McTighe, J., & Lyman, Jr., F. T. (1988, April). Cueing thinking in the classroom: The promise of theory-embedded tools. *Educational Leadership, 45*(7), 18–24.

McWaters, B. (Ed.). (1977). *Humanistic perspectives: Current trends in psychology*. Monterey, CA: Brooks/Cole.

Meek, A. (1999). *Communicating with the public: A guide for school leaders*. Alexandria, VA: Association for Supervision and Curriculum Development.

Mendler, A. N. (2000). *Power struggles: Successful techniques for educators*. National Educational Service.

Mendler, A. N. (2001). *Connecting with students*. Alexandria, VA: Association for Supervision and Curriculum Development.

Meyer, A., & Rose, D. H. (2002). *Teaching every student in the digital age: Universal design for learning*. Alexandria, VA: Association for Supervision and Curriculum Development.

Miller, J. P. (1981). *The compassionate teacher: How to teach and learn with your whole self*. Englewood Cliffs, NJ: Prentice-Hall.

Miller, J. P., Cassie, B., & Drake, S. (1991). *Holistic learning: A teacher's guide to integrated studies*. Toronto, Canada: OISE Press.

Miller, M., & Young-Eisendrath, P. (Eds.). (2000). *The psychology of mature spirituality: Integrity, wisdom, transcendence.* New York: Routledge.

Montessori, M. (1964). *The advanced Montessori method.* (A. E. George, Trans.). New York: Schocken Books.

Moorman, C. (2005). *Parent talk: How to talk to your child in language that builds self-esteem and encourages responsibility.* New York: Fireside.

Moorman, C., & Moorman, N. (1989). *Teacher talk.* Bay City, MI: Personal Power Press.

Moskowitz, G., & Hayman, J. (1976). Success strategies of inner-city teachers: A year-long study. *Journal of Educational Research, 69,* 283–289.

Moustakas, C. (1967). *Creativity and conformity.* Princeton, NJ: Van Nostrand.

Murphy, J. (1988, August). Contingency contracting in schools: A review. *Education and Treatment of Children, 11*(3), 257–269.

Murray, F. B. (1989). Explanations in education. In M. C. Reynolds (Ed.), *Knowledge base for the beginning teacher* (pp. 1–12). Oxford, England; New York: Pergamon Press.

National Commission on Excellence in Education. (1983). *A nation at risk: The imperative for educational reform.* Washington, DC: U.S. Department of Education.

Nave, B. (1990, December). *Self-esteem: The key to student success. A series of solutions and strategies* (No. 3). Clemson, SC: National Dropout Prevention Center.

Nelson, G. D. (2001, November). Choosing content that's worth knowing. *Educational Leadership, 59*(2), 12–16.

Nelson, R., & Carr, B. A. (1999). *Think Time strategy for schools: Bringing order to the classroom* (2nd ed.). Longmont, CO: Sopris West.

Newman, J. (1991). *Interwoven conversations.* Portsmouth, NH: Heinemann.

Newmann, F. (1988). *Higher order thinking in high school social studies: An analysis of classrooms, teachers, students, and leadership.* Madison, WI: University of Wisconsin, National Center for Effective Secondary Schools.

Nieto, S. M. (2003, May). What keeps teachers going? *Educational Leadership, 60*(8), 15–18.

Noddings, N. (1992). *The challenge to care in schools: An alternative approach to education.* New York: Teachers College Press.

North Central Regional Educational Laboratory. (2002). *Learning from TIMSS 1999: A guidebook for using TIMSS 1999 data for local school improvement.* Naperville, IL: Deborah Nelson.

Nucci, L. (1989). Knowledge of the learner: The development of children's concepts of self, morality and societal convention. In M. C. Reynolds (Ed.), *Knowledge base for the beginning teacher* (Ch. 10). Oxford, England; New York: Pergamon Press.

Nuthall, G. (1999). The way students learn: Acquiring knowledge from an integrated science and social studies unit. *Elementary School Journal, 99*(4), 303–341.

O'Connor, K. (1999). *How to grade for learning.* Arlington Heights, IL: Skylight.

Olson, M. W. (1991, January–March). Portfolios: Education tools (research into practice). *Reading Psychology, 12*(1), 73–80.

Ornstein, A. C. (1990). *Strategies for effective teaching.* New York: Harper & Row.

Ostrander, S., & Schroeder, L. (1994). *Super learning 2000.* New York: Delacorte Press.

Owens, R. (1991). *Organizational behavior in education* (4th ed.). Englewood Cliffs, NJ: Prentice-Hall.

Palincsar, A. S. (1986, October). Metacognitive strategy instruction. *Exceptional Children, 53*(2), 118–124.

Palincsar, A. S., & Brown, A. L. (1984). Reciprocal teaching of comprehension fostering and comprehension monitoring activities. *Cognition and Instruction, 1*(2), 117–175.

Palincsar, A. S., & Brown, A. L. (1985). Reciprocal teaching: Activities to promote reading with your mind. In T. L. Harris & E. J. Cooper (Eds.), *Reading, thinking and concept development: Strategies for the classroom* (pp. 147–158). New York: College Board.

Palincsar, A. S., & Brown, D. A. (1987, February). Enhancing instructional time through attention to metacognition. *Journal of Learning Disabilities, 20*(2), 66–75.

Patterson T. L., & Kelleher, P. (2005). *Resilient school leaders: Strategies for turning adversity into achievement.* Alexandria, VA: Association for Supervision and Curriculum Development.

Pedersen, E., Faucher, T. A., & Eaton, W. W. (1978, February). A new perspective on the effects of first-grade teachers on children's subsequent adult status. *Harvard Educational Review, 48*(1), 1–31.

Perini, M. J., Silver, H. F., & Strong, R. W. (2000). *So each may learn: Integrating learning styles and multiple intelligences.* Alexandria, VA: Association for Supervision and Curriculum Development.

Perls, F., Hefferline, R. F., & Goodman, P. (1977). *Gestalt therapy: Excitement and growth in the human personality.* New York: Bantam.

Piaget, J. (1970). Piaget's theory. In P. Mussen (Ed.), *Carmichael's manual of child psychology* (3rd ed., pp. 703–732). New York: Wiley.

Pilon, G. (1996). *Workshop way.* New Orleans, LA: Workshop Way.

Pinker, S. (2002). *Blank slate: The modern denial of human nature.* New York: Viking.

Pinnell G., & Deford, D. (1988). *Reading Recovery: Early intervention for at risk first graders.* Arlington, VA: Educational Research Service.

Pogrow, S. (2004, October). The missing element in reducing the learning gap. *Teachers College Record.*

Porro, B. (1996). *Talk it out: Conflict resolution in the elementary classroom.* Alexandria, VA: Association for Supervision and Curriculum Development.

Porro, B. (2002). *Teaching conflict resolution with the Rainbow Kids Program.* Alexandria, VA: Association for Supervision and Curriculum Development.

Pressley, M., Symons, S., McDaniel, M., Snyder, B. L., & Turnure, J. E. (1988). Elaborative interrogation facilitates acquisition of confusing facts. *Journal of Educational Psychology, 80*, 268–278.

Pressley, M., Wood, E., Woloshyn, V., King, A., & Menke, D. (1992). Encouraging mindful use of prior knowledge: Attempting to construct explanatory answers facilitates learning. *Educational Psychologist, 27*(1), 91–109.

Pulaski, M. A. S. (1980). *Understanding Piaget: An introduction to children's cognitive development* (2nd ed.). New York: Harper & Row.

Purkey, W., & Novak, J. M. (1984). *Inviting school success: A self-concept approach to teaching and learning.* Belmont, CA: Wadsworth.

Pysch, R. (1991). Discipline improves as students take responsibility. *NASSP Bulletin, 75*, 117–118.

Raths, L. E. (1972). *Meeting the needs of children: Creating trust and security.* Columbus, OH: Charles E. Merrill.

Redfield, D., & Rousseau, E. (1981, Summer). A meta-analysis on teacher questioning behavior. *Review of Educational Research, 51*, 234–245.

Redl, F., & Wattenberg, W. (1951; 1959). *Mental hygiene in teaching.* New York: Harcourt, Brace & World.

Render, G., Padilla, J., & Krank, H. (1989, March). What research really shows about assertive discipline. *Educational Leadership, 46*(6), 72–75.

Resnick, L. (1987). *Education and learning to think.* Washington, DC: National Academy Press.

Rickards, J. P. (1982). Homework. In H. E. Mitzel, J. Hardin Best, & W. Rabinowitz (Eds.), *Encyclopedia of educational research* (5th ed., pp. 831–834). New York: Free Press.

Riley, J. (1980). *The effects of teachers' wait-time and cognitive questioning level on pupil science development.* Paper presented at the annual meeting of the National Association for Research in Science Teaching, Boston.

Ripoll, T. (1999). Why this made me think that. *Thinking and Reasoning, 4*(1), 15–43.

Robbins, P. (1991). *How to plan and implement a peer coaching program.* Alexandria, VA: Association for Supervision and Curriculum Development.

Roe, M. F. (1991, December). *Portfolios: From mandate to implementation.* Paper presented at the annual meeting of the National Reading Conference, Palm Springs, CA.

Roettger, D., & Szymczuk, M. (Eds.). (1990). *Guide for developing student portfolios.* (Draft version). Johnston, IA: Heartland Area Education Agency 11.

Rogoff, B. (1990). *Apprenticeship in thinking.* New York: Oxford University Press.

Romesburg, C. (2001). *The life of the creative spirit.* Philadelphia: Xlibris.

Rosaen, C. L. (1989). Writing in the content areas: Reaching its potential in the learning process. In J. Brophy (Ed.), *Advances in research on teaching: Teaching for meaningful understanding and self-regulated learning* (Vol. 1, pp. 153–194). Greenwich, CT: JAI.

Rose, C., & Nicholl, M. J. (1997). *Accelerated learning for the 21st century: The six-step plan to unlock your master-mind*. New York: Dell.

Rosenholtz, S. (1989). *Teacher's workplace: The social organization of schools*. New York: Longman.

Rosenshine, B. (1968, December). To explain: A review of research. *Educational Leadership, 26*(3), 303–309.

Rosenshine, B. (1970). Enthusiastic teaching: A research review. *School Review 78*, 279–301.

Rosenshine, B. (1971). *Teaching behaviors and student achievement*. London: National Foundation for Educational Research in England and Wales.

Rosenshine, B. (1976). Classroom instruction. In N. Gage (Ed.), *Psychology of teaching: 77th yearbook of the National Society for the Study of Education* (pp. 335–371). Chicago: University of Chicago Press.

Rosenshine, B. (1979). Content, time and direct instruction. *Elementary School Journal, 83*, pp. 335–351.

Rosenshine, B., & Meister, C. C. (1994). Reciprocal teaching: A review of the research. *Review of Educational Research, 64*(4), 479–530.

Rosenthal, R., & Jacobson, L. (1968). *Pygmalion in the classroom: Teacher expectations and pupils' intellectual development*. New York: Holt, Rinehart & Winston.

Ross, J. A. (1988). Controlling variables: A meta-analysis of training studies. *Review of Educational Research, 59*(4), 405–437.

Rowe, M. B. (1974, Spring). Wait time and rewards as instructional variables: Their influence on language, logic, and fate control. *Journal of Research in Science Teaching, 11*(2), 81–84.

Rowe, M. B. (1986, January–February). Wait time: Slowing down may be a way of speeding up! *Journal of Teacher Education, 31*(1), 43–50.

Royce, J. R. (1981). *Humanistic psychology: Concepts and criticisms*. New York: Plenum.

Russo, J. E., & Schoemaker, P. J. H. (2002). *Winning decisions: Getting it right the first time*. New York: Currency/Doubleday.

Sachse, R. (1988). *From attitude to action: On the necessity of an action-oriented approach in client-centered therapy*. Bochum: Germany, Ruhr Universiat, Berichte aus der Arbeitseinheit Klinische Psychologie, Fakultat fur Psychologie, no. 64.

Sage, S., & Torp, L. (1998). *Problems as possibilities: Problem-based learning for K–12 education*. Alexandria, VA: Association for Supervision and Curriculum Development.

Sagor, R. (2003). *Motivating students and teachers in an era of standards*. Alexandria, VA: Association for Supervision and Curriculum Development.

Sanders, N. (1966). *Classroom questions: What kinds*. New York: Harper & Row.

Santa, C., Havers, L., & Maycumber, E. (1996). Creating independence through student-owned strategies. Dubuque, IA: Kendall/Hunt.

Saphier, J., & Gower, R. (1997). *The skillful teacher: Building your teaching skills*. Anton, MA: Research for Better Teaching.

Scherer, M. (Ed.). (1999). *A better beginning: Supporting and mentoring new teachers*. Alexandria, VA: Association for Supervision and Curriculum Development.

Schmoker, M. (1999). *Results: The key to continuous school improvement* (2nd ed.). Alexandria, VA: Association for Supervision and Curriculum Development.

Schmuck, R., & Schmuck, P. (1988). *Group processes in the classroom* (5th ed.). Dubuque, IA: William C. Brown.

Schneider, K. J., Bugental, J. F. T., & Pierson, J. F. (Eds.). (2001). *The handbook of humanistic psychology: Leading edges in theory, research, and practice*. Thousand Oaks, CA: Sage Publications.

Schults, D. (1977). *Growth psychology: Models of healthy personality*. New York: Van Reinhold.

Schweinhart, L. J., Montie, J., Xiang, Z., Barnett, W. S., Belfield, C. R., & Nores, M. (2005). *Lifetime effects: The High/Scope Perry Preschool study through age 40* (Monographs of the High/Scope Educational Research Foundaton, 14). Ypsilanti, MI: High/Scope Press.

Scott, J., & Sornson, R. (1997). *Teaching and joy*. Alexandria, VA: Association for Supervision and Curriculum Development.

Seligman, M. E. P. (1991). *Learned optimism*. New York: Knopf.

Sharan, Y., & Sharan, S. (1989, December–1990, January). Group investigation expands cooperative learning. *Educational Leadership, 47*(4), 17–21.

Shroyer, G., Wright, E., Kerr, E., & Weamer, D. (1996, April). *Expertise in elementary math and science teaching: Evaluating an innovative pre-service preparation model.* Paper presented at the National Association for Research in Science Teaching, St. Louis, MO.

Siccone, F. (1988). *Teacher as coach: Strategies for empowering students.* Self-published.

Sizer, N., & Sizer, T. (2000). *The students are watching: Schools and the moral contract.* Boston: Beacon Press.

Skinner, B. F. (1953). *Science and human behavior.* New York: Macmillan.

Skinner, B. F. (1971). *Beyond freedom and dignity.* New York: Knopf.

Slavin, R. E. (1981, May). Synthesis of research on cooperative learning. *Educational Leadership, 38*(8), 655–660.

Slavin, R. E. (1989, April). On mastery learning and mastery teaching. *Educational Leadership, 46*(7), 77–79.

Slavin, R. E. (1991, February). Synthesis of research on cooperative learning. *Educational Leadership, 48*(5), 71–82.

Slavin, R. E., & Madden, N. A. (2000). Research on achievement outcomes of Success for All: A summary and response to critics. *Phi Delta Kappan, 82*(1), 38–40, 59–66.

Slicker, E. K. (1998). Relationships of parenting style to behavioral adjustment in graduating high school seniors. *Journal of Youth and Adolescence, 27*(13), 345–372.

Smith, S. W., & Daunic, A. P. (2002). Using conflict resolution and peer mediation to support positive behavior. In R. Algozzine & P. Kay (Eds.), *Preventing problem behaviors: A handbook of successful prevention strategies* (Ch. 8). Thousand Oaks, CA: Corwin Press.

Sparks, D., & Hirsh, S. (1997). *A new vision for staff development.* Alexandria, VA: Association for Supervision and Curriculum Development.

Stevenson, H. W., & Stigler, J. W. (1992). *The learning gap: Why our schools are failing and what we can learn from Japanese and Chinese education.* New York: Simon & Schuster.

Stiggins, R. J. (2001). *Student-involved classroom assessment* (3rd ed.). Upper Saddle River, NJ: Merrill/Prentice Hall.

Stigler, J. W., & Hiebert, J. (1999). *The teaching gap: Best ideas from the world's teachers for improving education in the classroom.* New York: Free Press.

Strong, R., Silver, H., & Perini, M. (1999, March). Keeping it simple and deep. *Educational Leadership, 56*(6), 22–24.

Strong, R., Silver, H., Perini, M., & Tuculescu, G. (2003, September). Boredom and its opposite. *Educational Leadership, 61*(1), 24–29.

Sugai, G., & Colvin, G. (1996). Debriefing: A proactive addition to negative consequences for problem behavior. *Education and Treatment of Children, 20,* 209–221.

Sullivan, C. G. (1992). *How to mentor in the midst of change.* Alexandria, VA: Association for Supervision and Curriculum Development.

Swartz, R. J., & Perkins, D. N. (1990). *Teaching thinking: Issues and approaches.* Pacific Grove, CA: Midwest Publications.

Swick, K. J. (1985). *Disruptive student behavior in the classroom* (2nd ed.). Washington, DC: National Education Association.

Sylwester, R., & Choo, J. Y. (1992, December). What brain research says about paying attention. *Educational Leadership, 50*(4), 71–77.

Taba, H. (1965, May). Teaching of thinking. *Elementary English, 42*(2), 534.

Taba, H., Levine, S., & Elzey, F. (1964). *Thinking in elementary school children.* (Cooperative Research Project No. 15). San Francisco: San Francisco State College.

Thelen, H. A. (1960). *Education and the human quest.* New York: Harper & Row.

Thompson, M. (2001). *Best friends, worst enemies: Understanding the social lives of children.* New York: Ballantine.

Thornburg, D. (2002). *The new basics: Education and the future of work in the telematic age.* Alexandria, VA: Association for Supervision and Curriculum Development.

Tierney, R. J. (1991). *Portfolio assessment in the reading-writing classroom.* Norwood, MA: Christopher-Gordon.

Tillman, M. (1982). *Trouble-shooting classroom problems.* Glenview, IL: Scott Foresman.

Tomlinson, C. A. (2001). *How to differentiate instruction in mixed-ability classrooms* (2nd ed.). Alexandria, VA: Association for Supervision and Curriculum Development.

Trammel, D. L., Schloss, P. J., & Alper, S. (1994). Using self-recording and graphing to increase completion of homework assignments. *Journal of Learning Disabilities, 27*(2), 75–81.

Tyler, R. (1950). *Basic principles of curriculum and instruction.* Chicago: University of Chicago Press.

Van Dijk, T. A. (1980). *Macrostructures.* Hillsdale, NJ: Lawrence Erlbaum.

Van Dyke, H. T. (1984). Corporal punishment in our schools. *The Clearing House, 57,* 296–300.

Van Overwalle, F., & De Metsenaere, M. (1990). The effects of attribution-based intervention and study strategy training on academic achievement in college freshmen. *British Journal of Educational Psychology, 60,* 299–311.

Vars, G. F. (2000). Editorial comment: On research, high-stakes testing, and core philosophy. *The Core Teacher, 50*(1), 3.

Vogel, N. (2001). *Making the most of Plan-Do-Review: The teacher's idea book 5.* Ypsilanti, MI: High Scope Press.

Vygotsky, L. S. (1978). *Mind in society: The development of higher psychological processes.* Cambridge, MA: Harvard University Press.

Walberg, H. J. (1985, April). Homework's powerful effects on learning. *Educational Leadership, 42*(7), 76–79.

Walberg, H. J. (1986, September). What works in a nation still at risk. *Educational Leadership, 44*(1), 7–10.

Walberg, H. J. (1988, March). Synthesis of research on time and learning. *Educational Leadership, 45*(6), 76–85.

Walberg, H. J. (1999). Productive teaching. In H. C. Waxman & H. J. Walberg (Eds.), *New directions for teaching practice and research* (pp. 75–104). Berkeley, CA: McCutchen.

Walberg, H. J., & Greenberg, R. (1997, May). Using the Learning Environment Inventory. *Educational Leadership, 54*(8), 45–46.

Walker, H., & Sylwater, R. (1991, September). Where is school along the path to prison? *Educational Leadership, 49*(1), 14–16.

Walker, J. E., & Shea, T. M., & Bauer, A. M. (2004). *Behavior management: A practical approach for educators.* (8th ed.). Upper Saddle River, NJ: Merrill.

Wang, M., Haertel, G., & Walberg, H. J. (1993). Toward a knowledge base for school learning. *Review of Educational Research, 63*(3), 249–294.

Wasserman, S. (1988). *The asking of wonderful questions.* Bloomington, IN: Phi Delta Kappa.

Wasserman, S. (1991). *Serious players: Empowering children in the primary grades.* New York: Teachers College Press.

Wasserman, S., & Ivany, G. (1988). *Teaching elementary science: Who's afraid of spiders?* New York: Harper Row.

Welch, D., & Tate, G. A. (1987). *Self-actualization: An annotated bibliography of the theory and research.* New York: Garland.

Wenger, W. (1989). *A method for personal growth and development.* Gaithersburg, MD: Project Renaissance.

Wessler, S. L. (2003, September). It's hard to learn when you're scared. *Educational Leadership, 61*(1), 40–43.

Whimbey, A. (1980, April). Students can learn to be better problem solvers. *Educational Leadership, 37*(7), 560–565.

Whimbey, A., & Lochhead, J. (1986). *Problem solving and comprehension.* Hillsdale, NJ: Lawrence Erlbaum.

White, R. W. (1959). Motivation reconsidered: The concept of confidence. *Psychological Review 66,* 297–333.

Widaman, K. F., & Kagan, S. (1987, Winter). Cooperativeness and achievement: Interaction of student cooperativeness with cooperative versus competitive classroom organization. *Journal of School Psychology, 25*(4), 355–365.

Wiggins, G. (1993). *Assessing student performances: Exploring the purpose and limits of testing.* San Francisco: Jossey-Bass.

Wilburn, K. T., & Felps, B. C. (1983). *Do pupil grading methods affect middle school students' achievement? A comparison of criterion-referenced versus norm-referenced evaluation.* Jacksonville, FL: Wofson Senior High School. (ERIC Document Reproduction Service No. ED 229-451)

Wilde, J., & Sommers, P. (1978). Teaching disruptive adolescents: A game worth winning. *Phi Delta Kappan, 59,* 342–343.

Wilson. E. O. (2002). *The future of life.* New York: Knopf.

Wilson, T. D., & Linville, P. W. (1982). Improving the academic performance of college freshmen: Attribution theory revisited. *Journal of Research in Science Teaching, 20*(5), 415–425.

Wittrock, M. C. (1986). Students' thought processes. In M. C. Wittrock (Ed.), *Handbook of research on teaching* (3rd ed., pp. 297–314). New York: Macmillan.

Woessman, L. (Summer, 2001). Why students in some countries do better: International evidence on the importance of education policy. *Education Matters, 1*(2), 67–74.

Wolf, D. P. (1987, December–1988, January). Opening up assessment. *Educational Leadership, 45*(4), 24–29.

Wolf, D. P. (1989, April). Portfolio assessment: Sampling student work. *Educational Leadership, 46*(7), 35–39.

Wolfe, P. (2001). *Brain matters: Translating research into classroom practice.* Alexandria, VA: Association for Supervision and Curriculum Development.

Wolfgang, C. H. (1995). *Solving discipline problems: Methods and models for today's teachers* (3rd ed.). Boston: Allyn & Bacon.

Woloshyn, V. E., Willoughby, T., Wood, E., & Pressley, M. (1990). Elaborative interrogation facilitates adult learning of factual paragraphs. *Journal of Educational Psychology, 82*, 513–524.

Wong, H. K., & Wong, R. T. (1998). *The first days of school.* Mountain View, CA: Harry K. Wong Publications.

Zorfass, J. M., with Copel, H. (1998). *Teaching middle school students to be active researchers.* Alexandria, VA: Association for Supervision and Curriculum Development.

Zumwalt, K. (Ed.). (1986). *Improving teaching (1986 ASCD yearbook).* Alexandria, VA: Association for Supervision and Curriculum Development.

Index

Page numbers followed by an *f* indicate figures. Main entries that are capitalized indicate a strategy.

About the Authors

Merrill Harmin currently directs the Inspiring Strategy Institute, which specializes in practical ways of making schooling richer for students, more satisfying for teachers. He also teaches for the nonprofit American Meditation Society, which specializes in providing individualized meditation practices to adults. Earlier he spent 40 years as a professor of education at Rutgers University and Southern Illinois University. He's written several books and articles, received several research grants, and has several degrees, most notably a PhD in curriculum and instruction from New York University. Yet he is still searching because, he claims, "I can't remember where I left my favorite putter." He can often be contacted at 44 Midchester Avenue, White Plains, NY 10606. Phone: 914-946-5334. E-mail: mtharmin@optonline.net.

Melanie Toth began her career as a 4th grade teacher and is currently pursuing her doctorate in educational psychology at the City University of New York. She also works at the Inspiring Strategy Institute. Her focus is on developing ways to support teachers, particularly those new to the profession. In addition, she keeps busy writing, tutoring, doing yoga, and helping Merrill remember all the things he keeps forgetting. This is her first book. She can be contacted at 23-12 21st Avenue, Astoria, NY 11105. E-mail: mel_toth@yahoo.com.

For schools wishing assistance with inservice training programs, please contact Merrill. He would be happy to provide experienced trainers or recommendations for a self-directed training program. For more information about the Inspiring Strategy Institute, see www.inspiringonline.net.

Related ASCD Resources: Motivation and Classroom Management

At the time of publication, the following ASCD resources were available; for the most up-to-date information about ASCD resources, go to www.ascd.org. ASCD stock numbers are noted in parentheses.

Audio

Motivating the Hopeless, Disinterested, and Uninvolved Learner by Richard Curwin and Allen Mendler (CD #505276)

Motivation: Improving Negative Student Attitudes Toward School and Learning by Robert Bowman and Susan C. Bowman (CD #505302)

Student Motivation: What Do We Know? What Do We Need to Do? by Bea McGarvey (Audiotape #204074; CD #504108)

Reaching the Reluctant Learner by Jacquelyn Conti, Andrea Malafeew, and Elizabeth Walton (CD #505264)

Multimedia

Classroom Management Professional Inquiry Kit by Robert Hanson (8 Activity Folders and 1 Videotape #998059)

Networks

Visit the ASCD Web site (www.ascd.org) and click on About ASCD. Go to the section on Networks for information about professional educators who have formed groups around topics such as "Teaching Thinking" and "Character Education." Look in the Network Directory for current facilitators' addresses and phone numbers.

Online Courses

Visit the ASCD Web site (www.ascd.org) for the following professional development opportunities:

Classroom Management: Building Relationships for Better Learning by Marilyn Gootman (#PD00OC11)

Managing Challenging Behavior by Diane L. Jackson (#PD05OC46)

Print Products

Awakening Genius in the Classroom by Thomas Armstrong (#198033)

The Classroom of Choice: Giving Students What They Need and Getting What You Want by Jonathan C. Erwin (#104020)

Classroom Instruction That Works: Research-Based Strategies for Increasing Student Achievement by Robert J. Marzano, Debra J. Pickering, and Jane E. Pollock (#101010)

Connecting with Students by Allen Mendler (#101236)

Educational Leadership: Do Students Care About Learning? (Entire Issue #102305)

Educational Leadership: Building Classroom Relationships (Entire Issue #103385)

The Key Elements of Classroom Management: Managing Time and Space, Student Behavior, and Instructional Strategies by Joyce McLeod, Jan Fisher, and Ginny Hoover (#103008)

Motivating Students and Teachers in an Era of Standards by Richard Sagor (#103009)

Teaching Tips: 105 Ways to Increase Motivation and Learning by Spence Rogers (#301282)

Totally Positive Teaching: A Five-Stage Approach to Energizing Students and Teachers by Joseph Ciaccio (#104016)

Winning Strategies for Classroom Management by Carol Cummings (#100052)

Video

Classroom Management That Works Video Series: *Sharing Rules and Procedures, Developing Relationships,* and *Fostering Student Self-Management* (3 Videotapes and Facilitator's Guide #404038; DVD and Facilitator's Guide #604038)

Motivation: The Key to Success in Teaching and Learning Video Series: *Motivationally Anchored Instruction, Motivationally Anchored Classrooms,* and *Motivationally Anchored Schools* (3 Videotapes and Facilitator's Guide #403344)

A Visit to a Motivated Classroom (Videotape and Viewer's Guide #403384)

For more information, visit us on the World Wide Web (www.ascd.org), send an e-mail message to member@ascd.org, call the ASCD Service Center (1-800-933-ASCD or 703-578-9600, then press 2), send a fax to 703-575-5400, or write to Information Services, ASCD, 1703 N. Beauregard St., Alexandria, VA 22311-1714 USA.